COLORADO ADVENTURE GUIDE

The ultimate guide to the state's best hiking, biking, and cross country ski trails

PHOTOGRAPHY AND TEXT BY

CHARLIE NUTTELMAN

See you on the trail, Deb! Charlie Nuttelman

Jagged Mountain Publishing
www.jaggedmountainpublishing.com
Boulder, Colorado

Colorado Adventure Guide: Northern Edition
Copyright © 2012 by Charlie Nuttelman

Jagged Mountain Publishing
P.O. Box 3311
Boulder, CO 80307
info@jaggedmountainpublishing.com

ISBN: 978-0-615-57699-2

LCCN: 2012900188

Cover photo: Tina Lewis, Max Nuttelman, and Geoff Miller. Design by Charlie Nuttelman.

Please visit www.jaggedmountainpublishing.com to order additional copies of this book or to order selected photos from this guidebook. Central and Southern Editions to follow in subsequent years.

NOTE: Hiking, mountain biking, skiing, snowshoeing, backpacking, and climbing are all potentially hazardous activities and the mountains can be extremely dangerous. The user of this guidebook assumes all responsibilities related to involvement in outdoor activities described herein. To the best knowledge of the author and publisher, the trails and routes described in this guidebook are public and are open for the denoted uses. Ultimately, responsibilities related to trail usage, private property, mode of transportation allowed on a particular trail, and all parking and usage rules and regulations are those of the user. The author and publisher assume no responsibility for the certain unforeseen errors, inaccuracies, omissions, or inconsistencies herein. Please do not knowingly follow or encourage the formation of "renegade" trails. All maps provided in this guidebook are meant to act as locator maps and are not meant for navigation. Commercially-available, field-checked maps should always be carried in the backcountry and the user should know how to use a map and compass.

Although much time has gone into the preparation and proofreading of this book, there are bound to be mistakes in this first printing. The author will greatly appreciate the reporting of any and all tpyos and errers found in this guidebook. This includes not only spelling errors but also inconsistencies, omissions, or inaccuracies related to mileages, elevations, directions, etc. Please report errors directly to the author: charlie@jaggedmountainpublishing.com.

The author and publisher welcome positive or constructive feedback related to this guidebook that can be used to improve its quality. Submit feedback to: feedback@jaggedmountainpublishing.com.

Quantity discounts may be available on bulk purchases of this book for various outdoor or other groups. Please contact info@jaggedmountainpublishing.com for information.

First printing 2012.

Printed in China.

Acknowledgements

First and foremost, this book would not have been possible had I not grown up with the appreciation for the outdoors and nature that my parents bestowed upon me at an early age. I was lucky to be raised in Colorado and to have been introduced to hiking, camping, and skiing at such an early age. For this I am eternally grateful to my parents. My head is full of memories related to my family's "home away from home" pop-up camper, in which our family shared many fun and exciting trips together, exploring all corners of the state.

Secondly, I'd like to thank my high school buddies who struggled through the learning curves and challenges alongside me but at the same time realized the joys and rewards of backpacking, skiing, and climbing. These primarily include Matt Schenk, Dylan Yaney, Eric Lubell, Jamie Genuario, Phil Marsh, Michael Demmon, and Peter Eliassen. With all of you I have so many vivid memories of growing up in the Pikes Peak region - digging snow caves, winter camping in Stanley Canyon, hiking on Pikes Peak, and climbing our first Fourteeners - memories I would not trade in for the world. These camping trips founded in me a great respect and enjoyment for the outdoors. I'd also like to thank my twin brother Max who has for many years kept me grounded and tuned into things that are important in life. Together, we have done some pretty amazing outdoor adventures and climbs and I look forward to countless more.

Thirdly, while only a handful of the following were directly involved with adventures in this guidebook, I'd like to thank those who have shared my love and zest for the outdoors over the past decade or so: Stefan Griebel, Matt Seefeldt, Rex Headd, Dan Vega, Dave Mackey, Bob Schelly, Greg Dooley, John Ortega, Geoff Miller, and Alex Kostadinov.

Fourthly, I'd like to acknowledge the many organizations - public, private, and volunteer - that have helped protect, conserve, and preserve public lands for our enjoyment. I would like to especially thank the men and women of the United States Forest Service, National Park Service, United States Fish and Wildlife Service, and the Bureau of Land Management who, despite dwindling federal budgets, have proudly maintained and upheld a strong tradition of commitment to our federal lands.

Finally, special gratitude goes out to my lovely wife, Tina, who is a trooper. Without her patience, support, encouragement, and understanding over the past 18 months I never would have finished this book. Tina has carried me out of the slumps and maintained my motivation when I've wanted to throw in the towel on this arduous and frustrating at times project. She has kept things exciting and offered many corrections as the main "editor" of this book. It has been such a pleasure to share many of these adventures with my wife and I am excited to share many more. This book is dedicated to you, Tina.

Preface

For Christmas 1993 my brother received the spectacular book *To Walk in Wilderness* by T.A. Barron and John Fielder. Although not given to me, this book had a profound effect on me during my teen years. *To Walk in Wilderness* documents both in words and stunning photographs the authors' thirty-day backcountry trip in the Maroon Bells-Snowmass Wilderness. I'd steal the book from my brother but he'd quickly steal it back, equally as enthralled with the authors' experiences and photographic journey. This book left a permanent imprint on me, inspiring me immeasurably to get out and explore the

Wildflowers in the Indian Peaks Wilderness

sights, sounds, and smells of Colorado. I had done plenty of hiking and camping to that point, but I wanted to feel first-hand what the authors had experienced and I had a strong desire to immerse myself in wilderness. Soon after reading *To Walk in Wilderness*, my brother and I signed up for a volunteer, week-long trail crew with the Colorado Mountain Club for the following July in as close of a place to the setting of the book as possible: Avalanche Creek on the northwestern side of the Maroon Bells-Snowmass Wilderness. Just having obtained my drivers license, this was my first "real" road trip without my parents. The trail crew project involved a lot of physical labor but was in an extraordinary setting. When we weren't hauling dirt, digging ditches, and cutting geotech cloth, we were free to explore. And explore we did! On one of the days my brother and I climbed the 14,130-foot Capitol Peak. On another day we climbed Snowmass Peak from the north and I vividly remember the vulnerable, humble, and self-sufficient feelings of being so "out there" and alone in the wilderness This initial week-long backpacking trip in the mountains, combined with the hiking and camping journeys that my parents brought us on when we were young, solidified my love for the mountains and has no doubt been the main culprit in my stubbornness to leave the state of Colorado.

I have been "borrowing" *To Walk in Wilderness* from my brother for over a decade and it still occupies my closest bookshelf. I continue to flip through the pages of this book for inspiration during the winter months and I am forever indebted to the authors. It was especially gratifying to be able to be a "Sherpa" for John Fielder during the summer of 2004 on one of his photographic expeditions. Over the last several years, I have yearned for the opportunity to give back and inspire others to discover what I had - the solitude, challenges, and beauty that are found in wilderness - similar to the way *To Walk in Wilderness* inspired me.

In June of 2010 I decided to get serious about writing a guidebook. I began to document, photograph, and collect data that potentially could be used to create a Colorado guidebook emphasizing self-propelled adventure - hiking, mountain biking, cross country skiing, and snowshoeing. Soon thereafter, the project flourished. Although I have lived in Colorado my whole life, I was discovering more and more places each day and my desire to share many - but not all, I've kept numerous secret places to myself - of these places grew. In my opinion, the popularity of Colorado's 14,000-ft. "Fourteeners" has overshadowed many other incredibly beautiful and serene areas in the state and so I wanted this book to emphasize non-Fourteener options. In fact, of the 507 route descriptions in this guidebook only 3 are for Fourteeners. This project was no easy task and during the last two summers I have worked far harder than I would ever have imagined, waking up in the wee hours of the morning to photograph or begin my hikes, continuing well into the evening. There were definitely a few points along in this process where I was ready to call it quits. But after thousands of miles of exploring trails and hundreds upon hundreds of hours composing text and creating maps, I am happy to present the Northern Edition of the Colorado Adventure Guide. There are some obvious regions that are missing from this book - like Fort Collins, Cameron Pass, and the western side of Rocky Mountain National Park - but I think you will find that this guidebook is quite comprehensive in its coverage of the northern part of Colorado. I sincerely hope that this book will motivate and inspire and at least provide a starting point for numerous outdoor adventures with family and friends. Enjoy!

Charlie Nuttelman
Boulder, Colorado
December 2011

The author hiking in Summit County

Map
Detail

COLORADO

13

Craig

Rangely

Glenwood Springs

70

139

Carbondale

Loma
Fruita

Redstone

Palisade

Grand Mesa

133

Grand Junction

Cedaredge

Somerset

141

50   Delta

Paonia

Hotchkiss

Crested Butte

Crawford

92

Bob Lake, Indian Peaks Wilderness

Table of Contents

Lupine, near Rabbit Ears Pass

Chapter 1: Introduction

"Adventure is not in the guidebook, and beauty is not on the map. Seek and ye shall find."

- Terry & Renny Russell, "On the Loose"

There is nothing more enjoyable than packing up a lunch, lacing up the hiking boots, shouldering your backpack, and heading out on a mountain adventure. The diversity of climate, ecosystems, and geology make Colorado an extremely interesting and satisfying place to explore. Deserts, lush forests, high rocky ridges, tumbling rivers, alpine lakes, secluded canyons, and wildflower-studded meadows are waiting to be discovered. The continual turnover in the seasons ensures that there is never a dull moment in Colorado - each season temporarily transforms the landscape in a unique way, only lasting for a few months. On a daily basis, the ever-changing weather patterns keep us on edge and surprise us with spectacular sunsets, transitory arrangements of clouds, fog-filled valleys, and snow-covered evergreens.

What this guide-book is all about

With this book, I hope to motivate and inspire you to explore the outdoors via your own power - hiking, biking, skiing, snowshoeing. Discover a new place or push yourself to do something you never thought possible. The most impressive and amazing vistas, forests, and alpine lakes in Colorado are

Camping in the Vail area

only within reach if you get off the beaten path. Colorado is well-known for its 14,000-ft. mountains ("Fourteeners"), but there are so many other places to be explored in Colorado and no guidebook will ever come close to encompassing every trail possible. I hope that this book will provide numerous ideas and starting points for worthwhile adventures by yourself or with friends and family. Furthermore, I hope that the photos in this book will inspire you to get out and discover the sights that Colorado has to offer.

How to use the Colorado Adventure Guide

Early summer in the high country

I have attempted to make this book as user-friendly as possible. A lot of work has gone into making things understandable and clear and I have tried to present the most up-to-date information as possible and to the best of my ability. Things can change rapidly - trailhead and campground closures, parking regulations, policies, land privacy issues - so please make sure you are reading all posted signs and gather supplemental information on any activity you embark upon. There are plenty of additional trails and magical places that are not revealed in this guidebook. Using this guidebook as a starting point, you will undoubtedly stumble upon some special places of your own.

Organization

Each chapter is divided into several geographical sections, and each section has the following:

Maps: A list of commercially-available maps that cover the area presented. These are maps that you can purchase in typical outdoor retail stores and these maps can be found in many local bookstores.

Best time of the year: While every area in this book can in theory be explored any time of the year, I emphasize the *best* times of the year. There are certain areas of Colorado that become more aesthetically pleasing in the fall, for example, or trails that are muddy in the spring or impossible to travel in the winter. Conditions can vary from season to season so don't rely on my recommendations alone. Explore the various seasons for yourself.

Camping: A great way to interact and connect with the sights, sounds, and smells of nature is by camping. Allow a nearby stream to soothe you to sleep, wake up to the chirping of birds, get smacked in the face by falling aspen leaves as you cook breakfast on a crisp fall morning. I have listed common official and unofficial camping options in each area. It is recommended, especially if traveling from out of state or during busy summer holidays, to reserve campground sites well ahead of time. For additional options other than those provided, please contact the National Forest Service in the region you are visiting to learn about other dispersed camping options on federal lands.

Access

There's nothing quite like the crackle of a fire

The Access section provides information on how to get to a particular trailhead from popular towns in Colorado. All trailheads, unless marked with the jeep symbol below, are accessible by two-wheel drive (2WD) cars (low clearance). I have assumed that most visitors will not necessarily have high clearance vehicles so have kept this in mind when creating this guidebook. Most trailheads will not be crowded so parking is usually not an issue. However, parking in ski towns can be somewhat limited during busy parts of the year so I have tried to outline free parking spots and parking structures in these towns. In some mountain towns, public transportation is available (especially Summit County and Vail) and can be used very nicely to create point-to-point hikes or bike tours. I have also made an attempt to outline any special fee areas or other stipulations and regulations that apply.

Special symbols and abbreviations:

 Designates that a particular trailhead is not accessible in winter.

 Denotes that this trailhead is only accessible via a high clearance vehicle. Use caution as road conditions vary from year to year and may or may not be maintained regularly. Very few of the trailheads in this book require 4WD.

CR = County road   **HWY** = State highway

US = Federal highway   **FS** = Forest Service road

TH = Trailhead

Also presented in the Access section is information related to ski huts or other hike-to, bike-to, or ski-to cabins of interest. In particular, the extensive 10th Mountain Division hut system consists of a variety of huts that are found in the vicinity of mountain towns of northern Colorado. Primarily used in winter, some of these huts are open year-round.

Recommended Routes

I have provided, in my estimation, the best modes of travel on a particular trail and have rated the difficulty of each route. Obviously, there is some subjectivity involved here. On some routes that I find extremely fun or aesthetic, I have indicated this with a "thumbs up" or "two thumbs up". These are also based on my opinion - maybe it was a perfect day, perfect conditions when I traveled the route - and you may or may not have the same experience. Only one way to find out!

Here is a guide to the symbols used:

 Suitable for hiking.

 Excellent overnight backpacking trips can be set up on these routes.

 Mountain bikers can access this trail.

 Conditions permitting, this trail can be traveled via snowshoes in winter.

 Indicates that the trail is suitable for cross country skiing in the winter.

 Trail runners will enjoy this route.

Difficulty levels

The difficulty levels are subjective, but I have done my best to maintain consistency throughout the guidebook. Some trails may be rated "difficult" due to their technical nature, for example, even though they may be short in distance. Other trails or routes may be rated "difficult" because of length or strenuous nature. Take with a grain of salt.

 Easy   Moderate   Difficult

Aesthetic value

There are several routes or trails that are not to be missed in each particular area, and I've denoted these as follows:

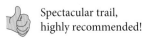 Spectacular trail, highly recommended!

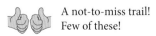 A not-to-miss trail! Few of these!

User Responsibilities

Hiking, biking, skiing, and snowshoeing are potentially dangerous activities. The goal of this guidebook is to inspire people to get out and explore nature and to present a wide variety of hiking, biking, and winter trails that can be traveled in the different seasons. A large number of folks enjoy human-powered outdoor recreational activities year-round and the safety record is exceptional. However, unforeseen accidents can and do occur in the backcountry. This guidebook is not meant to be a "how-to" book. It is up to the user to seek proper training before partaking in any of these aforementioned activities.

Many open space areas throughout northern Colorado, particularly along the front range areas in Boulder and Golden, are undergoing rapid changes in management plans. Consequently, trails that are in this guidebook *may* become off-limits, outdated, or possibly new trails may be built in some areas. The user assumes all responsibility related to travel on appropriate trails and for knowing what trails are off limits and what are not. Please do not create new trails or knowingly follow unofficial "renegade" trails, especially while on a mountain bike.

User Fees

Increasingly, user fees are being assessed to those who seek recreational opportunities on federal lands. Sometimes it can be a bummer to have to pay to go hiking, biking, cross country skiing or snowshoeing - activities that many are drawn to because of their simplistic and "free" nature - but the Forest Service has been quite strapped for funds during the last decade as their budget has dwindled as outdoor recreation has exploded in popularity. Implementation of user fees in popular destinations is the answer to addressing limited budgets of not only the Forest Service but also open space programs such as in the City of Boulder and others. You can count on many of the more popular areas in Colorado either to already have user fees in place or to be implementing user fees in the near future. If you visit national parks or visit federal or state lands quite frequently, consider purchasing a National Parks and Federal Lands Pass (12 consecutive months). This pass can be obtained online (http://store.usgs.gov/pass/index.html) or at various national parks and federal lands locations for $80. Places with known user fees at the time that this guidebook was written are denoted with a dollar sign: **$**

Maps

A tremendous amount of work has been devoted to creating the maps in this guidebook. I hope you find the maps both informative and visually appealing. I used a global positioning system (GPS) receiver to map out the exact location of over 95% of the trails in this book. Using mapping software, I then determined approximate mileages and elevation gain/loss for each route.

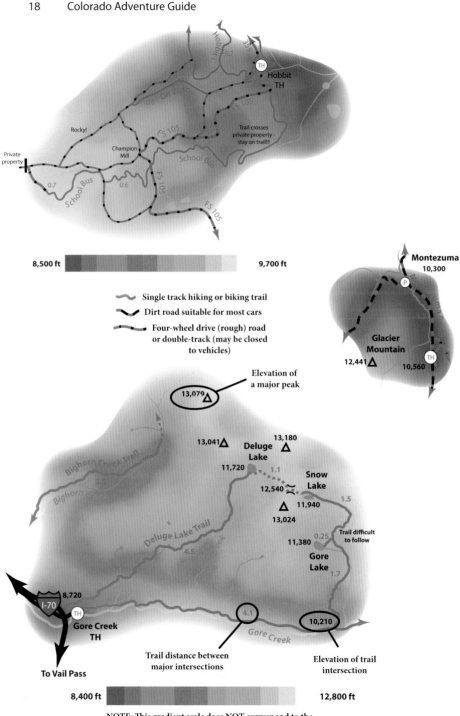

8,500 ft   9,700 ft

Single track hiking or biking trail
Dirt road suitable for most cars
Four-wheel drive (rough) road
or double-track (may be closed
to vehicles)

Montezuma
10,300

Glacier
Mountain
12,441 ▲   10,560

Elevation of
a major peak

13,079 ▲

13,041 ▲   Deluge   13,180 ▲
            Lake

11,720   1.1   Snow
                  Lake
         12,540   1.5
         11,940
13,024
                  Trail difficult
         11,380   0.25   to follow

                  Gore
                  Lake   1.7

Bighorn Creek Trail

Deluge Lake Trail   4.5

I-70   8,720
        TH
Gore Creek
TH

To Vail Pass   4.1   10,210
                Gore Creek

Trail distance between
major intersections

Elevation of trail
intersection

8,400 ft   12,800 ft

NOTE: This gradient scale does NOT correspond to the
same elevations for each map!

NOTE: Elevation gain/loss presented in the route descriptions includes all ups and downs, *not* the overall or net elevation gain/loss but cumulative gain/loss.

Maps have several components:

- Topography depicted by shading (NOTE: the colored gradient scale on one map is not necessarily the same as for another map - see the two examples on the previous page - and light color shading does not necessarily correspond to above treeline nor dark green to a forested region).
- Elevations of trailheads, major peaks, trail intersections, passes, and other geographic locations that will be encountered along the trail.
- Mileages of trail segments are denoted by a red number.
- Major geographical features like mountains, lakes, and streams.

The maps should not be used for navigation. You should always purchase a detailed, commercially available map when you embark on an adventure. Furthermore, you should know how to use a map in combination with a compass (see Navigation Basics below).

Navigation Basics

"Not all who wander are lost." - J.R.R. Tolkien

Getting Lost

Depending upon where you are, getting lost in the woods and mountains can be extremely dangerous. Every couple of years you hear a story of a hiker out for a short hike yet they descend the wrong drainage or trail and end up completely turned around and lost for days. Don't let this be you. On the other hand, some of the most memorable adventures can result from just following your nose and exploring the woods - "Not all who wander are lost." The landscape is chock full of little nooks and crannies, hidden waterfalls, and secret aspen groves that can only be stumbled upon by the adventurous spirit. If prepared for it - carrying the correct outerwear, food, map, and compass - getting lost can actually be quite fun... as long as you are able to find your way back.

Finding Your Way

Follow the tips below to minimize the chance that you get lost. These are infinitely more important for off-trail travel than on-trail travel, although it is not uncommon for people to get lost on well-marked trails. Here are general navigating tips:

- Look at the map ahead of time and try to visualize the terrain you'll encounter.
- Always look around and try to remember landmarks along the way. If you have a photographic memory then you'll be good at this and it will enable you to backtrack

Tina Lewis, Max Nuttelman, and Geoff Miller near the end of a great day in the mountains

if need be.

- Consider following a compass bearing. For instructions on how to navigate with a map and compass, see the section on "Using a Map and Compass".

- Estimate a pace that you are traveling at and keep track of your time. Your pace will vary depending upon terrain and fitness, but in general an average pace on trail is 2-3 miles per hour and 1-2 miles per hour off trail. Distance = speed x time, so you can estimate mileage traveled.

- Especially for off-trail travel, always know where on the map you are.

- An altimeter is a great tool that can add a third level or dimension to your navigational certainty, but only if you have properly calibrated it at the beginning of your excursion.

If you do get lost, experts say to stay still and don't go anywhere to conserve energy and food and wait until you are missed and help comes your way. Indeed, if you are deep within a wilderness area in Colorado and far away from towns or trailheads, you probably should play it safe and sit tight until someone finds you, assuming you've told someone, which is always a good idea. However, many popular hiking areas in Colorado are surrounded by roads or civilization and you can almost always reach a road or town by following creeks, stream beds, or rivers downhill. Better yet, train yourself to use a map and compass or GPS device to navigate yourself along your chosen route or back to familiar territory if you do indeed get lost.

GPS for Navigation

GPS receivers receive signals from satellites that hover over ten thousand miles above Earth and provide a relatively accurate two-dimensional (latitude and longitude) position of the receiver. GPS receivers are generally very accurate; manufacturers claim the accuracy to an average of about 15 meters (50 ft.). Today, you can load most GPS receivers with topographical maps of areas you are visiting and the GPS unit will essentially guide the user to a user-entered coordinate location. Keep in mind, however, that there are several potential issues that must be carefully considered when using GPS units. First, GPS receivers send you in a straight line to your destination. Oftentimes, there may be terrain in between you and your destination that will make this difficult - a big lake or canyon or a big peak that you'd have to climb. The GPS device would indicate that the best way is to go in a straight line, which will only get you in trouble and is not the most efficient or safe route. Second, while the error in GPS receivers is small, you need to be aware of human error in inputting the GPS coordinates. On two separate trips to ski huts that I've been on, either the GPS coordinates were entered wrong or the coordinates provided to us were wrong. Night came and on both occasions we spent almost an hour looking for the hut. We finally questioned the reliability of the GPS and coordinates, pulled out a compass and map and within 10 minutes had found the hut. Finally, navigating by map and compass will tune your perception of the geographical landscape and will make you more aware of your surroundings, and is a heck of a lot more fun than staring down at an electronic device when you are in the outdoors! And, what happens if the GPS batteries die?

Using a Map and Compass

Most backcountry travelers will choose to stay on well-traveled and well-marked trails. In these cases navigation is quite straightforward and, while you may find yourself confused as to how far you have traveled a particular trail or where a fork in the trail might lead to, it is quite difficult to get lost. However, if you decide to do any off-trail travel where navigation might be confusing or you have not been in that particular geographic area before, it is wise to carry a map and compass and know how to use them. For off-trail travel, a compass does little without a map, and a map is useless without a compass. Learning how to use a map and compass is the first step in learning to find your way in these difficult navigation situations.

The basis of map-and-compass navigation is the magnetic field of Earth, which is not situated exactly at the North Pole. For example, in Colorado magnetic north varies between 9-11° east of true north. True north means pointing straight to the North Pole. This is the notion of *declination*. Declination is the amount that you have to compensate for the difference between true north and magnetic north. What complicates things more is the fact that declination changes with

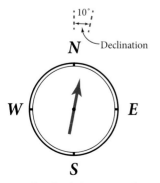

In Colorado, declination is about 10° east.

geographic location and also over time. Good maps provide the declination. All practical compasses allow you to adjust the declination manually.

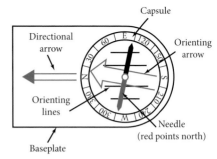

A typical compass.

Once declination is set, you are ready to navigate. To go directly north, turn the compass capsule (the rotatable part that has the fluid in it) until "N" is aligned with the directional arrow of your compass. Now, physically rotate and turn your body, holding the compass level, until the red part of the needle is aligned with the orienting arrow (see left diagram below). If you walk straight ahead at this point you will be going north. You can do the same thing to walk exactly east (middle) or at a random bearing, such as 210° (right).

What if you know where on a map you are and you want to get to some other location in a straight line by using your compass? Place your compass on your map and align one of the length-wise straight edges on the compass base from where you are to where you want to go (see diagram on following page). Without moving the compass' position relative to the map, rotate the capsule until the north-south lines on the capsule (orienting lines) are parallel to the north-south lines on your map and the north part of the capsule points towards north on the map. You have just taken a bearing from your map and now you just need to follow your bearing by making sure the red needle is aligned with the orienting arrow and walking in the direction of the directional arrow on the compass base. It is common to take small steps. Choose a distinct rock, tree, bush, or other landmark that is several hundred yards away and progress to that point, weaving around other natural obstacles as needed. Once at that landmark, take another sighting along your bearing, proceed to that next landmark, and continue the process.

"Red Fred is in the Shed":

Walking straight north.   *Walking straight east.*   *Heading towards a bearing of 210°.*

NOTE: Walk in the direction of the directional arrow on the compass base plate.

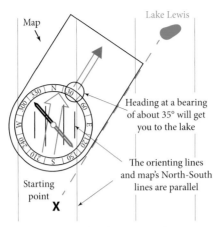

Taking a bearing from the map. Note that the orienting lines are parallel to the map's North-South lines. Also note that the needle does not need to line up with the orienting arrow.

Finding Your Position Using Triangulation

There's an easy way to find where you are if you become lost. This is known as triangulation and in order for it to work you need to be in sight of one major landmark if you are on-trail or two major landmarks if you are off-trail. Using your compass, site along the directional arrow and point to one of the landmarks (a nearby peak, for example, that you can identify on the map). Rotate the capsule until the needle is aligned in the orienting arrow. Place the compass on the map, align one end of a length-wise edge of the compass with the landmark you've sighted off of, then rotate the compass relative to the map until the orienting lines are parallel to the North-South lines of the map. Draw (or visualize) a line from the map to the intersection of the trail. Voila! This intersection is where you are on the trail. You can also do this if you are off-trail by choosing two landmarks, drawing a line across the map from one landmark then doing the same by taking a bearing off the other landmark and drawing a line on the map from the second landmark. Where the two lines cross is roughly where you are.

Routefinding

How you get from point A to point B will depend upon the route you choose. This is known as *routefinding*. Between point A and point B may lie some challenging terrain. For example, you may have to deal with navigating through mountains and valleys and rivers and lakes. Maybe there are dense forests or willows to be reckoned with and avoided. While a map has a lot of this information on it so a preliminary route can be planned ahead of time, some "on the fly" decisions will have to be made. Over time and once you gain experience with navigation, you will become efficient at routefinding. But while you are learning, just enjoy the process of acquiring a new outdoor skill.

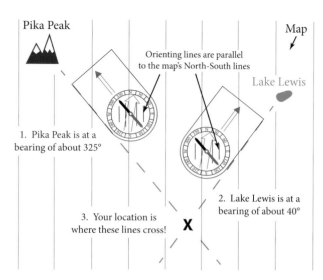

*Triangulation can be used to estimate your position. You need at least two visible **known** landmarks if you are off trail. If you are on a trail, only one of these lines is needed and your location is the intersection of the single line with the trail.*

Here are some routefinding tips:

- Open land (grasses, tundra) is faster to travel on than dense forests.

- Contouring (staying at same elevation) is more efficient than climbing and descending, but if a contouring route would take a long time then descend and ascend again.

- River crossings can be difficult; streams and rivers swell in the afternoon and evening but are lower flow in the morning.

- If a particular river is quite deep, wide, or fast-moving, continue upstream towards the source. Flow rate will decrease as you progress upstream.

- When climbing a peak, it is oftentimes better to ascend a gentle valley to a saddle and then take a ridge line to a peak rather than just bee-lining it to the summit.

- When the trail is difficult to follow (overgrown or covered in snow), look for signs that hint that the trail is near. These signs include visible saw-cut logs (recently removed fallen trees), cairns (piles of rocks), and tree markings, which can be either blue or orange diamonds or man-made markings (usually a small mark on top, longer mark on bottom - see photo).

Tree marking along the trail

Equipment

"It's not an adventure until something goes wrong."

– Yvon Chouinard

Hiking gear

Walking is just about the most basic human activity, and hiking is just one notch more involved. In contrast to other human-powered sports like Nordic skiing and mountain biking, hiking is pure and simple. No fancy gear necessary, no complicated techniques or skills required, no grease or oil to keep you moving, just plain freedom! All you need to hike is ... well... a sturdy pair of hiking shoes or boots and a backpack with some food and warm clothing! Of course, your list of gear will probably be more substantial in harsher weather conditions and will evolve as you gain more experience in the outdoors, but pretty much everyone can go for a hike with the gear they already have, more or less. Ankle-high, stiff leather hiking boots will prevent ankle twists and rolls and are relatively waterproof if treated correctly. However, I prefer to use trail running shoes since they allow me to feel and sense the terrain more acutely than bulky hiking boots. While they will get wet during a creek crossing, they dry out quickly. You'll definitely want heavier boots for extended backpacking trips when you have a loaded pack on your back. Good socks are important to prevent blisters and don't plan a really long day in new shoes - they take time to break in. Also, always carry a raincoat with you, even if the sky is blue. Colorado is known for its afternoon thunderstorms.

Backpacking gear

An overnight or multi-day trip to the high country is well worth the effort of lugging your camping gear on your back. You will be rewarded by spending the magical times of the day in a surreal setting. Keep in mind, however, that your body will be thankful if you keep things light. Not too light or your safety could be compromised (e.g., not enough food or warm clothing). Like other aspects of outdoor gear, there are decisions to be made and trade-offs to consider. Start simple and backpack just a mile or two from your car. Take note of things you used and what you

Camping in the Indian Peaks Wilderness

didn't. Refine your gear and learn what you can do without and what you should bring next time.

The first thing you'll need for backpacking is a sturdy internal or external frame backpack. Internal frame packs are more common nowadays. Be sure to use stuff sacks to compartmentalize your gear. Pack heavier stuff near the bottom and lighter stuff near the top. Place things that need to be readily accessible in the top pocket or side pockets of the pack.

A bunch of different types of tents are available. Three-season (spring, summer, fall) tents are more lightweight than the sturdy four-season tents so are preferable for all but the coldest conditions. And obviously, the 3-person tents will weigh slightly more than 2-person tents but will enable you to spread out a bit more at camp.

Sleeping bags also come in different varieties. Down is the preferred type of

Backpacking Essentials

- *Internal or external frame backpack*
- *Tent*
- *Sleeping bag*
- *Ground pad*
- *Headlamp & extra batteries*
- *Lightweight stove, fuel, matches, cookset, and utensils*
- *Sun protection*
- *Camera*
- *Dehydrated food*
- *Boots & extra socks*
- *Base & insulating layers*
- *Rain gear*
- *Water bottles & water purification*
- *First aid kit*

insulation but is more expensive than synthetic fills. Down is lighter but if it gets wet it will get batted down and will not insulate as well. Synthetic fill is heavier, not as compressible, but resists moisture better. For general Colorado summer conditions, a bag rated to 15-20 °F is fine, but if you are going to be camping above treeline, it is recommended to bring a bag rated down to around 0-5 °F - those clear, cold nights even in midsummer in the alpine zone can be extremely cold. Underneath your sleeping bag you'll want a ground pad, either inflatable or foam. You won't appreciate the ground pad until you have to sleep on rocks or it is a very cold night - the main purpose of the ground pad is to insulate you from the cold ground.

What to wear? Lightweight, synthetic clothing is preferable. Polypropylene or wool is the best material as it dries out quickly (see "Clothing" on p. 30). You'll want some good rain gear - don't skimp on this as it rains a lot in Colorado in the summer up high! Wear synthetic socks and bring extras.

Food should be dehydrated (only-add-water) or lightweight - don't bring canned food or a steak unless you are fit! Dehydrated soups and potatoes, granola bars and trail mix are good backpacking foods. You'll want a lightweight cook stove to prepare your food.

Other miscellaneous items the you might want to pack include lip balm, Ziploc bags, compass/GPS, trekking poles, cord/rope, pocket knife, first aid kit, and flip-flops or sandals.

Mountain Biking Gear

A great way to travel dirt roads and trails is on a mountain bike. While you won't be able to take a mountain bike into wilderness areas or other sensitive areas, they are allowed in a lot of places. What type of mountain bike should you ride? The answer to this question is… who cares, just get a mountain bike! You can have a great biking experience on any mountain bike. Sure, at some point you might want that nice, cushy full suspension bike and it is true that some of the mountain biking trails in this book might be more frustrating

A wide, knobby tire up front...

without some type of suspension system. Other equipment that is vital for mountain biking is a helmet and padded gloves for when you crash as well as for gripping the handlebars a bit more. You will probably want either some toe clips for your pedals or clipless pedals with shoes that enable you to clip directly to your pedals. With either of these options, you'll be able to pedal more efficiently. And it's always good to carry a spare tube, air pump, and tools in case something goes wrong. Be sure you know how to change a tire and use your tools! A "hands free" hydration backpack system like a Camelbak will enable you to stay hydrated and carry your gear and chain lube. More advanced folks will probably get a little carried away with the more "techy" details – weights of various components, the travel of your suspension, tire type, and whether you want to ride with tubed or tubeless tires. Narrower tires roll faster but don't grip nearly as well as

Mountain Biking Checklist

- *Multi-tool*
- *Chain lube*
- *Rain jacket*
- *Gloves*
- *Helmet*
- *Air pump (or CO_2 cartridges and inflator), extra tube, and tire levers*
- *Sunglasses to protect from sun and flying debris*
- *Sunscreen*
- *Hydration system*

the knobby ones; consider placing knobby tires up front to grip on the turns. Tubeless tires enable you to ride at lower pressures, providing a cushier ride. Recently, many bike companies have introduced 29-inch wheels (in contrast to the typical 26-inch wheels); these do a better job of rolling over logs and rocks but don't corner as well as the smaller tires. So wheel size is another consideration. Now that you're armed with the basics of mountain bike gear, just grab a bike and hit the trails!

... and a narrow, fast-rolling tire in back.

Trail Running Gear

The crunch of dirt and pebbles and pine needles and twigs underfoot is appealing to many, who enjoy putting in hard-earned "light and fast" miles in the backcountry. Some trail runners will elect to go very slow, chugging along just slightly faster than if they were hiking. Others will fly up and down the mountains at superhuman paces. Regardless, if you are capable of doing it, trail running is perhaps one of the most free and liberating activities that you can partake in. Done efficiently and if you are in the right shape for it, you can see a lot of wilderness in a short amount of time. But then again, why rush? Why not spend as much time as possible immersed in wilderness?!

Most trail runners will want to pare down the amount of equipment they bring with them. Important pieces of equipment include rain jacket, hat and light gloves if going above treeline, hydration system (water bottles or Camelbak-style backpack), a ball cap

Tina Lewis, Mountain View Trail, Steamboat

or visor to protect from the sun, sunscreen, and some food, depending upon distance. A method to purify water (either iodine tablets or water filter) also enables one to pick up water along the way, minimizing the weight of water that must be carried. I like to carry a hand-held ultraviolet (UV) light device that sterilizes the water by UV illumination. Finally, if you are going out for a super long run, you should bring some sort of food - energy bars, trail mix, peanut butter and jelly - something high in calories to prevent "hitting the wall". If you sweat a lot like me, you'll want to carry some salt tablets to replace electrolytes and prevent muscle cramps.

Trail Running Checklist

- **Hydration system**
- **Water filtration**
- **Hat & gloves**
- **Lightweight rain gear**
- **Sun protection**
- **Camera**
- **Food**
- **Electrolyte drink or electrolyte tablets**

Ski Equipment

No, not downhill skiing - cross country skiing! Schussing through a serene, snowy forest is probably one of the most enjoyable experiences, period. Skis prevent you from falling through the snow and allow you to slide effortlessly along. There are many types of skis that can be used. First, general cross country touring skis are the best for all-purpose skiing on easier terrain. These "waxless" skis have fish scale-like protrusions underfoot that grip the snow and allow the ski to, in general, slide easier forward than backward. Thus, you can propel yourself forward and grip the snow to prevent from sliding backward. Next, there is the "waxable" style of cross country touring ski. The base of the ski is completely flat along the length of the ski. These touring skis usually have something known as a "double camber". Weight the ski with about half a body weight and the middle part of the ski (underfoot) does not touch the ground. Press down on the ski with your entire body weight and the region underfoot touches the ground. This is useful because a "grip" wax can be placed on the ski underfoot; when unweighted, the ski can slide forward but when weighted, the grip wax sticks to the snow and allows the skier to propel himself or herself forward. The absence of the fish scales makes this type of ski faster than waxless skis. Waxing skis in this manner is a complex topic and the wax that you use is dependent upon factors such as snow temperature and humidity. There are entire books devoted to the subject! Many ski shops or outdoor shops will offer waxing clinics to get you started. While waxless skis are not recommended for beginners, more advanced skiers will appreciate the ease that these skis glide along the trails.

Ski Touring Checklist

- *Hydration system or water bottle*
- *Skies & Poles*
- *Grip wax/climbing skins*
- *Sun protection*
- *Camera*
- *Lunch*
- *Hand warmers*

What about ski width? Wider skis are more stable but slower than narrow skis; if you do a lot of up and down you might want something with metal edges or ¾-length metal edges. The stiffer the boot the better you'll be able to turn on the downhills but bulkier, heavier boots are more prone to causing blisters and will also slow you down. Boots have evolved from softer fabric and leather to far heavier,

The author skiing to the Ben Eiseman Hut

Winter trails are usually denoted by blue diamonds

but more supportive, plastic.   A variety of binding types have been introduced in the last two decades for use in the backcountry. These include 3-pin Telemark, New Nordic Norm   Backcountry   (NNN-BC), and various alpine touring (AT) setups like the Fritschi and Dynafit bindings.

Lots of trade-offs in the skiing business but just grab some equipment and go see what you like best. Over time and as you gain more experience, you will fine tune your gear and perhaps even have two or more different ski setups for different conditions and terrain. There is a lot of fun in learning all the nuances of backcountry and cross country skiing, so enjoy!

Snowshoes

Snowshoes allow us to explore the backcountry trails in winter with relative ease. While snowshoeing in fresh, unconsolidated snow can be frustrating and difficult, traveling partially packed trails or on consolidated snow via snowshoes can be extremely enjoyable.
Snowshoes come in a bunch of varieties ranging from the traditional wood-and-leather type to the more contemporary aluminum and neoprene versions.   There are even snowshoes specially designed   for running. Most snowshoers will want to use ski poles to assist with balance. Snowshoeing is an arduous activity and it is difficult to go very fast or far. Consequently, snowshoe trails in winter usually are not super long. Many of the summer trails in this guidebook can be snowshoed with varying success depending upon conditions. **NOTE:**  The large pits or holes that snowshoes create essentially destroy ski tracks, rendering ski waxes and the waxless scales on the bottom of skis ineffective. It is common etiquette for snowshoers to hike off to the side and parallel to ski tracks, making their own trail.

Clothing

Regardless of what you choose to wear in the outdoors, make sure it is wool or some sort of synthetic material. Polypropylene is a common material. My fabric of choice for the outdoors is merino wool. The stuff lasts forever and retains its new look for years. Great stuff but expensive – you pay for quality but you'll be glad you did. Wool might be too warm in the summer, but other "quick-dry" fabrics are available that are lightweight and breathable. Don't ever wear cotton in the backcountry unless it is a warm day. Even in summer, clear skies can give way to harsh thunderstorms. Cotton retains moisture and takes forever to dry out. Synthetic or wool garments are more "hydrophobic" (water-hating) and thus will dry quicker. In addition, they still insulate when wet.

Rain Gear

A typical Colorado summer day in the mountains involves rain showers (see Safety Concerns below). Start early but be prepared for

Always dress in layers

rain. Worst case, at least bring a small poncho. A lightweight rain jacket and rain pants will do wonders if it starts to rain. And, today's rain gear is extremely light and will take up just a small amount of space in your backpack.

Water Purification

Unfortunately, most streams, lakes, and rivers in Colorado are prone to *giardia* contamination. Giardia is caused by a small protozoa known as *Giardia lamblia*. When water containing this microorganism is consumed, the protozoa can infect the small intestine and victims of giardia will have diarrhea. Giardia spores are transmitted by both domesticated and non-domesticated animals such as cattle, elk, beavers, and others. Although a particular water source may be free of contamination, it is a good idea to treat all water in Colorado assuming that it is infected with giardia. This includes either boiling water from lakes and streams for at least 5 minutes, using iodine tablets or other water purification tablets, using a commercially available water filter specifically designed for this purpose, or by using an ultraviolet light designed for killing protozoans, such as a SteriPEN.

Safety Concerns in Colorado

Letting someone know your intended route and when to expect you home are probably two of the best things you can do when preparing for an outdoor adventure. Besides that, be careful if you are a male - according to the Colorado Department of Public Health, men are 3 times more likely to get injured in the woods, 8 times more likely to get killed in the mountains, and 17 times more likely to get killed by an avalanche! There's not much you can do about your sex, but everyone should be familiar with the following safety concerns that exist when visiting the mountains of Colorado.

Hypothermia

When the core body temperature drops below 95 °F this is defined as hypothermia, although the situation becomes more serious as body temperature decreases. During mild hypothermia (95 °F down to 90 °F), speech becomes slightly slurred, the victim will shiver as muscles attempt to create heat, and blood vessels constrict. During moderate hypothermia (90 °F down to 82 °F), shivering becomes much more vigorous, the victim can become confused but is still alert, and lips, ears, and extremities (fingers and toes) become blue as the body attempts to preserve its heat for the interior organs. As severe hypothermia (below 82 °F) sets in, shivering can actually stop, walking becomes almost impossible, and heart rate can plummet into the 30s. At the worst stages, victims have been known to undress in their confused state and sometimes the brain stem will elicit a "terminal burrowing" response in which the victim will burrow into an enclosed space before they die. Plan accordingly and don't let this be you!

In Colorado, cases of hypothermia involve individuals who are poorly prepared and/or who have an over-ambitious plan. Always hope for the best but plan for the worst. Perhaps more dangerous than cold temperatures is the combination of even moderately cold temperatures with rain or wet snow. Wet clothing will exacerbate the effects of hypothermia and will suck the heat from your body very rapidly. It is always a good idea to carry an extra dry layer and always carry a rain jacket and pants to fend off moisture.

If you are caught with hypothermia and you are with others, it is a good idea to get close to them. Cuddle up, place your hands and feet on their bare stomachs, and if it is really bad you might want to strip off your wet clothes and crawl into a sleeping bag with one of your buddies to warm up. Otherwise, try to build a fire (matches and fire starting material are good things to carry) or get back to civilization.

Frostbite & Wind Chill

Frostbite is the freezing of exposed and unprotected skin and can occur in temperatures that are below freezing. Your heart pumps warm blood throughout your extremities to keep them warm but when the temperature drops far below the freezing point, heat is lost faster than it can be replenished via blood circulation. In this case, the water in your skin may freeze. "Frostnip" is the initial stage where extremities become cold, sensation may be lost, but only the very superficial layer of skin near the surface may be frozen and damaged. Underlying tissue does not freeze at this point but superficial peripheral nerve damage may occur and in some times it may require weeks or months for nerve function to be completely restored. If circulation is not restored or skin re-warmed, the situation may get worse and the underlying tissue may start to freeze, resulting in blisters if the freeze is not too deep or may require amputation if a finger, toe, or extremity freezes solid. The best way to prevent frostbite is to wear adequate protective clothing in the winter. If your extremities become numb while in cold weather, stop your activity and make it a priority to restore circulation. Loosen boots to increase circulation to the toes. Wear a balaclava on the face to protect the ears and nose. It is also a good idea to carry hand and toe warmers.

The cold can be dramatically exacerbated by winds, causing "wind chill". Moving air across the skin causes a phenomenon known as "convection" in which heat loss from the skin is more rapid than if there were no moving air. In windy conditions, this results in it feeling a lot colder than the actual air temperature. For example, a 10 °F day with 30 mph winds feels equivalent to a calm air temperature of -33 °F. Bottom line, when winds are present in winter you need to dress warmer and protect exposed skin.

Altitude Sickness

Altitude sickness, also known as acute mountain sickness (AMS), afflicts many visitors to Colorado, especially those coming from sea level. The high elevations of the mountainous regions in Colorado mean lower oxygen content of the air. More than 20% of visitors to the mountains experience some type of altitude adjustment problems. Symptoms include difficulty sleeping, shortness of breath, headache, nausea, and rapid pulse. Pulmonary and cerebral edema are severe forms of altitude sickness and occur at higher elevations. To prevent altitude sickness and if you are flying from sea level, consider spending at least a day at a moderate elevation, like Denver, before heading to the higher mountain towns of Colorado. The drug Diamox has also been used preventively to decrease side effects of AMS when traveling to higher elevations. If you experience altitude sickness, be sure to drink lots of water and consider returning to lower elevations.

Aspen trees, early winter

Lightning

Few experiences are as humbling as being caught in an electrical rain storm in the mountains in Colorado during the summer. The sounds and vibrations of thunder are incredible! However, lightning can be dangerous. Between 1959 and 2009 there were 139 lightning casualties in Colorado. This averages to about 3 deaths per year from lightning, many of which are in the mountains above treeline. Additionally, there are about 16 injuries in Colorado each year from lightning. In general, it is a bad idea to be above treeline during a storm. If you are above treeline and you hear thunder, it is recommended to turn around and head to the trees to seek shelter. If you find yourself above treeline during an electrical storm, seek out low points in the terrain. Lightning strikes local high points and high passes. Hunker down in local low points or scramble down from a high summit. If lightning is crashing around you, squat down with your feet close together and wrap your arms around your legs to make yourself a tight ball with only your feet touching the ground. If necessary, cover your ears to protect them from the intense sounds. It is a bad idea to hide underneath an individual tree or small clump of trees since lone trees act to attract lightning and are the highest points around.

Wildlife

Dangerous encounters with wildlife in Colorado are extremely rare. In contrast to other parts of the Rocky Mountains, we don't have to worry about grizzly bears here in Colorado. Fortunately, we don't have to continually look over our shoulders and shout "Hey bear, hey bear" like you do in Canada, Alaska, and some places in Wyoming and Montana. So in these regards, Colorado is quite safe. However, we do have black bears, moose, and mountain lions.

Black bears become problematic when they associate humans with food. Bears are naturally unaggressive, but there is nothing stopping a bear on a mission for human food. When camping and backpacking, it is extremely important to store food and garbage in secure areas that are inaccessible to bears. In fact, bears' noses are 100 times more sensitive than human noses so they can smell food for very long distances, like the black bear that smelled a dozen chocolate energy gel packets and crawled through the open window of my brother's car one night to consume them! Store your food in bear-resistant containers, dispose of garbage in bear-resistant trash cans, keep a tidy camp and clean up after you cook. Store all cookware, stoves, and food in a locked car, camper, or RV (bears can open doors). When backpacking, store all food and cookware in bags hung from high up in trees to keep them out of reach of bears. While unfriendly encounters with bears are rare, there are some precautions you can take. First, stand still. Never run or climb a tree. Leave the area immediately if you see cubs. Wave your arms and talk calmly. Keep looking at the bear and back away slowly. If you are attacked, don't play dead - fight back! (If you are in grizzly bear country and a grizzly bear attacks, it is recommended to play dead.) But don't fret - in the last 20 years in Colorado there have been only 27 people injured by black bears and only one death.

There have been fewer than a dozen mountain lion deaths in North America over the last 100 years. Nevertheless, encounters with mountain lions are on the rise, particularly as foothill area developments expand into lion habitat. Mountain lions can be easily distinguished from other closely related species like bobcats by their long, bushy tail. If you do encounter a mountain lion, you should remain calm, stop or back away slowly while facing the lion, and do all you can to appear larger (raise hands in the air and slowly wave them). In the off chance that you are attacked, fight back with rocks, sticks, hiking poles, etc. You can reduce the chance of encountering a lion by avoiding hiking alone at dawn and dusk.

Encounters are rare, but know what to do if you run into a mountain lion

Thanks to recovery efforts over the last two decades, the state's moose population is thriving. Consequently, so are encounters with moose. Moose are curious creatures and tolerate humans for longer at closer distances than other wildlife. Do not be fooled by their seemingly friendly nature. Moose can be very dangerous animals, especially when they are with their young or during the mating season (fall). They will trample animals they feel are threatening to their young, including humans. Moose can run at speeds of up to 35 mph. In general, it is best to observe these animals from a distance.

Mosquitos

In many areas of the world, mosquitoes transfer viruses and parasites between individuals, leading to over 2 million worldwide deaths due to malaria, dengue fever, yellow fever, and others. However, other than the occasional incidence of West Nile virus, which is believed to be carried by the bugs, mosquitoes don't pose a significant health hazard *per se* in North America. Nevertheless, mosquitos can be extremely annoying and completely turn a trip upside down if you are not prepared to deal with them. Mosquitos flourish in damp, moist areas and are more prevalent during times of substantial rainfall. It is wise to carry DEET-containing bug repellents or other bug sprays. Other than chemical repellents, wear thick and long pants and shirts, even gloves if you have to. Purchase a head net that cinches tight around your neck to reduce the irritation and frustration when you are around these little buggers.

First Aid

First aid techniques are beyond the scope of this book. However, it is prudent to carry basic first aid materials in case of an accident in the backcountry. The longer the trip, the more extensive the first aid kit should be. Some good things to carry are antiseptic wipes, assorted bandages, gauze and sterile pads, antibacterial ointment, adhesive medical tape, wound closure strips (butterfly bandages), tweezers, antihistamine drugs, ibuprofen or other pain relief medications, and it's always good to carry a small first aid manual. Beyond that, two important things I have found useful time and time again are blister kits (moleskin and "second skin") and Ace bandages with safety pins. Be prepared, but hope you don't have to use your first aid kit.

Poison Ivy

Poison ivy is found in many places throughout Colorado, particularly low-lying, shady areas. The foothills around Boulder as well as the Black Canyon of the Gunnison are notorious for poison ivy. Poison ivy leaves contain urushiol oil, which most people are allergic to. If not washed off the affected area, urushiol oil can easily be spread to other areas of the body through itching and scratching (or from your pets). If you think you have been exposed, the best thing to do is immediately wash the affected skin with

"Leaves of three - let it be!"

hot water and soap. Wash any clothes that are suspected to have come in contact with the poison ivy. Calamine lotion and antihistamine creams can reduce the itching and allergic reactions. Zanfel™ is a product on the market that works well by reacting with the urushiol oil, eliminating the allergic reaction in people who have been exposed to poison ivy. But the best plan is to learn to identify poison ivy, which is easily characterized by its drooping leaves that are in groups of three. The urushiol oil is also found in dead leaves in the fall.

Falling Trees

Falling trees have increasingly become a concern in many mountain recreational areas due to the increased incidence of pine beetle infestation during the last decade or so. By 2010, nearly 3.6 million acres in northern Colorado and southern Wyoming had been affected. While the worst of the beetle kill has past, many dead trees remain standing in areas of northern Colorado. Falling trees present some significant hazards on many of the trails in these areas. Here are some tips from the White River National Forest web site for reducing the risk of being injured or killed by a falling tree:

- Avoid dense patches of trees. They can fall without warning.

- Stay out of the forest when there are strong winds. If you are in the forest and the winds kick up, head to a clearing out of reach of any trees.

- Place campers and tents in areas where they will not be hit by a falling tree.

- When driving in remote areas of the forest, park close to a main road rather than on a spur or one-way section. If trees fall across the road, you may be trapped

- Bring an ax or chainsaw to remove fallen trees from roads in case you become trapped.

- Do not rely on cell phones for safety as there is no coverage in many areas of the national forest.

Avalanches

The cross country ski and snowshoe trails outlined in this book are extremely safe since few of them proceed above treeline or on steep slopes and the very nature of cross country ski touring requires gentle slopes. Nevertheless, there is always a risk of an avalanche crashing down from above. Anyone who travels in the high country of Colorado in winter should be familiar with the basics of avalanches - where and how they form, risk factors, and how to avoid them. Avalanches kill on average 6 people a year in Colorado. Due to increased education and awareness, the numbers of avalanche victims each year has remained about the same despite increases in backcountry users. The majority of avalanche deaths are snowmobilers.

Wind is the most powerful agent that produces avalanches, moving snow from upwind slopes and deposits them on lee slopes. Snowstorms also deposit snow at a rapid rate. In either case, the weight of the snow can exceed the ability of the layers below it to support the snow. When this happens, an avalanche occurs. Slab avalanches (dry snow) occur either naturally or when triggered by a skier or snowshoer. They can not only be triggered from above but also from the sides and well below the avalanche-prone slope. These are most common in the heart of winter. In late winter, spring, and even early summer, rapidly melting snow during the day can cause an increase in the weight of snow layers while simultaneously degrading the bonds in the snow that hold those layers in place. Usually occurring later in the day, wet snow avalanches travel much more slowly than dry slab avalanches but can be far more destructive due to the heavy, concrete-like consistency.

While proper training on avalanches is beyond the scope of this book, there are a few things you can do to avoid being caught in an avalanche while traveling in the high country in winter:

- Before your trip to the mountains in the winter, check the Colorado Avalanche Information Center website for the most recent avalanche forecast and discussion: http://avalanche.state.co.us

- Avoid exposed areas if you see signs of recent avalanches, you observe instabilities in the snow ("whoomphing" sound and collapse of large areas), there has been heavy snowfall or rain in the last 24 hours, there have been or currently are significant winds, or there has been significant warming either over the last couple days or during the current day.

- Travel in groups. Each member should wear an avalanche beacon and carry a shovel and probe pole and know how to use their avalanche gear.

- Stay off of steep slopes. Most avalanches occur on slopes that are between 35 and 50 degrees in steepness. Avalanches on slopes less than 25 degrees are rare. Slope aspect - does it face north, east, south, west - can also have a dramatic impact on avalanche conditions.

- Avoid "terrain traps" - places where a snow slide may pin you and your party - like a gully or against a cliff, etc.

- A group should cross a suspected avalanche slope one member at a time and each member should loosen his or her pack's hip belt.

For more information, consult the excellent book *Staying Alive in Avalanche Terrain* by Bruce Tremper or visit the Colorado Avalanche Information Center (http://avalanche.state.co.us) or www.avalanche.org.

Marmots

Yes, they are cute and cuddly, but marmots can be extremely irritating and annoying, breaking into your campsite and gear and stealing food and chewing on backpack straps, etc. Popular places where marmots are accustomed to people are more problematic. Marmots enjoy the salty taste of anything that has sweat on it - shirts, socks, hats and visors, boots and shoes, and especially backpack straps. To protect your campsite or gear from marmots, the best thing to do is to hang your gear in trees or off rock cliffs or bury your gear underneath a bunch of large rocks while you are away from camp. There is anecdotal evidence that they are deterred by coyote urine (commercially available) or cayenne pepper, but probably best to leave those items out of the wilderness. Marmots have been known to crawl up into the undercarriage of cars to chew on brake lines and radiator hoses, so take a quick look underneath your car for any damage before you head down the mountain.

Be sure to marmot-proof your campsite or they'll git ya!

Sunrise in the Mount Evans Wilderness

Wilderness-Specific Regulations

Many of the routes in this guidebook are located within or pass through federally-designated wilderness areas. To limit human-caused impacts, ensure the protection of large areas of land for future generations to enjoy, and provide untouched, primitive land where "the earth and its community of life are untrammeled by man, where man himself is a visitor who does not remain", Congress passed the Wilderness Act in 1964. Special rules apply to wilderness areas and each wilderness area may have its own specific set of regulations. In all wilderness areas, mechanized and motorized transport is prohibited. This includes the use of motorized vehicles, chain saws, motorboats, bicycles, hang gliders, and carts. Most wilderness areas also restrict group size to not more than 12-15 people, require dogs to be on leashes, and prohibit camping and campfires within 200 ft. of all streams, lakes, and developed trails. Please be sure to read additional rules and regulations that are specific to the area you are visiting and remember to follow Leave No Trace outdoor ethics guidelines (see previous section).

The Leave No Trace Seven Principles

The Leave No Trace Seven Principles have been reprinted with the permission of the Leave No Trace Center for Outdoor Ethics. For more information: www.LNT.org.

Plan Ahead and Prepare

- Know the regulations and special concerns for the area you'll visit.
- Schedule your trip to avoid times of high use.
- Visit in small groups when possible. Consider splitting larger groups into smaller groups.
- Repackage food to minimize waste.
- Use a map and compass to eliminate the use of marking paint, rock cairns or flagging.

Travel and Camp on Durable Surfaces

- Durable surfaces include established trails and campsites, rock, gravel, dry grasses or snow.
- Protect riparian areas by camping at least 200 feet from lakes and streams.
- Good campsites are found, not made. Altering a site is not necessary
- In popular areas:
  - Concentrate use on existing trails and campsites.
  - Walk single file in the middle of the trail, even when wet or muddy.
  - Keep campsites small. Focus activity in areas where vegetations is absent.
- In pristine areas:
  - Disperse use to prevent the creation of campsites and trails.
  - Avoid places where impacts are just beginning.

Dispose of Waste Properly

- Pack it in, pack it out. Inspect your campsite and rest areas for trash or spilled foods. Pack out all trash, leftover food, and litter.
- Deposit solid human waste in catholes dug 6 to 8 inches deep at least 200 feet from water, camp, and trails. Cover and disguise the cathole when finished.

- Pack out toilet paper and hygiene products.

- To wash yourself or your dishes, carry water 200 feet away from streams or lakes and use small amounts of biodegradable soap. Scatter strained dishwater.

Leave What You Find

- Preserve the past: examine, but do not touch, cultural or historic structures and artifacts.

- Leave rocks, plants and other natural objects as you find them.

- Avoid introducing or transporting non-native species.

- Do not build structures, furniture, or dig trenches.

Minimize Campfire Impacts

- Campfires can cause lasting impacts to the backcountry. Use a lightweight stove for cooking and enjoy a candle lantern for light.

- Where fires are permitted, use established fire rings, fire pans, or mound fires.

- Keep fires small. Only use sticks from the ground that can be broken by hand.

- Burn all wood and coals to ash, put out campfires completely, then scatter cool ashes.

Respect Wildlife

- Observe wildlife from a distance. Do not follow or approach them.

- Never feed animals. Feeding wildlife damages their health, alters natural behaviors, and exposes them to predators and other dangers.

- Protect wildlife and your food by storing rations and trash securely.

- Control pets at all times, or leave them at home.

- Avoid wildlife during sensitive times: mating, nesting, raising young, or winter.

Be Considerate of Other Visitors

- Respect other visitors and protect the quality of their experience.

- Be courteous. Yield to other users on the trail.

- Step to the downhill side of the trail when encountering pack stock.

- Take breaks and camp away from trails and other visitors.

- Let nature's sounds prevail. Avoid loud voices and noises.

Trail Etiquette

There is nothing worse than having your day in the mountains ruined by another trail user or party. Other than the Leave No Trace ethics discussed in the previous pages, there are other "rules of the trail" that all users should follow:

- Above all, respect all trail signs, rules, regulations, and other users

- Downhill traffic should yield to uphill traffic - step off the trail and allow the uphill traveler to maintain his or her momentum.

Bikers and hikers yield to horses, bikers yield to hikers

- Bikers and hikers should always yield to horses; bikers always yield to hikers - this means stopping on the trail and putting a foot down to let the hiker pass.

- If someone is moving faster than you and approaches from behind, kindly offer for them to pass you and step aside.

- People are startled easily. Make noise as you are approaching and let them know your intentions - "On your left" or "Hi there, mind if I pass you?"

- Not everyone enjoys your dog or pet, even if it is a friendly kiss or sniff - keep your pet on a leash and step off the trail to let other users pass.

- Stay on the trail! Do not cut switchbacks, do not create new trails, and do not follow a trail that you feel is not an official trail. Don't let your irresponsible use of the forests cause the closure of great singletrack!

- When the trails are muddy, don't skirt around on dry terrain - this will cause the widening of trails. Stay in the mud - get muddy!

Don't be afraid to get muddy!

The view from Frigid Air Pass, Maroon Bells-Snowmass Wilderness near Aspen. Being here in person was ten times as spectacular!! My tent was perched at 12,500 ft. and nothing but howling coyotes for miles around that evening!

Going Faster & Setting Goals

"Your biggest challenge isn't someone else. Its the ache in your lungs and the burning in your legs, and the voice inside you that yells 'can't', but you don't listen. You just push harder. And then you hear the voice whisper, 'can'. And you discover that the person you thought you were is no match for the one you really are."

- Author Unknown

Once you gain experience in the outdoors, you will undoubtedly dream of bigger adventures. While each of us has different ideas of what these loftier goals are, there are several things that will better enable you to be comfortable and successful as your outdoor excursions become more involved. Remember that some of the best adventures do not really have an objective in mind - the journey *is* the destination. And many times the *process* of getting somewhere with a group of friends in an extraordinary place is more meaningful than actually getting to that summit or lake. However, if you truly have your heart set on a particular goal then here are some keys to making your adventure a success:

- Start early to avoid crowds and afternoon thunderstorms and to be certain you return by nightfall.

- Be organized. Know what your objective is ahead of time, purchase and peruse maps, and ask around for information.

- Have the proper gear and know how to use it, but don't bring superfluous gear.

- Bring enough food and water; consider bringing water purification tablets or filter.

- Don't bite off more than you can chew.

- Know what the consequences are and be prepared in case you do bite off more than you can chew - does your intended route have bail-out options?

- Sometimes, your safety can depend upon your speed. Choose partners wisely and make sure that your physical conditioning is adequate for the goal in mind.

- Refine your equipment – make a note of what you used and what you didn't. If it isn't safety-related gear, consider leaving the things you didn't use at home next time.

- Respect the mountains. Don't be afraid to turn back. In Ed Viesturs' words, "Getting to the top is optional. Getting down is mandatory." The mountains will always be there.

Last ride of the season

- Always bring a map and compass no matter how familiar you think you are with the area you will be visiting. Strange things happen and before you know it you can become lost. Know how to become un-lost (see pp. 19-24 - Navigation Basics).

- Don't be caught without a rain coat in Colorado on a summer afternoon!

Charlie's Picks

At the end of each chapter, I list a top-ten list of the most aesthetic *trails or places* in each chapter along with the most fun ways to travel on them. These include both summer and winter trails. This is my opinion and you may or may not agree with me. Nevertheless, if you are in an area for a limited amount of time then you may consider using Charlie's Picks as a starting point.

Clear Creek as it makes its way to the town of Golden

Chapter 2: Denver & Golden

The foothills to the west and southwest of Denver and Golden offer extraordinary recreational opportunities to folks of the metro Denver area and visitors alike. The Jefferson County Open Space program is incredible and the cities of Lakewood and Denver also have stellar open space programs. Golden Gate Canyon State Park is found within a half hour of Golden, offering another unique atmosphere to experience nature. The majority of these areas lie at the interface of plains and mountains, resulting in easy access and relatively mild climate, enabling the use of most of these parks throughout the year. The region has a rich homesteading history; you will undoubtedly run into historical relics on some of your adventures in many of the open space parks here. The eastern terminus of the 470-mi long Colorado Trail is found in the remote area to the south and west of Waterton Canyon, where hikers and bikers will experience diverse adventures and will yearn to see more of the Colorado Trail.

Golden & Denver

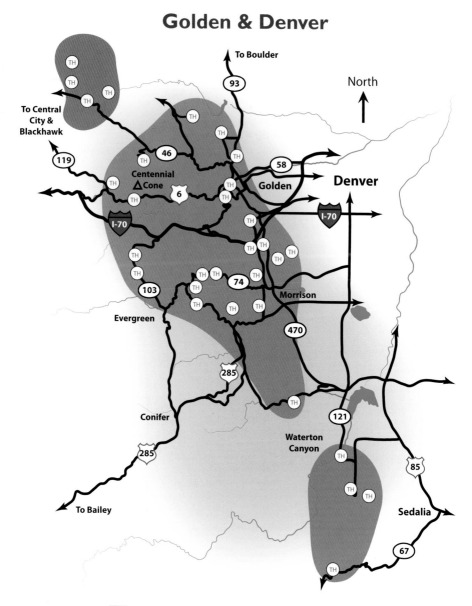

- To Boulder
- 93
- North
- To Central City & Blackhawk
- 119
- TH
- TH
- TH
- TH
- TH
- 46
- Centennial △ Cone
- 6
- TH
- TH
- TH
- 58
- Golden
- Denver
- I-70
- I-70
- TH
- TH
- TH
- TH
- TH
- TH
- TH
- TH
- TH
- TH
- TH
- TH
- TH
- 103
- 74
- TH
- TH
- TH
- Morrison
- Evergreen
- 470
- 285
- TH
- Conifer
- 121
- Waterton Canyon
- 85
- 285
- To Bailey
- TH
- TH
- TH
- Sedalia
- 67
- TH

Jefferson County Open Space (pp. 47-82)

Waterton Canyon, Roxborough State Park, & Douglas County Open Space (pp. 83-93)

Golden Gate Canyon State Park (pp. 94-97)

Jefferson County Open Space

The Jefferson County Open Space program is one of the premier "collections" of open space parks and ranches in the nation, comprised of many diverse recreational areas of Golden and the foothill areas west of Denver. Fortunately, foresight of county planners has ensured the preservation of many of these areas in the form of Open Space parks. More importantly, the trails are kept in great shape and, in contrast to the current situation in other neighboring areas such as the City of Boulder, many of these trails are open to mountain bikers. Not all areas are covered here, but some of the more popular Open Space parks in Jefferson County include:

- Apex & Windy Saddle Parks
- Centennial Cone Park
- Deer Creek Canyon Park
- Elk Meadow Park
- Lair 'o the Bear Park

- Matthews/Winters Park
- Mount Falcon Park
- North Table Mountain Park
- White Ranch Park

Looking north towards the hogback from White Ranch

Jefferson County Open Space

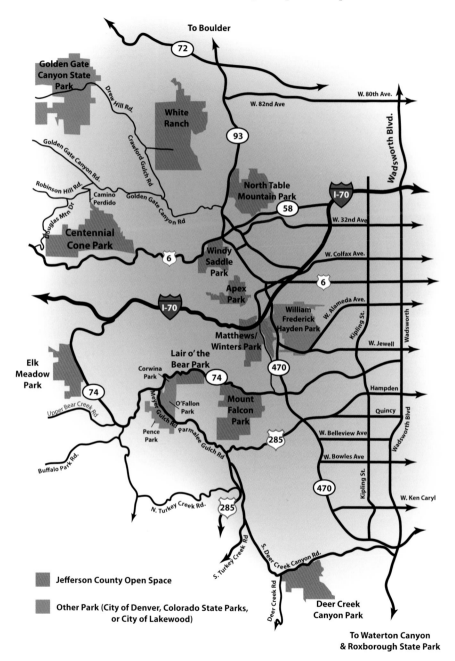

Information

Maps: Latitude 40° Maps "Colorado Front Range Trails" or National Geographic Trails Illustrated "Boulder/Golden" (#100). Some of these areas are covered on the "Buffalo Creek & Waterton Canyon" and "Golden to Evergreen" maps published by Sky Terrain as well as the "Golden Trails" map by Singletrack Maps.

Best time of the year: The conditions encountered in the Jefferson County Open Space parks can vary tremendously. In general, these are all great places to visit during the spring, summer, and fall. Areas that are lower down, such as North Table Mountain, White Ranch, Matthews/ Winters Park, and others, are quite warm in the summer, necessitating early or late activity during the hot times of the year. But even the higher areas like Bergen Peak in Elk Meadow Park can be snowshoed in the dead of winter. Furthermore, there are vast differences between south-facing (sun-exposed and much clearer of snow) and north-facing slopes in winter.

Camping: Unfortunately, there isn't much camping in the immediate Golden area. However, there is limited hike-in camping available at White Ranch and Reynolds Parks. Permits are free and can be obtained in advance or on a first come, first served basis on-site. The permits are valid for a maximum of three consecutive nights. For more information, contact the Jeffco Open Space

Pay attention to the signs!

camping hotline at (303) 271-5948. Plenty of camping is available at the nearby Golden Gate Canyon State Park, which can be accessed from the Golden area in less than a half hour. Take HWY 93 north from Golden one mile to Golden Gate Canyon Rd. then turn left (west) and drive approximately 13 mi. There are campsites as well as cabins and yurts that can be reserved by calling the reservations office at 1-800-678-2267.

More Information & Additional Resources: The Jefferson County Open Space web site has a great deal of information related to each of the Open Space parks including maps, directions, history, current news, closures, and trail maintenance activities and can be found at: http://www.co.jefferson.co.us/openspace. Or, call Jeffco Open Space at (303) 271-5925.

Apex & Windy Saddle Parks

Overlooking the town of Golden is Lookout Mountain and the sub-peak Mount Zion with its trademark "M" for Colorado School of **M**ines tattooed on its upper flanks. This is a popular recreation area and it is not uncommon to see paragliders sailing high above you. Despite the heavy traffic along US 6 at the base and neighborhoods encroaching the perimeters, there are many hidden and secluded nooks situated in the often-shaded drainages trickling down the north- and east-facing sides of Lookout Mountain. On the southeast side of Lookout Mountain is Apex Park, which contains many excellent yet rocky trails. Windy Saddle Park is a small open space park located on the north side of Lookout Mountain. One of the best mountain biking loops in the area connects these two parks and is described on p. 53 (Chimpex Loop).

Access

Chimney Gulch TH: Located off of US 6 at the base of Clear Creek Canyon near the intersection with HWY 93 and HWY 58, this trailhead provides access to the base of Lookout Mountain. The TH is located along the west side of US 6 just 0.2 mi to the south of the intersection of US 6/HWY 93/HWY 58. Use caution in this busy area.

Windy Saddle: The parking area at Windy Saddle provides access to the upper part of the Chimney Gulch Trail, as well as access to the hiker-only Beaver Brook Trail. From the intersection of US 6 and US 6/HWY 93/HWY 58 at the base of Clear Creek Canyon near Golden, drive southeast on US 6 for 1.0 mi to 19th street. Take a right (west) onto 19th street and continue on this. After 0.3 mi, 19th street turns into Lookout Mountain Rd. Continue up as the road ascends Lookout Mountain and after 2.4 mi from US 6 there will be a parking lot on your right (west side of road).

Lookout Mountain Nature Center: This 110-acre park has some great little trails to explore. Drive I-70 west of Denver to Exit 256 and turn right. If you are going eastbound on I-70, you should use Exit 254. Follow signs to the Lookout Mountain Nature Center, which uses Colorow Rd. **No dogs, bikes, or horses allowed on these trails.**

Along the Enchanted Forest Trail

Apex & Windy Saddle Parks

To Boulder (16 mi) 93

58 To Denver

Bike Path

To Clear Creek Canyon Trail

TH 5,800

Chimney Gulch TH

Golden

North

0.5 mi

6 19th St

Bike Path

Mount Zion 7,059 △

Lookout Mtn Road

6,200

0.9

1.4

SMB

Chimney Gulch Trail

To Idaho Springs

6

Windy Saddle TH 6,860

TH

0.25

6,990

Overlook 7,000

1.4

Overlook

7,520

0.6

0.3

P

Buffalo Bill Museum

Hiker only!!

Hiker only!!

Beaver Brook Trail

Kinney Run Trail (Bike Path)

To Denver

Heritage Road

Lookout Mountain Tr

Lookout Mtn. Nature Center

Lookout Mountain Road

1.1

Colorow Road

7,480

Apex

7,320

0.2

0.9

Apex Trail

Enchanted Forest Trail

1.4

Apex Trail

Apex TH

6,170

To Colfax

40

Heritage Square

To I-70

To I-70

Enlarged

0.8

◄ = One-way on odd calendar days

Grubstake Loop

6,850

0.3

7,150

Grubstake

Bonanza

6,930

Grubstake Loop

0.5

0.7

Apex TH

Argos Trail

0.25

TH

6,170

7,160

Pick n' Sledge

0.3

Hardscrabble

0.3

Sluicebox

0.6

0.7

6,500

Apex Trail

6,870

Enchanted Forest

0.2

6,810

0.3

Pick n' Sledge

6,950

0.3

6,420

0.2

0.7

0.7

Apex Trail

Apex TH: From central Golden, take US 6 south to the busy stoplight at Heritage Rd. Take a right (west) and continue along Heritage Rd. to just before Heritage Rd. intersects W. Colfax Avenue (US 40). Just before this intersection is a right turn into the lower parking lot of Heritage Square, and the trailhead and parking are found a short ways up. From the east (Denver), take I-70 west to Exit 259, take a right and drive north on W. Colfax Avenue for about a mile and take a left into Heritage Square. Make your way to the lower parking area (staying low and to the right) and follow signs to the Apex TH.

Recommended Routes

NOTE: On odd-numbered days (odd dates) there are several sections that are one-way only for mountain bikes. These trails include the Argos Trail, the section of the Apex Trail between Pick n' Sledge and Sluicebox, and the Enchanted Forest Trail. On ODD number days, these trails are all one-way UP if you are mountain biking. There are no restrictions on even-numbered days. For more information visit the Jeffco Open Space website.

Chimney Gulch Trail: Begin at the Chimney Gulch TH. You can actually start even lower if you'd like - the true bottom of this trail is located off the paved bike path near the HWY 93 bridge over Clear Creek. This trail switchbacks up Lookout Mountain before heading into the depths of the shaded and forested Chimney Gulch. If you can find someone to drop you off at the top of Lookout Mountain or Windy Saddle TH, this would be a great one-way descent. The Chimney Gulch trail takes a sharp right at a fork in the trail near the top as it turns into Lookout Mountain Trail; from here it is 0.3 mi to the top. The hiker-only Buffalo Bill Trail forks off to the left. It is approximately 3.5 mi and 1,750 ft. of elevation gain to ascend the Chimney Gulch Trail to the intersection with the Colorow Rd. at the top.

Beaver Brook Trail: Beginning at Windy Saddle TH, this hiker-only trail can be accessed by taking the Chimney Gulch Trail up (southwest) for a quarter of a mile to a sharp switchback. From here, the trail heads to the west as it contours along through forested slopes and provides access to some interesting terrain above Clear Creek Canyon. Ultimately, this trail leads to the Genesee Park area, but few folks will choose to go that far. There is a nice high lookout on a rocky outcropping about 1.4 mi from the start of the Beaver Brook Trail and this is a nice turn-around point.

Apex Park Trails: The trails that can be accessed in this area are great for hikers and bikers alike. While the Apex Trail is well-suited for hikers, bikers will prefer to ascend the route outlined below (see "NOTE for mountain bikers) due to the rocky terrain. Begin at the Apex TH at Heritage

Clear Creek Canyon

Square. The Apex Trail is a steep climb up a lovely drainage. Many other trails split off of the Apex Trail and will spark the curiosity within. Spend an hour here or explore for the whole day! The Enchanted Forest Trail is one of the most interesting parts of this area as it winds along a forested hillside and crosses several trickling creeks. Trail runners will enjoy the loops in this area. These trails are given the difficult rating due to the rocky nature and steep climbs, but hikers will encounter mainly moderate terrain.

NOTE for mountain bikers: The least frustrating way to ascend to the trails in the Apex Park area is via the new Argos Trail to Pick n' Sledge. At the three-way intersection of Grubstake, Pick n' Sledge, and Sluicebox there are many choices. The Grubstake Loop and Bonanza Trails are moderate and not too rocky. Hardscrabble Trail is super smooth, but Sluicebox is a jagged, rocky, frustrating mess of a trail.

Chimpex Loop: Begin at the Chimney Gulch TH at the base of Lookout Mountain. Ascend the Chimney Gulch Trail, crossing the Lookout Mountain Rd. after 0.9 mi. Continue up Chimney Gulch to Windy Saddle TH after another 1.4 mi (2.3 mi total). At the parking lot at Windy Saddle TH, cross the road yet again and climb through heavily wooded forests, taking a right onto the Lookout Mountain Trail at 3.2 mi (0.9 mi from Windy Saddle) and continue 0.3 mi to the top of the trail, which exits onto Colorow Rd. near the Lookout Mountain Nature Center. Follow the road to the right (west) and then south; the Lookout Mountain Trail parallels the Colorow Rd. for 1.1 mi to the intersection with the Lookout Mountain Rd. From this intersection, travel a short ways south, cross the road, and the upper end of the Apex Trail can be accessed. Continue down the Apex Trail 0.3 mi to the intersection with the Enchanted Forest Trail. Follow the Enchanted Forest Trail to the Apex Trail and to the Apex TH. Keep in mind that on odd-numbered days you will not be able to descend Enchanted Forest nor Apex; you'll have to descend upper Apex, Hardscrabble, Pick n' Sledge, and the very lower part of Apex. Just to the north of the trailhead you can pick up the Kinney Run Trail, a paved bike trail that can be taken north through neighborhoods and alongside US 6 to 19th street, where it is just a quick ride along the (dangerous!) US 6 back to your car. The route is 7.8 mi from Chimney Gulch TH to Apex TH (descent via Enchanted Forest and Apex); it is about 3 mi to return to the Chimney Gulch TH via the bike path. Total elevation gain about 2,000 ft.

Centennial Cone Park

Situated high above Clear Creek Canyon to the north, this Jeffco Open Space park is accessible from three different trailheads, including the newly-built Mayhem Gulch Trailhead off of Clear Creek Canyon. The trails in Centennial Cone Park are relatively smooth and rocky sections are few and far between, in contrast to the many technical and rocky trails characteristic of other Jeffco Open Space parks in the area. While the non-technical nature of the trails will entice the novice mountain biker, there are several strenuous climbs than must be negotiated, especially if starting from the Mayhem Gulch TH. The management plan of Centennial Cone Park has been drafted such that conflict

Looking down towards Clear Creek Canyon from the Travois Trail

between hikers and bikers is eliminated on weekends. **The trails are only open to hikers on odd-numbered weekend days and the trails are only open to mountain bikes on even-numbered weekend days.** The views from the Travois Trail and elsewhere are unparalleled.

Access

NOTE: Centennial Cone Park and the three trailheads below are closed each year for elk hunting from Dec. 1st to Jan. 31st.

Mayhem Gulch TH: From the intersection of US 6 and HWY 93 near Golden, take US 6 west up the scenic Clear Creek Canyon for about 10 mi, keep an eye out for the busy trailhead on the right side of the winding road a little over two mi after Tunnel 3. There are restroom facilities and maps available at the trailhead.

Centennial Cone TH: Follow the directions to Mayhem Gulch TH (above) but continue another 1.5 mi on US 6 to the stoplight at the intersection of US 6 and HWY 119. Continue straight onto HWY 119 and proceed about a half mile to Douglas Mountain Rd. on your right. After about a mile, turn right onto Centennial Cone Rd. and proceed to the parking area and trailhead.

Camino Perdido TH: This is a remote trailhead that provides access to the north part of Centennial Cone Park. From the Golden area, take HWY 93 north about a mile to Golden Gate Canyon Rd. Continue west for about 8 mi to Robinson Hill Rd. then take a left on Camino Perdido for about a mile to the trailhead.

Recommended Routes

Mayhem Gulch Lollipop

Mayhem Gulch Lollipop: This is a nice loop with easy access along US 6 (Clear Creek Canyon). Park at the Mayhem Gulch TH and ascend the well-maintained and relatively smooth switchbacks. After 1.5 mi, the trail intersects the Juniper Trail. Continue left on the Juniper Trail or right on the Mayhem Gulch Trail and you can make a nice loop by returning via the other route and back down the lower section of Mayhem Gulch Trail back to the trailhead. The lollipop is 4.6 mi.

Centennial Cone Park

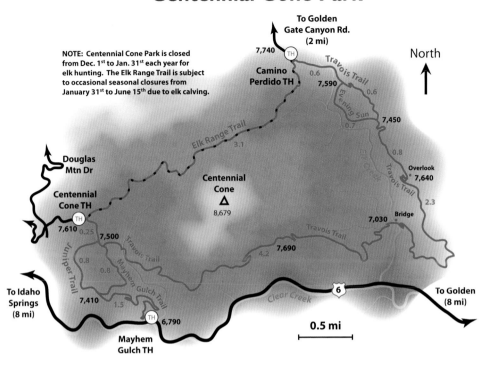

To Golden Gate Canyon Rd. (2 mi)

NOTE: Centennial Cone Park is closed from Dec. 1st to Jan. 31st each year for elk hunting. The Elk Range Trail is subject to occasional seasonal closures from January 31st to June 15th due to elk calving.

7,740   TH

Camino Perdido TH   7,590

Travois Trail   0.6   0.6

Evening Sun   0.7

7,450   0.8

North

Elk Range Trail   3.1

Douglas Mtn Dr

Centennial Cone △ 8,679

Overlook 7,640

Travois Trail   2.3

Centennial Cone TH   TH   7,610   0.25   7,500

Bridge   7,030   7,030...

Travois Trail

7,690   4.2

Juniper Trail

Mayhem Gulch Trail   0.8   0.8

Travois Trail

7,410   1.5

To Idaho Springs (8 mi)

TH   6,790

Mayhem Gulch TH

Clear Creek   6

0.5 mi

To Golden (8 mi)

Elk Range Trail: Connecting the Centennial Cone TH on the west side of the park with the Camino Perdido TH on the north side of the park, the Elk Range Trail is mainly double-track and climbs to a gradual saddle on the northwest side of Centennial Cone. There are magnificent views here of the impressive Centennial Cone looming above you. **NOTE: The Elk Range Trail is subject to occasional seasonal closures from January 31 to June 15 due to elk calving.** Up-to-date seasonal closure information can be obtained from the Jeffco Open Space website: http://www.co.jefferson.co.us/openspace.

Elk Range Trail

Travois Trail: Situated in a spectacular setting high above Clear Creek Canyon, the Travois Trail traverses along rocky slopes from the Camino Perdido TH to the Centennial Cone TH. This area was used by Arapaho peoples as a route from the plains to the mountains. Despite the traversing nature of this trail, don't be fooled - there are some significant climbs along this trail! Take this trail as an out-and-back or use as part of a bigger loop around Centennial Cone (see next page). Begin either at the north side (Camino Perdido TH) or access the southern terminus from the Mayhem Gulch Trail (Mayhem Gulch TH). The Travois Trail is a superb place for a trail run. The distance is 8.8 mi one-way; 2,300 ft. of elevation gain south to north, 2,170 ft. of elevation gain going north to south.

Travois Trail

Centennial Cone Loop: This loop can be started either at Mayhem Gulch TH (easiest access via car), Centennial Cone TH (more difficult access), or Camino Perdido TH (difficult access). Regardless, this loop takes the Elk Range Trail from the Centennial Cone TH at the

top of the Mayhem Gulch Trail to Camino Perdido TH then utilizes the Travois Trail back to the Mayhem Gulch area. Keep in mind that the Elk Range Trail is subject to seasonal wildlife closures (see opposite page). The loop can be done in either direction, but doing it clockwise will allow you to descend the few technical spots rather than ascend them. Great for trail runners. The loop itself (excluding the Mayhem Gulch Trail if you start from the south) is 11.9 mi and there is about 2,700 ft. of elevation gain. Using Mayhem Gulch Trail as an out-and-back to the loop will add on 4.6 mi and 1,100 ft. of elevation gain/loss.

Deer Creek Canyon Park

Located in a deep, secluded valley with forested slopes, Deer Creek Canyon Park is similar to other Jefferson County parks like White Ranch, Mount Falcon, and Apex Park in that it is situated where the plains meet the mountains. This results in a steep initial climb right from the trailhead. Once on top, however, the trails are easier as they traverse hillsides and encircle small mountains. Plenty of scrub oak is found in Deer Creek Canyon Park as well as fir and spruce trees. The canyon is shaded throughout the year, resulting in lush vegetation in the summer. The shaded nature and minimal sun exposure in the winter makes this a suitable place to snowshoe. The park has an interesting history as it was an occasional campsite for Native Americans and was homesteaded in the late 1800s. The infamous cannibal Alferd Packer spent time in the area after he was released from the state penitentiary.

Golden Eagle Trail with the hogback in the distance

Access

Deer Creek Canyon TH: Take C-470 south from I-70 or west from I-25 to Kipling Parkway (about 14 mi south of I-70 or 12 mi west of I-25 on C-470). Go south on Kipling for a tenth of a mile then turn right (west) onto W. Ute Ave. Proceed another 0.9 mi then take a right onto W. Deer Creek Canyon Rd. From here, continue just under 2 mi and take a left on Grizzly Drive. After 0.4 mi take a right into Deer Creek Canyon Park.

Recommended Routes

Plymouth Creek Trail: A difficult, rocky trail that climbs steeply along Plymouth Creek then climbs west then north to the intersection with the Red Mesa Loop.

Meadowlark Trail: A hiker-only trail that climbs a broad ridge from the trailhead then traverses southwest to join the Plymouth Creek Trail at Plymouth Creek.

Plymouth Mountain Trail: A moderate trail that contours around and encircles Plymouth Mountain. A short (0.4-mi) trail leads off of the Plymouth Mountain Trail to the summit of Plymouth Mountain.

Black Bear Trail: Not a through-trail, but this trail descends grassy and forested slopes and switchbacks from the east side of the Plymouth Mountain Trail down to the plains below. The trail currently ends at private property, necessitating an out-and-back and the long climb back up to the Plymouth Mountain Trail.

Homesteader Trail: This secluded trail contours along hillsides atop the park and crosses several small creeks. Off limits to bikes. 1.1 mi long.

Red Mesa Loop: A super cool loop that starts at the top of the Plymouth Creek Trail. The trail winds through meadows and forests with the occasional view of the grasslands below. Best done clockwise if you are on a bike.

Golden Eagle Trail: A hiker-only trail that leads from the Red Mesa Loop out to Bill Couch Mountain. Great views surround you on all sides.

Deer Creek Canyon Park

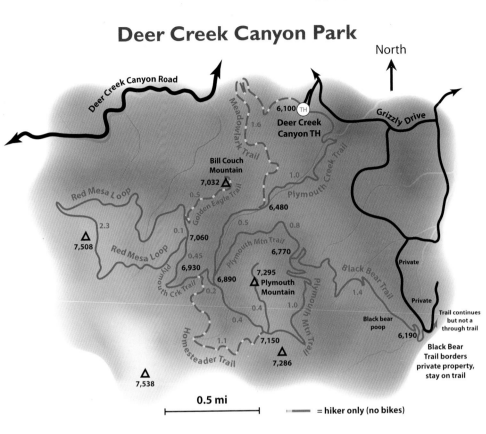

0.5 mi

= hiker only (no bikes)

Elk Meadow Park

Ranging from easy trails through high grassy meadows to steep, rocky climbs in ponderosa pine forests, the Elk Meadow Park has over 13 mi of stellar trails. This is a great place for mountain bikers and hikers alike, although the climb to the top of Bergen Peak is not recommended for bikes. Like many Jeffco Open Space parks, this park can get crowded, particularly on spring and fall weekends, so timing your visit early or late in the day may be advantageous. Once the snow falls, Bergen Peak must be accessed by snowshoe but many of the lower, sun-exposed trails are relatively clear even through the winter.

Access

Buchanan Ponds: This is a small parking area that provides access to the northeastern part of Elk Meadow Park. Take I-70 west from Denver and exit onto HWY 74 (Evergreen Parkway). Continue approximately 3 mi from I-70 to the stoplight at Squaw Pass Rd., take a left at this stoplight onto Ellingwood Trail, and proceed a short way to a parking area on the right next to Buchanan Ponds.

Old barn, Elk Meadow Park

Elk Meadow TH: Follow directions to the intersection of Evergreen Parkway (HWY 74) and the Squaw Pass Rd. as described on the previous page for Buchanan Ponds. Continue on Evergreen Parkway another 1.7 mi and take a right at the stoplight at Lewis Ridge Rd. Follow signs and continue a tenth of a mile to the Elk Meadow Park trailhead.

Stagecoach TH: From Lewis Ridge Rd. (see above "Elk Meadow TH"), continue an additional 0.9 mi to Stagecoach Rd. Take a right at the stoplight and continue up Stagecoach Rd. for 1.25 mi and there is a trailhead and parking area on your right (north side).

Recommended Routes

Meadow View Loop: If you enjoy easy to moderate trails and wide-open views, this loop is for you. Begin at the Elk Meadow TH off of Lewis Ridge Rd. Take the Painters Pause Trail from the parking area then the Founders Trail to the Meadow View Trail and stay on the Meadow View Trail as

Meadow View Loop

it ascends a bit, rolls in and out of the woods, and crosses Bergen Creek. Descend via the Elk Ridge Trail or the Meadow View Trail to the Sleepy "S" Trail back to the trailhead. This loop is about 4.4 mi for the return via Meadow View Trail. See route marked with green arrows on the opposite page.

Elk Meadow Park & Bergen Peak

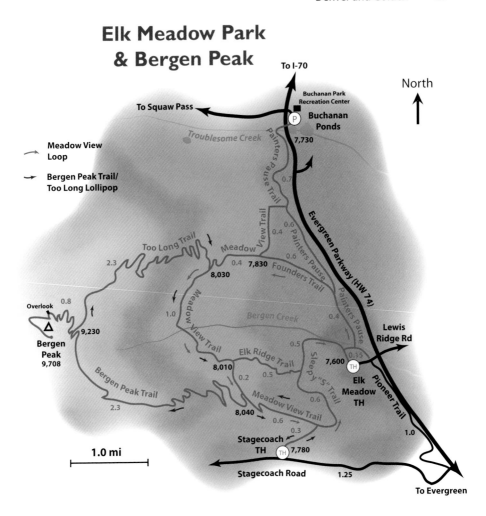

North

To I-70

To Squaw Pass

Buchanan Park Recreation Center

Buchanan Ponds

P

7,730

Troublesome Creek

Meadow View Loop

Bergen Peak Trail/ Too Long Lollipop

Painters Pause Trail

0.7

0.6

0.4

View Trail

Painters Pause

Evergreen Parkway (HW 74)

Too Long Trail

Meadow

0.4   7,830

8,030

0.6

Founders Trail

2.3

Painters pause

0.4

Lewis Ridge Rd

Bergen Creek

Overlook   0.8

9,230

Meadow View Trail

1.0

0.5

0.15

Bergen Peak 9,708

△

Elk Ridge Trail

8,010

0.2   0.5

Sleepy "S" Trail

0.6

7,600   TH

Elk Meadow TH

Bergen Peak Trail

2.3

Meadow View Trail

8,040   0.6

0.3

Pioneer Trail

1.0

1.0 mi

Stagecoach TH   TH   7,780

Stagecoach Road   1.25

To Evergreen

Bergen Peak

Bergen Peak: For hikers and mountain runners, the ascent of Bergen Peak is classic! Begin either at the Elk Meadow TH or the Stagecoach TH (slightly shorter). Regardless of where you start, make your way to the bottom of the Bergen Peak trail and ascend the very nice Bergen Peak Trail to the top of Bergen Peak, staying left at the intersection up high with the Too Long Trail. The Bergen Peak Trail climbs up an exquisite ridge, utilizes several nice switchbacks, then contours around the west side of the peak before the end of the trail. Return the way you came or for a longer trip return via the Too Long Trail. To the top of Bergen Peak it is 4.1 mi and 1,900 ft. of elevation gain via the Bergen Peak Trail from the Stagecoach TH.

Wintery aspens

Bergen Peak Trail/Too Long Trail Lollipop: This lollipop is great for mountain bikers as this loop comes close to the summit but avoids the final 0.7-mi rocky climb to the top of Bergen Peak. From Stagecoach TH, ascend the Meadow View Trail to the Bergen Peak Trail then descend the Too Long Trail. Return via the

Bergen Peak Trail/Too Long Lollipop

spectacular Meadow View Trail back to the trailhead. Not enough? Explore the other trails lower down, such as the Elk Ridge Trail, Painters Pause Trail, and others. 7.6 mi for the lollipop and about 2,600 ft. of elevation gain. See route marked with blue arrows on p. 61.

Lair o' the Bear Park

Bear Creek winds its way from the Evergreen area to Morrison. Situated to the south of Bear Creek and to the south and east of the small town of Kittredge are five open space parks: the Jeffco-owned Lair o' the Bear Park and four Denver Mountain Parks - Little, Corwina, O'Fallon, and Pence Parks. While Lair o' the Bear Park is the common name for this area, most of the area here is not the actual Lair o' the Bear Park, with most of the popular Bear Creek Trail occupying Corwina and O'Fallon Parks. This area is quite popular among "Front-Rangers" as it is less than a 15-minute drive from Morrison and less than an hour drive from Boulder and Denver. Depending upon conditions, parts of this area are excellent for snowshoeing once the snow falls.

Access

Lair o' the Bear Park: From the town of Morrison on the west side of Denver (a few mi north of the intersection of US 285 and HWY 470) take HWY 74 for about 4 mi to the tiny town of Idledale. Continue for another 3/4 mi beyond Idledale and the Lair o' the Bear Park is on the left hand side of the road. Continue down the dirt road a short ways to the parking area and the trailhead.

Corwina Park: From the town of Morrison, drive HWY 74 west for 7.1 mi. The turnoff to Corwina Park is shortly after a huge left-turning hairpin turn. The trailhead is located just off of the highway on the east side (left as you are driving up the canyon). If you get to O'Fallon Park or the town of Kittredge you have gone too far.

O'Fallon Park: Follow the directions to Corwina Park (above). Drive another 0.4 mi on HWY 74 and shortly after a water treatment pond on the right side of the highway you should see signs on the left to O'Fallon Park. Drive the gravel road a short ways to the parking area. This is a great place for a picnic as there are many picnic tables down by the creek. It is not obvious where the trailheads in this area are. One of them (providing access to the Meadow View Loop Trail) can be accessed by following a dirt road north and hiking past a gate for a quarter of a mile along Bear Creek. The other (providing access to the Picnic Loop and West Ridge Loop) can be accessed by making your way to the southwest side of the park on the west side of the creek.

Pence Park: From Morrison, drive HWY 74 for 7.9 mi to just before the town of Kittredge. Before Kittredge, turn left (south) on Myers Gulch Rd. (Rd. 120) and drive up Myers Gulch for about 1.8 mi. The parking area at Pence Park is on the right side (west side) of the road. Like O'Fallon Park, Pence Park is a great place for a picnic. The south terminus of the Bear Creek Trail can be accessed from this trailhead.

Bear Creek, early winter

Recommended Routes

NOTE: While the Bear Creek Trail is super popular among mountain bikers, the majority of the trails in the Lair o' the Bear, Corwina, and O'Fallon Parks are off limits to mountain bikers. Bikers have complained, but this has resulted in an agreeable arrangement for hikers as there are many superb hiking trails in this area. Even on the most popular weekend days, hikers will encounter off-the-beaten-path experiences.

Bear Creek Trail: This is what most folks know as "Lair o' the Bear". This out-and-back ride is a moderate ride. Beginners will enjoy the first 1.2 mi along Bear Creek. After this, bikers will be challenged on the climb from the river as the trail

switchbacks up a few rocky sections. After the first couple of miles, the trail is smooth and the trail contours and rolls along through hills and drainages. This trail can be crowded so start early or late to avoid congestion and keep your speed in check around the corners. Hikers may opt to travel the hiker-only trails (see below). This makes a great out-and-back run for trail runners. About 6 mi one-way from Lair o' the Bear Park to Pence Park.

Panorama Point Trail: An excellent 1-2 hour hike. The Panorama Point Trail follows a secluded drainage from Corwina Park up to the Bear Creek Trail and then utilizes the Bear Creek Trail for 0.15 mi, finishing with a short but steep climb to an overlook with a spectacular view. It is 1.4 mi with 750 ft. of elevation gain to Panorama Point.

Bergen Peak from Lair o' the Bear Park

Lair o' the Bear Park

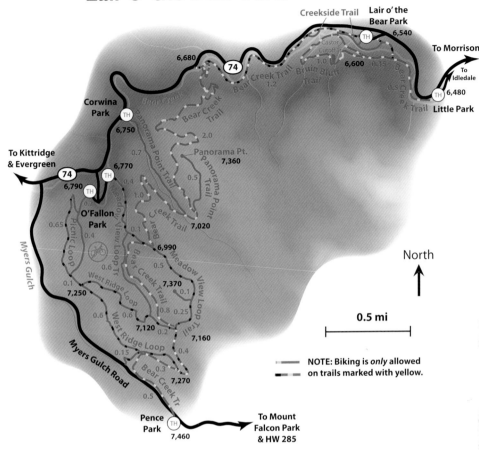

Picnic Loop: A short loop suitable for... well... picnickers! The loop begins from the southwest trailhead of O'Fallon Park, located on the west side of Bear Creek across a bridge. From the trailhead, hike up a drainage to a trail intersection. Either do the loop in the clockwise or counterclockwise direction. The latter is recommended since this leaves you with a nice hike down the drainage on the return. 1.5 mi round trip from the trailhead.

Picnic Loop

Meadow View Loop

Meadow View Loop: A longer loop that begins from the northern part of O'Fallon Park. From the parking area at O'Fallon Park, follow the dirt road north past a closure gate and parallel Bear Creek to the official trailhead. Hike up the beautiful drainage to a trail intersection. Continue straight (left), cross the Bear Creek Trail after a short distance, and

Tina Lewis running at Lair o' the Bear Park

continue up the doubletrack and way up to a high point. The trail then descends down and once again intersects the Bear Creek Trail near a trail information sign. Continue down the drainage through a meadow, staying right at the intersection of the West Ridge Trail and the Meadow View Loop Trail. The singletrack that parallels the creek is superb and in a great location. The loop closes and you can return to your car the way you came. 2.5 mi round trip.

Bruin Bluff Trail: A nice loop on the slopes above and to the south of the main parking area. A few technical and steep areas yet mostly nice singletrack with excellent views of Bear Creek from above.

Matthews/Winters Park & Red Rocks Park

Situated at the interface between the plains and foothills, the Matthews/Winters and Red Rocks Parks are quite unique. Grassy meadows, interesting geological formations, and ample vegetation make this area fun to explore. Matthews/Winters Park is a Jefferson County-owned park and the adjoining Red Rocks Park is owned by the City of Denver. Bikes are allowed on most of the trails in this area yet the biking can be extremely challenging. After your hike or bike, visit Dinosaur Ridge. Some of the most impressive dinosaur tracks in the world can be found here.

Access

Dakota Ridge TH/Stegosaurus Lot: Drive west on I-70 from Denver to Exit 259. This exit is just where the flatlands turn to foothills. Take a left (south) on CR 93 (Hogback Rd.) and proceed about a tenth of a mile and the Stegosaurus Lot is on your left. If this parking area is full you can park at the Matthews/Winters Park TH (see below). The Dakota Ridge Trail heads southeast up the hill to the south of the parking lot.

Matthews/Winters Park TH: This trailhead is located just south and across CR 93 (Hogback Rd.) from the Dakota Ridge TH/Stegosaurus Lot (see above). This trailhead can get busy on weekends.

Red Rocks TH: This trailhead can be accessed either from the town of Morrison or from I-70. From Exit 259 of I-70, travel south on CR 93 (aka Hogback Rd.) for 1.4 mi and take a right onto W. Alameda Parkway (signs for Red Rocks Park). Continue 0.7 mi and Red Rocks Trail Rd. will join from the left (east). At this intersection, there is a small parking area. The Red Rocks Trail can be accessed from just across the street. If approaching from Morrison, take CR 93 (Hogback Rd.) for 1.3 mi and take a left onto Red Rocks Park Rd. Continue 0.3 mi and take a right on Red Rocks Trail Rd. Continue on Red Rocks Trail Rd. until it intersects with W. Alameda Parkway. At this intersection, there is a small parking area and the Red Rocks Trail is just across the street.

Green Mountain TH: This trailhead provides access to the Zorro Trail. Take C-470 (on the west side of Denver) to its intersection with W. Alameda Parkway. This intersection is about 1.5 mi south of I-70/C-470 and 6.1 mi north of US 285/C-470. Take W. Alameda Parkway west for 0.3 mi, hang a sharp right onto S. Rooney Rd., and follow this for 0.6 mi

Red Rocks Park

to the obvious trailhead and parking area on the right (east side).

Recommended Routes

Red Rocks Trail: After beginning either on Village Walk (hikers) or Village Ride (bikers), this trail connects the Matthews/Winters Park TH to Red Rocks Park & TH. The trail skirts along grasslands and the occasional rocky spot and descends into a small canyon with red rocks looming above you as it makes its way to the Red Rocks TH in Red Rocks Park.

Morrison Slide Trail: Steep climbs on both ends of this trail provide access to a high, relatively flat area with excellent views of the Hogback and the city of Denver. A difficult mountain bike trail. This trail allows for a nice lollipop when taking the Red Rocks Trail south towards Red Rocks Park. Access the southern part of this trail from the Red Rocks TH or the northern part via the Matthews/Winters Park TH.

Dakota Ridge Trail: Relatively short but this trail is one of the rockiest trails around. Dakota Ridge is popular among both hikers and bikers but is a very difficult mountain biking trail. If biking, it is best to begin on the north end at the Dakota Ridge TH as this will give you more downhill than

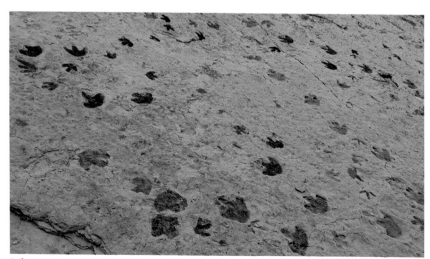

What creature made these tracks?!

Matthews/Winters Park
& Red Rocks Park

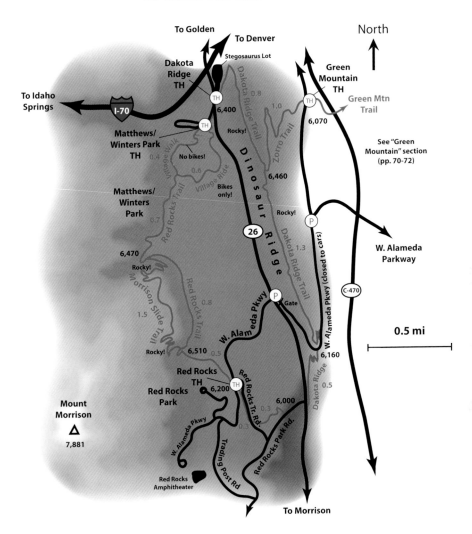

To Golden

To Denver

Stegosaurus Lot

North

Dakota
Ridge
TH

Green
Mountain
TH

Green Mtn
Trail

TH
6,400

TH
6,070

To Idaho
Springs

I-70

Dakota Ridge Trail

0.8

1.0

Zorro Trail

Matthews/
Winters Park
TH

TH

Rocky!

Dinosaur Ridge

See "Green
Mountain" section
(pp. 70-72)

0.4

Village Walk

No bikes!

0.6

6,460

Village Ride

Red Rocks Trail

Matthews/
Winters
Park

Bikes
only!

Rocky!

P

W. Alameda
Parkway

0.7

26

Dakota Ridge Trail

6,470

1.3

Rocky!

Red Rocks Trail

Morrison Slide Trail

0.8

P

Gate

C-470

0.5 mi

1.5

W. Alameda Pkwy

W. Alameda Pkwy (closed to cars)

Rocky!

6,510

0.5

6,160

Red Rocks
TH

TH

Dakota Ridge Trail

Red Rocks
Park

6,200

Red Rocks Tr. Rd.

0.5

6,000

Mount
Morrison

W. Alameda Pkwy

0.3

Red Rocks Park Rd.

△

7,881

Trading Post Rd

Red Rocks
Amphitheater

To Morrison

uphill. The Zorro Trail can be accessed readily from along the Dakota Ridge Trail. After 1.3 mi of the most technical trails around, you will end on a closed paved road; another 0.5 mi of dirt (1.8 mi total) will spit you out on CR 93 (Hogback Rd.).

Zorro Trail: Except for a short, steep technical section near the top, this trail is relatively easy and connects the Dakota Ridge Trail to the Green Mountain/Hayden Park area (see next section). Access the bottom of the Zorro Trail from the Green Mountain TH (see next page in "Green Mountain" section) or access the top of the Zorro Trail from along the Dakota Ridge Trail from a start at the Dakota Ridge TH.

Green Mountain (William Frederick Hayden Park)

This City of Lakewood park is formally known as William Frederick Hayden Park but most will refer to it simply as Green Mountain. A hot and exposed place in the summer but during the spring, fall, and winter these trails can be utilized easily by hikers, runners, and mountain bikers. The close proximity to Denver and Golden make this a popular area, and there are many fun and challenging trails at Green Mountain.

Near Rooney Valley, Green Mountain (Hayden Park)

Access

Green Mountain TH: Take C-470 (on the west side of Denver) to its intersection with W. Alameda Parkway. This intersection is about 1.5 mi south of I-70/C-470 and 6.1 mi north of US 285/C-470. Take W. Alameda Parkway west for 0.3 mi, hang a sharp right onto S. Rooney Rd., and follow this for 0.6 mi to the obvious trailhead and parking area on the right (east side).

Forsberg Park: From the intersection of C-470 and W. Alameda Parkway, take W. Alameda Parkway east for just over a mile and Forsberg Park is on your right (south side of road). Additional parking available just east along the road.

Utah & Florida THs: From the intersection of C-470 and W. Alameda Parkway, take W. Alameda Parkway for just over 2 mi, staying left after 1.5 mi. On the left side of the road across from W. Utah Ave is the Utah TH. Another quarter of a mile on the left is the Florida TH.

Recommended Routes

Green Mountain Trail: Doubletrack in parts, singletrack in parts, this loop ascends the west and east sides of Green Mountain and closes the loop with singletrack trails on the southern part of the mountain. Difficult and strenuous to get to the top of Green Mountain, but the sections down low are moderate in difficulty. Suitable for trail runners, too.

Box O' Rox: A technical and rocky-at-times trail. Great for a technical mountain bike descent.

Summit Loop Trail: Hikers and bikers alike will enjoy this easy singletrack trail that parallels the Green Mountain Trail. Rocky towards the northwest end.

Rooney Valley Trail: A nice singletrack trail that begins on its east side near Forsberg Park and traverses along the southwest side of Green Mountain before descending into Rooney Valley. The trail then climbs up and out of Rooney Valley to meet the Green Mountain Trail.

Green Mountain (Hayden Park)

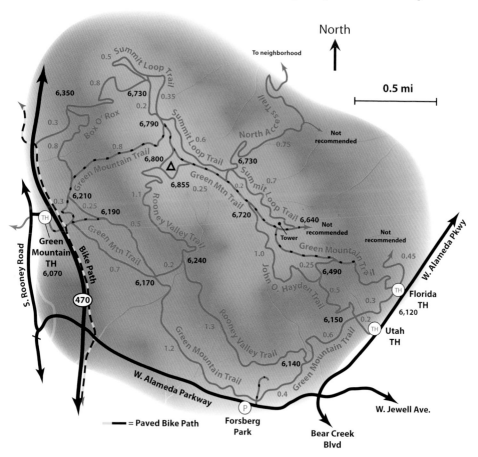

North

To neighborhood

0.5 mi

0.5 Summit Loop Trail

0.8

6,350

6,730

0.35

0.2

0.3

Box O' Rox

6,790

Access Trail

North Access

0.6

Not recommended

0.8

0.8

Green Mountain Trail

6,800

0.75

6,730

6,855

Green Mtn Trail

0.25

Summit Loop Trail

0.2

0.7

6,210

0.25

6,190

1.1

6,720

6,640

Not recommended

Not recommended

0.3

Rooney Valley Trail

0.5

Tower

Green Mountain Trail

0.25

0.45

TH

Green Mountain TH 6,070

Green Mtn Trail

0.2

6,240

1.0

0.25

6,490

W. Alameda Pkwy

0.7

6,170

John O. Hayden Trail

0.5

0.3

TH

Florida TH

6,120

470

Bike Path

0.2

TH

Utah TH

6,150

0.6

6,140

0.4

Green Mountain Trail

1.3

Rooney Valley Trail

1.2

Green Mountain Trail

S. Rooney Road

W. Alameda Parkway

W. Jewell Ave.

= Paved Bike Path

P

Forsberg Park

Bear Creek Blvd

John O. Hayden Trail: A fun, challenging trail that ascends switchbacks from the Utah TH then traverses into a large drainage before climbing up to join the Green Mountain Trail.

John O. Hayden Trail

Mount Falcon Park

This lofty park sits high above the town of Morrison and has a rich history. Much of this land was owned in the early 1900s by a man named John Brisben Walker, who built himself an elaborate mountain castle made of stone. He also planned and began construction of a Summer White House for the presidents of the United States, even soliciting donations of 10 cents from each of thousands of Colorado schoolchildren. However, only the foundation was ever built of the Summer White House. Remains of both structures can still be seen today - quite incredible. There are trails for both hikers and bikers and for beginners and experts. Park up top at the Parmalee Gulch TH if you are looking for easier trails; climb up the steep Castle Trail or Turkey Trot Trail from near the town of Morrison if you are looking for a challenge. Bikes are allowed on all trails except for the Turkey Trot Trail, which makes it nice for hikers to ascend Mount Falcon from the east. Depending upon snow coverage, the upper part of the park can provide an excellent setting for winter snowshoeing.

Access

Mount Falcon TH: Located just to the south of the quaint town of Morrison, the Mount Falcon TH provides access to the east side of Mount Falcon Park. Anywhere you go from here is up, so if you are a beginner or are not feeling up for a challenge, consider driving to the Parmalee Gulch TH for easier trails. Take C-470 southwest of Denver to Morrison Rd. (HWY 8). This is located about 4.6 mi south of I-70 and about 23 mi west of I-25 in southern Denver. Proceed west to the town of Morrison, then continue on HWY 8 south from Morrison for 0.9 mi and take a right onto Forest Ave. After 0.2 mi take a right on Vine St. and the trailhead and parking area are located after a quarter of a mile.

Parmalee Gulch TH: Provides access to the west side and top of Mount Falcon Park. It is a very easy hike from here to the top of Mount Falcon. From the intersection of C-470 and US 285, drive a little more than 4 mi to the Parmalee Gulch Rd., take a right and proceed about 2.7 mi to Picutis Rd. From here, follow signs east to Mount Falcon Park.

Recommended Routes

Castle Trail: An easy old doubletrack road at the top of Mount Falcon Park yet this trail continues as singletrack as it drops off the top and down the front of Mt. Falcon to the Mount Falcon TH near Morrison. It is a challenging 1,500-ft. climb over 2.6 mi from the base to the

Castle Trail

top. Start from Parmalee Gulch TH if you want to explore the relatively flat, easy terrain atop the park or start at the Mount Falcon TH if you are looking for a stout climb.

Eagle Eye Shelter near the summit of Mount Falcon

Turkey Trot Trail: A hiker-only trail that winds its way up a small valley, traverses to the northwest side of a high ridge (excellent views to the north) into an idyllic valley, then switchbacks east to regain the ridge at the intersection with the Castle Trail. Begin at the Mount Falcon TH.

Parmalee Trail: A difficult trail that drops down onto the south side of Mount Falcon to a low point at a stream crossing. If biking, you might consider doing this counterclockwise to maximize singletrack descent. 2.2 mi and 500 ft. of elevation gain if done this way. Access from the Parmalee Gulch TH.

Meadow Trail: An easy trail that skirts the south and east sides of a large meadow. Access the Meadow Trail via the Castle Trail from the Parmalee Gulch TH.

Devil's Elbow Trail: A stellar singletrack trail lollipop that traverses a high ridge and leads to an incredible spot overlooking US 285 and Turkey Creek Canyon. Begin at the Parmalee Gulch TH.

Tower Trail: A moderate but short climb to the top of Mount Falcon and a covered wooden platform on which you can stand. Access from

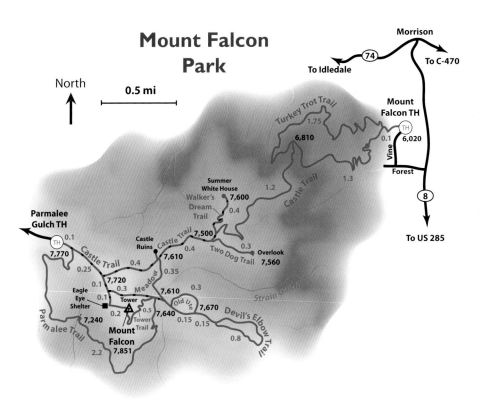

Mount Falcon Park

the Parmalee Gulch TH via the Castle Trail.

Old Ute Trail: A nice but rocky at times loop around a small mountain. Combine with the Devil's Elbow Trail for a nice out-and-back hike. Access from the Parmalee Gulch TH via the Castle Trail.

Two Dog Trail: A short trail leading to an overlook.

Walker's Dream Trail: From the Castle Trail just before it drops off to the east from atop the park, the Walker's Dream Trail is a short out-and-back trail that takes you to the remains of Walker's Summer White House. An awesome ridge and high point overlooking Bear Creek Canyon to the north; Red Rocks can be seen from here as well as much of the Golden/Denver area.

The steep doubletrack leading to the top of North Table Mountain

North Table Mountain Park

North Table Mountain forms a unique landscape. Floating close to a thousand feet above Golden and the surrounding areas, the broad flat area on top is quite stellar. Trails ascend and penetrate through cliff bands and once on top, many of the urban areas surrounding North Table Mountain disappear from view, leaving behind interesting rock structures and grasslands with an incredible backdrop of high snowy peaks. The trails up top are easy and perfect for beginners, yet those required to get to the top of the mesa are steep and strenuous. Nevertheless, those who put in the effort will be rewarded with an exceptional outdoor experience. Jefferson County has plans to improve and build additional trails in the next several years, particularly on the southern side of North Table Mountain Park. In fact, as this book nears completion, construction is underway on these trails.

Access

North Table Mountain TH: The main trailhead in the area located just off of HWY 93. Take HWY 93 for 1.1 mi north of HWY 93/Washington Ave. or take HWY 93 south for 1.4 mi from the HWY 93/W. 58th Ave. intersection.

Golden Cliffs Preserve TH: Off limits to bikes, this small property owned by the Access Fund is popular among climbers and hikers. There is a trail leading up to the cliffs and a

North Table Mountain

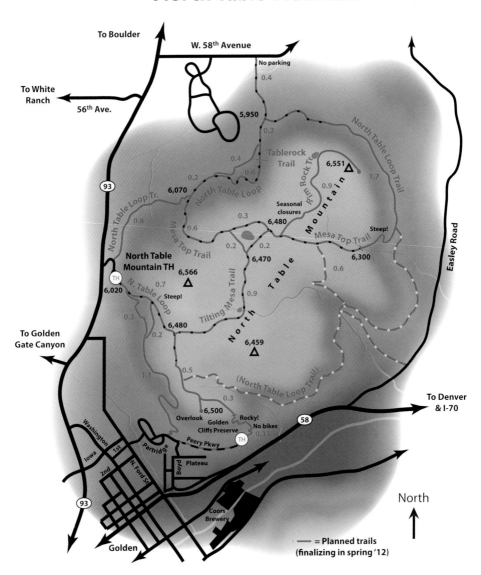

small trail leads through the cliff bands to the top of North Table Mountain, where the Jeffco North Table Mountain park can be accessed.

Recommended Routes

North Table Loop Trail: Only the northern half of this loop is complete; construction of the southern part is underway as of publication of this book. This trail includes the very steep doubletrack trail leading up from the North Table Mountain TH to the top of the mesa. Easy otherwise. The rest of this trail skirts the northeastern and northern side of North Table Mountain on both doubletrack and singletrack trails.

Tilting Mesa Trail: A doubletrack trail traversing some great, wide-open terrain. This trail connects the North Table Loop Trail with the Mesa Top Trail.

Mesa Top Trail: A doubletrack trail perpendicular to the Tilting Mesa Trail that bridges the North Table Loop Trail. Both ends of this trail are difficult. It is a grueling climb to gain the top of the mesa using this trail. In particular, the eastern side is quite rocky and the ascent from this side is not recommended for bikes.

Rim Rock Trail: A spectacular singletrack trail that leads to an overlook. This trail is closed seasonally due to bird nesting, so please read and obey all posted regulations. Easiest access is via the North Table Loop Trail to the Tilting Mesa Trail.

Tablerock Trail: A very short, 0.4-mi long section of singletrack contouring in the grass on the north side of North Table Mountain.

Meadows and trees, White Ranch Park

White Ranch Park

White Ranch is a great place to hike but in places can be a tough place to mountain bike. Terrain varies from rocky and exposed to forested with trickling creeks to wide open meadows. The climb of Belcher Hill is steep, rocky, and loose. However, the trails up high near the west and northwest sides of the park are relatively mellow. As such, beginner hikers and mountain bikers should utilize the Crawford Gulch TH. Snowshoers will have a hard time finding good snow in the winter, the exception may be up high on the treed trails near the Crawford Gulch TH. Regardless of your technical or fitness level, you will be rewarded with excellent vistas and serene forests.

Access

Crawford Gulch TH: From the intersection of HWY 58 and HWY 93 near Golden, take HWY 93 north for about 1.4 mi and turn west on Golden Gate Canyon Rd. If driving from the north, Golden Gate Canyon Rd. is approximately 2.1 mi south on HWY 93 from the stoplight north of Golden at the intersection of HWY 93 and W. 58th Avenue. Take Golden Gate Canyon Rd. for approximately 3.9 mi then take a right on Crawford Gulch Rd. (CR 57). Drive an additional 3.9 mi on Crawford Gulch Rd. and turn right onto Belcher Hill Rd. After 1.9 mi on Belcher Hill Rd. you will arrive at the parking area at the end of the dirt road. Additional parking can be found west of the trailhead alongside the road at the intersection of the road with the Belcher Hill Trail.

Pine Ridge TH: From the intersection of HWY 58 and HWY 93 near Golden, take HWY 93 north 3.2 mi, turn left (west) on W. 56th Ave. If approaching from the north, W. 56th Ave is approximately 0.3 mi south along HWY 93 from the stoplight at the intersection of HWY 93 and W. 58th Ave north of Golden. Drive for 1.1 mi west on W. 56th Ave to the intersection with Pine Ridge Rd. At this intersection, turn right but then stay left and it is a short distance to the parking lot and trailhead.

Recommended Routes

Belcher Hill Trail: This is one of the more brutal climbs around. The Belcher Hill Trail climbs 1,730 vertical ft. over 3.7 mi. On top of that, the steep doubletrack trail is super rocky and loose in places. Nevertheless, this trail provides access to the meat of White Ranch when parked on the east side (Pine Ridge TH) and regardless of where you bike, you always have a screamin' downhill ride to your car. Rated difficult for technical difficulty and steepness, but this trail isn't too long.

Shorthorn-Longhorn Lollipop: This is a great intermediate loop for hikers and mountain bikers. Begin at the Pine Ridge TH and ascend the Belcher Hill Trail to the intersection with the Longhorn Trail. Follow the Longhorn Trail to the intersection with the Shorthorn Trail. Continue down (fun!) the Longhorn Trail (rocky at times) to the intersection with the Whippletree Trail, then climb the steep singletrack and switchbacks to the intersection with the Shorthorn Trail. Follow the Shorthorn Trail along the forested hillside (rocky at times); this area is spectacular! Return via the southern end of the Longhorn Trail to the Belcher Hill Trail. The lollipop is 6.4 mi total, 1800 vertical ft. of climbing. Other variations are definitely possible and encouraged! This makes a nice trail run, too.

Rawhide Loop: Hikers and intermediate mountain bikers will enjoy this loop. Begin at the Crawford Gulch TH. This loop follows the Rawhide Trail as it loops around the northern part of White Ranch. It is recommended to do this loop in the clockwise direction so that, in general, you are ascending more doubletrack and descending more singletrack. There are a few very rocky spots (get off your bike!) along the eastern side of this loop. Be sure to avoid the Waterhole Trail as the best part of the Rawhide Loop is perhaps the very northwest tip. The loop is approximately 4.6 mi.

The Burly Cowboy: So you think you are tough? This loop links up many of the better trails in White Ranch for a semi-epic mountain bike ride or long hike/trail run. From Pine Ridge TH, follow Belcher Hill Trail all the way

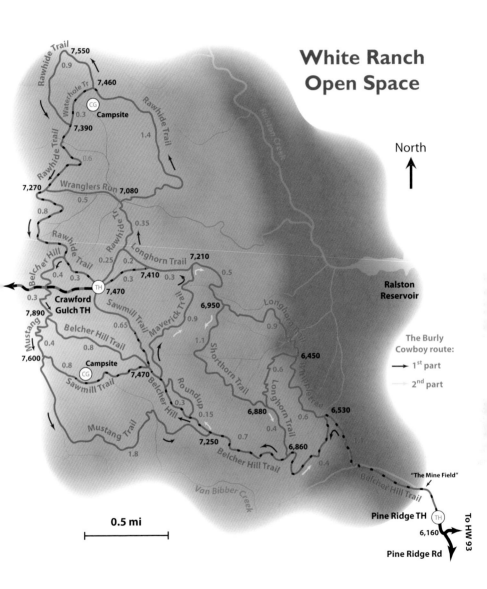

White Ranch
Open Space

North

Rawhide Trail 7,550
0.9
7,460
Waterhole Tr
CG
0.3 Campsite
7,390
0.6
Rawhide Trail 1.4
7,270
Wranglers Run 7,080
0.5
0.8
0.35
Rawhide Trail
Longhorn Trail 7,210
0.25 0.2
0.4 0.3 7,410 0.3
TH 7,470
0.3 Crawford
Gulch TH
7,890
Mustang
0.4 Belcher Hill Trail 0.8
7,600
0.8 Campsite
CG 7,470
Sawmill Trail

Rawhide Tr

Belcher Hill
Rawhide Trail

Maverick Tr
6,950
0.9
0.65
Shorthorn Trail 1.1

Longhorn Trail 0.5

Ralston
Reservoir

The Burly
Cowboy route:
→ 1st part
→ 2nd part

6,450

Longhorn Trail 0.9

Rippletree
6,530
0.6
6,880
0.4
6,860 0.4
7,250 0.7
Belcher Hill Trail 1.1

Mustang Trail 1.8

Roundup
0.3
0.15

Belcher Hill

Belcher Hill Trail

"The Mine Field"

Van Bibber Creek

0.5 mi

Nelson Creek

Pine Ridge TH TH
6,160
To HW 93
Pine Ridge Rd

up to the Maverick Trail, take the Maverick Trail over to upper Longhorn Trail, take a left on upper Longhorn Trail, then intersect and descend the Rawhide Trail, continuing right on the Rawhide Trail at the creek and intersection with Wranglers Run. Continue counterclockwise on Rawhide Trail (bypassing Waterhole Trail) and take Rawhide all the way to the intersection with the Belcher Hill Trail. Ascend the short section of Belcher Hill Trail to the south of the road then bomb down the somewhat technical but stunningly fun Mustang Trail, finishing Mustang with a few short climbs back to the Belcher Hill Trail. Ascend Belcher Hill Trail a short ways back up to Maverick, traverse along Maverick down to the Longhorn Trail, but this time descend Longhorn or Shorthorn back to Belcher Trail and return to the trailhead. The ride is about 16 burly miles if you return via Shorthorn; 4,200[+] vertical ft. of elevation gain.

NOTE: There are many other options in White Ranch Park! Grab a backpack, lunch, and hiking boots or mountain bike and go exploring!

Summary of White Ranch Trails

Easy trails include:
- Whippletree Trail
- Maverick Trail
- Rawhide Trail (west part of loop)
- Waterhole Trail
- Wranglers Run
- Roundup Trail

Moderate trails include:
- Shorthorn Trail
- Longhorn Trail (upper parts)
- Rawhide Trail (east part of loop)
- Sawmill

Difficult trails include:
- Belcher Hill Trail
- Longhorn Trail (lower parts)
- Mustang Trail

Along the Roxborough Loop Trail

Waterton Canyon, Roxborough State Park, & Douglas County Open Space

Snowmelt from the mountains of the Front Range is carried to the plains by the mighty South Platte River, which spills out of Waterton Canyon southwest of Denver. Waterton Canyon is also the northern/eastern terminus of the Colorado Trail, a mostly singletrack trail making its way through the Colorado mountains from Denver to Durango. Also found in the hills above Waterton Canyon is the Indian Creek Loop, a spectacular 16-mi loop that is popular among mountain bikers. So close to Denver but you will feel like you are in the heart of the Colorado Rockies. Red rocks jut out of the grassy hills at Roxborough State Park, which is unique in that it is one of the only state parks that is also designated by the Department of the Interior as a National Natural Landmark. There are plenty of hiking trails in the area, including the relatively challenging Carpenter Peak Trail. Bikes are not permitted on any of the park trails except on the Powerline Trail to the west of Carpenter Peak. Douglas County has some excellent open space parks located southwest of Denver, including the Pike Hill, Nelson Ranch, and Sharptail Ridge Open Space areas to the south and east of Roxborough State Park. Several hiking and biking options exist in this region, including the stellar Ringtail Trail for mountain bikers and the Sharptail Ridge Trail, which is off-limits to bikes. Bigger adventures in this area can incorporate trails from the adjoining Roxborough State Park and Pike National Forest to the west.

Maps: "Buffalo Creek & Waterton Canyon" map by Sky Terrain, "Buffalo Creek Trails" by Singletrack Maps, and National Geographic Trails Illustrated "Deckers/Rampart Range" (#135). There are also very good paper maps provided when you enter Roxborough State

Park, which are fine for hiking in the park.

Best time of the year: Waterton Canyon and Roxborough State Park are low-lying and exposed to the sun. As such, the summer months can be extremely hot. The most pleasurable hiking conditions are in spring and fall or in the early morning/late evening during the summer. The Colorado Trail and sections of the Indian Creek Loop are higher in elevation, resulting in slightly cooler temperatures in the summer but they can also retain snow later into the spring. By late April to mid May these higher trails are usable until sometime in November, in general. After this time, snowshoes can be used on some of these trails.

Camping: There isn't much camping in the Roxborough State Park area. However, there are three National Forest campgrounds located to the west of Sedalia, one of which is near the Indian Creek TH (see next page). These three campgrounds include the Devil's Head, Flat Rocks, and Indian Creek campgrounds. Call the South Platte Range district at (303) 275-5610 for more information or visit www.recreation.gov for reservations.

More Information & Additional Resources: Additional information can be obtained at the Roxborough State Park website (www.parks.state.co.us/parks/roxborough) and at the Douglas County Open Space website (www.douglas.co.us/openspace).

Roxborough State Park

Tina Lewis running the Indian Creek Loop

Waterton Canyon & Indian Creek Loop

Access

Waterton Canyon TH: From the intersection of C-470 and Wadsworth Blvd. in southwestern Denver, take S. Wadsworth Blvd. (HWY 121) south for 4.2 mi to Waterton Rd. (clearly marked with signs to Waterton Canyon). Take a left onto Waterton Rd. and shortly (0.1 mi) thereafter, there is an obvious large parking area on the left (north) side of the S. Platte River. The Waterton Canyon Rd. (S. Platte Canyon Rd.) begins just across Waterton Rd. to the west. It is 6 mi along this dirt road to the start of the Colorado Trail.

Indian Creek TH: 💲   This trailhead provides access to the southern part of this area and is about a 45-minute drive from south Denver. From the intersection of Santa Fe Drive and C-470 in southwest Denver, take Santa Fe Drive, which turns into US 85, 10 mi to the town of Sedalia. Turn west and take HWY 67 (Jarre Canyon Rd.) as it winds its way up to the mountains. After 10 mi, you will see signs for the Indian Creek Campground. Turn here (north side of highway) and there is a parking area and trailhead. There is a fee to park here.

Recommended Routes

Waterton Canyon Road: This is popular among runners and bikers. A great beginner mountain bike ride. Closed to cars, the road starts to the west of the Waterton

Canyon TH and follows the South Platte River to a point with Strontia Springs Reservoir Dam looming high overhead. Just beyond is the official start of the Colorado Trail, about 6 mi from the trailhead. Enjoy a picnic next to the South Platte River.

Indian Creek Loop: Using dirt roads and the Indian Creek Trail (#800), this absolutely awesome loop is rather close to the metro Denver area yet you will feel quite "out there". In fact, you are quite isolated in much of the area. Access either via Waterton Canyon by biking the easy Waterton Canyon Rd. from the Waterton Canyon TH or park west of Sedalia at the Indian Creek TH. The Indian Creek TH is close to the high point of the ride so keep that in mind when deciding your route. The loop is about 14.5 mi long and it can be made slightly easier (less elevation drop/gain) by taking the Roxborough Loop Trail instead of descending to Waterton Canyon and subsequently ascending the Colorado Trail. The route is marked with green arrows on the map on the opposite page. Hikers and trail runners will also enjoy this loop immensely! Snowshoers can access the Indian Creek Trail from the Indian Creek TH but the full loop will probably be too much in winter.

Colorado Trail: At the end of the Waterton Canyon Rd. is the official start of the Colorado Trail (cars are not allowed on the Waterton Canyon Rd. so you will need to park at the Waterton Canyon TH). An out-and-back bike, hike, snowshoe, or backpack

The view from Lyons Overlook, Roxborough State Park

Waterton Canyon & Indian Creek Loop

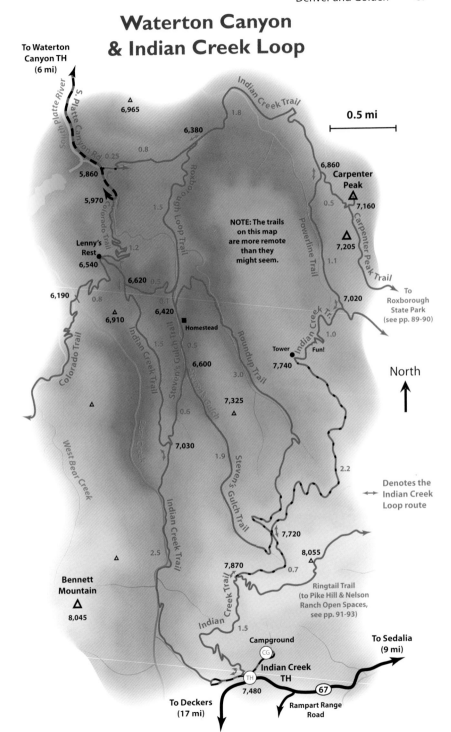

To Waterton
Canyon TH
(6 mi)

S. Platte River

S. Platte Canyon Rd.

6,965

Indian Creek Trail

1.8

6,380

0.8

0.25

5,860

0.5 mi

6,860

Carpenter
Peak

7,160

5,970

Colorado Trail

Roxborough Loop Trail

Carpenter Peak Trail

7,205

1.5

Lenny's
Rest
6,540

1.2

NOTE: The trails
on this map
are more remote
than they might seem.

Powerline Trail

1.1

To
Roxborough
State Park
(see pp. 89-90)

6,620

6,190

0.8

0.1

7,020

Colorado Trail

6,910

6,420

Homestead

Indian Creek Trail

Indian Creek Trail

1.1

North

1.5

0.5

Tower
7,740

Fun!

1.0

6,600

Stevens Gulch Trail

Roundup Trail

3.0

7,325

0.6

Denotes the
Indian Creek
Loop route

West Bear Creek

7,030

Bear Creek

1.9

Stevens Gulch Trail

2.2

7,720

8,055

2.5

7,870

0.7

Ringtail Trail
(to Pike Hill & Nelson
Ranch Open Spaces,
see pp. 91-93)

Bennett
Mountain

8,045

Indian Creek Trail

Indian

1.5

Campground
CG

To Sedalia
(9 mi)

Indian Creek
TH

TH
7,480

67

Rampart Range
Road

To Deckers
(17 mi)

Homestead at Roxborough Park

trip on the Colorado Trail is well worth it. This section of the Colorado Trail ultimately links to the South Platte town site after about 10 mi.

Roxborough Loop Trail: A stellar, secluded trail that connects the Lenny's Rest area to the northern part of the Indian Creek Trail. Can be done as a loop from Waterton Canyon combined with the Colorado Trail.

Steven's Gulch Trail: The Steven's Gulch Trail essentially has two forks (east and west) and connects the east and west sides of the Indian Creek Loop with the Roxborough Loop Trail. About a half mile below this intersection, you can find an interesting old homestead. Just below the homestead, a short connector trail can be followed to intersect the Roxborough Loop Trail.

Roundup Trail: A difficult-to-follow and somewhat overgrown trail that begins near the homestead (see description above for the Steven's Gulch Trail) and ascends a long valley to the eastern side of the Indian Creek Loop near the eastern fork of the Steven's Gulch Trail. Not recommended for bikes, especially in the uphill direction.

Roxborough State Park

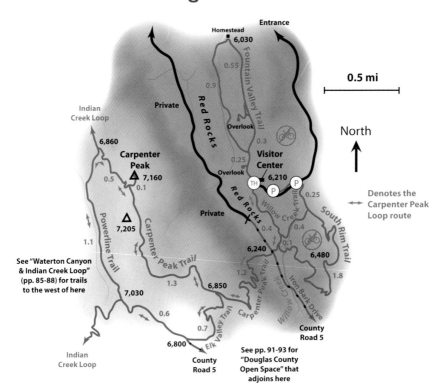

Roxborough State Park

Access

Roxborough State Park Visitor Center: 💲 If approaching from west Denver, take C-470 south to Wadsworth, then take Wadsworth Blvd. (HWY 121/S. Platte Canyon Rd.) south for 4.2 mi and take a left onto Waterton Rd. Continue an additional 1.6 mi (you will pass by the Waterton Canyon TH and the South Platte River) and take a right on N. Rampart Range Rd. at a T-junction. Continue on N. Rampart Range Rd. for 2.2 mi. Take a left then immediate right and follow signs to Roxborough Park, passing through the gate. If approaching from central, south, or east Denver, take I-25 south to C-470, proceed on C-470 west to Santa Fe Drive, and take Santa Fe south for just over 4 mi to Titan Rd., go west on Titan Rd. for about 3 mi and Titan Rd. will make a sharp turn left and turns into N. Rampart Range Rd. Continue from this point for 3.7 mi, take a left and immediate right and follow signs to Roxborough State Park. **There is a fee to enter the park.** Continue to the end of the road, where there are several parking lots below the Visitor Center.

Recommended Routes

Fountain Valley Trail: A short, 2-mi lollipop that takes you to an old homestead and through a valley with extraordinary views of the red rock formations. Visit Lyons Overlook for a spectacular view north of Fountain Valley from above.

South Rim Trail: Excellent views of the rock formations from above. A moderate trail that switchbacks up to a high ridge then descends back to the valley. 1.8 mi long.

Willow Creek Trail: A short trail that can be hiked by itself or utilized to access either the Carpenter Peak Trail or the South Rim Trail. This trail is about a mile long.

Carpenter Peak Trail: A long yet not-too-steep trail that begins at the Willow Creek Trail and ascends 3.2 mi with 1,150 ft. of elevation gain to the top of Carpenter Peak. The lower parts of the trail are quite sun-exposed, so start early and bring water. Excellent views of the red rocks from above.

Elk Valley Trail: A short trail connecting CR 5 with the Carpenter Peak Trail that winds through a scrub oak grove. Use this by itself or as part of the Carpenter Peak Loop (see below).

Carpenter Peak Loop: Climb Carpenter Peak via the Carpenter Peak Trail but then you can add on some great hiking by continuing northwest on a trail that begins just below the summit and connecting to the Powerline Trail (part of the Indian Creek Loop). Continue south on Powerline (mostly doubletrack) until you reach a trail intersection, then descend this trail to near the end of CR 5 (see map). Take Elk Valley Trail for 0.7 mi to the intersection with the Carpenter Peak Trail, then return via the lower part of Carpenter Peak Trail. The loop has 8 mi and 1,800 ft. of climbing. See map for detailed route (depicted by arrows).

Swallowtail Trail area, Nelson Ranch Open Space

Douglas County Open Space

Access

Indian Creek TH: $ See directions to this trailhead on p. 85. Plowed in winter.

Sharptail Ridge TH: From C-470 and Santa Fe Drive, take Santa Fe for about 4 mi to Titan Rd. Proceed on Titan Rd. 2.0 mi, turn left onto Roxborough Park Rd. (dirt), and the trailhead is located about 3.7 mi on the left off of Roxborough Park Rd.

Roxborough State Park Visitor Center: $ See directions on p. 89 to get to the Roxborough State Park trails. There is a fee to park here.

Recommended Routes

Ringtail Trail: Passing through the Pike National Forest and the Pike Hill Open Space and connecting to the Nelson Ranch Open Space, this stellar trail starts at the Indian Creek Loop (see p. 86) and ends near the Swallowtail Trail. It is 5.6 mi long and all singletrack.

The only way to access this trail by bike, unfortunately, is via the Indian Creek Trail (bikes are prohibited both in Roxborough State Park and on the Sharptail Ridge Trail).

Max Nuttelman descending the Ringtail Trail

Swallowtail Trail: From the Roxborough State Park Visitors Center, hike the Willow Creek Trail to Iron Bark Drive (CR 5) (see map). A connector trail can be taken that leads to the Nelson Ranch Open Space and the Swallowtail Trail, which is actually composed of two mile-long loops that meander through meadows, scrub oak, and small rocky sections. From CR 5, it is a 3.4-mi lollipop. **Bikes are allowed, although bikes cannot be ridden in via Roxborough Park. All bikes must access either from Indian Creek Trail or via the Ringtail Trail.**

Ringtail-Roxborough-Indian Creek Loop: Several longer (even epic) mountain bike or trail running loops can be created in the area. One such loop is the Ringtail-Roxborough-Indian Creek Loop, which combines the Ringtail Trail with CR 5 and the Indian Creek Trail, part of the Indian Creek Loop. From the Indian Creek TH,

take the Indian Creek Trail or CR 5 north to the Ringtail Trail, descend the Ringtail Trail to just outside Roxborough State Park, then find the Swallowtail Trail and take it northwest to CR 5. A gate with a no biking sign separates the Swallowtail Trail from CR 5. **If you are on a bike, disregard this sign but do not proceed onto the Sharptail Trail!** Climb CR 5 to the Indian Creek Trail and return via the eastern part of the Indian Creek Loop (clockwise) back to the Indian Creek TH. See the map on the opposite page for the Ringtail-Roxborough-Indian Creek Loop, denoted with green arrows. This loop is 15.2 mi long with 3,400 ft. of elevation gain/loss. Want a little more? Instead of returning clockwise on the Indian Creek Loop, return counterclockwise from the top of CR 5 via the Roxborough Loop Trail and west side of the Indian Creek Trail (see p. 86). This extended loop is 18.9 mi long with 4,300 ft. of elevation gain/loss.

Douglas County Open Space

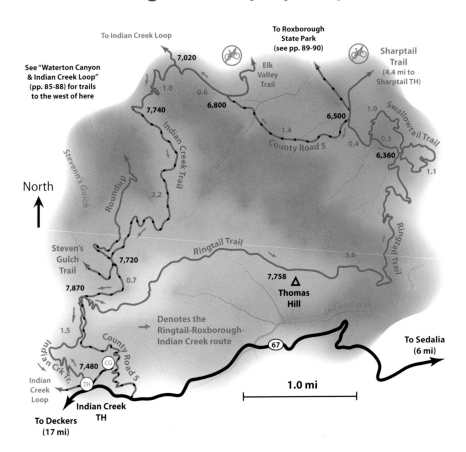

To Indian Creek Loop

To Roxborough
State Park
(see pp. 89-90)

Sharptail
Trail
(4.4 mi to
Sharptail TH)

7,020

Elk
Valley
Trail

See "Waterton Canyon
& Indian Creek Loop"
(pp. 85-88) for trails
to the west of here

1.0   0.6

7,740   6,800

1.0   Swallowtail Trail

6,500

1.4   0.3

County Road 5   0.4

6,360

Indian Creek Trail

Stevenn's Gulch

2.2

North

1.1

Ringtail Trail

Ringtail Trail

5.6

Steven's
Gulch
Trail   7,720

7,758 △
Thomas
Hill

7,870   0.7

Indian Creek

1.5   Denotes the
Ringtail-Roxborough-
Indian Creek route

County Road 5

67   To Sedalia
(6 mi)

Indi'n Crk Tr.

7,480   CG

1.0 mi

Indian
Creek
Loop   TH

Indian Creek
TH

To Deckers
(17 mi)

Sharptail Ridge Trail

Sharptail Ridge Trail: A 4.4-mi trail along a broad ridge.
This trail connects the Sharptail Ridge TH with the south
side of Roxborough State Park. Off limits to bikes.

Matt Schenk at Golden Gate Canyon State Park

Golden Gate Canyon State Park

Golden Gate Canyon State Park is a relatively large chunk of wild land situated within a half hour from Golden. Abundant wildlife, interesting terrain, fishing ponds, picnic sites, and campgrounds make this a great place for a weekend escape. The views of high peaks like Mt. Evans and Mt. Bierstadt are phenomenal from points in the park. Both hikers and mountain bikers will find 35 miles of challenging trails, many of them are rocky and steep. The park is also great for overnight backpacking trips as there are 20 remote tent sites and 4 camping shelters that can only be reached by foot. Furthermore, 5 cabins and 2 yurts that can be accessed by car are nestled among aspen and pine trees and can be reserved year round. In winter, Golden Gate Canyon State Park is a great place to cross country ski and snowshoe. Mountain Base Rd. is closed to vehicles in winter, making this a great ski trail. Many of the other trails can be skied or snowshoed.

Maps: Latitude 40° Maps "Colorado Front Range Trails" or National Geographic Trails Illustrated "Boulder/Golden" (#100). In addition, "Buffalo Creek & Waterton Canyon" and "Golden to Evergreen" maps published by Sky Terrain as well as the "Golden Trails" map by Singletrack Maps cover Golden Gate State Park.

Best time of the year: There are activities at Golden Gate State Park year round. Hiking, mountain biking, and picnicking are popular during the spring, summer, and fall. In winter, Mountain Base Rd. is closed but can be skied or snowshoed. Gap Rd. can still be accessed in winter by continuing on HWY 46 west to HWY 119 and driving north to Gap Rd.

Camping: Plenty of camping is available at Golden Gate Canyon State Park. There are campsites as well as cabins and yurts that can be reserved by calling the reservations office at 1-800-678-2267. Backcountry permits can also be obtained.

Access

$ Golden Gate Canyon State Park is accessed most readily from Golden. From the intersection of HWY 58 and HWY 93 in Golden, take HWY 93 north for about 1.4 mi and turn west on Golden Gate Canyon Rd. Proceed approximately 13 mi on Golden Gate Canyon Rd. to the park. There is a fee to use the park. Several trailheads and campgrounds provide access points to the trails. Consult the map on the opposite page or obtain a map from the Visitors Center for directions to the various trailheads and campgrounds. Camping and hiking information can be obtained in the Visitors Center. For more information, visit www.parks.state.co.us/Parks/GoldenGateCanyon.

Recommended Routes

There are 35 miles of trails in Golden Gate Canyon State Park. Most of them are steep and rocky but there are some moderate trails as well. Here are some recommended routes for hikers and bikers.

Hikers/Trail Runners

Horseshoe-Black Bear Loop: This is a moderate loop. From the Horseshoe TH, hike up the Horseshoe Trail for 1.5 mi to the intersection with the Mule Deer Trail. Be sure to stay straight at a 4-way trail intersection. Turn left on Mule Deer for a short ways and then turn left (east) onto Black Bear Trail. Descend this trail back to Ralston Roost. Return via the connector trail back to your car. 4.9 mi round trip.

Horseshoe-Black Bear Loop

Coyote Trail

Coyote Trail: A nice but strenuous out-and-back from Bootleg Bottom to the intersection with the Mule Deer Trail. Climb a steep, forested slope to a rocky ridge then the trail descends gradually to Frazer Meadow. 2.0 mi one way.

Golden Gate Canyon State Park

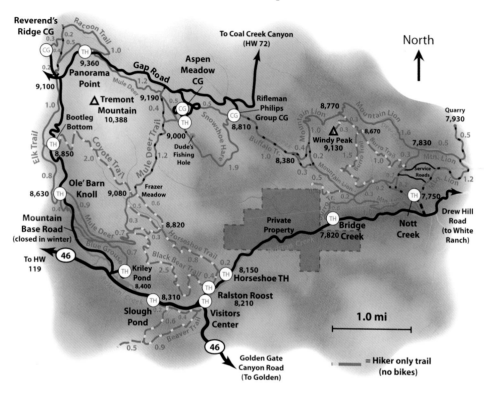

Easy trails include:

- Blue Grouse Trail
- Buffalo Trail
- Elk Trail
- Horseshoe
- Mule Deer Trail
- Raccoon Trail

Moderate trails include:

- Burro Trail
- Mountain Lion Trail
- Snowshoe Hare Trail

Difficult trails include:

- Beaver Trail
- Black Bear Trail
- Coyote Trail

Windy Peak Lollipop: This is a long, strenuous hike but you will be rewarded with some interesting terrain and nice views. From Bridge Creek, take the Burro Trail past the Mountain Lion Trail to the intersection with the south fork of the Burro Trail. Continue uphill for 1.5 mi on

Windy Peak Lollipop

the south fork of the Burro Trail as the trail climbs steeply through meadows, forests, and beneath a few rock cliffs before leveling out and traversing north to the intersection with the north fork of the Burro Trail. From here, go left and ascend 0.3 mi to a trail intersection. It is 0.3 mi to the top of Windy Peak with excellent views all around!! Return via the north fork of the Burro Trail and back to your car. 6.1 mi round trip from Bridge Creek.

Mountain bikers

Tremont Loop

Tremont Loop: This moderate ride makes a loop around Tremont Mountain. Begin at the Kriley Pond parking area. Ascend Blue Grouse Trail for 0.7 mi to the Mule Deer Trail. Take a right on Mule Deer and continue to Frazer Meadow. Keep going on doubletrack on the Mule Deer Trail past the Aspen Meadow Campground. The trail will parallel Gap Rd. and after some frustrating technical sections the trail will intersect Gap Rd. Continue across the road on the Raccoon Trail going east then northwest and the trail will make a rocky descent to a doubletrack road. Climb this road (still the Raccoon Trail) south back up to Gap Rd. to the southwest of Panorama Point. Descend the super fun singletrack Elk Trail to Ole' Barn Knoll then take the Mule Deer and the Blue Grouse Trails back to Kriley Pond. This loop is about 10 mi.

Mountain Lion Loop: A difficult and technical route that also makes a good trail run. Begin at Nott Creek. Take the Mountain Lion Trail west on singletrack. Continue on the Mountain Lion Trail past the Burro Trail and ascend the valley to Forgotten Valley, where there is a small pond

Mountain Lion Loop

and homestead. Continue right on the Mountain Lion Trail and shortly the trail turns to singletrack. Climb loose and frustrating trail for about a mile to a high point to the north of Windy Peak. At a trail intersection, continue down (left) and be careful as much of the next 1.6 mi is extremely technical; consider riding with others. The trail follows a rocky stream bottom and crosses Deer Creek about a dozen times on Ewok bridges. Continue past the intersection with the Burro Trail then you will intersect an old jeep trail (trail to quarry goes left). Climb the jeep trail and a short descent will spit you out at the Nott Creek trailhead. About 6.3 mi for the loop.

Charlie's Picks for Golden & Denver

1.   Indian Creek Loop (p. 86)

2.   Centennial Cone Loop (p. 57)

3.   Turkey Trot Trail (p. 74)

4.   Chimpex Loop (p. 53)

5.   Bergen Peak Trail (p. 61)

6.   Bear Creek Trail (p. 64)

7.   Red Mesa Loop (p. 58)

8.   Parmalee Trail (p. 74)

9.   Ringtail Trail (p. 91)

10. Devil's Elbow Trail (p. 74)

Gamble oak

Boulder Creek in early fall

Chapter 3: Boulder Foothills

There is certainly no lack of outdoor activities to do in Boulder and the surrounding areas, thanks to both the City of Boulder Open Space & Mountain Parks (OSMP) and the Boulder County Parks and Open Space (BCPOS) programs. A variety of trails ranging in difficulty provide access to the mountainous foothill regions to the west of town. The OSMP program has 144 miles of trails, 48 of which are open to mountain bikes. The county (BCPOS) allows mountain biking on all but a small fraction of its trails that are found on almost 48,000 acres. Hiking and trail running are the premier activities in these open space parks throughout the year. When conditions allow, snowshoes or even cross country skis can be donned to access all but the most difficult of these trails. South Boulder Creek winds its way down from the mountains south of Nederland and meets the plains just after Eldorado Canyon State Park, where it has carved away the rock and left massive rock walls.

Information

Maps: "Trails & Recreation Map of Boulder County" produced by the Boulder Area Trails Coalition (BATCO), Latitude 40° "Boulder County Trails", Sky Terrain "Boulder/Nederland Trails", National Geographic Trails Illustrated "Boulder/Golden" (#100), and Singletrack Maps "Fort Collins & Lyons" for Heil and Hall Ranches.

Best time of the year: By far the most popular time to visit OSMP trails is spring through fall, yet you will just about find someone on every trail on every weekend even in the heart of winter. Trails in these areas can become muddy in early spring and during times of winter snowmelt, so during mud season start early while the ground is still frozen and remember to get muddy and don't shortcut or widen the trails. Or, consider using a different trail.

Camping: You can basically forget about trying to camp within 20 miles or so of Boulder. The nearest camping is probably White Ranch Park, Reynolds Park, or Golden Gate Canyon State Park near Golden (see p. 95) or West Magnolia Rd. near Nederland (see the Nederland and Caribou section on p. 177). Alternatively, there are several campgrounds in Rocky Mountain National Park (see p. 190). However, Boulder is a great little town for an overnight hotel stay - get out and explore the trails then explore the eclectic Pearl Street.

More Information & Additional Resources: The City of Boulder OSMP web site (www.bouldercounty.org) has information related to various topics such as trail maps, closure information, rules and regulations, how to rent a shelter for group picnics, and what to do if you happen to encounter a bear or mountain lion. The Boulder County Parks and Open Space website address is www.bouldercounty.org/play/recreation. This website also has important information about rules and regulations, maps, and updated trail conditions.

Welcome to the Boulder Mountain Parks

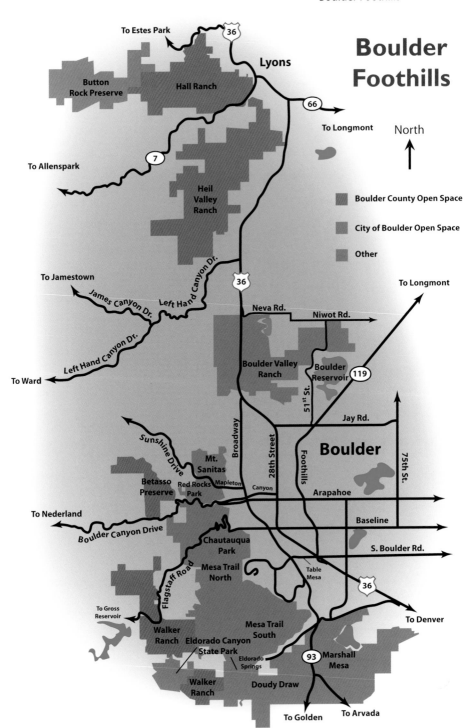

Boulder Foothills

Red Rocks Park

City of Boulder Open Space & Mountain Parks

Red Rocks Park & Mount Sanitas

Located near the west side of downtown, Mount Sanitas and Red Rocks Park are popular places for hikers. There is something here for everyone - take an early morning stroll on the Sanitas Valley Trail, explore the intimate trails of Red Rocks Park, or tackle the challenging climb up Mount Sanitas. And you can always start the day with coffee or end the day perusing shops and bars of the exciting Pearl Street Mall.

Access

Centennial TH: This trailhead provides access to the Mt. Sanitas area to the west of Boulder and is located a half mile west of 4th St. on Mapleton Avenue. If this parking lot is full, there is some public parking back down Mapleton near the hospital (be sure to read signs). Many of the trails are accessed from the Mount Sanitas TH (old parking area, see map).

Settler's Park/Red Rocks TH: This trailhead is located at the far west end of Pearl Street with its intersection with Canyon Blvd. in Boulder.

Recommended Routes

Sanitas Trail: This very popular, steep and rocky trail climbs the long, continuous south ridge of Mt. Sanitas, gaining approximately 1,200 ft. in 1.2 mi. An incredible view overlooking downtown Boulder awaits you! Begin at the Mount Sanitas TH (park at Centennial TH).

Sanitas Valley Trail: A gentle, easy and wide trail that parallels the Sanitas Trail in the valley to the east of Mount Sanitas. Excellent views of Green Mountain to the south. Start at the Mount Sanitas TH (park at Centennial TH).

East Ridge Trail: A steep, rocky trail that connects the top of the Sanitas Valley Trail to the top of Mount Sanitas. Use this trail and the Sanitas Trail to make a nice loop hike of Mount Sanitas.

Goat Trail: Mountain goats only on this steep trail! This trail connects the neighborhoods of west Boulder with the top of the Sanitas Valley Trail. Easy to moderate near the bottom but difficult near the top. Access the bottom of the Goat Trail from just west of 4th St. at the end of Hawthorn or from the top of the Sanitas Valley Trail.

Dakota Ridge Trail: A singletrack trail that parallels the Sanitas Valley Trail to the east. Use this in combination with the Sanitas Valley Trail to create a nice easy loop hike. Somewhat more aesthetic than the Sanitas Valley Trail as it skirts a wooded ridge instead of a broad valley. Access from the Mount Sanitas TH (park at Centennial TH).

Red Rocks Trail: A small network of trails great for a morning walk or evening stroll connecting the Settler's Park/Red Rocks TH with the Centennial TH.

Anemone Trail: From the high point of the Red Rocks Trail, the Anemone Trail heads west up slopes to a ridge. The trail ends after 0.4 mi. Access from either the Centennial TH or the Settler's Park/Red Rocks TH.

Mount Sanitas

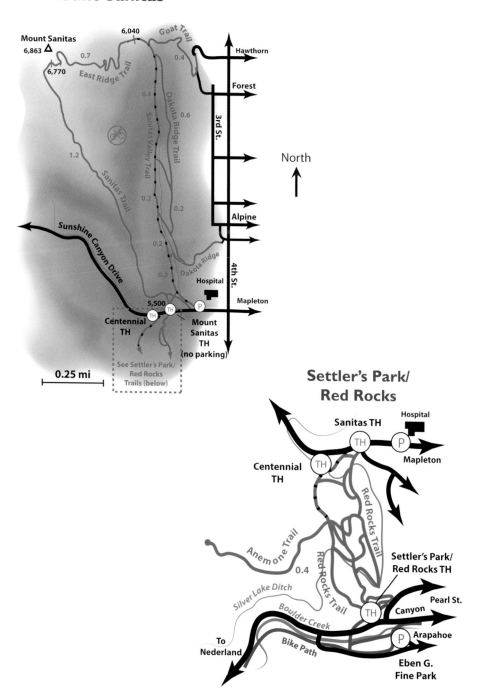

Settler's Park/ Red Rocks

The Flatirons from Chautauqua Park

Chautauqua Park & Northern Mesa Trail Area

There is perhaps nothing that symbolizes the town of Boulder more than the jagged Flatirons that emerge from the plains to the west of town. Chautauqua Park lies directly below the Flatirons and is extremely popular amongst visitors, for good reason. There is much to do in the area - picnicking, hiking, climbing, and evening summer concerts on the large lawn of Chautauqua Park. **Mountain bikes are not allowed on any of the trails in this area** 🚲.

Access

NOTE: Park visitors who park at the trailheads along Flagstaff Rd. must pay a parking fee if their license plates are not registered to Boulder County. These trailheads include the Gregory Canyon, Panorama Point, Realization Point, Flagstaff Summit, and Long Canyon trailheads, among others not listed here. Daily passes are $5 and can be purchased at five self-service stations along Flagstaff Rd. All of the trailheads below are accessible in winter.

Gregory Canyon TH: 💲 From the busy intersection of Baseline Rd. and Broadway Street in Boulder, take Baseline Rd. west for about 1.5 mi to a right-turning hairpin turn. At this turn, take a left and follow the narrow paved road for a short ways to the parking area and trailhead.

Mule deer, Green Mountain

Chautauqua Park: Chautauqua Park is located on the west side of Boulder, just south of the intersection of Baseline Street and Grant Street. It can be difficult to find parking here during fall, summer, and spring weekends, so start early! Additional parking can be found in the surrounding neighborhoods but be sure to follow all parking regulations.

Enchanted Mesa TH: This trailhead is located just south of the Chautauqua Auditorium, which is south of the lawn at Chautauqua Park. There are limited parking spots here or you can park at the main Chautauqua Park parking lot (see above) and walk south to this trailhead.

NOTE: For the next five trailheads, mileages are given for distances along Flagstaff Rd. from Chautauqua Park, and these distances coincide with mile markers along Flagstaff Rd. See above for directions to Chautauqua Park.

Panorama Point TH: **$** This trailhead is located about a mile up Flagstaff Rd.

Realization Point TH: **$** Located 3.4 mi up Flagstaff Rd., this trailhead is at the turnoff to the Flagstaff Summit Rd. There is parking on both sides of the road.

Flagstaff Summit TH: **$** From Realization Point TH (above), turn right (north) and take the Flagstaff Summit Rd. 0.5 mi to this trailhead.

Long Canyon TH: **$** Limited parking here at the top of the Long Canyon Trail. 4.6 mi up Flagstaff Rd.

Green Mountain West Ridge TH: Also limited parking here (parking along the road only), this trailhead is located 5 mi up and at the high point of Flagstaff Rd. at the west border of the park.

Viewpoint TH: This trailhead is located near the western end of Arapahoe Avenue in Boulder. From the intersection of Broadway Street and Arapahoe Avenue, continue west on Arapahoe for about 0.8 mi to Eben G. Fine Park. There is no parking at the trailhead; rather, you must park at Eben G. Fine Park or along Arapahoe Ave (read parking regulations). The Viewpoint TH can be accessed just south of the traffic circle at the entrance of the park.

NCAR TH: From the intersection of Table Mesa Drive and Broadway Street in south Boulder, continue up Table Mesa Drive for 2.5 mi to the National Center for Atmospheric Research (NCAR). There is plenty of public parking here and the trails emerge from the woods on the north side of NCAR on the northwest side of the parking lot.

Recommended Routes

There are a lot of trails in the Chautauqua and Mesa Trail area. Descriptions of some of the most popular trails are provided here. **Bikes are not allowed on these trails.**

A snowy ponderosa pine in the foothills west of Boulder

Summer sunset along the West Ridge of Green Mountain

Mesa Trail: The classic trail in the area. Leading south from Chautauqua Park, this popular trail rolls along the foothills. For the most part, the hiking is moderate but there are several sustained climbs along the way. 6.5 mi and 1,700/1,800 ft. of elevation gain/loss on the one-way trip to the South Mesa TH (see in the next section "Southern Mesa Trail"). Can be snowshoed when conditions permit.

Chautauqua Trail: A popular trail connecting Chautauqua Park with the Flatirons. A myriad of unnamed trails exist in this area. You will be humbled by the Flatirons looming high above you! It is 0.6 mi from Chautauqua Park to the Bluebell-Baird Trail.

Bluebell-Baird Trail: Linking the Gregory Canyon TH to the Mesa Trail, the Bluebell-Baird trail climbs a short ways to the top of the Chautauqua Trail then traverses south to the Bluebell Shelter. An excellent picnic option is to take the Chautauqua Trail to the Bluebell-Baird Trail to the Bluebell Shelter, where you can eat lunch with the 1st, 2nd, and 3rd Flatirons watching over you.

NCAR Trail: From the NCAR TH, this easy to moderate trail heads west and provides easy access to the heart of the Mesa Trail area. An amphitheater of mountains will surround you and the views to the east and southeast are incredible. The NCAR trail also descends northeast through trees and meadows from NCAR (moderate in difficulty).

Royal Arch Trail: A difficult and rocky trail to a natural stone arch. You will be rewarded with a spectacular view of the southern Mesa Trail area. About 1.2 mi one way from the Bluebell Shelter (see map). In some places it is easy to lose the trail. Access via the Mesa Trail from Chautauqua Park.

Mallory Cave Trail: A short but steep trail in the NCAR area that ascends west from the Mesa Trail to a small cave. Start at the NCAR TH, take the NCAR Trail west, then cross the Mesa Trail, following signs for the Mallory Cave Trail. A strenuous climb but the views are well worth the effort.

Gregory Canyon Trail: A moderate to difficult, rocky-at-times trail on the northern side of Green Mountain that makes its way from the Chautauqua area (Gregory Canyon TH) to the ranger cabin on Flagstaff Mountain.

Chautauqua Park & Mesa Trail North

0.5 mi

North

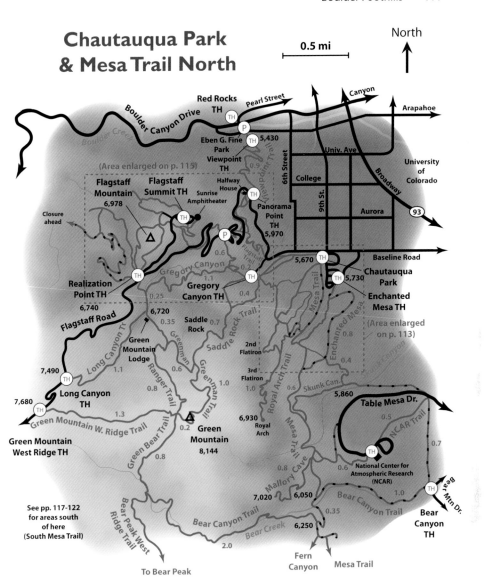

Red Rocks TH

Pearl Street

Canyon

Boulder Canyon Drive

Arapahoe

Boulder Creek

Eben G. Fine Park Viewpoint TH

5,430

Univ. Ave.

6th Street

College

University of Colorado

(Area enlarged on p. 115)

Flagstaff Mountain 6,978

Flagstaff Summit TH

Halfway House

Sunrise Amphitheater

Panorama Point TH 5,970

9th St.

Aurora

93

Closure ahead

Gregory Canyon

Realization Point TH 6,740

Gregory Canyon TH

5,670

Baseline Road

5,730

Chautauqua Park

Enchanted Mesa TH

Flagstaff Road

6,720

Saddle Rock

0.25

0.6

1.1

0.4

Mesa Trail

(Area enlarged on p. 113)

Green Mountain Lodge

0.35

0.7

Saddle Rock Trail

2nd Flatiron

Enchanted Mesa

0.8

0.4

Long Canyon Tr.

Ranger Trail

Greenman Trail

0.6

1.0

3rd Flatiron

Royal Arch Trail

0.6

Skunk Can.

5,860

Table Mesa Dr.

7,490

1.1

0.8

7,680

Long Canyon TH

Green Mountain W. Ridge Trail

1.3

0.2

Green Mountain 8,144

6,930 Royal Arch

Mesa Trail

NCAR Trail

0.5

0.7

Green Mountain West Ridge TH

Green Bear Trail

0.8

0.8

Cave

0.6

National Center for Atmospheric Research (NCAR)

Bear Mtn Dr.

1.0

See pp. 117-122 for areas south of here (South Mesa Trail)

Bear Peak West Ridge Trail

7,020

6,050

Mallory

Bear Canyon Trail

Bear Canyon TH

Bear Canyon Trail

2.0

Bear Creek

6,250

0.35

To Bear Peak

Fern Canyon

Mesa Trail

Saddle Rock Trail

Saddle Rock Trail: From the Gregory Canyon TH, this steep and strenuous trail begins along the Gregory Canyon Trail but then splits off to the southwest as it switchbacks up wooded slopes, climbs along trickling streams to the high lookout of Saddle Rock, then contours southwest and south to the intersection with the Greenman Trail. It is 1.1 mi and 1,400 ft. to the intersection with the Greenman Trail.

Ranger Trail: A steep trail that heads south from the Green Mountain Lodge (see map) and gains a ridge protruding northwest from Green Mountain before a few steep switchbacks to the intersection with the Green Mountain West Ridge Trail and Green Bear Trail. Best to access from the Realization Point TH. It is 1.5 mi and 1,250 ft. of climbing from the Realization Point TH to the Green Mountain West Ridge Trail.

Greenman Trail: A strenuous but spectacular trail leading from the Green Mountain Lodge area south and southeast along a secluded drainage, ultimately switchbacking to gain the northeast ridge of Green Mountain and finishing at the top of Green Mountain. Most readily accessed from the Realization Point TH or combine with a hike of the Saddle Rock Trail from the Gregory Canyon TH. It is a climb of 1,600 ft. over 2.4 mi from the Realization Point TH to the summit of Green Mountain.

Green Mountain West Ridge Trail: This is one of my favorite trails in all of Boulder! A moderate trail that connects the Green Mountain West Ridge TH to the summit of Green Mountain. It is about 1.5 mi and 700 vertical ft. (250 ft. of elevation loss) to

the summit of Green Mountain from the Green Mountain West Ridge TH. For an excellent loop hike, take the Gregory Canyon Trail from the Gregory Canyon TH to Long Canyon to the Flagstaff Rd., then ascend the Flagstaff Rd. for a short ways to the Green Mountain West Ridge TH, then take the Green Mountain West Ridge Trail to the summit of Green Mountain. Return to Gregory Canyon or Chautauqua Park via the Saddle Rock Trail. This loop is 6.4 mi long with 2,750 ft. of elevation gain/loss and is a difficult route.

Chautauqua Park area from Flagstaff Trail

Chautauqua Park Trails

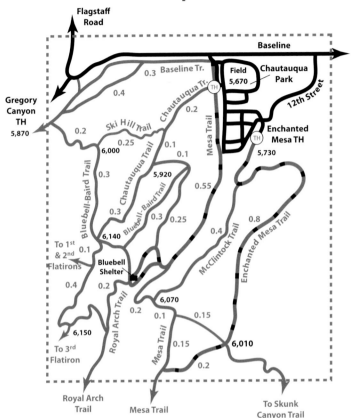

Long Canyon Trail: Another favorite! Long Canyon is located along the northern slopes of Green Mountain and stays relatively cool and lush throughout the summer. This 1.1-mi trail connects the Green Mountain Lodge area with the Flagstaff Rd. at the Long Canyon TH as it climbs gradually westward 800 vertical ft. through secluded forests along a creek. In the spring, there are oftentimes springs trickling down along the trail. Access the bottom of the Long Canyon Trail from the Realization Point TH and the bottom of the Ranger Trail.

Flagstaff Summit Trails: The Ute, Tenderfoot, Range View, and Boy Scout Trails provide a network of easy to moderate trails atop the Flagstaff Mountain area. Several

Poppies below the Flatirons, Chautauqua Park

overlooks offer excellent views of both the city of Boulder and the jagged Indian Peaks to the west.

Flagstaff Trail: Crossing Flagstaff Rd. several times, this trail winds its way up from near Gregory Canyon TH to the Flagstaff Summit area in 1.7 mi. A fairly big climb from base to top (1,250 ft.), but the switchbacks make it relatively moderate and manageable.

Viewpoint Trail: A moderate trail that begins to the south of Eben G. Fine Park at the Viewpoint TH. This trail switchbacks up through meadows and trees, climbs to the Panorama Point TH, then crosses the Flagstaff Rd. and continues to intersect the Flagstaff Trail after 1.4 mi and 800 ft. of climbing.

Tina Lewis on the Ranger Trail

Summary of Chautauqua/Northern Mesa Trail area trails:

● Easy trails include:
- Mesa Trail
- Chautauqua Trail
- NCAR Trail
- Boy Scout Trail
- Range View Trail
- Enchanted Mesa Trail
- Kohler Mesa Trail
- Ute Trail
- Viewpoint Trail

■ Moderate trails include:
- Bear Canyon Trail
- Crown Rock Trail
- Tenderfoot Trail
- Green Bear Trail
- Skunk Canyon Trail
- Long Canyon Trail
- Royal Arch Trail
- Flagstaff Trail

◆ Difficult trails include:
- Ranger Trail
- Saddle Rock Trail
- Gregory Canyon Trail
- Greenman Trail
- Amphitheater Trail
- Green Bear Trail
- Fern Canyon Trail
- Bear Peak West Ridge Trail
- Mallory Cave Trail

The South Boulder area on a frosty winter morning - yes, those are cross country ski tracks!

Southern Mesa Trail Area

Quieter and less busy than the northern Mesa Trail, Chautauqua Park, and Flagstaff Mountain areas, the southern part of the Mesa Trail is a diverse area with trails ranging from wide open meadow walks to steep climbs to rocky summits. This region is to the north of Eldorado Springs Drive and west of HWY 93.

Access

NOTE: Visitors whose cars are not registered in Boulder County must pay a $5 parking fee at the South Mesa, Doudy Draw, and Flatirons Vista trailheads. As of fall of 2011 this is a pilot program at these trailheads and the fee system may or may not continue in 2012.

South Mesa TH: **$** From the last stoplight on Broadway (at Greenbriar Blvd.) as you drive south out of Boulder, take HWY 93 south 1.7 mi to the stoplight at the intersection with HWY 170 (Eldorado Springs Drive). Turn right (west) and proceed 1.7 mi. The trailhead is located just off Eldorado Springs Drive on the right (north) side of the road. Don't confuse this with the Doudy Draw TH, which is located on the left (south) side of the road.

South Boulder Creek West TH: From the stoplight at the intersection of Broadway and Greenbriar on the south side of Boulder, continue south on HWY 93 for just over a mile to this trailhead, which is located in a dirt parking area just off the right (west) side of the highway.

Bear Canyon Trailhead: From the intersection of Table Mesa Drive and Broadway Street in Boulder, take Table Mesa 0.7 mi west to Lehigh St. Take a left (south) and after about 0.15 mi take a right onto Bear Mountain Drive. Continue about a half mile to a broad left turn in the road and park along the road. A trail leads into the woods and is marked with a post.

Shanahan Ridge Trailhead: Follow directions above for the Bear Canyon TH but instead of turning on Bear Mountain Drive, continue on Lehigh St. for 0.9 mi. Just at the top of a steep hill and as the road turns left there is a trailhead on the south side of the road. You may park along the street here, but there are very few parking spots. Additional parking may be found in nearby neighborhoods but follow all parking regulations.

Recommended Routes

Mesa Trail: The classic trail in the area. Leading north from the South Mesa TH, this popular trail rolls along the foothills. For the most part, the hiking is moderate but there are several sustained climbs along the way. 6.5 mi and 1,800/1,700 ft. of elevation gain/loss on the one-way

Lush forests in the Boulder Mountain Parks

Mesa Trail South

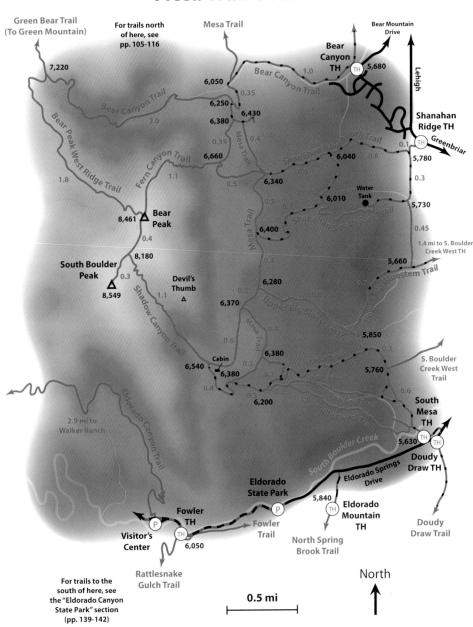

Green Bear Trail
(To Green Mountain)

For trails north
of here, see
pp. 105-116

Mesa Trail

Bear Mountain
Drive

Bear
Canyon
TH   5,680

7,220

Bear Canyon Trail   1.0

Lehigh

Shanahan
Ridge TH

6,050

0.35

Greenbriar

Bear Canyon Trail   2.0

6,250

6,430

0.1   5,780

6,380

0.4

0.6

6,040

0.3

0.35

6,660

5,730

Fern Canyon Trail

1.1

0.5

6,340

Shanahan North Fork Trail

5,660

0.5

0.7

6,010

Water
Tank

0.45

1.4 mi to S. Boulder
Creek West TH

1.8

Bear Peak West Ridge Trail

Mesa Trail

0.5

Shanahan South Fork Trail

8,461   Bear
Peak

6,400

0.4

0.3

8,180

6,280

5,850

Big Bluestem Trail

South Boulder
Peak

0.4

Devil's
Thumb

6,370

0.2

5,760

S. Boulder
Creek West
Trail

8,549

0.3

1.1

Upper Big Bluestem Trail

0.8

0.3

Shadow Canyon Trail

Mesa Trail

0.6

0.4

6,380

South
Mesa
TH

6,540

Cabin

0.3

0.1

Mesa Trail

5,630

0.6

2.9 mi to
Walker Ranch

Eldorado Canyon Trail

6,380

0.4

0.2

6,200

1.0

Homestead Trail

Doudy
Draw TH

Eldorado Springs Drive

South Boulder Creek

Eldorado
State Park

Eldorado
Mountain
TH

Doudy
Draw Trail

Fowler
TH

5,840

Visitor's
Center

Fowler Trail

6,050

North Spring
Brook Trail

Rattlesnake
Gulch Trail

For trails to the
south of here, see
the "Eldorado Canyon
State Park" section
(pp. 139-142)

0.5 mi

North

trip to Chautauqua Park (see previous section).

Bear Canyon Trail: A moderate trail that parallels Bear Creek as it cascades from the mountains to the west of Boulder. Huge rock walls hover above you as this rocky-at-times trail meanders through meadows, switchbacks up hillsides, and crosses Bear Creek several times before its intersection with the Green Bear and Bear Peak West Ridge Trails after 3.3 mi and 1,800 ft. of elevation gain from Bear Canyon TH. The bottom of this trail is quite easy.

Green Bear Trail: A moderate to difficult trail that connects the West Ridge of Green Mountain to the Bear Canyon Trail. Use this as part of a longer hike combined with the Bear Peak West Ridge Trail to connect Bear Peak and Green Mountain. This trail is 0.8 mi long.

Bear Peak West Ridge Trail: A spectacular trail traversing a high ridge at the head of Bear Canyon. Excellent views of Bear Peak and the town of Boulder far below. Steep, technical, and rocky near the top of Bear Peak. This trail begins at the top of the Bear Canyon Trail (see map). If you have the time, this is the best way to climb Bear Peak but is a little longer than the Fern Canyon Trail ascent, time-wise and distance-wise.

Fern Canyon Trail: One very direct way to climb Bear Peak. If you like challenging hikes and climbs, this trail is for you.

Scrambling the summit ridge of Bear Peak with the University of Colorado in the background

Begin at the Bear Canyon TH, take the Bear Canyon Trail to the Mesa Trail, and then go south on the Mesa Trail to the base of the Fern Canyon Trail. Steep, loose, and rocky, this short and not-so-sweet trail gains an incredible 2,050 ft. in 1.45 mi. Probably the most bang for the buck as far as steep hiking goes in Boulder.

North Shanahan Trail: A wide, double track trail that climbs 550 ft. over 1.1 mi from the Shanahan Ridge TH to the intersection with the Mesa Trail. The trail continues for another 0.5 mi on singletrack as it passes beneath The Slab (rock formation) and joins the Fern Canyon Trail.

South Shanahan Trail: The lower half of this trail follows a doubletrack road to a large water storage tank then heads south then west again on singletrack to the intersection with another doubletrack trail that ascends to the Mesa Trail. Best accessed from the Shanahan Ridge TH.

Lower Big Bluestem Trail: Starting at the South Boulder Creek West TH on the west side of HWY 93, this trail follows a dirt road then doubletrack for 1.4 mi to a trail intersection then the trail continues southwest towards the Mesa Trail, becoming singletrack. It is about 2.2 mi long.

Upper Big Bluestem Trail: A singletrack trail connecting the upper part of the Lower Big Bluestem Trail with the Mesa Trail. Ascends a small creek valley through meadows and forests as it gains 420 ft. over 0.85 mi. Access via the Mesa Trail from the South Mesa TH.

Shadow Canyon: A beautiful but steep climb that winds its way up through a dense forest with occasional views of the Devil's Thumb, a rock formation to the east. This trail gains 1,650 ft. over 1.1 mi from the cabin at the base of the trail to the saddle between Bear Peak and South Boulder Peak. It is another 0.3 mi and 360 vertical ft. to the summit of South Boulder Peak. At 8,549 this is the highest point in the mountain parks. This is one of my wife's all-time favorite trails.

Towhee Trail: Connecting the South Mesa TH area with the Mesa Trail, the Towhee Trail traverses the north side of an idyllic valley then ascends a trickling-at-times creek. Great to combine with the Homestead Trail (next page) for a nice loop.

Homestead Trail: The Homestead Trail climbs from near South Boulder Creek up a rather steep set of rocky stairs then mellows out a bit as it ascends a broad ridge with views of Eldorado Canyon and the Doudy Draw area to the south. Ultimately, the trail descends slightly to a creek, where it intersects the Towhee Trail.

Doudy Draw & Marshall Mesa

The Doudy Draw & Marshall Mesa area is just south of Boulder along HWY 93. Five well-maintained trailheads permit access to a variety of easy to moderate singletrack and doubletrack trails that tour wide open meadows, rolling hills, rocky ridges, and ponderosa forests. Hike, bike, or run for just an hour or make a longer day of it. One of the best viewpoints of the area is near the top of the Doudy Draw Trail. From here, you can view the spectacular Eldorado Canyon to the west. Better yet, take the Fowler Trail from the Eldorado Mountain TH west into Eldorado Canyon State Park; the Fowler Trail drops you right into the heart of Eldorado Canyon. **The Fowler and Goshawk Trails are off limits to bikes.**

Access

NOTE: Visitors whose cars are not registered in Boulder County must pay a $5 parking fee at the South Mesa, Doudy Draw, and Flatirons Vista trailheads. As of fall of 2011 this is a pilot program at these trailheads and the fee system may or may not continue in 2012.

Doudy Draw TH: **$** From the last stoplight on Broadway (at Greenbriar Blvd.) in Boulder as you drive south out of town, take HWY 93 south 1.7 mi to the stoplight at the intersection with HWY 170 (Eldorado Springs Drive). Turn right (west) and proceed 1.7 mi. The trailhead is located just off Eldorado Springs Drive on the left (south) side of the road. Don't confuse this with the South Mesa TH, which is located on the right (north) side of the road.

Eldorado Mountain TH: Follow directions to the Doudy Draw TH (above) but continue on Eldorado Springs Drive (HWY 170) for another 0.7 mi. Take a left on CR 67 (look for signs to the yoga ashram). Continue up the steep hill for about a quarter of a mile to a closure gate. Be aware of the parking signs.

Flatirons Vista TH: **$** Drive south from Boulder on HWY 93. After the stoplight at the intersection of HWY 93 and Eldorado Springs Drive, continue 1.8 mi up the big hill to the stoplight at the intersection of HWY 93 and HWY 128. Continue a quarter of a mile south from this stoplight on HWY 93 and the Flatirons Vista TH is located on the right

Doudy Draw Trail

(west) side of the road. Can also be accessed from Golden along HWY 93.

Greenbelt Plateau TH: Follow directions as indicated in above (Flatirons Vista TH) to the stoplight at the intersection of HWY 93 and HWY 128. Turn east on HWY 128 for a short distance and the Greenbelt Plateau TH is located on the north side of the highway just off the road.

Marshall Mesa TH: From the last stoplight on Broadway (at Greenbriar Blvd.) in Boulder as you drive south out of town, take HWY 93 south 1.7 mi to the stoplight at the intersection with HWY 170 (Eldorado Springs Drive). Take a left (east) onto Eldorado Springs Drive and almost immediately take a right into a dirt parking area. This is the Marshall Mesa TH.

Recommended Routes

NOTE: These trails are a great option in the winter as they are usually less icy since many, but not all, of these trails are quite sun-exposed. However, they can be muddy when others are snow-covered or icy.

Doudy Draw Trail: An easy to moderate trail that begins at the Doudy Draw TH. The trail skirts south along the side of a small ridge, traverses a meadow to a stream crossing,

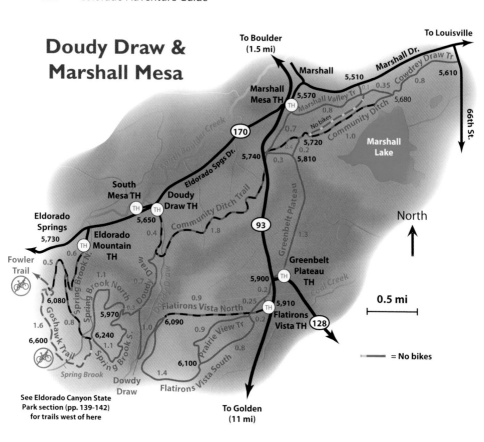

Doudy Draw & Marshall Mesa

then climbs a hillside before switchbacking northeast to its intersection with the Flatirons Vista Trail. Excellent views.

Community Ditch Trail: An easy trail paralleling a water ditch connecting the Doudy Draw area to the private Marshall Lake. Begin either at the Doudy Draw TH or at the Marshall Mesa TH and access via the Doudy Draw Trail or Coal Seam Trail. Cross the busy HWY 93 with caution!

Spring Brook Lollipop: The Spring Brook South and Spring Brook North Trails make a great lollipop loop in combination with the Doudy Draw Trail. A great fun, rolling route. Begin at the Doudy Draw TH and hike or bike the loop clockwise or counterclockwise. The lollipop is about 5 mi round trip.

Ponderosa pines and pinecones

Goshawk Ridge Trail: Off-limits to bikes, this moderate to difficult trail climbs to a high point atop Goshawk Ridge as it winds through forests and seasonal streams. Access the east end of the Goshawk Trail at the top of the Spring Brook Loop or access the west end of the Goshawk Trail from the Fowler Trail. From end to end the Goshawk Trail is about 1.6 mi. Best accessed from the Eldorado Mountain TH.

Fowler Trail: From the Eldorado Mountain TH, take the Spring Brook North Trail 0.6 mi to a trail intersection. The Fowler Trail leads to the right on doubletrack and continues west for another 0.5 mi to another trail intersection where the Fowler Trail heads west.

Flatirons Vista South Trail: An easy trail with views to the south and west. Take the southern-most trail near the small pond located 0.2 mi west of the Flatirons Vista TH. This trail is 2.2 mi long.

Flatirons Vista North Trail: This 1.1-mi long trail climbs from the Flatirons Vista TH to the top of a broad plateau where spectacular views of the Eldorado Canyon area to the west await you. At its west end, this trail intersects the top of the Doudy Draw Trail and the Flatirons Vista South Trail.

Prairie View Trail: A short yet fun trail skirting a hillside just to the south of the Flatirons Vista North Trail. Take the middle of a 3-way fork 0.2 mi west of the Flatirons Vista TH and continue southwest. This trail is 0.9 mi long.

Greenbelt Plateau Trail: An easy, doubletrack trail that climbs south from the Community Ditch Trail over the Greenbelt Plateau to the Greenbelt Plateau TH.

Marshall Valley Trail: A fun, easy trail connecting the Marshall Mesa TH to near Marshall Lake. Fun, easy, and great for beginners.

Coal Seam Trail: A moderate trail connecting the Marshall Mesa TH to the Community Ditch Trail near HWY 93.

Marshall Trail: Off-limits to bikes, this short trail connects the east side of the Marshall Valley Trail to the Community Ditch Trail.

Cowdrey Draw Trail: An easy trail connecting the east end of the Community Ditch Trail to 66th Street.

Green Mountain from near the summit of Bear Peak

Max Nuttelman on the Benjamin Loop Trail, Betasso Preserve

Boulder County Parks & Open Space

Betasso Preserve

Betasso Preserve was the first major open space purchase made by Boulder County back in the year 1975. A quick ride or drive from Boulder, Betasso Preserve has some excellent trails that are perfect for a morning hike or an evening ride.

NOTE: Mountain biking is not allowed at Betasso Preserve on Wednesdays and Saturdays.

Access

Betasso TH: From the intersection of Broadway and Canyon near downtown Boulder, drive approximately 5.2 mi west of Boulder along Boulder Canyon Drive. Take a right onto Sugarloaf Rd. (CR 122) and drive about a mile. Take a right on Betasso Rd. and follow signs to the Betasso Preserve parking area.

Via the Bike Path From Town: Betasso Preserve can be accessed from the town of Boulder via bike. Navigate to the Boulder Creek Bike Path in the town of Boulder. Take this west past Eben G. Fine Park and just keep going, taking a right onto a bridge after 0.8

mi and reaching Boulder Canyon Drive after 2.3 mi. Unfortunately, you must ride the shoulder of the highway west for just over a mile. Just before a tunnel, the steep, loose, rocky Betasso Link Trail heads up a hill to the right. There is a limited amount of parking at the base of this rocky climb.

Recommended Routes

Betasso Link Trail: This trail connects Boulder Canyon Drive to the Canyon Loop Trail. See "Via the Bike Path From Town" on the previous page for directions to the bottom of this trail. A difficult trail. If on bike, your buddies will buy you a six-pack of beer if you can clean this from the highway without stopping. It is about 1.2 mi from the highway to the Canyon Loop Trail (see below).

Canyon Loop Trail: An excellent singletrack trail great for bikers and hikers alike. Begin at the Betasso TH or from the town of Boulder. 3.2 mi for the loop. Bikes are not allowed on this trail on Wednesdays and Saturdays.

Benjamin Loop Trail: Completed in the spring of 2011, this 3.1-mi multi-use loop winds its way along rocky slopes and open meadows to an enchanted forest at

the north part of the loop. Extremely smooth, fun, and very few technical spots. Plans are in the works to possibly link this loop north to Four-Mile Canyon. One of the best trails in the Boulder area!

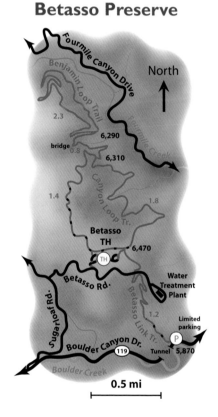

Betasso Preserve

North

Fourmile Canyon Drive

Benjamin Loop Trail

2.3

6,290

bridge   0.8   6,310

1.4   Canyon Loop Tr.   1.8

Betasso TH

6,470

Betasso Rd.

Sugarloaf Rd.

Betasso Link Tr.

1.2

Water Treatment Plant

Limited parking

Boulder Canyon Dr.   119   Tunnel   5,870

Boulder Creek

0.5 mi

Mt. Meeker and Longs Peak from Hall Ranch

Hall Ranch & Button Rock Preserve

There are over 3,000 acres and 13 mi of moderate to difficult trails to be explored west of the town of Lyons in Hall Ranch. A variety of trails are accessible to users, including trails that are open to mountain bikes as well as trails that are off-limits to bikes. The lower areas of Hall Ranch are south-facing and receive ample sunlight throughout the year, making this a good place to play even in winter. The upper parts, however, can be quite muddy at times. Mountain bikers will find challenging terrain along the Bitterbrush Trail yet the Nelson Loop is quite moderate and non-technical. Hikers will enjoy the solitude and superb views of the Nighthawk Trail. Directly to the west of Hall Ranch is Button Rock Preserve, owned by the City of Longmont. Button Rock Preserve is a public sanctuary developed to protect the water supply for the town of Longmont. Several hiking trails can be found here and Hall Ranch can be accessed from the west side through Button Rock Preserve.

Access

NOTE: Dogs are not allowed at Hall Ranch. Dogs must be on leash in Button Rock Preserve. Also, watch out for horses.

Hall Ranch TH: From the town of Lyons (12 mi north of Boulder on US 36 or about 16 mi west of I-25 on HWY 66), take HWY 7 west towards Allenspark for about a mile and a

Hall Ranch & Button Rock Preserve

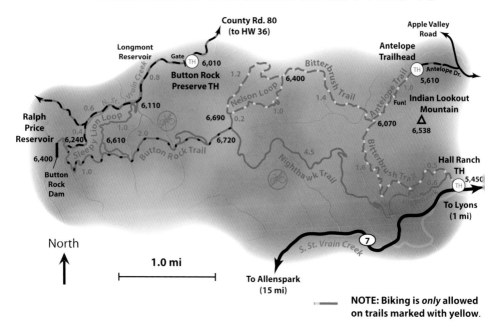

North

1.0 mi

NOTE: Biking is *only* allowed on trails marked with yellow.

quarter. The Hall Ranch TH is on the right (north) side of the highway.

Antelope TH: From the town of Lyons, take US 36 west for 0.4 mi. Just before a bridge over N. St. Vrain Creek, then take a left on Apple Valley Rd. and continue for 0.7 mi. Take a left on Antelope Rd. After half mile you will reach the trailhead and parking area.

Button Rock Preserve TH: From the town of Lyons, take US 36 west to CR 80. Take a left and proceed to the closure gate.

Recommended Routes

Bitterbrush Trail: A rocky-at-times trail that winds its way up from the grasslands near the Hall Ranch TH through rock gardens to a broad meadow area. 3.7 mi each way and 1,200 ft. of elevation gain from the bottom to the intersection with Nelson Loop.

Bitterbrush Trail

Sunrise at Hall Ranch with the North St. Vrain valley below

Antelope Trail: A steady climb that provides easy access to Hall Ranch from the town of Lyons via the Apple Valley Rd. This is an easier alternative to the Bitterbrush Trail for mountain bikes since it is not nearly as technical.

Nelson Loop Trail: A moderate loop atop Walker Ranch accessed either from the Bitterbrush Trail (bikers) or the Nighthawk Trail (preferred for hikers).

Nighthawk Trail: A great trail, off limits to bikes. Begin at the Hall Ranch TH and the trail proceeds west through a large meadow below the Bitterbrush Trail. The trail ascends a broad valley, switchbacks up to the top of a ridge, then meanders through ponderosa forests and meadows to a high point near the intersection of the Button Rock Trail and the Nelson Loop Trail just beyond. 4.5 mi from the trailhead to the Button Rock Trail; 1,500 ft. of elevation gain.

Button Rock Trail: This trail begins near the top of the Nighthawk Trail and proceeds west for 2.0 mi where it intersects the Sleepy Lion Trail. Sections of singletrack and doubletrack. Combine with the Nighthawk Trail for a nice hike.

Sleepy Lion Trail: This trail was named when a ranger stumbled across a mountain lion sleeping on a trailside rock! The loop starts on the Button Rock Dam Rd. (begin at the Button Rock Preserve TH) and switchbacks up forested slopes, traverses a high meadow, and continues through rocky terrain to the intersection with the Button Rock Trail, which leads to Hall Ranch. A final descent on doubletrack leads to the bottom of the Button Rock Dam. Return via the Button Rock Dam Rd. along the N. St. Vrain Creek.

Heil Valley Ranch

North St. Vrain Creek near Lyons

Located in some interesting terrain along the foothills between Left Hand Canyon to the south and the town of Lyons to the north, Heil Valley Ranch is spectacular, secluded, and has an awesome variety of trails ranging from the lightly forested terrain on the south side to the sweeping meadows and vistas found along the Picture Rock Trail. As the BCOS website puts it, "It only takes one visit to this 5,020-acre property to turn a sedentary person into an outdoor enthusiast." This is a great place for all seasons but can become quite muddy during late fall and early spring. Mountain bikers may find these trails a bit on the rocky side yet the northern part of the Picture Rock Trail is rather smooth and exceptionally fun.

Ruins along the Wapiti Trail, Heil Valley Ranch

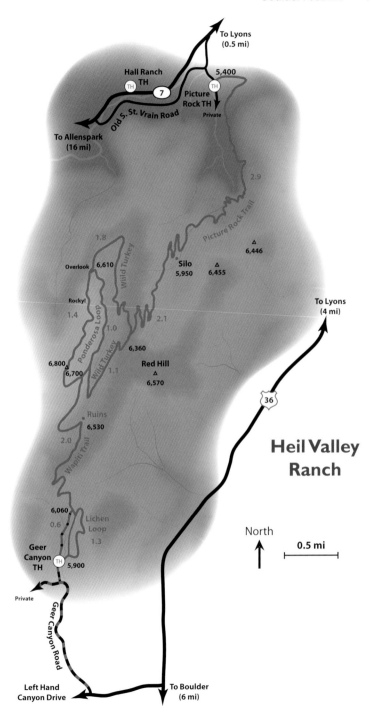

To Lyons
(0.5 mi)

Hall Ranch
TH

5,400

7

Picture
Rock TH

Old S. St. Vrain Road

Private

To Allenspark
(16 mi)

2.9

Picture Rock Trail

1.8

6,446 △

Overlook   6,610

Wild Turkey

Silo
5,950

6,455 △

Rocky!   1.4

Ponderosa Loop

1.0

Wild Turkey

2.1

6,360

6,800 △
6,700 △

1.1

Red Hill
△
6,570

To Lyons
(4 mi)

36

Ruins   6,530

2.0

Wapiti Trail

**Heil Valley
Ranch**

6,060

0.6

Lichen
Loop

1.3

Geer
Canyon
TH

TH   5,900

North

0.5 mi

Private

Geer Canyon Road

Left Hand
Canyon Drive

To Boulder
(6 mi)

Access

NOTE: Dogs are not permitted at Heil Valley Ranch.

Rex Headd and Carolyn Adams at Walker Ranch

Geer Canyon TH: From northeast Boulder at the intersection of Broadway and US 36, travel north on US 36 for 4.8 mi and take a left (west) on Left Hand Canyon Drive. Continue for about 0.7 mi and take a right onto Geer Canyon Drive (dirt). Follow signs to Heil Valley Ranch. The trailhead and parking area are just over a mile up this road.

Picture Rock TH: From the west end of Lyons (approximately 12 mi north of Boulder on US 36), take HWY 7 south for about a half mile and take a left onto Old South St. Vrain Rd. Continue 0.3 mi and at a road intersection take a left onto Red Gulch Rd. Continue a short ways up the hill and the trailhead is on your right.

Recommended Routes

Lichen Loop: A short, 1.3-mi loop that begins from the Geer Canyon TH. The perfect hike before a summer picnic. Bikes are not permitted on this trail.

Wapiti Trail: A moderate but rocky at times trail that connects the Geer Canyon TH with the Ponderosa Loop. The trail is 2.6 mi each way and has 800 vertical ft. of elevation gain.

Ponderosa Loop: A loop that winds its way through ponderosa trees and meadows. The loop is about 2.5 mi long and is rocky at times.

Wild Turkey Trail: A stellar trail that essentially forms another loop to the east of the Ponderosa Loop. This loop is a bit more challenging and slightly more aesthetic than the Ponderosa Loop to the west. It is 2.9 mi from the start to end of this trail.

Picture Rock Trail: Absolutely not to be missed! The bottom portion of the Picture Rock Trail near the Picture Rock TH is easy then the trail becomes a bit steeper and more technical as it makes its way up to the intersection with the Wild Turkey Trail. Begin at the Picture Rock TH or connect to this trail from the southern part of Heil Valley Ranch. This trail also makes for an excellent trail run. Frustrating at times for mountain bikes, especially past the silo.

Walker Ranch

Walker Ranch is located in the foothills to the west of Boulder and is a land of meadows, forests, and canyons. Four trailheads provide access to this area and all trails in this area are open to mountain bikes. Both the Meyer's Homestead Trail and the Walker Ranch Loop Trail are moderate to difficult but quite different from one another. The Eldorado Canyon Trail can be accessed readily from the east side of the Walker Ranch Loop but bikes are not allowed.

Access

Meyer's Homestead TH: Start your odometer from Broadway St. and Baseline Rd. in Boulder. Take Baseline Rd. west past Chautauqua Park and proceed up Flagstaff Rd., all the

Fir trees near South Boulder Creek, Walker Ranch

A large portion of Walker Ranch burned in a forest fire in 2000

way to the top near the west boundary of the park (about 6 mi). Continue on Flagstaff Rd. for an additional 2.2 mi (8.2 mi total) and the Meyer's Homestead TH will be on your right.

Walker Ranch Loop TH: Follow directions above to the Meyer's Homestead TH. About 0.4 mi after the Meyer's Homestead TH, there is a sharp right turn in the road and a dirt road heads left and proceeds a short distance to the Walker Ranch Loop TH.

Ethel Harrold TH: Follow directions above to the Meyer's Homestead TH. About 0.25 mi after the Meyer's Homestead TH, there is a dirt road on the left (east side) called Pika Rd. Continue on this for 1.1 mi then take a right on Bison Dr. and the Ethel Harrold TH is found after a short distance.

Crescent Meadows TH: Providing access to the southwest side of White Ranch, the Crescent Meadows TH is more difficult to get to. Follow directions to the Walker Ranch Loop TH but instead of taking a left into the parking area at the sharp right turn after 8.6 mi up Flagstaff Rd., continue on Flagstaff Rd. an additional 1.3 mi (9.9 mi total on Flagstaff Rd.) to a left turn onto Gross Dam Rd. (dirt). From here, continue approximately 3.8 mi to the Crescent Meadows TH.

Walker Ranch

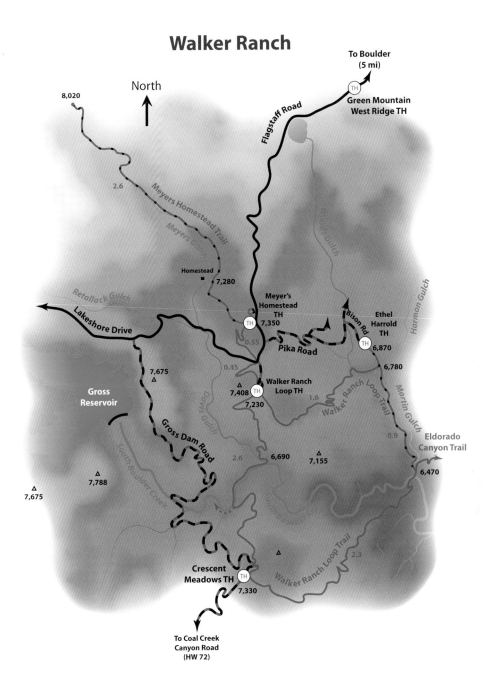

North

8,020

To Boulder
(5 mi)

TH Green Mountain
West Ridge TH

Flagstaff Road

2.6

Meyers Homestead Trail

Meyer's Gulch

Homestead   7,280

Retallack Gulch

Lakeshore Drive

Meyer's
Homestead
TH
7,350

0.55

Pika Road

Bison Rd

Ethel
Harrold
TH
6,870

6,780

Harmon Gulch

0.45

7,675

Walker Ranch
Loop TH
7,230

7,408

1.6

Walker Ranch Loop Trail

Martin Gulch

Gross
Reservoir

Davis Gulch

0.9

Eldorado
Canyon Trail

Gross Dam Road

2.6   6,690   7,155

6,470

South Boulder Creek

7,788

7,675

Walker Ranch Loop Trail

2.3

Crescent
Meadows TH
7,330

To Coal Creek
Canyon Road
(HW 72)

Recommended Routes

Meyer's Homestead Trail: A doubletrack trail that leads to a high point overlooking Boulder Canyon after 2.6 mi. The first 0.5 mi are quite easy but then it gets steeper for the remainder of the climb. Mountain lion country.

Walker Ranch Loop Trail: The Walker Ranch Loop Trail has tremendous variety as it winds its way through meadows, over rocky outcroppings, across streams and rivers, through canyons, and along forested hillsides. If you are biking this loop, there is a mandatory hike-a-bike as you negotiate the deep canyon carved out by South Boulder Creek. A steep staircase leads from the creek back up to the forests above. Be careful! It is best to park at either the Walker Ranch Loop TH or the Ethel Harrold TH. 7.4 mi for the loop with 1,700 ft. of elevation gain.

Walker Ranch Link Trail: A fun, 1.0-mi trail connecting the Meyer's Homestead TH to the Walker Ranch Loop TH. Easy to moderate in difficulty but short.

An evening stroll along the Fowler Trail

Eldorado Canyon Trail: A 3.5-mi trail connecting the east side of the Walker Ranch Loop Trail to Eldorado Canyon State Park. A spectacular trail and is accessed most quickly from the Ethel Harrold TH. Excellent views to the south and east and of Eldorado Canyon. An excellent long

hike or trail run is to begin in Eldorado Canyon State Park (see next section) and take this trail, complete the Walker Ranch Loop, then return via the Eldorado Canyon Trail.

Eldorado Canyon State Park

There's nothing quite as humbling as sitting at the bottom of the huge rock walls of Eldorado Canyon and listening to South Boulder Creek as it cascades down from the mountains to the west of Boulder. Eldorado Canyon State Park has something for everyone and is a great place to get out and enjoy nature. Hikers will enjoy three excellent hiking trails ranging in difficulty from easy (Fowler Trail) to difficult (Eldorado Canyon Trail and Rattlesnake Gulch Trail). Mountain bikes are allowed on the Rattlesnake Gulch Trail, although bikers may want to stay off this trail during the busy weekends. Spend some time here watching the rock climbers as they dangle on cliffs high above you. The hike up Rattlesnake Gulch will reward you with a stellar view of the canyon below.

Access

Eldorado Canyon TH: $ Located just inside Eldorado Canyon State Park. From the southern-most stoplight in Boulder along Broadway St. (at Greenbriar Blvd.), take HWY 93 south 1.7 mi to the stoplight at the intersection with HWY 170 (Eldorado Springs Drive). Turn right (west) and proceed about 3 mi to the town of Eldorado Springs. Continue straight through town on a dirt road and you will enter Eldorado Canyon State Park. You will need to pay the entrance fee, which is $8 per day.

Fowler TH: $ Located 0.5 mi up the dirt road from the Eldorado Canyon TH on the left hand side of the road. Provides access to the Rattlesnake Gulch Trail and the Fowler Trail.

Eldorado Mountain TH: $ This trailhead provides access to the west end of the Fowler Trail as well as the Rattlesnake Gulch Trail. Follow directions above to Eldorado Canyon State Park. From the parking area just inside the park, follow the dirt road for about a half mile. There is limited parking here at the Fowler TH. You can also walk to this TH from the parking area below or from the Visitor Center (see below).

Visitor Center: $ This parking area provides access to the Eldorado Canyon Trail. From inside the park, drive the dirt road for about 0.7 mi and veer left after cross the bridge over South Boulder Creek.

The Redgarden Wall as viewed from the southern side of Eldorado Canyon

Eldorado Canyon State Park

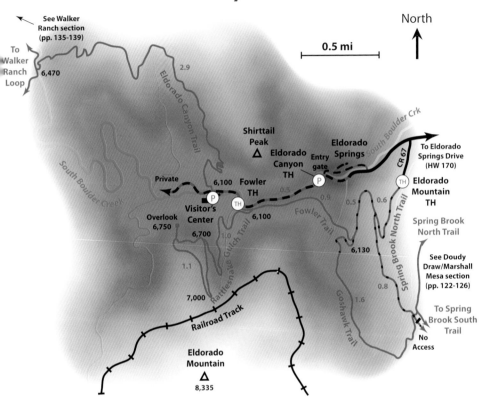

Recommended Routes

Fowler Trail: An easy trail with spectacular views of the rock walls of Eldorado Canyon. Several benches line this trail and are great places to watch climbers ascend the steep canyon walls. When approaching the canyon from the east, you will come around a corner at one point and the rock walls and deep canyon are splayed out in front of you, like "opening a Christmas present" in the words of my wife.

Rattlesnake Gulch Trail: A steep, rocky at times trail that zigzags up the south side of Eldorado Canyon to a high overlook. After 1.0 mile there are the remains of the historic Crags Hotel. From here, you can complete the 1.1-mi loop and return the way you came; approximately 1,300 ft. of elevation gain for the loop. Open to mountain bikes, but mountain bikers will want to do the loop counterclockwise. This is a very challenging mountain bike trail and, consequently, is not very popular for biking.

Eldorado Canyon Trail: This excellent and challenging trail begins just north of the Visitor Center and connects Eldorado Canyon with Walker Ranch Park (see page 139). Excellent views of Eldorado Canyon and exciting terrain. 2.9 mi to the Walker Loop Trail and 1,500 ft. of elevation

gain; requires an additional 400 ft. of climbing on the return trip to Eldorado Canyon.

Charlie's Picks for the Boulder Foothills

1. Benjamin Loop Trail (p. 128)

2. Green Mountain West Ridge Trail (p. 112)

3. Picture Rock Trail (p. 135)

4. Long Canyon Trail (p. 113)

5. Bear Peak (West Ridge, Fern Canyon, or Shadow Canyon) (p. 120)

6. Royal Arch Trail (p. 110)

7. Sleepy Lion Trail (p. 132)

8. Nighthawk Trail (p. 131)

9. Eldorado Canyon Trail (this page)

10. Walker Ranch Loop (p. 138)

Bob Lake with Rollins Pass in the distance

Chapter 4: Northern Front Range

When approaching the Rocky Mountains from the east, the Great Plains abruptly slam into a north-south line of mountains known as the Colorado Front Range, which spans essentially the entire state from Wyoming border to New Mexico border. After a short stretch of intermediate foothill regions, mountains reach skyward at elevations of greater than 14,000 feet. Stretching from the James Peak Wilderness in the south to Rocky Mountain National Park and beyond to the north, the Northern Front Range area is a relatively lengthy yet narrow expanse of mountains encompassing some wild and surreal places. This chapter is comprised of the mountainous areas to the west of Boulder and Golden, which includes the Indian Peaks Wilderness, Nederland, and the James Peaks Wilderness - areas in the Front Range that are to the north of I-70, east of the Continental Divide, and south of Rocky Mountain National Park. Rocky Mountain National Park is treated as its own chapter (see the next chapter, pp. 185-222). Keep in mind that the areas in this chapter are further west and higher in elevation than the foothill regions covered in Chapter 2 (Denver and Golden) and Chapter 3 (Boulder Foothills). There is a tremendous variety of outdoor activities to partake in, ranging from the easily accessible hiking and biking trails near Nederland and Caribou Lake to the high alpine, remote excursions into the Indian Peaks Wilderness and the James Peak Wilderness. Access is easy - most of the recreational opportunities along the Northern Front Range are only within an hour or two of the Denver/Boulder area.

Northern Front Range

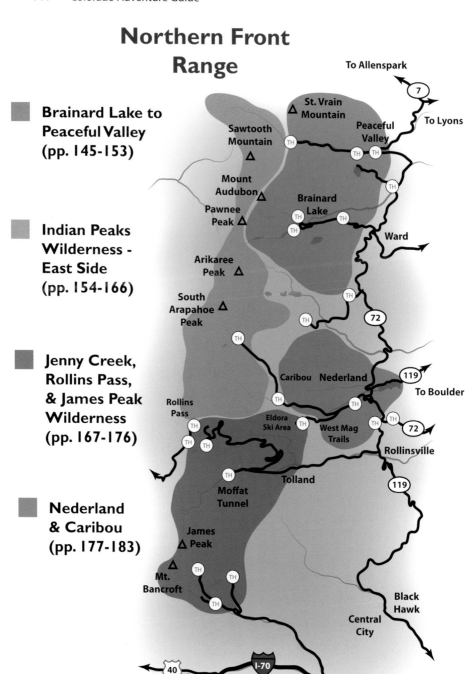

Brainard Lake to Peaceful Valley (pp. 145-153)

Indian Peaks Wilderness - East Side (pp. 154-166)

Jenny Creek, Rollins Pass, & James Peak Wilderness (pp. 167-176)

Nederland & Caribou (pp. 177-183)

To Allenspark

7

To Lyons

St. Vrain Mountain

Peaceful Valley

Sawtooth Mountain

Mount Audubon

Brainard Lake

Pawnee Peak

Ward

Arikaree Peak

72

South Arapahoe Peak

Caribou   Nederland

119

To Boulder

Rollins Pass

Eldora Ski Area

West Mag Trails

72

Rollinsville

Tolland

Moffat Tunnel

119

James Peak

Mt. Bancroft

Black Hawk

Central City

40   I-70

Idaho Springs

The lovely Lake Isabelle

Brainard Lake to Peaceful Valley

The Brainard Lake Recreation Area is popular among hikers, bikers, and picnickers in the summer and cross country skiers and snowshoers in the winter. Many of the Brainard Lake area trails lead into the neighboring Indian Peaks Wilderness, whose high jagged peaks provide a phenomenal setting in such places as Lake Isabelle and the Buchanan Pass areas. The Sourdough Trail is a spectacular singletrack trail that links the Rainbow Lakes area to Peaceful Valley. Several bike-'n-hike adventures can be set up to the west of Peaceful Valley by biking on dirt roads and hiking into the northern part of the Indian Peaks Wilderness. In winter, ski or snowshoe to the Colorado Mountain Club (CMC) cabin near Brainard Lake, where you can warm up with a hot drink in exchange for a small donation.

Maps: Boulder Area Trails Coalition (BATCO) "Trails and Recreation Map of Boulder County", Latitude 40° "Boulder/Nederland Trails" or "Boulder County Trails", Sky Terrain's "Southern Rocky Mountain National Park and Indian Peaks Wilderness", or Trails Illustrated "Indian Peaks/Gold Hill" (#102).

Best time of the year: The Brainard Lake area is a place for all seasons except for "mud" season - typically late April through mid June; don't expect to be hiking or biking these trails until late June at the earliest, depending upon snowfall the winter prior. You can find spectacular recreational activities in summer, early to mid fall, and winter. The conditions can vary wildly from one year to the next - for example, you may find yourself hiking or mountain biking on the Sourdough Trail in October of one year but snowshoeing in October of the next year.

Camping: Forest Service campgrounds that are in the vicinity of the Sourdough Trail and Brainard Lake include the Pawnee, Camp Dick, and Peaceful Valley Campgrounds. Reservations can be made for these three campground 5-240 days in advance. To make reservations for any of these campgrounds, please visit www.recreation.gov or call 1-877-444-6777. Additional information can be obtained by calling the Boulder Ranger District of the Arapaho-Roosevelt National Forest at (303) 541-2500. Besides these options, there is plenty of free camping in the West Magnolia area (see "Nederland and Caribou" section on p. 177-178) along West Magnolia Rd. Backcountry permits are not granted for the Four-Lakes area of the Indian Peaks Wilderness (the drainages near Brainard Lake); however, dispersed camping is permitted here from Nov. 15 to April 30.

Access

NOTE: From mid to late June through September, there is a fee to use the Brainard Lake Recreation Area. The Red Rocks/Sourdough TH parking area is free but if you'd like to enter the Brainard Lake Recreation Area there is a fee for a 5-day pass; hikers and bikers who enter the recreation area are asked to pay $1. **Other regulations:** From May 1 to November 14 dogs must be on leash and dispersed camping is prohibited; from November 15 to April 30 dogs are prohibited on all singletrack trails in the Brainard Lake area except for the Sourdough Trail and dispersed camping is permitted.

Brainard Lake: **$** Brainard Lake can be accessed most easily from the towns of Boulder or Lyons. **From Boulder:** From the north end of Boulder, drive US 36 north for 4.8 mi

Trees along the Sourdough Trail in winter

and take a left on Left Hand Canyon Drive. Proceed an additional 16.7 mi to the town of Ward, making sure to take a left at an intersection just after 5 mi. Drive through the town of Ward, take a right onto HWY 72 for about a hundred yards, then take a sharp left onto the Brainard Lake Rd. (well marked). **From Lyons:** Take HWY 7 west for about 14 mi to the intersection with HWY 72. Turn left (south) and travel just under 10 mi to the beginning of the Brainard Lake Rd. Continue 2.7 mi to the entrance station. The Brainard Lake Rd. area is generally closed late September through mid to late June but is plowed to the Red Rock/Sourdough TH in winter (see below).

S. Sourdough TH: This trailhead is located at the southern terminus of the Sourdough Trail. From Nederland, travel 7.0 mi north on HWY 72 and take a left onto Rainbow Lakes Rd. (CR 116). Nederland is located 16 mi west of Boulder on Boulder Canyon Drive. There is a sign here for the University of Colorado Mountain Research Station. Proceed 0.5 mi and there is a very large parking area and restroom on the left and across the road on the right is the start of the Sourdough Trail.

Red Rock/Sourdough TH: Follow directions above to the Brainard Lake Rd. The Red Rock/Sourdough TH is located about 2.5 mi up the Brainard Lake Rd. on the right hand side. The Sourdough Trail can be found close to this trailhead area.

Mitchell Lake TH: From the bottom of the Brainard Lake Rd. (see directions above), follow the road west about 2.7 mi to the entrance station (fees apply, see above). Proceed an additional 3 mi to the Mitchell Lake TH (follow signs).

Long Lake TH: Located within a few tenths of a mile further along the Brainard Lake loop than the Mitchell Lake TH (see above).

South St. Vrain TH: Drive to the town of Ward as described in the description for Brainard Lake above. Continue past Ward, intersect HWY 72, and take a right (north) onto HWY 72. Proceed just over 2.5 mi and take a left (west) onto CR 96. The trailhead is located on your left after about a hundred yards or so.

N. Sourdough TH: Follow directions to CR 96 as described above for the South St. Vrain TH. Continue on the dirt road past the South St. Vrain TH, staying right at an intersection after 1.3 mi from HWY 72. After about 2.0 mi the Sourdough Trail crosses the road and parking is available here. This road is plowed to Beaver Reservoir in winter.

Peaceful Valley TH: From Ward (see description for the Brainard Lake Rd. above), continue north on HWY 72 for about 5.9 mi. At a large right-turning hairpin turn, you should see signs for Peaceful Valley/Camp Dick. Take a left here onto CR 92. The Peaceful Valley TH is located within a quarter mile up this road and the Buchanan Pass Trail emerges from the woods. Alternatively, this trailhead can be accessed from the town of Lyons by driving HWY 7 for just over 14 mi to the intersection with HWY 72, then proceeding south on HWY 72 for roughly 4 mi. The turnoff for CR 92 will be on your right at the hairpin. In winter, this TH is open and skiers and snowshoers can access either the Buchanan Pass Trail or travel the Middle St. Vrain Rd.

Buchanan Pass TH: From the Peaceful Valley TH (see previous page), continue on CR 92 (Middle St. Vrain Rd.) for 1.2 mi. This trailhead is located in a large parking area that is on the west end of the Camp Dick Campground.

Upper Middle St. Vrain TH: Follow the directions above to the Buchanan Pass TH. With a *sturdy* 4WD vehicle, you can drive an additional 3.7 rocky miles to a small parking area and trailhead on the south side of Middle St. Vrain Creek. Hikers without a 4WD vehicle can access this trailhead by hiking the lower part of the Buchanan Pass Trail. Alternatively, you can get here from the north side of Beaver Reservoir (along CR 96), but from the reservoir it is 3.8 rocky miles (4WD required) to the Upper Middle St. Vrain TH.

Coney Flats TH: This seldom-used trailhead requires a *very good* four wheel drive vehicle. Directions are included to this trailhead primarily for hikers and mountain bikers to access the upper Buchanan Pass Trail and the Coney Creek and Beaver Creek Trails. About a tenth of a mile before reaching the Upper Middle St. Vrain TH (see above), turn south (left) onto Coney Creek Rd. After 0.7 mi of rocky terrain, you will reach the Coney Flats TH.

Tina Lewis hiking Mount Audubon

Recommended Routes

Sourdough Trail: Stretching for 12 mi, the multi-use Sourdough Trail connects the Rainbow Lakes Rd. in the south to the Camp Dick area to the north and passes through the Brainard Lake area. Much of the trail is quite

Blue Lake from near Paiute Peak

rocky and technical, so beginner mountain bikers may want to stay away from this trail. Hikers will love it. There are 5 popular access points - the S. Sourdough TH, Red Rock/ Sourdough TH, N. Sourdough TH, the Buchanan Pass TH, and the Peaceful Valley TH. From south to north, there is approximately 1,950 ft. of elevation gain and 2,690 ft. of elevation loss over the 12.2 mi.

Buchanan Pass Trail: Starting from Buchanan Pass TH, the Buchanan Pass Trail heads west along the north side of Middle St. Vrain Creek. Many small waterfalls are found along the creek, making this area spectacular. The trail emerges at the west end of the Middle St. Vrain Rd. near the Upper Middle St. Vrain TH but the Buchanan Pass Trail continues west and enters the Indian Peaks Wilderness (see p. 159). Suitable for mountain bikes up to the wilderness boundary, but bikes are not allowed in areas designated as Wilderness.

Peaceful Valley Mountain Bike Loop: Begin at Buchanan Pass TH. Choose your poison - either bike up the super rocky and loose Middle St. Vrain Rd. (FS 104) or bike up the super rocky and loose Coney Flats Rd. (FS 507) - both will require legs of steel. Regardless, end up at the Upper Middle St. Vrain

TH. Cross the bridge just past the trailhead, continue east, and persevere through a half mile of technical hike-a-bike. It would be easy to dislocate a shoulder or fracture a clavicle or wrist in here! You will be glad you stuck with it – the 3 ½ mi back to the Buchanan Pass TH are stellar singletrack along a beautiful creek. Be on the lookout for hikers (remember, bikers yield to hikers!) as this can be a crowded area, especially on the weekends.

Brainard Lake Area

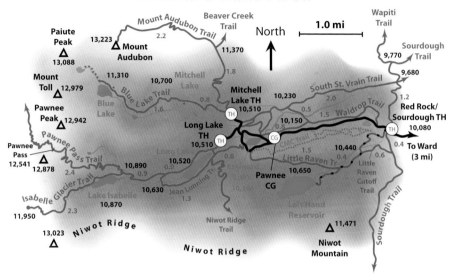

Little Raven Trail: The Little Raven Trail is a moderate trail traversing through some spectacular forests.   In winter, this trail is only open to cross country skiers (no snowshoes and no dogs).   Recently, the trail was improved to make it more suitable for mountain biking.

Little Raven Cutoff Trail: A short 0.5-mi trail connecting the Sourdough Trail south of the Brainard Lake Rd. to the Left Hand Reservoir Rd.   Steep and rocky, open to skiers and snowshoers in winter.

CMC Trail: This fun, skier-only trail (**no snowshoes and closed to dogs**) is only open in the winter and essentially parallels the Brainard Lake Rd. to its south.   Snowshoers should use the Snowshoe Trail (see below)

CMC Snowshoe Trail: The "Snowshoe Trail" begins just west of the winter closure gate to the west of the Red Rock TH and parallels the Brainard Lake Rd. yet is north of the CMC Trail.   As you continue west on this trail, it spits you out at the

Brainard Lake to Peaceful Valley

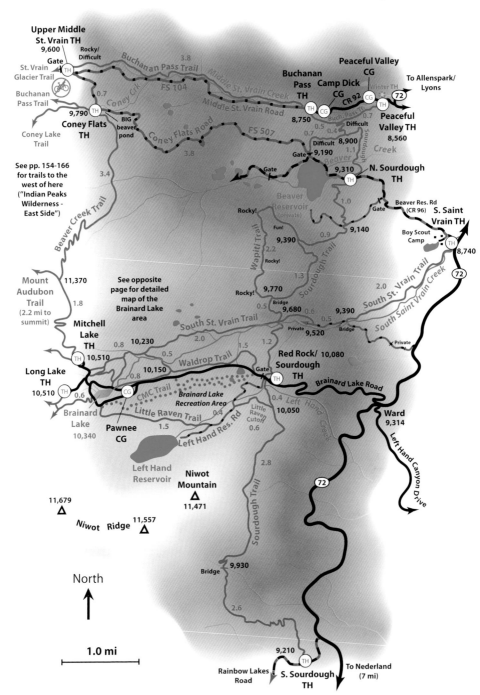

Brainard Lake Rd. Cross the road and re-enter the woods. After a short distance the trail intersects the Waldrop Trail. Snowshoers can continue west on the Snowshoe Trail all the way to the east end of Brainard Lake.

Waldrop Trail: In winter, this trail is fun for both skiers and snowshoers. This trail begins just west of the winter closure gate and gradually climbs west and descends to a creek before a short ascent where it joins the South St. Vrain Trail. Hikers will enjoy the Waldrop Trail in the summer. It is open to mountain bikes, although the surface is quite rocky and it is a technical ride. 2.0 mi one way.

South St. Vrain Trail: Recently re-routed to bring this trail out of the Indian Peaks Wilderness, the sweet singletrack of the South St. Vrain Trail is not to be missed. Open to mountain bikers, this trail connects the Brainard Lake area with HWY

72 at the South St. Vrain TH and crosses the Sourdough Trail. Portions of this trail are rocky and technical. Open to skiers and snowshoers in winter. Going eastbound from the Sourdough Trail, the South St. Vrain Trail traverses some rocky terrain for 0.6 mi, connects with a doubletrack road for 0.5 mi, then heads northeast for 2.0 mi along South St. Vrain Creek to the South St. Vrain TH. Moderate for hikers but difficult for mountain bikers.

Wapiti Trail: A fun trail that loops off the northern Sourdough Trail. The Wapiti Trail is rocky and technical but has some fun, smooth sections interspersed among rocky ones. Moderate for hikers but difficult for bikers.

Mount Audubon Trail: There are few high, accessible 13,000-ft. peaks in the Northern Front Range, but Mount Audubon is one of them. The hike up Mount Audubon is strenuous but the trail is well-worn except for the last push to the summit ridge, which requires some easy scrambling

on boulders. Excellent views await you. Mount Audubon is in a supreme location with jagged peaks to the south and Rocky Mountain National Park and Longs Peak to the north. Well worth the effort. The summit is 4.0 mi from the Mitchell Lake TH with 2,730 ft. of elevation gain.

Blue Lake Trail: A lovely, moderate trail that passes by several large and small lakes with Mount Audubon on the north side of the valley. Mitchell Lake is reached after 0.8 mi (230 ft. of elevation gain) and Blue Lake is reached after 2.4 mi (920 ft. of elevation gain). Continue up the drainage past Blue Lake to Upper Blue

Josh Emdur and Stefan Griebel traversing to the summit of Algonquin Peak

Lake with the impressive Mount Toll looming high above.

Lake Isabelle: There are few scenes as representative of the Rocky Mountains as the panorama laid out before your eyes when you visit Lake Isabelle. It is a fairly easy 2.0-mi hike to the eastern end of Lake Isabelle from the Long Lake TH. For a nice loop, return via the Jean Lunning Trail (see below).

Jean Lunning Trail: A peaceful, gentle trail that takes you along the south side of Long Lake through forests and meadows, ultimately intersecting the Isabelle Glacier Trail after 1.4 mi. Excellent for skiing and snowshoeing but quite far from the winter trailhead.

Niwot Ridge Trail: A moderate hike that climbs and traverses a broad ridge past the Niwot Ridge research station. Excellent views of the Indian Peaks. Start at the Long Lake TH, take the Jean Lunning Trail, then turn south and up at a fork.

Diamond Lake from the Arapaho Glacier Trail

Indian Peaks Wilderness - East Side

Located within an hour's drive of the foothill regions of Boulder and the surrounding areas, the Indian Peaks Wilderness provides a retreat from the hot summertime temperatures. Inhabitants of the Front Range are lucky to have such magnificent wilderness experiences available so close to them. Venture off-trail and explore the intricate nooks and crannies in the Indian Peaks, which looms high over the metropolitan areas in the plains far below. Day hiking is quite popular in the Indian Peaks on summer weekends; however, to fully appreciate the Indian Peaks Wilderness one must spend a night or two up here, take in the unfettered view of the stars and galaxies, and experience waking up in a high alpine ecosystem. Like all wilderness areas, the Indian Peaks Wilderness is closed to bikes.

NOTE: Keep in mind that this section only describes the popular trails that are most readily accessible from the *east* side of the Indian Peaks Wilderness. Since the *west* side of the Indian Peaks Wilderness is best entered from the Winter Park area (Rollins Pass and northeast of Fraser), trails on the west side of the wilderness area are described in Chapter 10: Winter Park and Fraser (see pp. 434-443). Many options exist to link the east and west side through long hikes and/or backpacking trips.

Maps: "Trails & Recreation Map of Boulder County" produced by the Boulder Area Trails

Coalition (BATCO), Latitude 40° "Boulder/Nederland Trails" or "Boulder County Trails", Trails Illustrated "Indian Peaks/Gold Hill", or Sky Terrain's "Southern Rocky Mountain National Park and Indian Peaks Wilderness."

Best time of the year: Snowfall in the Indian Peaks can vary tremendously from year to year and most of the trails in the Indian Peaks Wilderness are only accessible once the snow has melted and mud season has ended. This is generally mid June but can be as early as late May (especially the lower trails) and as late as early to mid July (for the more alpine trails). Like many areas in Colorado, fall is a wonderful time to be in these mountains with crisp, clear days. The season ends with the first snows, usually in early November. Snowshoers and cross country skiers can travel the lower trails in this area once the first snows arrive.

The trail to South Arapaho Peak

Camping: The Buckingham Campground located just past the Fourth of July TH (see p. 159) has 10 first-come, first-served tent sites (no water, grills and fires prohibited). There is plenty of camping (designated campsites) in the West Magnolia area (see "Nederland and Caribou" section on pp. 177-178) along West Magnolia Rd. If you are visiting the Indian Peaks Wilderness near the Brainard Lake area, the Pawnee, Camp Dick, and Peaceful Valley Campgrounds are rather close, as is the Rainbow Lakes Campground. For reservations and information about campgrounds, visit www.recreation.gov.

Backcountry Camping: Backcountry permits are required for all overnight trips to the Indian Peaks Wilderness from June 1st through September 15th each year. The fee is $5 per group regardless of duration and there are restrictions on locations where backpackers may camp. Other restrictions apply to large (8+) groups. Call the Boulder Ranger District for more information at (303) 541-2500 or the Sulphur Ranger District at (970) 887-4100. Alternatively, day-of permits can be obtained conveniently at the Indian Peaks Ace Hardware store in Nederland (303-258-3132, open 8 am - 7 pm M-Sa and 9 am - 5 pm Su) or the Monarch and Junco Lake Wilderness Stations near Lake Granby (open every day in summer from 8 a.m. to 5 p.m.). Contact www.fs.fed.us.gov and search for "Indian Peaks Wilderness" for the most recent information regarding permits and other topics of interest to visitors to the Indian Peaks Wilderness,

Access

Directions to Nederland: It is about a 16-mi drive to Nederland from Boulder along HWY 119 (Boulder Canyon Drive). If approaching from Denver or Golden, take HWY 93 about 8 mi north of Golden, drive west on HWY 72 up Coal Creek Canyon for 18.5 mi, and then take a right onto the Peak to Peak Highway (HWY 119/HWY 72) for 3.0 mi to Nederland.

Buchanan Pass TH: From Ward (for directions to Ward see the directions to Brainard Lake on p. 146), continue north on HWY 72 for about 5.9 mi. At a large right-turning hairpin turn, you should see signs for Peaceful Valley/Camp Dick. Take a left here onto CR 92. Continue on CR 92 (Middle St. Vrain Rd.) for 1.4 mi. This trailhead is located in a large parking area that is on the west end of the Camp Dick Campground.

Upper Middle St. Vrain TH: Follow the directions above to the Buchanan Pass TH. With a sturdy 4WD vehicle, you can drive an additional 3.7 rocky miles to a small parking area and trailhead on the south side of Middle St. Vrain Creek. Hikers without a 4WD vehicle can access this trailhead by hiking the lower part of the Buchanan Pass Trail. Alternatively, you can get here from the north side of Beaver Reservoir (along CR 96), but from the reservoir it is 3.8 rocky miles (4WD required) to the Upper Middle St. Vrain TH.

Paiute Peak from near the summit of Mount Audubon

Mount Neva, early Fall

Coney Flats TH: This seldom-used trailhead requires a *very good* four wheel drive vehicle. Directions are included to this trailhead primarily for hikers and mountain bikers to access the upper part of the Buchanan Pass Trail and the Coney Creek and Beaver Creek Trails. About a tenth of a mile before reaching the Upper Middle St. Vrain TH (see previous page), turn south onto the Coney Flats Rd. After 0.7 of the rockiest miles around, you will reach the Coney Flats TH. To access this by foot, the best way is to utilize the Buchanan Pass Trail from Camp Dick (see p. 159).

Mitchell Lake TH: **$** From the bottom of the Brainard Lake Rd. (see directions on p. 146), follow the road west about 2.7 mi to the entrance station (fees apply, see p. 146). Proceed an additional 3 mi to the Mitchell Lake TH (follow signs).

Long Lake TH: **$** Located within a few tenths of a mile further along the Brainard Lake loop than the Mitchell Lake TH (see above).

Glacier Rim TH/Rainbow Lakes TH: From Nederland (Nederland is located about 16 mi west of Boulder on HWY 119), take the Peak to Peak Highway (HWY 119) for 6.7 mi to CR 116/FS 298 (you will see signs for the Mountain Research Station). Take a left and proceed for 5.0 mi along CR 116 to the Rainbow Lakes Campground and a parking area. The Glacier Rim TH is on the north side of the campground and the Rainbow Lakes TH is on the west side of the campground. Not accessible in winter.

Indian Peaks North

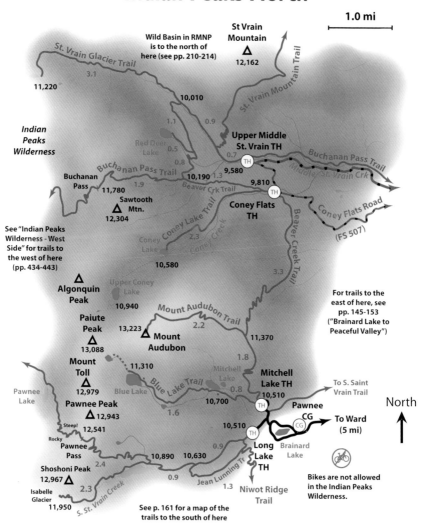

1.0 mi

Wild Basin in RMNP
is to the north of
here (see pp. 210-214)

St Vrain
Mountain
△
12,162

St. Vrain Glacier Trail
3.1

11,220

10,010

St. Vrain Mountain Trail

Indian
Peaks
Wilderness

Red Deer
Lake   0.5

1.1   0.9

Upper Middle
St. Vrain TH

0.7

Buchanan Pass Trail

Buchanan Pass Trail

0.8

9,580   TH

Buchanan
Pass

11,780

10,190   1.3

Beaver Crk Trail

9,810   TH

Middle St. Vrain Crk

Sawtooth
△   Mtn.
12,304

1.9

Coney Flats
TH

Coney Flats Road

(FS 507)

See "Indian Peaks
Wilderness - West
Side" for trails to
the west of here
(pp. 434-443)

Coney Lake Trail

Coney
Lake

2.3

Coney Creek

Beaver Creek Trail

△
Algonquin
Peak

10,580

3.3

10,940

Upper Coney
Lake

For trails to the
east of here, see
pp. 145-153
("Brainard Lake to
Peaceful Valley")

Paiute
Peak
△
13,088

13,223

Mount Audubon Trail

2.2

△ Mount
Audubon

11,370

Mount
Toll
△
12,979

11,310

1.8

Blue Lake Trail

Mitchell
Lake

Mitchell
Lake TH

Pawnee
Lake

Blue Lake   0.8

10,510

To S. Saint
Vrain Trail

North

Pawnee Peak
△ 12,943

1.6

10,700   TH

Pawnee
CG   To Ward
(5 mi)

Steep!   12,541

10,510   TH

Rocky

Pawnee
Pass

10,890   10,630

0.9   Long
Lake
TH

Brainard
Lake

2.4

Shoshoni Peak
12,967 △

0.9

Jean Lunning Tr

1.3   Niwot Ridge
Trail

Bikes are not allowed
in the Indian Peaks
Wilderness.

Isabelle
Glacier
11,950

2.3

S. St. Vrain Creek

See p. 161 for a map of the
trails to the south of here

Hessie TH: From the southwest end of Nederland (see directions on p. 156), take CR 130 west towards Eldora. Continue on CR 130 through town and the road will turn to dirt. After a total of 4.8 mi, there is an obvious parking area along the road. This is an extremely popular trailhead so you will likely have to park quite a bit down the road. If you have a 4WD vehicle, you can take a left off of CR 130 and proceed about 0.4 mi to the true Hessie TH; otherwise, there is a nice singletrack hiking trail on the north side of this road that leads to the trailhead.

Fourth of July TH:  Follow directions to the Hessie TH (previous page) but continue up CR 130, which turns into Fourth of July Rd. At 4.5 mi from the Hessie TH parking area is the Fourth of July TH. Suitable for most 2WD vehicles.

Recommended Routes

St. Vrain Glacier Trail: A lengthy trail leading to a high cirque containing Gibraltar Lakes. Begin at the Buchanan Pass TH (most folks) or the Upper Middle St. Vrain TH (if you have a burly 4WD vehicle). Proceed west then northwest along Middle St. Vrain Creek. The trail progresses through forests and high meadows before arriving at the lakes, requiring some minor routefinding. From the Upper Middle St. Vrain TH, it is a climb of 1,750 ft. in 4.7 mi to the lake.

St. Vrain Mountain Trail: This trail leaves the St. Vrain Glacier Trail (above) after 0.7 mi and heads up forested slopes to a high flat area below St. Vrain Mountain and Meadow Mountain. Ultimately, the trail continues east and down to Ski Rd. in the Allenspark area.

Buchanan Pass Trail: This trail starts out easy but the difficulty increases to moderate then difficult near Buchanan Pass. The trail proceeds up a broad drainage to a high point along the

Continental Divide where you can peer to the west towards Lake Granby and east towards the Front Range. The trail is quite long, beginning near HWY 72 at the Peaceful Valley TH (see p. 147) and proceeding through forests on the south side of the valley before traversing to the north side of the valley at Camp Dick. West of Camp Dick, the trail winds along the Middle St. Vrain

Ryan Cooper in the Indian Peaks Wilderness

Bob Schelly traversing from Diamond Lake to Jasper Lake, S. Arapaho Pk in the distance

Creek to meet the Upper Middle St. Vrain TH (3.8 mi from Camp Dick). The Buchanan Pass Trail then heads west then northwest then climbs out of the creek drainage to the south (the St. Vrain Glacier Trail continues northwest). Finally, the trail joins the Beaver Creek Trail (3.5 mi from Upper Middle St. Vrain TH) and it is a stout climb of 1.9 mi from here to the top of Buchanan Pass. From the Buchanan Pass TH, it is 9.2 mi to Buchanan Pass with 2,600 ft. of elevation gain. Add in a side trip to the scenic Red Deer lake if you wish.

Coney Lake Trail: Begin at the Coney Flats TH. Most folks will have to hike here; the lower Buchanan Pass Trail/Coney Flats Rd. from Camp Dick is a nice choice (see p. 159).   Take the Beaver Creek Trail west from the trailhead but within 0.4 mi hang a left onto the Coney Lake Trail. The trail progresses on a combination of singletrack and old doubletrack for 2.5 mi to Coney Lake, which requires a small descent to reach. Upper Coney Lake can be reached after about another mile, but there is no good trail to this lake.

Beaver Creek Trail: A 4.8-mi trail through forested slopes connecting the Buchanan Pass Trail in the Coney Flats area with the Mount Audubon Trail.

Mount Audubon Trail and Blue Lake Trail: See these trail descriptions in the Brainard Lake section (see p. 152). The hike of Mount Audubon is a popular endeavor!

Pawnee Pass Trail: The hike up to Pawnee Pass is difficult yet rewarding. The trail starts out quite mellow from Long Lake TH to just east of Lake Isabelle but quickly becomes steep as the trail switchbacks up rocky slopes and through cliff bands. Follow the trail west from the top of Pawnee Pass and the terrain gets even more interesting! You'll be amazed at how the trail zigzags down towards Pawnee Lake and makes its way down rocky cliff bands. Pawnee Lake is a spectacular destination in a wild setting. 4.4 mi to Pawnee Pass with 2,100 ft. of elevation gain; an additional 1.8 mi to Pawnee Lake with a loss of 1,650 ft.

Pawnee-Buchanan Superloop: A big loop that is best done as a backpacking trip or a *long* day for hikers or trail runners. Start at the Long Lake TH and hike past Long Lake and up to Pawnee Pass (4.4 mi). Continue down the spectacular, rugged switchbacks to Pawnee Lake, descend to the intersection with the

Cascade Creek Trail (7.9 mi total), then to the intersection with the Buchanan Pass Trail (11.3 mi total). Hang a right and ascend the Buchanan Pass Trail all the way to Buchanan Pass (17.0 mi total), descend east from the pass to the Coney TH via the Beaver Creek Trail (20.4 mi total), then make your way to the Mitchell Lake TH (25.5 mi total) via the Beaver Creek Trail and Mount Audubon Trail. It is an easy 0.7 mi from the Mitchell Lake TH to the Long Lake TH where you began. 26.2 mi for the loop - a perfect mountain marathon! - with approximately 7,700 ft. of elevation gain/loss.

Rainbow Lakes Trail: A short and easy trail that heads west from the Rainbow Lakes TH to several small lakes. It is about 0.9 mi to the farthest lake and a climb of about 300 ft.

Arapaho Pass Trail: This trail begins at the Fourth of July TH and ascends west along the north side of the valley. The Arapaho Glacier Trail leaves the Arapaho Pass Trail after 2.1 mi (pass the Diamond Lake Trail after 1.2 mi) and can be continued to South Arapaho Peak (see below). After 3.2 mi

and 1,780 ft. of climbing, the trail comes to a trail intersection near the top of Arapaho Pass. Continue left to Caribou Pass and beyond or take the right fork, which takes you to Caribou Lake and elsewhere.

South Arapaho Peak: Follow the Arapaho Pass Trail 2.1 mi to the Arapaho Glacier Trail, climb the steep Arapaho Glacier Trail 1.8 mi and 1,530 ft. to a saddle. From here, the summit is clearly visible about 700 vertical ft. above you. Continue left (west) from the saddle, scrambling at times and following a cairned route, ultimately gaining the summit (13,397 ft.) after 4.3 mi total. A difficult climb.

A stream disappears into a cave of snow, Indian Peaks Wilderness

Indian Peaks South

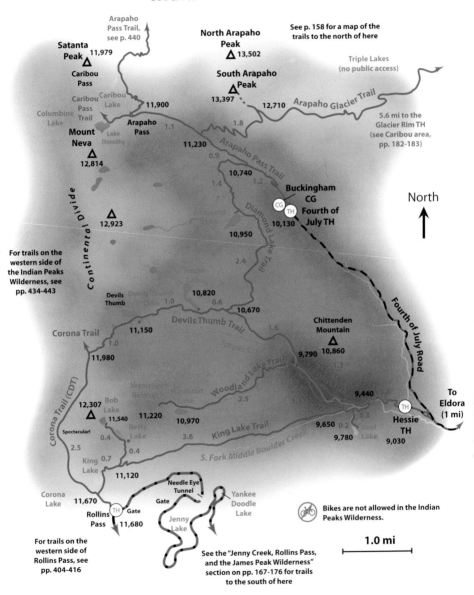

Arapaho
Pass Trail,
see p. 440

**North Arapaho
Peak**
△ 13,502

See p. 158 for a map of the
trails to the north of here

**Satanta
Peak** △ 11,979

Triple Lakes
(no public access)

Caribou
Pass

**South Arapaho
Peak**
△ 13,397

Caribou
Pass
Trail

Caribou
Lake

11,900

12,710

Arapaho Glacier Trail

Columbine
Lake

Arapaho
Pass

1.1

1.8

5.6 mi to the
Glacier Rim TH
(see Caribou area,
pp. 182-183)

**Mount
Neva**
△ 12,814

Lake
Dorothy

11,230

Arapaho Pass Trail

0.9

10,740

1.4   1.2

**Buckingham
CG**
CG TH
**Fourth of
July TH**

North

↑

△ 12,923

Continental Divide

Diamond
Lakes

Diamond Lake Trail

10,950

10,130

For trails on the
western side of
the Indian Peaks
Wilderness, see
pp. 434-443

2.4

10,820

Devils
Thumb

Devils Thumb
1.0   0.6

10,670

**Chittenden
Mountain**
△ 10,860

Fourth of July Road

Corona Trail

Devils Thumb Trail

1.6

11,150

1.0

11,980

Corona Trail (CDT)

Woodland Lake Trail

9,790

1.3

Skyscraper
Reservoir

Woodland
Lake

2.5

9,440

To
Eldora
(1 mi)

△ 12,307

Bob
Lake

11,540   11,220

10,970

0.3   TH

Spectacular!

Betty
Lake

3.6

King Lake Trail

9,650   0.2   Lost
Lake

9,780   **Hessie
TH**

9,030

0.4

S. Fork Middle Boulder Creek

2.5

King
Lake

0.7

0.4

11,120

Needle Eye
Tunnel

Bikes are not allowed in the Indian
Peaks Wilderness.

Corona
Lake

11,670

TH Gate

**Rollins
Pass**   11,680

Gate

Yankee
Doodle
Lake

Jenny
Lake

1.0 mi

For trails on the
western side of
Rollins Pass, see
pp. 404-416

See the "Jenny Creek, Rollins Pass,
and the James Peak Wilderness"
section on pp. 167-176 for trails
to the south of here

Diamond Lake Trail: A relatively easy grade trail with a moderate but rocky and rooty climb to the lake. Begin at the Fourth of July TH and after 1.2 mi on the Arapaho Pass Trail head left on the Diamond Lake Trail. The trail descends to the N. Fork of Middle Boulder Creek before ascending to the Diamond Lake area (1.4 mi); it is a short side

Diamond Lake Trail

trip to Diamond Lake, situated in a stellar alpine setting. The Diamond Lake Trail continues an additional 2.4 mi to intersect the Devils Thumb Trail; this is a challenging hike over rocky terrain.

Campsite near Devils Thumb Lake

Arapaho Glacier Trail: From the saddle on the east side of South Arapaho Peak (see p. 161), the Arapaho Glacier Trail continues 5.6 mi to the east and northeast to the Glacier Rim TH (see p. 157). Spectacular views to the south and east can be had from this ridge overlooking the Eldora and

Arapaho Glacier Trail

Nederland areas. As the Arapaho Glacier Trail continues to the northwest side of the ridge, the hiker is treated with magnificent views of the northern Indian Peaks towering high above the lakes and valleys below.

Devils Thumb Trail: Making its way to the ultra-scenic Jasper and Devils Thumb Lakes, the Devils Thumb Trail climbs from the King Lake Trail through wildflower-covered meadows and forests with high peaks all around. Devils Thumb is a natural rock formation to the north of Devils Thumb Lake; this

Devils Thumb Trail

rock formation is also visible from the west side of the Continental Divide near the town of Tabernash and has a distinctive "thumb" appearance. Start at Hessie TH, take the King Lake Trail west for 1.2 mi to the Devils Thumb Bypass Trail then head northwest then west to the lakes. Jasper Lake is reached after 4.5 mi (1.890 ft. of climbing) from Hessie TH; Devils Thumb Lake is an additional 1.0 mi and 400 vertical ft. A great place for an overnight trip. The Devils Thumb Bypass Trail makes the trip just slightly easier as it heads along the north side of Jasper Creek.

Corona Trail (Continental Divide Trail): Spectacular! From the east side of the divide, it is quite difficult to approach the Corona Trail, which is part of the Continental Divide Trail (CDT). But it can be accessed from either the King Lake Trail near Rollins Pass or the Devil's Thumb Trail above

Devil's Thumb Lake. However, you can drive to Rollins Pass via the Rollins Pass Rd. from the Winter Park area to the west (see p. 407). Regardless, the Corona Trail rolls along the Continental Divide and, besides the initial climb north from Rollins Pass, is a quite enjoyable trail with no big climbs. The Continental Divide Trail can be taken south from the Rollins Pass Rd. to Rogers Pass and beyond (see p. 175).

Woodland Lake Trail: Begin at the Hessie TH and hike west up the doubletrack King Lake Trail, past the turnoff to Lost Lake. Continue north on the Devils Thumb Trail just after a bridge crossing in a meadow. After 1.1 mi from the King Lake Trail, the Woodland Lake Trail forks off of the Devils Thumb Trail and continues 2.5 mi past Woodland Lake to Skyscraper Reservoir. The trail is steep in spots with a few flat sections to ease the climb. It is a total of 4.8 mi to the reservoir.

King Lake Trail: Connecting the Hessie TH area with Rollins Pass, the King Lake Trail follows the South Fork of Middle Boulder Creek more or less all the way up to King Lake. Higher up, the trail traverses lush, wildflower-filled meadows before ascending willow-covered slopes to King Lake. Beyond King Lake, the trail traverses

rocky slopes to intersect the Corona Trail (part of the Continental Divide Trail) just north of Rollins Pass. It is a hike of 5.4 mi from Hessie TH to King Lake and a climb of 2,400 ft.

Siblings Bob and Erica Schelly climbing above Devils Thumb Lake

The trail starts out easy near the bottom but becomes quite steep and rocky near and above King Lake.

Betty & Bob Lakes: They are easiest accessed from the west side via the Rollins Pass Rd. (see p. 407), but the Betty & Bob Lakes can also be added onto an adventure on the east side of the Indian Peaks. Situated in a high alpine setting, these lakes make a great addition to a hike in the King Lake area.

Devils Thumb Loop: A stunning, 15-mi loop taking you through a variety of wilderness subalpine and alpine terrain. Be prepared for anything! The loop can be done in either direction, although it is recommended to do it in the clockwise direction so you descend rather than climb the most difficult and rocky terrain. Begin at Hessie TH, take the King Lake Trail west all the way to the intersection with the Corona Trail near Rollins Pass and above the mighty King Lake. Proceed north (right) on the Corona Trail to the intersection with the Devils Thumb Trail. Climb to the high point along the ridge and descend to Devils Thumb Lake, continue past Jasper Lake, and make your way down the drainage, staying right at a trail intersection below Jasper Lake and taking the Devils Thumb Bypass Trail down and back to the Hessie TH. 14.5 mi round trip with approximately 3,600 ft. of elevation gain (another 1.1 mi added if parked at the Fourth of July Rd.). Great for either a long hike or run or a multi-day backpacking trip.

Sunset near Devils Thumb Lake

James Peak from the Winter Park area

Jenny Creek, Rollins Pass, & the James Peak Wilderness

South of Nederland and Eldora, north of the busy I-70 corridor, and east of the Continental Divide lies a pocket of unspoiled terrain that has much to offer the outdoor enthusiast. Easy, year-round access makes this an enticing place to visit. Mountain bikers will enjoy the Rollins Pass and Jenny Creek areas. The numerous lakes just east of the Continental Divide in the James Peak Wilderness provide scenic and peaceful destinations for hikers and backpackers. In winter, snowshoe and cross country ski trails penetrate deep into the surrounding forests.

Maps: Latitude 40° "Boulder/Nederland Trails" or "Boulder County Trails", Sky Terrain's "Boulder and Nederland" or "Southern Rocky Mountain National Park and Indian Peaks Wilderness", or Trails Illustrated "Indian Peaks / Gold Hill". For the southern part of this region (James Peak Wilderness), you will need Trails Illustrated "Winter Park, Central City, and Rollins Pass" (#103).

Best time of the year: Access to the Jenny Creek TH and East Portal TH is maintained throughout the year. The ski touring season usually lasts through late March or early April. After the mud season, trails are generally usable by mid June. The alpine areas at and above treeline can be covered with snow into early to mid July in some years. A month or two of nice, crisp fall weather usually ends with the first snowfall in mid to late October.

Camping: The Kelly-Dahl Campground near Rollinsville is a nice campground in the area. Other than this, there is quite a bit of free camping in the West Magnolia Rd. area (see pp. 178). Informal campsites can be found on National Forest land near the base of Rollins Pass and along the Rollins Pass Rd. In the James Peak area, campsites can be found along Rainbow Rd. and on the road to Loch Lomond (if you have 4WD).

Access

Directions to Nederland: It is about a 16-mi drive to Nederland from Boulder along HWY 119 (Boulder Canyon Drive). If approaching from Denver or Golden, take HWY 93 about 8 mi north of Golden, drive west on HWY 72 up Coal Creek Canyon for 18.5 mi, and then take a right onto the Peak to Peak Highway (HWY 119/HWY 72) for 3.0 mi to Nederland.

Jenny Creek TH: From the west side of Nederland, take CR 130 (Eldora Rd.) for 1.5 mi, past the Nederland High School. Veer left onto Shelf Rd., following signs to Eldora Mountain Resort. After 2.6 mi on Shelf Rd., you will come to a parking area and the Jenny Creek TH on the left side of the road, just before the Eldora entrance gate.

Aspen trunks in late fall

East Portal TH: Take HWY 119 south from Nederland for not quite 5 mi to the town of Rollinsville. Turn right (west) onto the Tolland Rd. (East Portal Rd.). Travel 8.1 mi on the dirt road, passing by the town of Tolland after about 5 mi and staying left at the intersection with the Rollins Pass Rd. after 7.3 mi. There is a large parking area at the East Portal of the Moffat Tunnel. Accessible in winter.

Forest Lakes TH: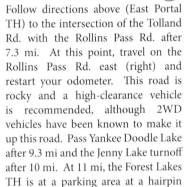
Follow directions above (East Portal TH) to the intersection of the Tolland Rd. with the Rollins Pass Rd. after 7.3 mi. At this point, travel on the Rollins Pass Rd. east (right) and restart your odometer. This road is rocky and a high-clearance vehicle is recommended, although 2WD vehicles have been known to make it up this road. Pass Yankee Doodle Lake after 9.3 mi and the Jenny Lake turnoff after 10 mi. At 11 mi, the Forest Lakes TH is at a parking area at a hairpin curve.

Wildflowers near the Continental Divide

James Peak TH: From Idaho Springs (Idaho Springs is located on I-70 19 mi west of I-70 & C-470 in west Denver), proceed west on I-70 for about 2 mi to Exit 238 (Fall River Rd.). Continue northwest along Fall River Rd. (CR 275) for 6.6 mi to an obvious right-turning hairpin curve. At this curve, a dirt road (Rainbow Rd.) continues; proceed on Rainbow Rd. for 1.6 mi to an obvious parking area where the Continental Divide Trail emerges from the woods on the north side of the road. Some 2WD vehicles will have trouble getting here. If this is the case, follow directions to the Upper James Peak TH (see below).

Upper James Peak TH: Follow directions to the James Peak TH (above), but instead of driving all 1.6 mi on Rainbow Rd. from CR 275, take a sharp right after about 1.25 mi. After another couple of switchback (1.0 mi from Rainbow Rd.) you will reach a parking area on the east side of a seasonal closure gate (see map). The CDT is just south and down the hill from here. 4WD vehicles can proceed as far as Loch Lomond (next page).

The Continental Divide Trail heading south towards James Peak

Loch Lomond: From the Upper James Peak TH (see previous page), continue 2.0 rocky miles on the dirt road to Loch Lomond. Park on the west side of the dam; the James Peak Cutoff Trail begins near the northeast end of the dam.

St. Mary's Glacier TH: From Exit 238 on I-70 (see directions in the "James Peak TH" description on the previous page), take Fall River Rd. for 9.0 mi through the town of Alice to the well-marked St. Mary's Glacier TH on the left (west) side of the road. There is a fee to park here; additional parking is found down the road.

James Peak Lake TH: From the town of Nederland (see p. 168), take HWY 119 south from for about 5 mi to the town of Rollinsville. Turn right (west) onto the Tolland Rd. (East Portal Rd.). Travel 5.0 mi on the dirt road to the town of Tolland. Just east of Tolland, find the Mammoth Gulch (sign misspelled "Mammouth") road (CR 4N). This road is not recommended for 2WD vehicles. Continue about 3.5 mi (stay left after 1.6 mi) to FDR 353 (4WD), take a right, and continue west on FDR 353 for 3.3 mi to a fairly small parking area at a high, scenic point overlooking the impressive James Peak Lake basin.

Kingston Saddle TH: A somewhat difficult trailhead to get to but nevertheless a great starting point for James Peak if you have a 4WD vehicle. Drive to Alice, which is located 8.3 mi from Exit 238 along CR 275 (Fall River Rd.). Just before Alice, take a left (west) onto Alice Rd. and follow this road for 0.7 mi and take a right. From here, it is best to follow the map on p. 173 as the roads and turns are quite confusing. Once on Hilltop Rd., it is about 3.5 mi on rocky terrain to an obvious pullout and trailhead.

Recommended Routes

Jenny Creek Trail: The Jenny Creek Trail is excellent for skiing and good for hiking, but is quite difficult for mountain bikes due to the rocky nature. Begin at the Jenny Creek TH. The trail makes its way through the Eldora Nordic Center trails before descending west to

Jenny Creek, where the trail intersects the Jenny Creek Rd. (FS 502) after 2.1 mi.

NOTE: The Eldora Ski Resort is on private property and the *only* summer access is via the Jenny Creek Trail; all other hiking or mountain bike access is prohibited, including the Nordic center trails.

Jenny Creek Road (FS 502): A popular route in winter when combined with the Jenny Creek Trail. The road is quite rocky, especially the higher you go, and is not recommended for bikes west of the Guinn Mountain Trail. Climbing through forests, the road intersects the Rollins Pass Rd. 3.2 mi east of the Jenny Creek Trail near Yankee Doodle Lake. If the goal is to ride up the Rollins Pass Rd. from the Jenny Creek area, bikes will want to take the southern spur of FS 502, which begins at a creek crossing just south of the intersection of the west fork of the Guinn Mountain Trail and the Jenny Creek Rd. Skiers will absolutely love this road when snow cover is adequate.

Rollins Pass Road: The Rollins Pass Rd. has a rather gentle grade, a result of its history as a railway bed, as it snakes its way

Guinn Mountain Cabin

up from the South Boulder Creek drainage near the east portal of the Moffat Tunnel to near Rollins Pass. Despite the gentle grade, the road is quite rocky and rough. Most 2WD vehicles can make it to about the Yankee Doodle Lake area but it is slow going. Some 2WD vehicles with high clearance can easily make it to the closure gate above the Forest Lakes TH. The Rollins Pass Rd. makes a great, relatively easy place to bike in summer and fall and cross country ski in winter (avalanche terrain

Rollins Pass Road, late fall

encountered around the Yankee Doodle Lake area). The views are spectacular the higher you get, especially if you can hike past the closure gate to near the old Needle Eye Tunnel. In winter, park either at the base of the Rollins Pass Rd. (please read all signs as there is no parking along county roads) or park at the nearby East Portal TH (Moffat Tunnel). From the East Portal area, it is 12.1 mi to the gate below the old tunnel.

Arestua Hut (aka Guinn Mt. Cabin) via the Guinn Mountain Trail:

Owned by the Colorado Mountain Club (CMC), the Arestua Hut (also known as the Guinn Mountain Cabin) makes a great winter destination. The hut operates on a first come, first served basis. Reservations are not required and are not accepted; however, there is an

online reservations calendar so folks can let others know when they are planning on being there so that the hut is not too crowded. As the CMC website notes, "It is a crowded night or a long ski out when two parties both show up to use the cabin, so to keep from being the one who sleeps on the floor." For more information and a link to the online calendar, visit www.cmcboulder.org/cabins.html. To get to the hut, take the Jenny Creek Trail for 2.3 mi to the Guinn Mountain Trail and continue an additional 2.2 mi up a steep drainage. The hut sits at about 11,000 ft. and it is a climb of about 2,000 ft. (loss of 300 ft.) over 4.5 mi.

Rollins Pass Road/Guinn Mountain Lollipop:

This is a big mountain bike ride with lots of variety. Begin at the Jenny Creek TH. Ascend the rocky-at-times Jenny Creek Trail west from Eldora (please see note about private property on p. 171 in the description for the Jenny Creek Trail) then descend to Jenny Creek (2.1 mi). From here, continue right on a mixture of singletrack and doubletrack for an additional mile (you will see signs/forks for the Guinn Mountain Cabin after 0.2 and 0.9 mi, but stay left at both of these) to a major creek crossing

Rollins Pass, Jenny Creek, and the James Peak Wilderness

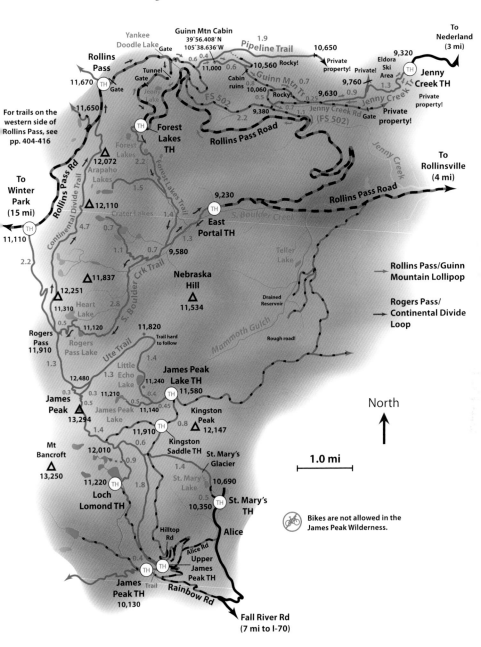

Yankee Doodle Lake

Rollins Pass
11,670 TH
Gate
Tunnel Gate
Gate
11,650

Guinn Mtn Cabin
39°56.408′N
105°38.636′W
0.6 0.4
11,000
Cabin ruins
Pipeline Trail 1.9
10,650

To Nederland (3 mi)

9,320
Eldora Ski Area
Jenny Creek TH

10,560 Rocky!
0.7
Private property!
Private! Private!
9,760
1.3
0.8
10,060
0.5 Rocky!
9,630 0.25
0.9
Guinn Mtn Trl
Private property!

For trails on the western side of Rollins Pass, see pp. 404-416

Forest Lakes TH

FS 502
9,380 0.7 1.1
Jenny Creek Rd (FS 502)
Gate
2.2
Rollins Pass Road
Private property!

Jenny Creek

To Rollinsville (4 mi)

12,072
Arapaho Lakes
Forest Lakes
2.2

To Winter Park (15 mi)
Rollins Pass Rd
Continental Divide Trail
12,110
1.5
Forest Lakes Trail

9,230
TH
Rollins Pass Road

Crater Lakes 1.4
East Portal TH

S. Boulder Creek

11,110
4.7 0.7
1.3
9,580
Teller Lake

2.2
1.1 0.7
Nebraska Hill
11,534
Drained Reservoir

11,837
S. Boulder Crk Trail
2.8
Rough road!

12,251
11,310 Heart Lake
0.5 11,120
11,820
Mammoth Gulch

Rogers Pass
11,910
Rogers Pass Lake
Ute Trail
Trail hard to follow

1.3
12,480 1.3 Little Echo Lake 1.4
James Peak Lake TH
11,240 11,580

James Peak
13,294
0.3 0.3 11,210
0.5
James Peak Lake
11,140 0.45
0.4 Kingston Peak
12,147

1.4
11,910 0.8
TH
0.6
Kingston Saddle TH

Mt Bancroft
13,250
12,010
0.9
1.4
St. Mary's Glacier

11,220 TH
1.8
St. Mary's Lake
10,690
Loch Lomond TH

0.5
10,350 TH St. Mary's TH

North

1.0 mi

Bikes are not allowed in the James Peak Wilderness.

Rollins Pass/Guinn Mountain Lollipop

Rogers Pass/Continental Divide Loop

Alice

Hilltop Rd
0.4
TH TH
Alice Rd
Upper James Peak TH

James Peak TH
10,130
James Peak Trail
Rainbow Rd

Fall River Rd (7 mi to I-70)

and the intersection with FS 502. Go left (east) and take this rideable doubletrack for 1.1 to the Rollins Pass Rd. Take the Rollins Pass Rd. up (west) all the way past Yankee Doodle Lake (3.9 mi from FS 502) and the Forest Lakes TH (5.6 mi from FS 502) to the closure gate (6.6 mi from FS 502). Proceed past the gate and just before the Needle Eye Tunnel is a steep, loose, rocky trail that heads up (left) for several hundred ft. (0.1 mi). You will be rewarded with a spectacular view of James Peak to the south. Find the cairns and a faint singletrack trail that brings you back to north of the north side of the tunnel to an old parking area and gate. Descend west on some loose terrain and switchbacks then traverse west and ascend a short ways (Yankee Doodle Lake will be far below you) along the doubletrack. Near some metal railings (12.3 mi total into the ride) the singletrack Pipeline Trail exits to the left (the Boulder Wagon Rd. continues straight and down and intersects the upper part of the Jenny Creek Trail/FS 502); follow the Pipeline Trail for only 0.4 mi as it descends and traverses some meadows. It is of utmost importance that you find the Guinn Mountain Cabin, which is in some trees several hundred yards south of the Pipeline Trail and you will NOT be able to see it from the Pipeline Trail. This might take some searching. If you miss the hut then you will keep going to Eldora Ski Resort and it is illegal to enter and descend the ski area. If you have a GPS, plug in the coordinates (see map). Bushwhack or find the very faint trail from the Pipeline Trail to the Guinn Mountain Trail. Once at the cabin (11,000 ft.), descend singletrack and doubletrack all the way down to the Jenny Creek Trail and return the way you came. 17.2 mi for the lollipop with 3,040 ft. of elevation gain/loss.

Rollins Pass to Winter Park: An awesome ride for folks looking for a long day! Or reserve a place to stay in Winter Park and make it a two-day event. Follow directions above (Rollins Pass Road/Guinn Mountain Lollipop) to just north of the old Needle Eye Tunnel. From here, head west along the Rollins Pass Rd. (closed to motor vehicles) over the old trestle bridges and ultimately you will reach the parking area atop Rollins Pass after a total of 13.2 mi. There are several ways to reach Winter Park, but the easiest and most straightforward way is down the Rollins Pass Rd. to Winter Park. It is about 27 mi and 3,200 ft. gain/3,400 ft. loss to Winter Park. Spend some time or the night in Winter Park and return to the Needle Eye Tunnel the same way, completing the over-and-back journey either by biking down the Rollins Pass Rd. or finishing the Rollins Pass Road/Guinn Mountain Lollipop (described above).

Rollins Pass to Winter Park

South Boulder Creek Trail

South Boulder Creek Trail: The South Boulder Creek Trail begins at the East Portal TH and ascends forested slopes and meadows along South Boulder Creek. Off-limit to mountain bikes, this trail enters the James Peak Wilderness. After 5.0 mi and 2,800 vertical ft. of elevation gain the trail intersects the Continental Divide Trail atop Rogers Pass. The Moffat Tunnel area is popular in winter among backcountry and cross country skiers as well as snowshoers.

Forest Lakes Trail: Take the Rollins Pass Rd. to the Forest Lakes TH. The Forest Lakes Trail heads south as it descends

Forest Lakes Trail

into the woods, passes a few small lakes, and ultimately intersects the South Boulder Creek Trail after 3.6 mi.

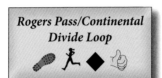

Rogers Pass/Continental Divide Loop: A superb overnight or multi-day backpacking trip or even a one-day long hike/run. Begin at the East Portal TH. Take the South Boulder Creek Trail (see previous page) to Rogers Pass. Tag on James Peak to the south if you wish. From Rogers Pass travel north on the Continental Divide Trail all the way to Rollins Pass. From here, travel north on the Rollins Pass Rd. to Rollins Pass then east past the closure gate to the east side of the divide. Find the singletrack trail over the old Needle Eye Tunnel. Descend the Rollins Pass Rd. to the Forest Lakes TH then pick up the singletrack Forest Lakes Trail, which intersects the South Boulder Creek Trail. Return to the East Portal TH. It is 18.5 mi for the loop with 3,900 ft. of elevation gain/loss.

James Peak Trail/Continental Divide Trail: The Continental Divide Trail (CDT) goes up and over James Peak (13,294 ft.). A nice way to hike James Peak is via the CDT from Rainbow Rd. Start at the James Peak TH, find the James Peak Trail/CDT on the north side of Rainbow Rd.,

then follow this trail all the way to the top of James Peak (4.6 mi and 3,200 ft. of climbing from the James Peak TH; the Upper James Peak TH eliminates 0.4 mi). There are several spurs and old doubletrack roads but the trail is well-marked with signs or cairns. Enjoy the view from the top! For a somewhat more difficult return, take the Ute Trail on the north face of James Peak then return south past the James Peak Lake drainage and over Kingston Saddle (see map).

Looking east from the summit of James Peak

James Peak Cutoff Trail: If you have a 4WD vehicle, you can start from Loch Lomond. The James Peak Cutoff Trail begins on the northeast end of the dam. Ascend this trail until it intersects the James Peak Trail/CDT at around 12,000 ft. It is 2.4 mi and 2,100 ft. of elevation gain to the summit of James Peak via this approach. A seldom-used spur heads west from this trail to several idyllic lakes that hang in the basin between James Peak and Mt. Bancroft.

James Peak Lake Trail: A relatively short yet steep descent from the James Peak Lake TH to James Peak Lake and Little Echo Lake. A very scenic basin. Continue on the Ute Trail for a longer hike. About a mile to James Peak Lake.

Ute Trail: The Ute Trail links the James Peak Lake area with the Continental Divide Trail on the north side of James Peak. A rather mellow trail with few steep climbs. Stellar views all around!

St. Mary's Glacier Trail: Park at the St. Mary's Glacier TH. Just down the road from the parking area is a sign that reads "Glacier Hike". Follow the doubletrack road as it climbs, staying left at two forks. The road reaches St. Mary's Lake after about 0.5 mi; the glacier can be found after an additional quarter mile by traversing around the north side of the lake. The trail keeps going all the way to the Continental Divide Trail after 1.8 mi total.

Rogers Pass Lake, James Peak Wilderness

Early morning, early fall near Nederland

Nederland and Caribou

Nederland is a quaint yet eclectic town perched on the shores of Barker Reservoir. While this area has always attracted hikers and skiers from Boulder and elsewhere, the mountain biking opportunities have grown in recent years. In particular, the West Magnolia area is booming with exciting singletrack trails. Just west of Nederland is the ghost town of Caribou, an old silver-mining town situated at about 10,000 ft. The nearby Caribou Ranch and Mud Lake Open Spaces offer easy to moderate hiking trails in historic settings. In winter, skiers and snowshoers enjoy the trails of the Eldora Nordic Center as well as the Jenny Creek Trail, Rollins Pass Rd., and Caribou areas.

Maps: "Trails & Recreation Map of Boulder County" produced by the Boulder Area Trails Coalition (BATCO), Latitude 40° "Boulder/Nederland Trails" or "Boulder County Trails, Sky Terrain's "Boulder and Nederland Trails", or Trails Illustrated "Indian Peaks / Gold Hill".

Best time of the year: Many of these areas are tree covered and high in elevation. Depending upon seasonal conditions, the trails may be usable without skis or snowshoes as early as late April or early May, but early June is more typical. Generally, many of these trails remain dry until mid to late October.

Camping: Plenty of designated campsites exist along West Magnolia Rd. From the first roundabout when entering Nederland, continue on HWY 119 south for 2.0 mi to West Magnolia Rd. Take a right and continue on West Magnolia Rd. After 3/4 mi, there are many designated campsites along FS 355 and others. First come, first served. In the Caribou area, there are several designated, dispersed campsites to the north and west of the Caribou TH (see next page) along FS 505.

Access

Directions to Nederland: It is about a 16-mi drive to Nederland from Boulder along

HWY 119 (Boulder Canyon Drive). If approaching from Denver or Golden, take HWY 93 about 8 mi north of Golden, drive west on HWY 72 up Coal Creek Canyon for 18.5 mi, and then take a right onto the Peak to Peak Highway (HWY 119/HWY 72) for 3.0 mi to Nederland.

West Magnolia TH: This trailhead is located at the beginning of the West Magnolia Rd., 2.0 mi south of Nederland along the west side of HWY 119.

Nederland High School TH: From the southwest end of the town of Nederland, take a right onto CR 130. After about a half mile the high school will be on your left. Just before the high school is a dirt road and trailhead right off the road to the left (south side).

Tina Lewis biking the West Magnolia trails

Park along either side of CR 130 near the trailhead.

Observatory TH: From the West Magnolia TH (above), follow the West Magnolia Rd. for 1.0 mi to FS 355T. After less than a tenth of a mile the trailhead and start of the Observatory Trail is on your right (west side of road). In winter, park along West Mag. Rd.

Hobbit TH: While it takes a little bit of time driving to this trailhead, this unofficial trailhead is located at roughly the intersection of Hobbit II and FS Rd. 355. Take West Magnolia Rd. (see directions on previous page) about 1.4 mi to the intersection with FS Rd. 355. Take a left on 355 and continue (okay for 2WD vehicles to the trailhead) for approximately 0.9 mi to an obvious parking area with a trailhead sign and map. This provides easy access to trails in the southwest region of the West Magnolia area.

West End of West Magnolia Road: At the west terminus of the West Magnolia Rd. there is a parking area. This provides easy access to Sugar Magnolia and the Lookout Trail, among others.

Jenny Creek TH: From the southwest end of Nederland along HWY 72/HWY 119, take a right onto CR 130. Continue along CR 130 for 1.5 mi, then take a left (following signs to Eldora Ski area) and drive up the Shelf Rd. (CR 140). At 2.3 mi up CR 140 you will come to the Eldora Ski area gate; park just before the gate at the obvious trailhead on your left.

Caribou TH: From the roundabout in Nederland at the intersection of HWY 72 and HWY 119, proceed north on HWY 72 for 0.4 mi and take a left onto Caribou Rd. (CR 128). After 5.2 mi, you will come to a parking area. FS 505 can be accessed from here, which can be taken south towards the town of Eldora or north towards the Rainbow Lakes Rd.

Mud Lake Open Space: From the roundabout in Nederland at the intersection of HWY 72 and HWY 119, proceed north on HWY 72 for 1.9 mi to CR 126. Travel west on CR 126 for 0.3 mi to the obvious parking area on the south side of the road.

Caribou Ranch: Follow directions to Mud Lake Open Space (above) but continue on CR 126 an additional 0.6 mi to the parking area on the north side of the road.

Recommended Routes

West Magnolia Trails

Get yourself lost in these trails! Be sure to bring a map and maybe a compass of GPS receiver if you have trouble finding your way back to where you start. There are lots of trails heading this way and that. Suitable for hiking, trail running, and biking. The Nederland High School and the West Magnolia TH are good starting points for adventures. Among my favorites are Re-Root (Root Canal re-route), the Hobbit Trails (I, II, and III), Sugar Magnolia, and the stellar School Bus Trail. Great in summer and even late into the fall until significant snowfall accumulates. For the best experience, stay away from the double track jeep roads in the interior of this area, which can become sandy and loose. However, some of these dirt roads provide easy access to the singletrack areas so can be quite helpful.

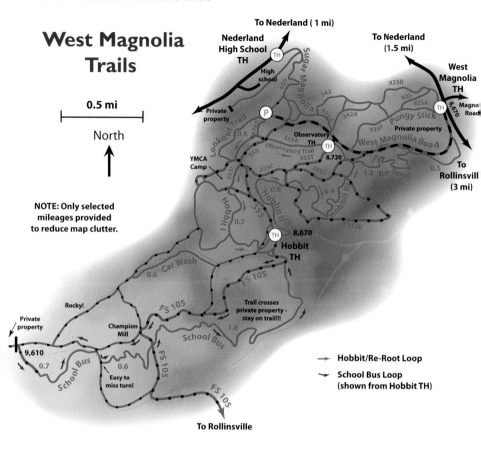

West Magnolia Trails

0.5 mi

North

NOTE: Only selected mileages provided to reduce map clutter.

→ Hobbit/Re-Root Loop

↝ School Bus Loop (shown from Hobbit TH)

Hikers will find nice trails from all of the trailheads in this area; here are two nice loops for bikers:

Hobbit/Re-Root Loop

Hobbit/Re-Root Loop: A nice, moderate ride. Start at Observatory TH and take the Observatory Trail west past FS 355, continuing on a singletrack trail to the west of a small pond. Make your way to FS 355I (see map) and the start of Hobbit I. From here, continue to the Hobbit TH and find Hobbit II (behind a sign to the east) then Hobbit III after a crossing of FS 355D. After yet another crossing of FS 355D, pick up Re-Root and follow this east to the intersection with West Magnolia Rd. Return west to your car via West Magnolia Rd. 5.6 mi round trip. Trailrunners and snowshoers (when conditions are good) will also enjoy this loop.

School Bus Loop: A stout climb up a Forest Service road then an unbelievable singletrack descent through spruce, fir, pine, and aspen

School Bus Loop

forests. Park either at the West Magnolia TH or the Observatory TH and make your way to the Hobbit TH via FS 355. There is a sign with a map on it at this location. Continue south a short ways on FS 355 then the road takes a turn to the west and goes up. Climb this loose-at-times road all the way to the old Champion Mill (obvious mill site). From here, continue west on a dirt road (not FS 355, which continues south and down) past two road/trail intersections and you will reach a high meadow area and a closure gate on the far west end near the top. Veer left (southeast) and the dirt road descends slowly and ultimately ends in singletrack; this is the top of the School Bus Trail. Enjoy over 3 mi of continuous singletrack descent! After the first road intersection (0.7 mi from the top), make sure you keep an eye out for the singletrack trail that goes left and up a short hill. Otherwise, the trail is quite straightforward and drops you off near the Hobbit TH. 5.3 mi round trip from the Observatory TH with 1,060 ft. of elevation gain/drop.

FS 355/105: In winter, park along the West Magnolia Rd. near the Observatory TH or at the road's western terminus (all gates are closed so the roads in this area are not accessible by vehicle). Ski or snowshoe FS 355 and FS 105 all the way to near Rollinsville. It is about 4.2 mi from West Magnolia Rd. to the Rollins Pass Rd. west of Rollinsville.

Dot Trails

These trails link the Nederland, West Magnolia, and Reynold's Ranch Open Space. Hikers will find moderate

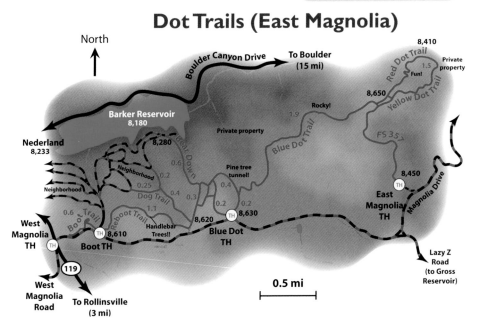

Dot Trails (East Magnolia)

trails with the occasional short but steep and rocky hill. Mountain bikers will encounter intermediate and advanced riding with a few technical spots. Don't let the few rocky areas discourage you or turn you around. Magnolia Rd. provides a good avenue for returning from or getting to these trails. Suggested routes in this area include the Boot and Re-Boot Trails or a link-up of the Blue, Red, and Yellow Dot Trails from the Blue Dot TH. There are many possibilities here and you are never too far from your starting point.

Caribou Area

Caribou Ranch: A Boulder County Open Space park located to the north of Nederland. A nice place for a hike or trail run. The DeLonde Trail leads through aspen groves and pine forests to intersect an old railroad grade after 0.8 mi. The railroad grade continues another

0.4 mi to a beautiful meadow and a fork. Go left along the old railroad grade or right and the trail becomes singletrack after the old ranch buildings. The loop is about 1.8 mi. Closed April 1 through June 30 every year. Biking is not allowed here.

Mud Lake Open Space: A small Boulder County Open Space park just south of Caribou Ranch. Great for a short hike in a spectacular setting. The Kinnickinnick Loop and Tungsten Loops penetrate through aspen, pine, and spruce forests; check out the scenic Mud Lake on the east side of the Tungsten Loop.

FS 505: In summer and fall, FS 505 provides a nice subalpine atmosphere for easy to moderate hiking and biking outings. In winter, cross country skiers and snowshoers enjoy the frosty landscape with the snow-covered summits of the Indian Peaks Wilderness nearby. Park at the Caribou TH and go north or south along FS 505.

Caribou Big Ride: Begin either in the town of Nederland (day parking available in several places in town) along CR 130 just east of Nederland High School. Ride Rd. 130 west 2.7 mi to the town of Eldora. Proceed to Huron Ave, which appears as a main dirt road as you enter town. Take a right onto 5th St.; it will appear as if you are going up someone's driveway, but you aren't. Go up the hill and take a right at the top of 5th St., which turns into CR 505. Climb 505, rocky at times, all the way up to a high point just west of Caribou Hill then descend to a parking area near Caribou. Continue north on 505, make a wet-at-times crossing of Caribou Creek, and continue to the intersection with the Rainbow Lakes Rd. Proceed north. Continue north on the Sourdough Trail (see p. 148) to the Peaceful Valley TH (28.3 mi) and return via HWY 72. Can be made shorter by eliminating the Sourdough Trail portion. 47.1 mi for the longer option with 7,300 ft. of gain/loss.

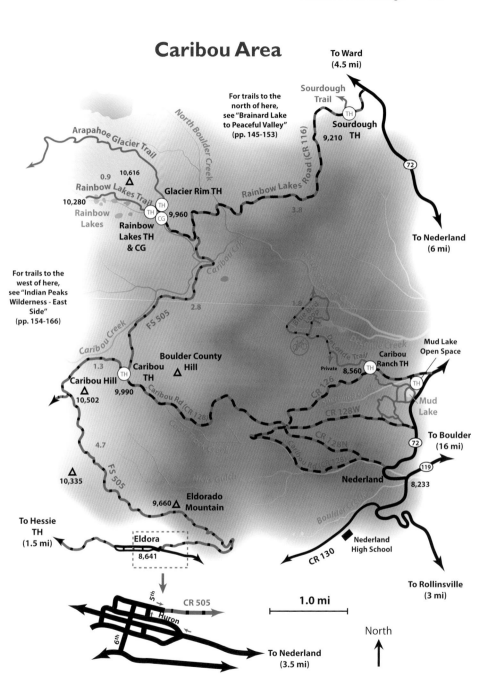

Caribou Area

To Ward
(4.5 mi)

Sourdough Trail

For trails to the north of here, see "Brainard Lake to Peaceful Valley" (pp. 145-153)

Sourdough TH
9,210

Arapahoe Glacier Trail

North Boulder Creek

Rainbow Lakes Road (CR 116)

72

0.9   10,616

Rainbow Lakes Trail

Glacier Rim TH

10,280

Rainbow Lakes

Rainbow Lakes TH & CG

9,960

Rainbow Lakes

3.8

To Nederland
(6 mi)

Caribou Cr.

For trails to the west of here, see "Indian Peaks Wilderness - East Side" (pp. 154-166)

2.8

1.8

FS 505

Caribou Creek

1.3

Boulder County Hill

Caribou TH

Caribou Hill

Mud Lake Open Space

Delonde Trail

Private

Caribou Ranch TH

8,560

9,990

Caribou Hill

10,502

Caribou Rd (CR 128)

CR 126

CR 128W

Mud Lake

4.7

CR 128N

To Boulder
(16 mi)

10,335

FS 505

Caribou Road (CR 128)

Nederland

72

119

8,233

9,660

Eldorado Mountain

To Hessie TH
(1.5 mi)

Eldora

8,641

Nederland High School

CR 130

5th

CR 505

Huron

6th

To Nederland
(3.5 mi)

1.0 mi

North

To Rollinsville
(3 mi)

Additional Wintertime Activities

❄️ ***Eldora Nordic Center:*** **$** Additional winter-time fun can be found at the Eldora Nordic Center, part of the Eldora Ski Resort. There are over 40 km of trails suitable for classic and skate skiing as well as snowshoeing. The Nordic center has ski and snowshoe rentals and sells snacks and drinks and ski accessories. Ski lessons available. For more information, visit www.eldora.com.

Charlie's Picks for the Northern Front Range

1. School Bus Loop (p. 180)

2. Devils Thumb Loop (p. 166)

3. Pawnee Pass Trail (p. 161)

4. South Boulder Creek Trail to Rogers Pass (p. 174)

5. Little Raven Trail (p. 150)

6. Betty & Bob Lakes (p. 166)

7. Lake Isabelle, return via Jean Lunning Trail (p. 153)

8. Hobbit/Re-Root Loop (p. 180)

9. Sourdough Trail (p. 148)

10. Rollins Pass/Guinn Mountain Lollipop (p. 172)

Sunset over Longs Peak

Chapter 5: Rocky Mountain National Park

The "living showcase of the grandeur of the Rocky Mountains" as the National Park Service eloquently puts it, Rocky Mountain National Park is the most visited national park in the state and one of the top 10 most visited parks in the nation and for good reason. The park has many hidden treasures: jagged peaks, serine alpine meadows, trickling streams, cascading waterfalls, and abundant wildlife. Topographical relief is immense, ranging from the 14,259-ft. Longs Peak to the lush riparian regions of Moraine Park, situated at an elevation of around 8,000 ft. Consequently, the diversity in terrain and vegetation is tremendous. One moment you may be hiking through thick, enchanted spruce forests yet a few miles away find yourself hiking through wide open meadows with views of the divide. Several trails traverse above treeline, a harsh place where the growing season is only a few weeks a year. Each season brings something new and places that are easy to get to in summer can provide challenging yet rewarding destinations in winter. In mid summer, wildflowers transform grassy meadows to a state of photogenic, brilliant perfection. By late summer, crowds disappear, giving rise to spectacular fall colors, the captivating bugle sounds of elk, and crisp, cool days filled with cloudless, blue skies. Fall does not last long; early snows lay down a soft blanket of snow and tuck the park in for a long, cold winter. This chapter presents the more popular places on the east side of the park. The west side of Rocky Mountain National Park is equally as impressive yet is not discussed here.

Wildflowers at sunset

Rocky Mountain National Park

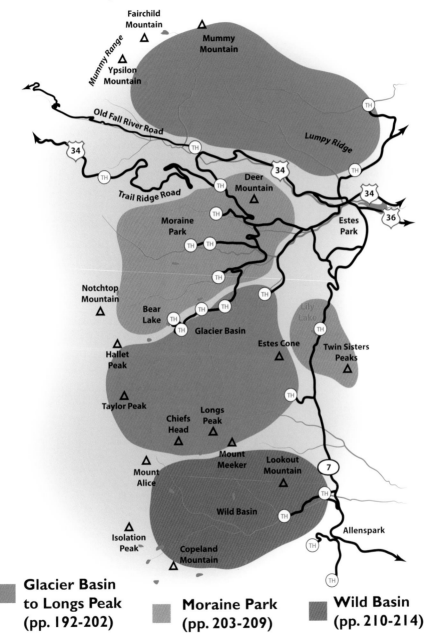

Fairchild Mountain

Mummy Range

Ypsilon Mountain

Mummy Mountain

Old Fall River Road

Lumpy Ridge

34

Trail Ridge Road

34

Deer Mountain

Moraine Park

34

Estes Park

36

Notchtop Mountain

Bear Lake

Glacier Basin

Lily Lake

Estes Cone

Twin Sisters Peaks

Hallet Peak

Taylor Peak

Chiefs Head

Longs Peak

Mount Meeker

Lookout Mountain

7

Mount Alice

Wild Basin

Allenspark

Isolation Peak

Copeland Mountain

Glacier Basin to Longs Peak (pp. 192-202)

Moraine Park (pp. 203-209)

Wild Basin (pp. 210-214)

Lumpy Ridge & Mummy Range (pp. 215-219)

Lily Lake & Twin Sisters (pp. 220-222)

Information

Directions to Estes Park: Estes Park is best accessed from the town of Lyons, which is located west of I-25 along HWY 66. From Exit 243 of I-25, take HWY 66 about 16 mi to Lyons. Continue west on US 36/HWY 66 for 20 mi to Estes Park. Lyons is also 15 mi north of Boulder on US 36.

Entrance Fee: **$** There is an entrance fee to enter Rocky Mountain National Park. The fee is currently $20 for 7 consecutive days. You can also purchase an annual pass for $40 or the *America the Beautiful - National Parks and Federal Recreation Area* annual pass for $80, which provides access for a year from the last day of the month of purchase to all federal lands requiring a fee.

Maps: Latitude 40° Maps "Front Range Trails", Sky Terrain Maps "Southern Rocky Mountain National Park & Indian Peaks Wilderness", or National Geographic Trails Illustrated "Rocky Mountain National Park" (#200). If you are just visiting the east side of the park, pick up the National Geographic Trails Illustrated "Longs Peak/Bear Lake" (#301) map. USGS topographical quad maps are available at visitor centers.

Best time of the year: Rocky Mountain National Park is a spectacular place to visit in the summer, yet it can get rather crowded. To beat the crowds, start early or visit in the evening.

Hallett Peak and Flattop Mountain from the Bear Lake TH

The imposing east face (aka "The Diamond") of Longs Peak from Chasm Lake

During busy times, you will likely need to take the shuttle bus into the park from town (see below) or will need to park at the Glacier Basin Park 'n Ride and use the shuttle bus. If you are willing to plan your trip for late spring (late May and June) or fall (September), there are far fewer people on a typical day. For those who are willing to face the cold, Rocky Mountain National Park is a serene, quiet place in winter. Grab snowshoes or cross country skis and explore!

Shuttle Service: An extensive and well-managed free shuttle bus service has been in operation in the park for years. There are currently three shuttles that serve visitors: the Visitor Shuttle, the Hiker Shuttle, and the Bear Lake and Moraine Park Shuttle. The Visitor and Hiker Shuttles generally operate daily from late June through early September with additional weekend service; the Bear Lake and Moraine Park Shuttle generally operates earlier and later in the season than the Visitor and Hiker Shuttles. Visit the link below for more information.

Visitor Shuttle: The Visitor Shuttle has three different routes: the Brown, Blue, and Red Routes. Each of them uses the Estes Park Visitor Center as its central hub. The Brown Route is a common way for folks to get to the Beaver Meadows and Estes Park (in town) Visitor Centers from hotels and lodging in town, including the Mary's Lake and YMCA areas. From the Beaver Meadows Visitor Center, visitors can pick up the Hiker Shuttle to get into the park. The Blue Route provides transportation from lodging on the north side of

Lake Estes to the Estes Park Visitor Center and other points in town. The Red Route links Estes Park to the Fall River Visitor Center with ample lodging stops along the way.

Hiker Shuttle: The Hiker Shuttle departs from the Estes Park Visitor Center, stops at the Beaver Meadows Visitor Center, then arrives at the Glacier Basin Park & Ride. A park pass, which can be obtained at automated machines outside the Estes Park and Beaver Meadows Visitor Centers, is required to board the bus. Campers who are camped at the Glacier Basin Campground can take this bus into town.

Bear Lake and Moraine Park Shuttle: This shuttle might more appropriately be named the "hiker" shuttle as many hikers utilize it to set up one-way hiking adventures, for example from Bear Lake to either the Glacier Gorge or Bierstadt Lake areas or even Bear Lake to Fern Lake area. The Bear Lake Route provides access to Glacier Gorge and Bear Lake from the Glacier Basin Park & Ride. The Moraine Park Route links the Glacier Basin Park & Ride to the Fern Lake TH with stops at Hollowell Park, the Moraine Park Museum, the Moraine Park Campground, and others.

For schedules, maps, and hours of operation of each of the shuttles, please visit www.nps.gov/romo/planyourvisit/shuttle_bus_route.htm.

Camping: It can be a battle finding a campsite in the park during the summer so advanced reservations are strongly recommended. There are five campgrounds in Rocky Mountain National Park; three of them (Moraine Park, Glacier Basin, and Aspenglen Campgrounds)

take advanced reservations and two of them (Timber Creek and Longs Peak Campgrounds) are first come, first served. The latter campgrounds are usually full by late morning or early afternoon except in spring and fall. The Longs Peak Campground accommodates tents only and all campgrounds have stay limits of 7 days from June 1 to September 30. The Timber Creek, Moraine Park, and Longs Peak Campgrounds are open year-round, yet water is not available at these campgrounds in the winter. The Timber Creek Campground is located on the west side of the park. Camping information can be obtained by calling (888) 448-1474 or by visiting www.nps.gov/romo/planyourvisit/camping.htm. Reservations can be made online or by phone: (877) 444-6777.

Ferns along the Cub Lake Trail

Arnica near Bear Lake

Backcountry Camping: To truly experience the park, plan an overnight trip. Throughout the park are numerous designated campsites. Permits are required for all overnight trips and are available at the Beaver Meadows Visitor Center Backcountry Office. The number of permits issued each day is limited. Permits can be obtained day-of for any day of the year at the Backcountry Office or reserved in advance after March 1st for any day of that calendar year. Backcountry sites are categorized by individual or group. Individual sites are limited to 7 people; group sites are for parties of 8 to 12 individuals. There is a $20 fee for each permit, which can be issued for up to 7 nights from June through October and up to 14 nights between October and May. For more information, visit www.nps.gov/romo/planyourvisit/backcntry_guide.htm or contact the Backcountry Office by phone at (970) 586-1242.

Additional Information: *Rocky Mountain National Park: The Complete Hiking Guide* (Westcliffe Publishers), written by my friend Lisa Foster, is by far the most detailed hiking guidebook for Rocky Mountain National Park and provides extensive information on pretty much every trail, nook, and cranny of the park. For additional online information about Rocky Mountain National Park, please visit www.nps.gov/romo or call (970) 586-1206.

Bicycles: Bicycles are allowed on park roads but are prohibited on all trails.

Dogs: Dogs are not permitted on any trails or in the backcountry of Rocky Mountain National Park. They are, however, allowed on leash in areas used by vehicles (parking areas, picnic areas, and campgrounds).

Alex Kostadinov approaching Black Lake, Glacier Gorge

Glacier Basin to Longs Peak

Stretching from Mt. Lady Washington and Longs Peak in the east and circling west then north towards Flattop Mountain, the rocky peaks of central Rocky Mountain National Park form an impressive horseshoe punctuated with several deep, glacier-carved alpine valleys each containing small, idyllic lakes and ponds. Winter snowmelt channels its way down the steep valley walls and into Sprague Lake via Glacier Creek and Boulder Brook. Perhaps the most remarkable of all basins in the park is Glacier Gorge, whose towering peaks and rock walls surround with authority and encase the upper reaches of the basin. Down below, hiking trails weave through lush forests and beside gurgling mountain streams. Hiking trails in this area range in difficulty and there are hiking options for everyone. Among the more popular destinations for day hikes are Bear Lake, Nymph Lake, and Alberta Falls. The road to Bear Lake is plowed in winter and snowshoeing is a popular wintertime activity on the trail of Glacier Basin.

Access

Bear Lake and Moraine Park Shuttle: This free shuttle provides access to Bear Lake and Moraine Park from the Glacier Basin Park & Ride. A great way to set up one-way hikes, which can be designed to be overall downhill if desired. See pp. 189-190 for more information on the park shuttles.

Beaver Meadows Entrance Station: From Elkhorn Ave. (downtown Estes Park), go south on Moraine Ave. at the main downtown stoplight (following directions for US 36). Continue for 3.6 mi west on US 36 and well outside of town you will arrive at the entrance station, just past the Beaver Meadows Visitor Center and park headquarters.

Glacier Basin Park & Ride: From the Beaver Meadows Entrance Station, proceed a quarter of a mile and take a left (south) onto the Bear Lake Rd. Travel just under 5 mi on this road to an obvious 4-way intersection. Take a right here and park.

Glacier Basin TH: The trailhead for access to Bierstadt Lake from the east is located at the southwest corner of the large parking area at the Glacier Basin TH.

Sprague Lake TH: Follow directions to the Glacier Basin TH and parking area but continue an additional 0.7 mi south on Bear Lake Rd. Take a left here and proceed a short ways to the parking area at Sprague Lake. Several easy trails can be accessed here.

Storm Pass TH: The Storm Pass TH provides access to the Storm Pass and Boulder Brook Trails but there are only spots here for several cars. If the lot is full, park down the road at either the Sprague Lake TH or Glacier Basin TH and hike a trail on the west side of the Bear Lake Rd. Alternatively, take a shuttle bus from Glacier Basin or elsewhere. The Storm Pass TH is located 6.4 mi along the Bear Lake Rd. from US 36.

Air bubbles trapped in ice, early winter

Mountain reflection near Glacier Gorge

Glacier Gorge TH: Located near some large switchbacks in the Bear Creek Rd., 8.4 mi from US 36 and 1.8 mi past the Bierstadt Lake TH. This lot fills quickly. The shuttle stops here en route to Bear Lake.

Bear Lake TH: A popular destination. Start early if you want a parking spot here! If the lot is full, park at Glacier Basin and take the shuttle bus to Bear Lake. Bear Lake is located about 9.2 mi from US 36 at the end of the Bear Lake Rd. There are restrooms here and a self-guided nature hike. The shuttle from Glacier Basin stops here.

East Portal TH: This trailhead is just outside the park and provides access to the Wind River Trail. Not as popular as other trailheads in the park and not as much space for parking. Take the Brown Route of the Visitor Shuttle to access this trailhead if the parking lot is full. From the intersection of HWY 66 and US 36 on the west side of Estes Park, follow signs for the YMCA camp. Drive HWY 66 (Tunnel Rd.) for 3.2 mi to a parking area and trailhead.

Longs Peak TH: From the intersection of US 36 and US 34 on the east side of Estes Park, take US 36 for 0.5 mi to the stoplight at the intersection with HWY 7. Proceed on HWY 7 for 9 mi to the Longs Peak Rd., and the trailhead is located about a mile up this road.

Recommended Routes

Bear Lake: The Bear Lake area is an extraordinary area in a unique location. Readily accessible, the lake can be accessed within a few minutes from the Bear Lake TH. The lake is nestled at the base of Tyndall Gorge. Hallett Peak and Flattop Mtn. reign supreme above the lake. The trail around the lake is 0.7 mi long and is suitable for anyone. A perfect place to snowshoe in winter when conditions permit.

Nymph, Dream, and Emerald Lakes: The parking area at Bear Lake gets you very close to some very fine alpine lakes. Begin at the Bear Lake TH and follow signs towards Nymph, Dream, and Emerald Lakes. Nymph Lake lies just above Bear Lake and makes a great excursion by itself, or continue on the trail to Dream and Emerald Lakes, both wedged down in the bottom of the deep and narrow Tyndall Gorge. From either lake, you'll have neck-breaking views of peaks looming high above. Nymph Lake is reached after 0.5 mi, Dream Lake after 1.0 mi, and Emerald Lake after 1.6 mi.

Lake Haiyaha: Lake Haiyaha is located in Chaos Canyon and the lake is surrounded by large boulders. Visible from the lake are Hallett and Otis Peaks. Follow directions to Dream Lake (above) from the

Bear Lake TH. Just below and east of Dream Lake is a trail intersection. Continue south here (follow signs to Lake Haiyaha) and the trail climbs a bit, skirts around some rocky cliffs with superb views of Longs Peak, then levels out just before another trail intersection. Turn right here and it is a short quarter of a mile to the lake, some of which is over rocky terrain. The lake is located 1.9 mi from Bear Lake with a climb of 1,000 ft. (230 ft. descent). To make a nice loop hike, proceed southeast from Lake Haiyaha to the Loch Vale Trail and return by passing by Alberta Falls; a trail parallels the Bear Lake Rd. and climbs back up to Bear Lake.

Flattop Mountain Trail: A steep hike to the broad, flat summit of Flattop Mountain. Begin at the Bear Lake TH and contour around the east side of the lake. Follow signs for the Flattop Mountain Trail. After 0.4 mi, take a left at the trail intersection, following signs for Flattop Mountain. The Flattop Mountain Trail is reached after an additional 0.5 mi. The trail switchbacks numerous times and the grade eases near the top. Absolutely spectacular views along the trail and once you arrive on top. The actual summit is difficult to discern but it is just east of the intersection with the Continental Divide Trail. It is 4.2 mi with 3,100 ft./260 ft. of elevation gain/loss to the top of Flattop Mountain from Bear Lake.

Alberta Falls: Begin at the Glacier Gorge TH. Hike south from the trailhead and follow signs towards Loch Vale (check photos for trail signs). Within 0.3 mi continue straight (south) at a 4-way intersection, following signs for Alberta Falls. The falls are reached after 0.9 mi. There are several great overlooks of Glacier Creek along the trail to the falls and beyond as it tumbles down the rocky canyon.

Perfect lodgepole pines in Glacier Basin (pp. 198-199: Fall near Bear Lake)

Glacier Basin to Long's Peak

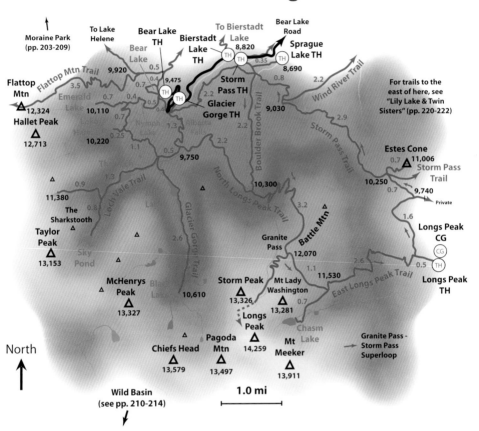

North

1.0 mi

Wild Basin
(see pp. 210-214)

Glacier Gorge Trail

Glacier Gorge Trail: Continue past Alberta Falls (see above); the intersection with the North Longs Peak Trail is reached after 1.6 mi from the Glacier Gorge TH. Proceed another 0.5 mi to a 4-way intersection; the Glacier Gorge Trail heads left (south) and the Loch Vale Trail heads straight (west). The Glacier Gorge Trail climbs gently up Glacier Gorge along the base of a long ridge extending north from Longs Peak. Mills Lake is reached after a total of 2.6 mi from the Glacier Gorge TH; Black Lake is reached after 4.7 mi and 1,800 ft. of total elevation gain. The immense rock walls of McHenrys Pk., Chiefs Head Pk., Pagoda Mtn., and Longs Pk. surround you at Black Lake, which is one of the finest alpine locations in the entire park.

The Loch and Sky Pond: Follow directions to the 4-way intersection of Loch Vale Trail and Glacier Gorge

The Loch & Sky Pond

Tina Lewis along the Boulder Brook Trail

Trail above Alberta Falls (see "Glacier Gorge Trail description above). Continue west on the Loch Vale Trail. After a moderate climb, the trail levels out and skirts around The Loch, a superb lake in a surreal setting with the omnipresent Sharkstooth overlooking the valley. Continue up the valley past Timberline Falls to Glass Lake and Sky Pond, with a few moderately difficult sections of trail. The Loch is reached after 2.9 mi (1,260 ft. of climbing), Glass Lake after 4.3 mi, and Sky Pond after 4.6 mi (2,060 ft. of total climbing).

Glacier Creek Trail: This trail winds its way down along Glacier Creek from the Glacier Gorge TH past Sprague Lake to the Glacier Basin Campground and beyond. The Glacier Creek Trail and others lower down in the park are heavily used by horse packers.

Unfortunately, this trail has been severely damaged to the east of the Storm Pass Trail but this trail is spectacular from the Glacier Gorge TH to Sprague Lake. Great for snowshoeing and cross country ski touring in winter.

Sprague Lake: A nice place for all seasons. In summer, the grass surrounding the lake glows in a superb, greenish-yellow. Explore the trails in this area or hike around the lake.

Boulder Brook Trail: Steep at times but a direct route to treeline. Start at the Storm Pass TH. The babbling Boulder Brook keeps you company as you climb towards treeline and the intersection with the North Longs Peak Trail after 2.5 mi and 1,500 ft. of climbing.

North Longs Peak Trail: Branching east off the Loch Vale Trail above Alberta Falls, the North Longs Peak Trail climbs forested slopes to the intersection with the top of the Boulder Brook Trail then switchbacks several times above treeline to Granite Pass. At this lofty point, the trail intersects the East Longs Peak Trail. It is 5.3 mi from the Loch Vale Trail to Granite Pass with 2,500 ft. of climbing.

Storm Pass Trail: Begins at the Storm Pass TH along Bear Lake Rd. Only a few parking spots available here so start early or you'll need to take the shuttle. Hike south across Glacier Creek and follow signs for the Storm Pass Trail. The trail switchbacks and climbs steeply at times and moderately at other

Stefan Griebel approaching Chasm Lake

times to Storm Pass, just below Estes Cone. For bonus points, climb steeply to the top of Estes Cone. It is 4.4 mi and 1,800 ft. of climbing to Storm Pass from the Storm Pass TH.

Granite Pass-Storm Pass Superloop: A spectacular yet difficult hiking or trail running loop. Start early as this route spends significant time above treeline. From the Storm Pass TH, follow the Boulder Brook Trail and the North Longs Peak Trail to Granite Pass. Drop down the East Longs Peak Trail to just up from the Longs Peak TH, take the Eugenia Mine Trail to Storm Pass, and descend the Storm Pass Trail back to the Storm Pass TH. The loop is 15.9 mi with 4,500 ft. of climbing/descending. See map on p. 197 for the route (green arrows).

East Longs Peak Trail: The climb of the 14,259-ft. Longs Peak is a popular endeavor. On a given day in the summer, hundreds of people are headed up towards the summit. The climb is actually quite difficult and is not a hike. Many visitors are caught unprepared and an average of 2 people die on the peak each year. If you wish to climb Longs Peak, start early and make sure you are prepared. Visit www.nps.gov/romo/planyourvisit/longspeak.htm for more information about climbing Longs Peak. Although many visitors are headed up towards the summit,

Chasm Lake from halfway up the Diamond face on Longs Peak with the Twin Sisters in the distance

the trail is also spectacular for those not wishing to summit the peak and is a great way to explore the tundra areas of the park and to get up close to some of the jagged, stoic peaks of Rocky Mountain National Park. Begin at the Longs Peak TH, which can be quite crowded in the summer, and follow the obvious trail towards Longs Peak. It is 7.0 mi and a total climb of 5,300 ft. to the summit of the peak; Granite Pass is reached after 4.4 mi and 2,800 ft. of net climbing. The lower sections of this trail are popular for snowshoeing in winter.

Chasm Lake: Possibly the most humbling place in Colorado, with rock walls on three sides of you. You will feel like you are an ant among giants. The hike to Chasm Lake is well worth the effort. While the Longs Peak Trail is quite crowded, relatively

few people make it to Chasm Lake. Start at the Longs Peak TH and hike the Longs Peak Trail for 3.4 mi to Chasm Junction, then it is a rather short 0.9 mi to the lake. 2,600 ft. of elevation gain from the trailhead.

Estes Cone Trail: Start at the Longs Peak TH on the East Longs Peak Trail. After a half mile turn right onto the Eugenia Mine Trail. The trail passes the mine remnants and descends towards a trail intersection. Take a left and climb to the 4-way intersection atop Storm Pass. Continue straight as the trail climbs 750 ft. in 0.7 mi. Great views of Longs Peak, the Twin Sisters, and the Estes Valley. Can also be hiked from the Lily Lake TH (see p. 220). 3.3 mi and 1,800 ft. of climbing to the top of Estes Cone.

Wind River Trail: A moderate trail connecting the East Portal TH with Glacier Basin. The trail follows the Wind River up to the Storm Pass Trail. Lower down, a spur heads west to intersect the Glacier Creek Trail near the Glacier Basin Campground. It is 2.2 mi from the East Portal TH to the Storm Pass Trail.

Wind River Trail

Bierstadt Lake with the Continental Divide in the distance

Moraine Park

Rocky Mountain National Park has been carved by glaciers several times in recent geological times and nowhere is this more evident than in the Moraine Park area. The valleys of Forest Canyon, Spruce Canyon, and Odessa Gorge once were filled with extensive glaciers. These rivers of ice were fed by snowfall high above and as they flowed down the valleys they ground away rocks and debris, depositing them on the sides (lateral moraines) and termini of the glaciers. These huge glaciers melted in the broad, flat area of Moraine Park and ample evidence of this glaciation can be observed in Moraine Park. The high ridges on the north and south sides of Moraine Park were formed by lateral moraines and rocks were pushed up against Eagle Cliff on the east side of the park, forming a terminal moraine. Because of these unique geological activities, hiking opportunities in Moraine Park are quite interesting. Trails climb the lateral moraines and several small lakes are found atop these moraines. Moraine Park is situated at relatively low elevations, making this a popular area for ski touring and snowshoeing in winter. The park shuttle service has stops at Glacier Basin, Hollowell Park, and the Cub Lake and Fern Lake Trailheads. Consequently, if you are just looking for easy to moderate hikes through forests and past lakes, you will not be disappointed with the trails in Moraine Park.

Access

Beaver Meadows Entrance Station : $ For full directions, see p. 193. The Beaver Meadows Entrance Station is located 3.6 mi west of Estes Park on US 36. The Beaver Meadows Visitor Center is located just over a mile east of the entrance station. Visit the

Hollowell Park with Longs Peak in the distance

various visitor centers in the park for historical, ecological, and geological information.

Bear Lake and Moraine Park Shuttle: The shuttle can be used to set up one-way hikes in Rocky Mountain National Park or can be used to access trailheads whose parking lots fill quickly. In the Moraine Park area, the Bear Lake, Bierstadt Lake,

In the Tuxedo Park area

Glacier Basin, Hollowell Park, Cub Lake, and Fern Lake Trailheads can all be accessed via the Bear Lake and Moraine Park Shuttle. For more information on the park shuttles, see pp. 189-190.

Cub Lake TH: Travel west on US 36 a quarter of a mile from the Beaver Meadows Entrance Station then take a left onto the Bear Lake Rd. Proceed 1.3 mi and take a right just after the Moraine Park Visitor Center onto Moraine Park Rd., following signs towards the Moraine Park and Fern and Cub Lakes. Drive an additional 1.8 mi to the Cub Lake TH, taking a left turn at the campground after 0.5 mi.

Fern Lake TH: The Fern Lake TH is located just less than a mile west from the Cub Lake TH (see above) along a dirt road. There isn't much parking here; if the lot fills up then there is overflow parking 0.6 mi east of the trailhead. The shuttle bus drops passengers off at this lower parking area so if you are planning on hiking from or hiking to the Fern Lake TH and utilizing the shuttle, you will need to hike the 0.6 mi between the bus stop and the trailhead.

Upper Beaver Meadows TH: From the Beaver Meadows Entrance Station, travel west on US 36 for about 0.7 mi to a hairpin curve, take a left, and follow signs and the dirt road to the Upper Beaver Meadows TH, which is located 1.5 mi from US 36.

Deer Mountain TH: From the Beaver Meadows Entrance Station, follow US 36 for 3 mi to a parking area and trailhead at the intersection of US 36 and Fall River Rd. (US 34).

Hollowell Park TH: A quarter mile past the Beaver Meadows Entrance Station, take a left onto the Bear Lake Rd. Continue about 3.6 mi on Bear Creek Rd. to a left-turning hairpin curve and turn onto the road to Hollowell park (well marked with signs). The trailhead and parking area is located just up the road. The Moraine Park Shuttle stops here.

Bierstadt Lake TH: Located just past the Storm Pass TH on the north side of the Bear

Creek Rd., 6.6 mi from US 36.

Bear Lake TH: Bear Lake is located about 9.2 mi from US 36 along the Bear Lake Rd. Get here early as this parking area fills quickly during most summer days and fall and spring weekends.

Recommended Routes

Cub Lake Trail: An easy to moderate trail that begins at the Cub Lake TH, traverses south across the Big Thompson River and a wide-open meadow, then the trail climbs west through the fern-filled, lush creek drainage to Cub Lake. There are only a few lakes in the park that are covered in lilies and Cub Lake is one of them. It is 2.4 mi and 770 ft. of net elevation gain to the east end of the lake.

The Pool: The Big Thompson River, Spruce Creek, and Fern Creek flow swiftly down the mountains and crash together at a roiling, churning spot called The Pool. The rock has been carved out and this is a popular destination for day hikes, even in winter. The Pool is 1.7 mi west along the Fern Lake Trail from the Fern Lake TH.

Fern and Odessa Lakes: Follow the Fern Lake Trail west from the Fern Lake TH. Near The Pool is a trail intersection; follow the right fork (signs for Fern Lake) and climb moderately past Fern Falls then Marguerite Falls to Fern Lake (1,500 ft. and 3.8 mi). The lake is a great destination by itself or continue to Odessa Lake, which is a steep climb of about 500 ft. from Fern Lake over 0.9 mi. If you have more energy, you can keep going to Lake Helene and stare at the impressive rock walls of Notchtop Mtn. and Little Matterhorn splayed out before you.

Spruce Lake: From Fern Lake (see above), the start of the trail to Spruce Lake is located just below the lake to the north of the patrol cabin. It is a steep and rocky trail and sometimes hard to follow, but the lake is situated in a surreal setting. It is 0.9 mi and 300 ft. of climbing to the lake from Fern Lake.

Ute Trail: The Ute Trail begins at the Upper Beaver Meadows TH and heads southwest then climbs steeply at times northwest up Windy Gulch past Timberline Pass on its way to meet Trail Ridge Rd. The trail in spots becomes hard to follow but usually the trail has cairns where it is difficult to find. It is 6.3 mi and 3,400 ft. of climbing to Trail Ridge Rd.

Moraine Park

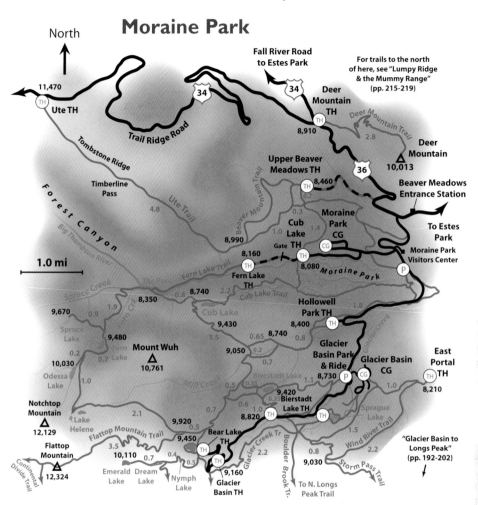

North

**Fall River Road
to Estes Park**

For trails to the north
of here, see "Lumpy Ridge
& the Mummy Range"
(pp. 215-219)

34

34

11,470

Ute TH

**Deer
Mountain
TH**

8,910

Deer Mountain Trail

2.8

**Deer
Mountain**
10,013

Trail Ridge Road

Tombstone Ridge

Timberline
Pass

**Upper Beaver
Meadows TH**
8,460

36

**Beaver Meadows
Entrance Station**

F o r e s t   C a n y o n

Beaver Mountain Trail

Ute Trail

4.8

8,990

0.3

**Cub
Lake
TH**
8,160

1.0

1.4

**Moraine
Park
CG**

CG

**To Estes
Park**

Moraine Park
Visitors Center

Big Thompson River

Gate

8,080

Moraine Park

P

1.0 mi

The Pool

Spruce Creek

Fern Lake Trail

**Fern Lake
TH**

0.8

8,740

2.2

Cub Lake Trail

Cub Lake
9,430

**Hollowell
Park TH**
8,400

TH

1.8

Glacier Creek

9,670

1.9

8,350

Fern Creek

Spruce
Lake

0.9

9,480

1.5

0.65

8,740

TH

Spruce
Lake

0.2

Mount Wuh
10,761

Fern
Lake

0.7

9,050

0.2

0.7

**Glacier
Basin Park
& Ride**
8,730

**Glacier Basin
CG**

CG

**East
Portal**
TH

10,030

Odessa
Lake

1.0

Mill Creek

Bierstadt Lake

P

1.1

8,210

0.5

0.35

**Notchtop
Mountain**
12,129

Lake
Helene

2.1

9,920

0.6

0.5

9,420

0.35

**Bierstadt
Lake TH**
8,820

TH

Sprague
Lake

TH

Wind River Trail

2.2

**"Glacier Basin to
Longs Peak"**
(pp. 192-202)

**Flattop
Mountain**
12,324

Flattop Mountain Trail

3.5

10,110

0.7

0.4

9,450

0.5

**Bear Lake
TH**

TH

Glacier Creek Tr

2.2

Boulder Brook Tr.

0.8

9,030

Storm Pass Trail

1.5

Continental
Divide Trail

Emerald
Lake

Dream
Lake

Nymph
Lake

TH

9,160

**Glacier
Basin TH**

To N. Longs
Peak Trail

Deer Mountain Trail: The low elevation and southern exposure of Deer Mountain allow for year-round hiking on Deer Mountain (and Lumpy Ridge, see pp. 215-219). Begin at the Deer Mountain TH and the trail heads east then switchbacks up to gain the broad ridge of the mountain. 2.8 mi and a climb of 1,300 ft. to get to the southeastern summit from the Deer Mountain TH.

Deer Mountain

Mill Creek Trail

Mill Creek Trail: Hollowell Park is a unique spot in Rocky Mountain National Park. Great views of Longs Peak and the verdant meadows encourage elk to frequently forage in this area. A worthwhile hike begins at the Hollowell Park TH and gradually ascends along Mill Creek. After 1.2 mi, choose to go

Notchtop Mountain

left or right; left continues to Bierstadt Lake and the right fork ascends then descends to Cub Lake.

Cub Lake to Hollowell Park: Use the Moraine Park Shuttle to set up a one-way hike from the Cub Lake TH to Hollowell Park. This is a moderate hike. From the Cub Lake TH, hike to Cub Lake (see p. 206) then continue southeast towards Mill Creek and descend the Mill Creek Trail to Hollowell Park. This trip is 6.0 mi with 1,650 ft./1,300 ft. of elevation gain/loss.

Bierstadt Lake Loop: Bierstadt Lake can be accessed from either the Glacier Basin TH at the Glacier Basin Park & Ride or from the Bierstadt Lake TH. The latter TH has very limited parking yet can be accessed easily by parking at Glacier Basin and taking the shuttle bus. In fact, the one-way hike

from the Bierstadt Lake TH to Glacier Basin is very popular and for good reason. Bierstadt Lake is located atop the Bierstadt Moraine, which was formed from intense glaciation as rocks and debris was pushed up from glaciers in Glacier Gorge. Hike to the east end of the lake and look west across the lake for a spectacular view of the Continental Divide. The trip from Bierstadt Lake TH to Glacier Basin is 2.7 mi with 630 ft. of elevation gain and 900 ft. of elevation loss. In winter, begin at Glacier Basin and snowshoe or cross country ski towards the Bierstadt Lake area.

Bierstadt Lake to Hollowell Park: Similar to the route above, the one-way trip from Bierstadt Lake TH to Hollowell Park is a nice hike. If parking at either trailhead is full, you can take the shuttle from Glacier Basin to the Bierstadt Lake TH, do the hike, then return from Hollowell Park to Glacier Basin by the Shuttle. This route is 4.5 mi long with 900 ft. of climbing/1,350 ft. of descent.

Lake Helene: Lake Helene is situated in an incredible alpine valley. From the Bear Lake TH, follow signs for the Flattop Mtn. Trail and Lake Helene. Continue past the Flattop Mtn. Trail turnoff (right) and the trail traverses easily towards a sharp switchback at the head of Fern Creek with Notchtop Mountain looming above. From this sharp switchback, a rudimentary trail heads south less than a tenth of a mile to the uber-scenic Lake Helene. It is 3.0 mi and 1,270 ft. of elevation gain to the lake.

Bear Lake to Bierstadt Lake: This is a popular one-way hike due to the fact that it is mostly downhill. Begin at Bear Lake, climb a short ways to a trail intersection, and take a right (northeast), following signs towards Bierstadt Lake. The trail climbs a short ways then very gradually descends to Bierstadt Lake. Continue towards Hollowell Park or descend the switchbacks to the Bierstadt Lake TH. Return to your car via the shuttle. The route is 3.4 mi with 500 ft. of climbing and 1,200 ft. of descent.

Bear Lake to Fern Lake: A somewhat lengthy route but one that brings you through a variety of terrain is the one-way traverse from Bear Lake to the Fern Lake TH. From Bear Lake, follow directions to Lake Helene (see above). Continue down Fern Creek towards Odessa Lake then Fern Lake. Descend to The Pool and return via the Fern Lake Trail to the Fern Lake TH. 8.4 mi with

1,500 ft./2,800 ft. of ascent/descent. 0.6 mi east of the official trailhead along a dirt road is another parking area, where you can pick up a shuttle bus and return to where you started. Spectacular! Rated difficult for the length, but the hiking is moderate and sometimes quite easy.

Bear claw marking?

Pear Lake, late spring

Wild Basin

In contrast to other parts of Rocky Mountain National Park, Wild Basin is far less crowded, perhaps because it is quite distant from Estes Park and the more popular destinations and visitors centers. Hiking trails are substantially longer in Wild Basin than in other areas of the park. During times of spring and summer snowmelt, Calypso Cascades and Ouzel Falls roar with massive energy. The lush riparian regions found near the Wild Basin entrance contrast starkly with the harsh alpine climates found in the higher basins, such as the Lion Lake and Bluebird Lake areas. Wild Basin is open in winter and access roads as well as a handful of the lower-lying trails can be snowshoed or cross country skied with relative ease.

Camping: There are two National Forest Service campgrounds near Wild Basin: the Olive Ridge Campground just south of the Wild Basin entrance and the Meeker Park Overflow Campground, which is located 1.5 mi north of the Wild Basin entrance just off HWY 7. If these campgrounds are full, the Peaceful Valley and Camp Dick Campgrounds are nearby to the south of Allenspark on HWY 72. Call the Boulder Ranger District at (303) 541-2500 for more information or visit www.recreation.gov for reservations for these campgrounds.

Access

Wild Basin Entrance Station: **$** Allenspark is easily accessed from the town of Lyons, which is located 15 mi north of Boulder. If coming from Denver or Fort Collins, Lyons can be approached by traveling west of I-25 along HWY 66. From Exit 243 of I-25, take HWY 66 about 16 mi to Lyons. At the west end of town, take a left (south) onto HWY 7 and travel up the S. St. Vrain canyon for about 19 mi to the town of Allenspark. Continue 2.1 mi on HWY 7 and take a left onto Wild Basin Rd. If approaching from Estes Park, find the intersection of US 34 and US 36 on the east side of town. Go east on US 36 for 0.5 mi then take a right (south) onto HWY 7. From here, follow HWY 7 as you climb out of Estes Park. After 12.5 mi, take a right onto Wild Basin Rd., following signs. Regardless of how you approach Wild Basin Rd., proceed for 0.4 mi to the obvious entrance station area.

Sandbeach Lake TH: The Sandbeach TH is located on the north side of the Wild Basin Entrance Station area, just a hundred feet or so from the entrance gate.

Finch Lake TH: From the Wild Basin Entrance Station, continue west on the Wild Basin Rd., following signs for the Wild Basin Trailhead and Ranger Station. The road crosses to the south side of N. St. Vrain Creek then gets narrower as it climbs gradually westward. The Finch Lake TH is located on the left (south) side of the Wild Basin Rd. 2.0 mi from the entrance station.

Wild Basin TH: Follow directions to the Finch Lake TH (above). The Wild Basin Ranger Station and trailhead is located less than a quarter of a mile further up the Wild Basin Rd. There is plenty of parking here but occasionally it can be full.

The lower part of Wild Basin from the Sandbeach Lake Trail

Wild Basin

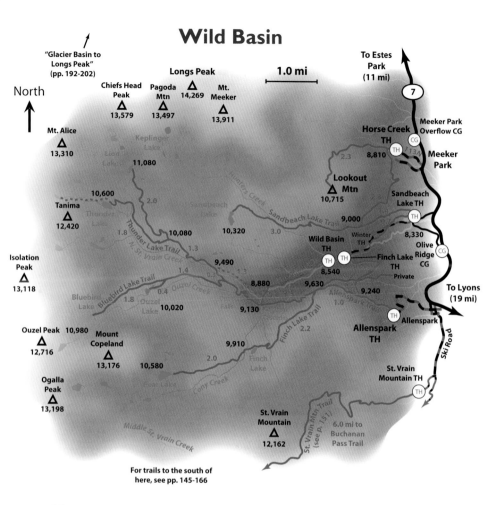

North

"Glacier Basin to Longs Peak" (pp. 192-202)

To Estes Park (11 mi)

Longs Peak

1.0 mi

Chiefs Head Peak △ 13,579

Pagoda Mtn △ 13,497

14,269 △

Mt. Meeker △ 13,911

Meeker Park Overflow CG

Mt. Alice △ 13,310

Horse Creek TH   8,810

Meeker Park

Keplinger Lake

Lion Lake

11,080

Lookout △ Mtn 10,715

Sandbeach Lake TH

10,600

Hunters Creek

Sandbeach Lake Trail

9,000

8,330

Tanima △ 12,420

2.0

Sandbeach lake

3.0

Wild Basin TH

Winter TH

Olive Ridge CG

Thunder Lake

10,080

10,320

Private

Isolation Peak △ 13,118

1.8

Thunder Lake Trail

N. St. Vrain Creek

1.3

1.4

9,490

8,540

Finch Lake TH

9,240

To Lyons (19 mi)

Bluebird Lake Trail

0.4

Ouzel Creek

8,880

9,630

Allenspark Trail

1.0

Bluebird Lake

1.8

Ouzel Lake

10,020

9,130

Finch Lake Trail

Allenspark TH

Allenspark

Ouzel Peak △ 12,716

10,980

Mount Copeland △ 13,176

10,580

9,910

2.2

Allenspark TH

Ski Road

Ogalla Peak △ 13,198

2.0

Bear Lake

Cony Creek

Finch Lake

St. Vrain Mountain TH

Middle St. Vrain Creek

St. Vrain Mountain △ 12,162

St. Vrain Mtn Trail (see p. 151)

6.0 mi to Buchanan Pass Trail

For trails to the south of here, see pp. 145-166

Wild Basin Winter TH: Shortly after the Wild Basin Rd. crosses south over the N. St. Vrain Creek is the winter parking area, which is located about 1.3 mi from the entrance station.

Allenspark TH: The Allenspark TH provides access to the southern side of Wild Basin. In Allenspark (see directions in the description to the Wild Basin Entrance Station above), find the post office and immediately take a right (west) onto CR 90. Proceed on this dirt road for 1.5 mi and the Allenspark TH is on the right side of the road as the road takes a left turn.

Horse Creek TH: From the intersection of US 36 and US 34 on the east side of Estes Park, drive east on US 36 for 0.5 mi to HWY 7. Take HWY 7 just under 12 mi to Meeker Park.

Look for CR 113N (also labeled with Dead End). Follow the dirt road west and up for about 0.7 mi. The Lookout Mountain Trail can be accessed here.

Recommended Routes

Sandbeach Lake Trail: The trip to Sandbeach Lake is a worthwhile endeavor and is particularly shorter than hikes to other lakes in the Wild Basin area. Situated on the southern slopes of Mt. Meeker, Sandbeach Lake affords striking views all around. The name of the lake is fitting; go there and you will see why! It is 4.4 mi and a climb of 2,000 ft. to the lake.

Sandbeach Lake

Calypso Cascades, Ouzel Falls, &
Thunder Lake: From the Wild Basin TH, pick up the Thunder Lake Trail. The trail passes by the Lower and Upper Copeland Falls after about a quarter of a mile. After 1.7 mi you will reach Calypso Cascades, a huge, roaring waterfall. Cross

the bridges and continue west. Ouzel Falls is reached after 2.5 mi. If you still have energy, continue west along the N. St. Vrain Creek, passing the turnoff to the Bluebird Lake Trail (2.9 mi) and the Lion Lake Trail (4.5 mi) further up. After 6.3 mi, the stunning Thunder Lake is reached after 2,400 ft. of energy. If you still have energy, you can climb west for about a thousand feet to Lake of Many Winds. The bottom portions of this trail are popular for snowshoeing and ski touring in winter.

Lion Lakes: The jagged rock walls of Mt. Alice, Chief's Head Pk., Pagoda Mtn., Longs Pk., and Mt. Meeker surround you in this high basin. Several lakes can be found here with the first Lion Lake being the most popular destination. The 3.6-mi hike to Lion Lakes from the Thunder Lake Trail is steep and rocky and the trail is not maintained. Nevertheless, you will be rewarded for the climb. Follow directions to Thunder Lake (see above) but 4.5 mi from the trailhead take the Lion Lakes Trail to the north. 6.6 mi and 2,900 ft. of elevation gain to the first Lion Lake from Wild Basin TH.

Ouzel and Bluebird Lakes:
Follow directions to Ouzel Falls
(see above).   0.4 mi after the
falls, take a left (west) onto the
Bluebird Lake Trail. The trail
climbs to the top of a moraine
then gradually ascends through
an area that was burned in a 1978
fire to the intersection with the
Ouzel Lake Trail. Continue left
to Ouzel Lake, which is reached
after 4.8 mi (1,700 ft. of elevation
gain), or continue straight for a

Colorado Columbine along N. St. Vrain Creek

substantially more challenging climb to the spectacular
alpine setting of Bluebird Lake (6.2 mi with 2,800 ft. of
climbing from the trailhead). Moderate to Ouzel Lake;
difficult to Bluebird Lake.

Finch Lake Trail: The Finch Lake Trail begins at the Finch
Lake TH and ascends forested slopes as it traverses to the
south side of a ridge before intersecting the Allenspark Trail.
From here, the trail continues southwest to Finch Lake (4.6
mi). Continue an additional 2.0 mi up a lovely drainage to
Pear Lake, which sits in an open basin surrounded by forested slopes and high mountains.

Allenspark Trail: An easy trail climbing gradually from the
Allenspark TH west to the intersection with the Finch Lake Trail.
The trail then descends gradually to the magnificent Calypso
Cascades. 3.1 mi to the Calypso Cascades.

Ouzel Falls

Wild Basin Road: In winter,
ski touring and snowshoeing
on the Wild Basin Rd. is quite
popular with high snowy peaks
all around. You will be able to
start at the Wild Basin Winter
TH and you can continue past
the Wild Basin TH towards the
Thunder Lake Trail if desired.

Mount Ypsilon and Fairchild Mountain, Mummy Range

Lumpy Ridge & the Mummy Range

Remote and wild, the Mummy Range stretches from Trail Ridge Rd. to the northern border of Rocky Mountain National Park. Sitting below and to the east of the range is Lawn Lake, situated in a spectacular alpine environment with an incredible backdrop. The Dark Canyon Trail leads southeast and down from Lawn Lake through Black Canyon towards Lumpy Ridge, whose globular granite rock piles seem somewhat out of place. While the alpine areas of the Mummy Range see significant snowfalls during the winter, the south-facing slopes of the low-lying Lumpy Ridge permit hiking excursions late into fall and early in the spring. For a scenic and moderate hike, weave your way beneath bus-size granite boulders as you make your way to the distinctive Gem Lake area.

Access

Fall River Entrance Station: $ From the intersection of US 36 and US 34 on the east side of Estes Park, take US 34 (Fall River Rd.) for 5 mi to the entrance station. Just east of the entrance station is the Fall River Visitor Center. A park pass is required to enter Rocky Mountain National Park.

Lumpy Ridge TH: From the intersection of US 36 and US 34 to the east of downtown Estes Park and west of Lake Estes, proceed 0.5 mi west on US 34 (E. Wonderview Ave) past

Elk near Trail Ridge Road

the historic Stanley Hotel and take a right onto MacGregor Ave. Proceed 1.3 mi on this road to Lumpy Ridge Rd. (follow signs for Lumpy Ridge TH); MacGregor Ave will take a sharp right after 0.8 mi and turn into Devils Gulch Rd. It is a quick 0.3 mi to the parking area and trailhead. There is no fee to park here.

Cow Creek TH: Follow directions to the Lumpy Ridge TH (above) but instead of turning onto Lumpy Ridge Rd., continue on Devils Gulch Rd. Drive 2.7 mi on Devils Gulch Rd. and take a left onto McGraw Ranch Rd. (dirt). Proceed 2.2 mi on this road as it climbs then descends to the Cow Creek TH and the old McGraw Ranch. Parking is not available right at the trailhead but is available on the south side of the creek along the road (read signs). There is no fee to park here. Plowed in winter.

Lawn Lake TH: From the Fall River Entrance Station, proceed west on Fall River Rd. for 2.2 mi. Take a right, following signs to the Lawn Lake TH and the Old Fall River Rd. After a tenth of a mile the Lawn Lake TH and parking area is found just off the road. There is no fee to park here.

Recommended Routes

NOTE: Many of the trails of Lumpy Ridge, with the exception of the upper Black Canyon Trail and the upper part of the Cow Creek Trail, are passable most of the year due to the

Lumpy Ridge & the Mummy Range

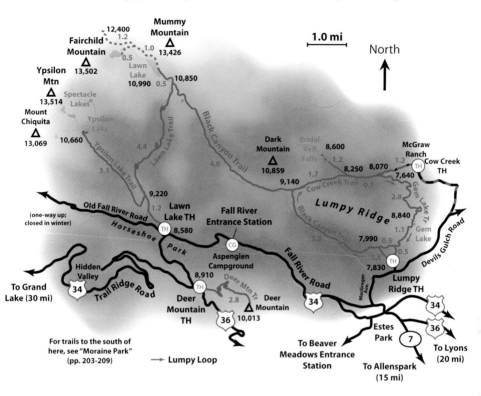

relatively low elevation and southern exposure.

Black Canyon Trail: Starting at the Lumpy Ridge TH, the Black Canyon Trail contours along the base of the cliffs of Lumpy Ridge with several climbers trails leading up towards the rocks. The trail descends a bit and crosses through meadows before entering lodgepole forests and climbing steeply at times towards the intersection with the west end of the Cow Creek Trail (3.8 mi from Lumpy Ridge TH). From this intersection, the Black Canyon Trail continues west and gets narrower and is used far less than other trails in the area. After an additional 4.8 mi of winding through thick forests interspersed with a few open meadows, the trail intersects the Lawn Lake Trail just below Lawn Lake, near treeline. It is a climb of 4,000 ft. to this intersection at the end of the Black Canyon Trail.

Gem Lake Trail: A super fun trail that winds its way through the monstrous boulders of Lumpy Ridge. If you have some extra

time you may want to play around on some of these rocks, or enjoy your lunch atop a choice boulder. Nestled in a rocky cleft near the top of Lumpy Ridge is Gem Lake, a unique, shallow lake with rock slabs as beaches. It is a climb of 1,300 ft. (loss of 230 ft.) over 1.6 mi to Gem Lake. Continue north from Gem Lake towards Cow Creek if you wish, or hike to Gem Lake from the Cow Creek TH, which is a hike of 4.0 mi and 1,500 ft. of climbing.

Balanced Rock Trail: A side trip from the Gem Lake Trail 1.2 mi north of Gem Lake. From the Gem Lake Trail, it is about a mile to Balanced Rock, a truck-sized rock balancing on a small pedestal.

Cow Creek Trail: Cow Creek Trail skirts along the base of the north side of Lumpy Ridge. From the Cow Creek TH, the trail ascends gradually to the intersection with the Bridal Veil Falls Trail then crosses Cow Creek and ascends more steeply to the saddle between Dark Mountain and Lumpy Ridge near the intersection with the Black Canyon Trail. It is a climb of 1,300 ft. over 3.6 mi to the Black Canyon Trail. The north side of Lumpy Ridge would make a fine place to camp; there are three designated backcountry campsites along Cow Creek (see p. 191 for more information about backcountry camping in the park).

Bridal Veil Falls: A worthy side trip from the Cow Creek Trail. 1.9 mi up the Cow Creek Trail, the Bridal Veil Falls Trail can be taken to Bridal Veil Falls, which is a 20-ft. falls that is more impressive in the spring than other times of the year. From the

Gem Lake with the Twin Sisters in the distance

An interesting hole in the rock along the Gem Lake Trail

Cow Creek Trail, it is 1.2 mi to the falls.

Lumpy Loop: A nice 10.6-mi hike or trail run with varied terrain. From the Lumpy Ridge TH, take the Black Canyon Trail west and northwest to the intersection with the Cow Creek Trail. Turn right (east) and descend through fir and spruce forests then along aspen forests and cross Cow Creek. Continue down towards the Gem Lake Trail. Climb rocky slopes through pine forests to Gem Lake, perched atop Lumpy Ridge with spectacular views of Estes Valley, Longs Peak, and the Twin Sisters. Descend the southern part of the Gem Lake Trail back to the Lumpy Ridge TH. The loop has 2,850 vertical ft. of climbing/descending.

Lawn Lake Trail: An overall moderate, well-traveled trail after an initial steep climb. The trail follows Roaring River to the scenic Lawn Lake, which is right at treeline. Lawn Lake lies at the base of a large cirque framed by Mummy Mountain, Hagues Peak, and Fairchild Mountain. From the Lawn Lake TH, it is 6.1 mi and

2,500 ft. of climbing to the lake. There are several designated campsites about halfway up this trail (see p. 191 for information on backcountry camping in the park).

Ypsilon Lake Trail: Begin at the Lawn Lake TH and head up the Lawn Lake Trail. After the initial climb, take a left after 1.2 mi and the Ypsilon Lake Trail heads southwest across Roaring River. The trail eases slightly in difficulty but it is a consistent climb to Ypsilon Lake, which lies just below treeline. It is 4.3 mi over 2,300 ft. of elevation gain to Ypsilon Lake.

The Mummy Range as seen from the Lily Lake area

Lily Lake & the Twin Sisters

Perched in a unique location just before the mountains drop off to the Estes Valley, Lily Lake is in the far northeastern corner of the park. Across HWY 7 from Lily Lake are the Twin Sisters, a 2-mile ridge running north to south, part of which is part of Rocky Mountain National Park. The climb of the Twin Sisters is short yet steep but those who make the effort are rewarded with spectacular views of Longs Peak, the Continental Divide, and the Estes Valley. Stop at the Lily Lake area for a picnic and explore the nearby trails for a couple of hours. Unlike most of Rocky Mountain National Park, there is no fee to park in the Lily Lake area.

Access

Lily Lake TH: Lily Lake is located about 6 mi south of Estes Park along HWY 7 on the west side of the road. Alternatively, if approaching from the south, the trailhead is located about 8.5 mi north of Allenspark on HWY 7. This area is part of Rocky Mountain National Park yet there is no park fee to park or use the trails in this area.

Twin Sisters TH: Follow directions to the Lily Lake TH (above). The Twin Sisters TH is just across HWY 7 on the east side. Park at the trailhead or alongside the road.

Lily Mountain TH: The Lily Mountain TH is located just a half mile north of Lily Lake and there is room for half a dozen or so cars.

Lily Lake & the Twin Sisters

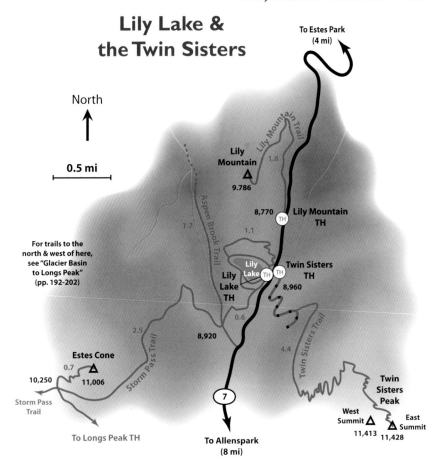

North

0.5 mi

To Estes Park
(4 mi)

Lily Mountain Trail

Lily Mountain
△
9,786

1.8

8,770   Lily Mountain
TH

Aspen Brook Trail

1.7

1.1

For trails to the
north & west of here,
see "Glacier Basin
to Longs Peak"
(pp. 192-202)

Lily
Lake

Lily
Lake
TH

Twin Sisters
TH
8,960

0.6

2.5

8,920

Storm Pass Trail

Estes Cone
0.7   △
10,250   11,006

Storm Pass
Trail

To Longs Peak TH

7

To Allenspark
(8 mi)

Twin Sisters Trail

4.4

Twin
Sisters
Peak

West
Summit △
11,413

East
△ Summit
11,428

Recommended Routes

Lily Lake: The Lily Lake Trail encircles Lily Lake and is 1.4 mi long. The Lily Ridge Trail is a 1.1-mi long trail that forms a loop with the Lily Lake Trail and traverses up on the hillside to the north of Lily Lake. Both trails are easy and suitable for anyone.

Lily Lake

Storm Pass Trail to Estes Cone

Storm Pass Trail: From the Lily Lake TH, head south and follow trails for the Storm Pass Trail. The Storm Pass Trail heads southwest to intersect the Aspen Brook Trail then climbs steeply on the eastern flank of Estes Cone to Storm Pass. It is 3.4 mi to Storm Pass and a climb of 1,650 ft. from Lily Lake. Estes Cone is a steep 0.7 mi, 750-ft. climb from Storm Pass.

Aspen Brook Trail: An easy trail descending along a creek from the Storm Pass Trail (see above). Views of the Mummy Range permeate from the north. The trail ends at the park boundary, which is about 1.7 mi from the Storm Pass Trail.

Lily Mountain Trail: Located just outside Rocky Mountain National Park, the Lily Mountain Trail starts from the Lily Mountain TH off of HWY 7. The first section of the trail is quite easy as it contours north but then the trail switchbacks left (south) and climbs steeply to the summit. This latter section of trail is rocky and is marked mostly with cairns. It is 1.7 mi and a gain of about 1,200 ft. to the summit.

Twin Sisters Trail: From the Twin Sisters TH, this trail follows a dirt road then shortly after a gate takes a left onto a singletrack trail. The trail climbs steeply through lodgepole forests that turn to the typical spruce and fir forests higher up. Once treeline is reached, scramble up rocky terrain to either the west summit or the east summit. The east summit is just slightly higher than the west summit and is more popular. It is 4.4 mi and a climb of 2,700 ft. to the east summit.

Charlie's Picks for Rocky Mountain National Park

1. The Loch and Sky Pond (p. 197)

2. Nymph, Dream, and Emerald Lakes (p. 195)

3. Gem Lake (p. 217)

4. Glacier Gorge Trail (p. 197)

5. Lumpy Loop (p. 219)

6. Bear Lake to Bierstadt Lake (p. 209)

7. Storm Pass Trail (p. 201)

8. Lily Lake (p. 221)

9. Thunder Lake Trail (p. 213)

10. Cub Lake Trail (p. 206)

Sunset from the summit of Mount Evans

Chapter 6: Mount Evans

Mount Evans towers high above the plains to the west of Denver and is one of many peaks in the area extending Colorado's Front Range southward from the northern part of the state (see Chapters 4 and 5). The trip to the top of Mount Evans via the Mount Evans Rd. is an invigorating and rewarding experience and a great opportunity to see the alpine zones of Colorado up close. Several hiking trails are easily accessible in the Echo Lake area and make popular destinations for day hikers. Despite the popularity of the Mount Evans Rd., surprisingly few people explore the remote wilderness experiences nearby. Surrounding the busy corridor of the roadway is an expansive wilderness area. Containing over 74,000 acres, the Mount Evans Wilderness is diverse, wild, and biologically unique. The rare, slow-growing bristlecone pine is found near treeline. Growing extremely slowly, these trees live between 1,500 and 2,000 years and thrive in the harsh conditions found near treeline on Mount Evans. Furthermore, there are few places south of the Arctic Circle where arctic tundra can be found and the Mount Evans area is one of them. Unlike most alpine tundra found in Colorado that is dry and firm, arctic tundra harbors many small pools of water and does not dry out completely like alpine tundra. The marshy nature is difficult to travel on. You can experience arctic tundra on the east side of Guanella Pass and near Summit Lake, among other places. Come explore the craggy peaks, wide open tundra, and enchanted spruce and pine forests of the Mount Evans area!

Near Summit Lake, Mount Evans

Information

Map: National Geographic Trails Illustrated "Idaho Springs, Georgetown, and Loveland Pass" (#104). The Forest Service also provides a very nice general map of the area with admission to the Mount Evans Rd.

Best time of the year: The Mount Evans area is one of the first to melt out in the spring. By late May or early June, in general, most of the trails are passable. Some of the lower trails in the eastern part of the area (Captain Mountain, Beaver Meadows, and Meridian Trails) may be usable significantly earlier in the season. Fall is a great time to explore these trails as they are relatively dry. Usually the first significant snowfalls arrive in late October to mid November; however, snowshoes and cross country skis can be used on many of the trails once the snow flies, especially in the Echo Lake and Guanella Pass areas.

Camping: There are several campgrounds on the periphery of the Mount Evans Wilderness within the Clear Creek and South Platte Ranger Districts. These include the Echo Lake and West Chicago Creek Campgrounds on the north side (closest to the Echo Lake/Mount Evans Rd. area); the Clear Lake, Guanella Pass, Geneva Park, Burning Bear, and Whiteside Campgrounds along the Guanella Pass Rd. on the west side; and the Deer Creek, Meridian, and Camp Rock Campgrounds on the southeastern side of the Mount Evans Wilderness. The Columbine, Cold Springs, Pickle Gulch, and the Mizpah Campgrounds are also in the vicinity if the campgrounds above are full. Camping and building of fires is prohibited

Mount Evans

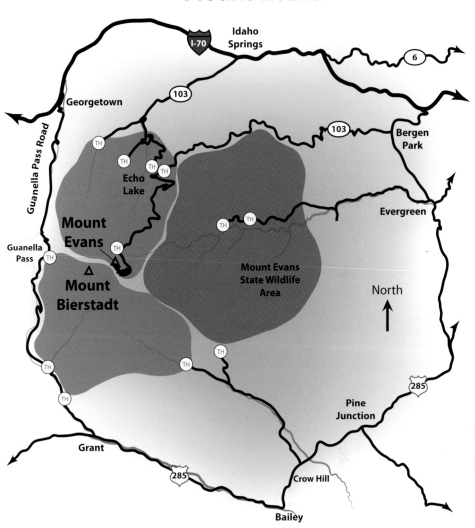

Echo Lake, Chicago Creek, & the Mount Evans Road (pp. 227-231)

Mount Evans East (pp. 231-238)

Guanella Pass & Mount Evans South (pp. 238-242)

within a half a mile of the Mount Evans Rd. There is also limited dispersed, primitive camping available along the Guanella Pass Rd., the West Chicago Creek Rd., and FS 102 (near the Meridian TH), among others.

More information related to camping can be obtained by contacting the Clear Creek Ranger District (Echo Lake, West Chicago Creek, Clear Lake, Guanella Pass Campgrounds) at (303) 567-3000 or the South Platte Ranger District (Burning Bear, Deer Creek, and Meridian Campgrounds) at (303) 275-5610. Some of these campgrounds accept advance reservations; visit the National Forest Service Reservation System online at www.recreation. gov or call 1-877-444-6777.

Showers (and other fun activities including indoor rock climbing) are available at the Buchanan Park Recreation Center in Bergen Park for a very reasonable fee. This is located just west of the intersection of Evergreen Parkway (HWY 74) and the Squaw Pass Rd.

More Information & Additional Resources: For more information related to the Mount Evans Rd. and recreational opportunities in the Mount Evans area, visit www. mountevans.com. For up-to-date conditions on the Mount Evans Rd., call the Clear Creek Ranger Station at (303) 567-3000. The Mount Evans Rd. is typically open by Memorial Day (depending upon snowfall) and closes in early October, after the first significant snowfall. There is a fee to access the road. For other questions related to the national forests in this area, contact the South Platte Ranger District at (303) 275-5610.

NOTE: A mandatory, self-issuing permit system has been implemented in the Mount Evans Wilderness for all access. The permits are free, easy to fill out, and can be obtained at each trailhead.

Sunset at Echo Lake

Sunrise on Gray Wolf Mountain

Echo Lake, Chicago Creek, and the Mount Evans Road

Echo Lake and the Chicago Creek area are by far the most popular areas to visit in the vicinity of Mount Evans. Providing easy access to the mountain, the Mount Evans Rd. is the highest paved road in North America and is a remnant of a long-ago dream to connect Longs Peak in the north with Pikes Peak in the south by driving up and over Mount Evans. This proved to be an overly-ambitious goal yet the Mount Evans Rd. remains. Today, you can drive to the parking area and hike the remaining 130 ft. to the summit. In 1942, the Crest House was built, which contained a restaurant and gift shop. Unfortunately, the Crest House burned down in 1979, but the remains are still visible today. Visitors to the highway also enjoy Summit Lake, which is managed by Denver Mountain Parks. Climbing Mount Evans is a popular endeavor, as well as some of the hikes in the Echo Lake area.

Access

Hell's Hole TH: From the Mount Evans exit (Exit 240) of I-70 in Idaho Springs, take HWY 103 (Chicago Creek Rd.) for 6.5 mi to a sharp left-turning hairpin turn. Turn right onto the dirt West Chicago Creek Rd. (CR 114) and drive about 3 mi. Just past the West Chicago Creek Campground is found the Hell's Hole TH.

Echo Lake TH: The most popular trailhead in the area most easily accessed from Idaho Springs. Idaho Springs is located roughly 25 mi west of the intersection of I-70 and C-470 west of Denver. From the west, Idaho Springs is located about 36 mi east of Silverthorne. Regardless, from the Mount Evans exit (Exit 240) in Idaho Springs, take HWY 103 south for 13 mi. Alternatively, drive HWY 103 28 mi west of Bergen Park, which is located just south of I-70 (Exit 251/252). Near the east end of the lake, turn onto the Mount Evans Rd. near the Mount Evans Lodge and there is a parking area just down the dirt road on your left (south). If you are accessing the Chicago Lakes Trail, you can also park at the picnic area on the north side of Echo Lake; the Chicago Lakes Trail can be accessed by hiking west from the picnic area along the north shore of the lake.

South Chicago Creek TH: ❄ Take the Mount Evans exit (Exit 240) of I-70 and continue on HWY 103 (Chicago Creek Rd.) for about 8.7 mi to CR 113 (Hefferman Gulch Rd.). There is a Dead End sign here. Continue 1.2 mi to a parking area. In winter, there is limited parking back along HWY 103 and the Hefferman Gulch Rd. is great for cross country skiing.

Mount Goliath TH: ❄ $ This trailhead is located at about the 3-mi marker of the Mount Evans Rd. (follow directions to the Echo Lake TH above; the Mount Evans Rd. begins by the Mount Evans Lodge) at an obvious, sharp switchback. Hike the Walter Pesman/Mount Goliath Trail from here or explore some of the other smaller trails. A famous stand of bristlecone pine sits in the vicinity.

Upper Goliath TH: ❄ $ The Upper Goliath TH is located approximately 4.8 mi up the Mount Evans Rd. on the east side of the road. This trailhead provides access to the top of the Walter Pesman Trail as well as the Walter Pesman Alpine Garden, a short, 1/4-mi hiking loop.

Summit Lake: ❄ $ Located approximately 9 mi up the Mount Evans Rd. (follow directions to the Echo Lake TH above; the Mount Evans Rd. begins by the Mount Evans Lodge) is the parking area for Summit Lake. You can estimate your progress along the road by using the mile markers. From here, hike around the lake, to the top of Mount Evans, or southeast on the Summit Lake Trail. A great place for a picnic or rest stop while driving up the Mount Evans Rd.

Recommended Routes

Chicago Lakes Trail: A popular trail starting at Echo Lake and descending to Chicago Creek before a gradual ascent past the Idaho Springs Reservoir to the lower and upper

Chicago Lakes Trail

Echo Lake & Chicago Creek

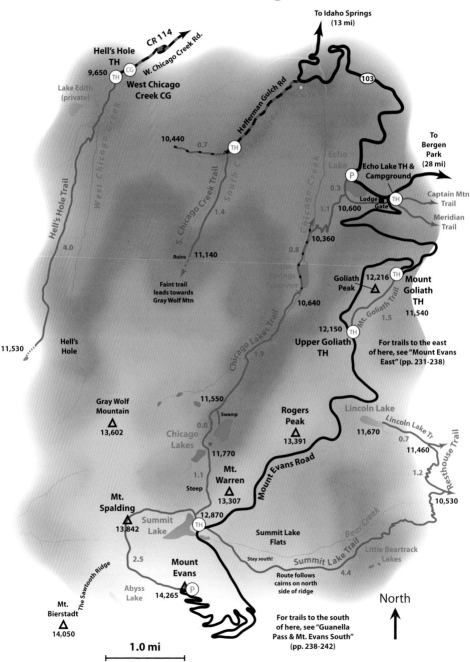

Hell's Hole TH
9,650

CR 114
W. Chicago Creek Rd.

West Chicago Creek CG

Lake Edith (private)

To Idaho Springs (13 mi)

103

To Bergen Park (28 mi)

Echo Lake TH & Campground

P

0.3

Lodge
Gate

10,600

Captain Mtn Trail

Meridian Trail

10,440   0.7   TH

Hefferman Gulch Rd.

Echo Lake

1.1

10,360

0.8

10,640

Goliath Peak   12,216   TH   Mount Goliath TH   11,540

Mt. Goliath Trail   1.5

Upper Goliath TH   12,150   TH

For trails to the east of here, see "Mount Evans East" (pp. 231-238)

West Chicago Creek

Hell's Hole Trail

S. Chicago Creek Trail

South Chicago Creek

Chicago Creek

1.4

4.0

Ruins   11,140

Faint trail leads towards Gray Wolf Mtn

Idaho Reservoir

Hell's Hole   11,530

11,530

11,550

Chicago Lakes Trail

7.9

Swamp

0.6

Gray Wolf Mountain   13,602

Chicago Lakes

11,770

1.1

Steep

Mt. Warren   13,307

Rogers Peak   13,391

Lincoln Lake

11,670

Lincoln Lake Tr

0.7

11,460

1.2

10,530

Resthouse Trail

Mount Evans Road

Mt. Spalding   13,842

Summit Lake

12,870   TH

Summit Lake Flats

Stay south!

Summit Lake Trail   4.4

Bear Creek

Little Beartrack Lakes

The Sawtooth Ridge

2.5

Abyss Lake

Mount Evans   14,265   P

Route follows cairns on north side of ridge

Mt. Bierstadt   14,050

For trails to the south of here, see "Guanella Pass & Mt. Evans South" (pp. 238-242)

North

1.0 mi

Chicago Lakes. The reservoir is reached after 1.8 mi (10,620 ft.), the lower lake (11,420 ft.) after 4.0 mi, and the upper lake (11,770 ft.) after 4.6 mi. 1,750 ft. of elevation gain to the upper lake and 640 ft. of elevation loss. Continue south on a rocky trail above and to the east of the upper lake on the western flanks of Mt. Warren to Summit Lake (additional 1.1 mi and 1,300 ft.), which can even be taken higher to the top of Mt. Evans (see Mt. Evans Trail on the next page).

Hell's Hole Trail: Begin at the Hell's Hole TH. Climbing through aspen then pine then spruce, this trail leads to a small lake above treeline. The trail starts easy then quickly becomes surprisingly steep until about the last mile or so. It is about 4.0 mi and 1,900 ft. of elevation gain to the small pond at the end of the trail.

Walter Pesman Trail (aka Mount Goliath Trail): The somewhat rocky Walter Pesman Trail connects the Mount Goliath Natural Area at the bottom with the Walter Pesman Alpine Garden (near the Upper Goliath TH) at the top. The trail is 1.5 mi long and gains about 600 ft. Have someone drop you off and you can walk down this trail quite easily.

Summit Lake Trail: Instead of going to Summit Lake, this trail starts at Summit Lake and descends southeast through the Summit Lake Flats, ultimately making its way below treeline to Resthouse Meadows (see also p. 234).

Upper Chicago Lake

The start of the Beaver Meadows Trail

Mount Evans Trail: The Mount Evans Trail ascends to the top of Mount Evans, one of Colorado's "Fourteeners". From Summit Lake, hike northeast past the restrooms towards a saddle between Mt. Warren and Mt. Spalding. The obvious trail heads up the east ridge of Mt. Spalding then traverses south to gain the west ridge of Mt. Evans before climbing and meeting the popular Summit Loop Trail just below the summit. This is a difficult hike over rocky terrain and climbs approximately 1,400 ft. in 2.5 mi. Can be dangerous when snow or ice is present.

S. Chicago Creek Trail: From the S. Chicago Creek TH a short (1.4-mi) trail climbs steadily up to some old ruins at around 11,140 ft. In winter, park near HWY 103 and ski/snowshoe the Hefferman Gulch Rd. and beyond.

Mount Evans East

Accessible at several points along the Mount Evans Rd. and from points west of Evergreen and Bergen Park, the east side of the Mount Evans Wilderness is a great place to explore in late spring and early summer as the area usually melts out fairly early in the season. Aspen groves and spruce forests are abundant. Several forest fires in the area during the last 50 years have altered the landscape in spots, providing interesting ecosystems. Forest succession can be observed as younger forests return. Regardless of where you are, the ever-present Mount Evans can be seen high above you.

Access

Echo Lake TH: In the area to the east of Mount Evans, the Echo Lake TH provides access to the Captain Mountain and Resthouse Meadows Trails. See directions to the Echo Lake TH on p. 228.

Summit Lake: The Summit Lake Trail can be taken from Summit Lake east to the Resthouse Meadows area. See directions to Summit Lake on p. 228.

NOTE: The following three trailheads are closed annually to all human activities from January 1st to June 14th due to wildlife closures in the Mount Evans Wildlife Management Area.

Mount Evans State Wildlife Area: From Evergreen Lake, which is 0.5 mi west of the town of Evergreen (Evergreen is 7.3 mi south of I-70 along HWY 74, 11 mi west of Morrison on HWY 74, or 8.8 mi north of Conifer on CR 73), take Upper Bear Creek Rd. (CR 74, which turns into CR 480) for 9.7 mi. Along the way, be sure to stay left after 4.4 mi and right after 6.0 mi, at which point the road turns to dirt.

Captain Mountain TH (Bear Creek Guard Station) & Lost Creek TH: Follow directions to the Mount Evans State Wildlife Area (above) but continue west from the parking

The Captain Mountain Trail descends this valley from the vicinity of Echo Lake

area on FS 195 (Camp Rock Rd.) for an additional 2.3 mi to a trailhead area on the east end of a large clearing. The Lost Creek TH is on the left (south) side; the Captain Mountain TH is on the right (north) side. Access the Lost Creek and Captain Mountain Trails here.

Camp Rock TH: Access the Captain Mountain TH (above), continue on CR 480 for an additional 2.3 mi to a rather

Along the Captain Mountain Trail

rudimentary parking area. There is a steep descending hill the last quarter of a mile that may be too rough for passenger cars; in this case, there are some pull-offs back along the road (read all signs). The road may not be plowed all the way to the trailhead in winter.

Recommended Routes

Resthouse Meadows Trail: Beginning at the Echo Lake TH near the campground just to the east of the Echo Lake Lodge, the Resthouse Meadows Trail begins on rather easy terrain, traversing forested slopes as

it rolls along south with a few short climbs and descents along the way. Eventually, the trail enters a burn area (Lincoln Lake Fire of 1962), intersects the Lincoln Lake Trail, and descends steeply through a burn area to the Resthouse Meadows area. It is 6.1 mi to the intersection with the Beaver Meadows and Cub Creek Trail. This makes a great ski or snowshoe in the winter as well, at least until the intersection with the Lincoln Lake Trail.

Lincoln Lake Trail: Take the Resthouse Meadows Trail for 4.9 mi to a junction at the top of a burn area. Proceed west on the Lincoln Lake Trail for 0.7 mi to a scenic lake. The Lincoln Lake Fire of 1962, ironically, did not burn trees near the lake.

Captain Mountain Trail: A diverse trail connecting the Echo Lake area to the Mount Evans Wildlife Management Area on the east side of the Mount Evans Wilderness. From the Echo Lake TH, the Captain Mountain Trail descends the Beaverdam Creek drainage then traverses faint trails

through meadows. The trail becomes very difficult to navigate as it crosses south over Vance Creek (GPS coordinates provided for point of creek crossing - see map). The route then climbs on faint trails to the top of some rock outcroppings (see map for GPS coordinates where the trail resumes) and a good trail continues through aspen groves, along an enchanted spruce forest to the south of Captain Mountain, down to Pedee Creek, and up and over a hill through ponderosa trees to the Captain Mountain TH. 9.2 mi from end to end.

Burnt tree trunk

Beaver Meadows Trail: This spectacular trail begins at the Camp Rock TH. After ascending gradually through forests and switchbacks in spruce forests, the trail emerges into a wide open, lush valley with beaver ponds. An old campground with two somewhat usable shelters is reached after   1.3

mi. At the end of the large meadow, the trail continues through forests as it climbs rocky terrain to the intersection with the Cub Creek Trail and the Resthouse Meadows Trail after 3.5 mi. The beaver meadows would provide an excellent beginner backpacking trip.

Summit Lake Trail: The Summit Lake Trail leads from just east of Summit Lake south and southeast across the Summit Lake Flats, staying on the south side of the broad drainage to avoid soggy terrain. The trail is very faint, but cairns (rock piles) mark the way. The trail then descends east into the trees and switchbacks north to the west end of Resthouse Meadow.

Shortly after, the trail joins with the Resthouse Meadows Trail. It is 4.4 mi from Summit Lake to the intersection with the Resthouse Meadows Trail and a drop of 2,500 vertical ft.

Cub Creek Trail: This trail provides the spine for many of the trails in the area, as most other trails branch off of the Cub Creek Trail. Unfortunately, land ownership issues are such that the far east end of this trail is no longer accessible. Rolling through meadows, forests, hills, and valleys, this trail connects the Beaver Meadows Trail to trails in the far southeast corner of the Mount Evans Wilderness. The Cub Creek Trail itself is quite rocky and loose but is nice in that there are no super big climbs or descents. A fine example of forest succession can be observed along

Mount Evans East

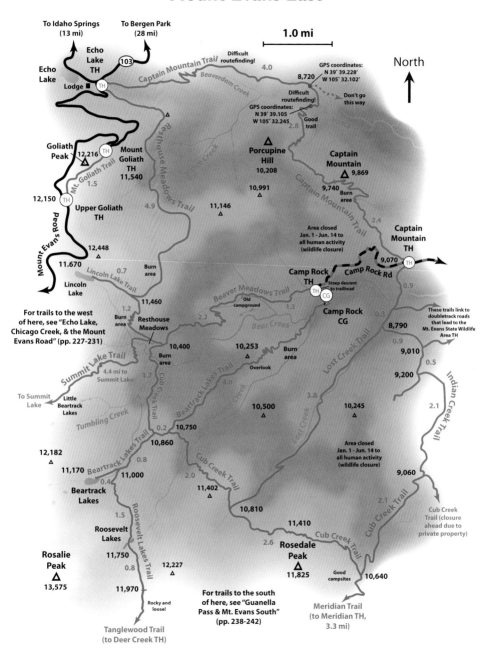

To Idaho Springs
(13 mi)

To Bergen Park
(28 mi)

1.0 mi

North

Echo
Lake
TH

103

Echo
Lake

Lodge

TH

Captain Mountain Trail

Beaverdam Creek

Difficult
routefinding!

4.0

8,720

GPS coordinates:
N 39° 39.228'
W 105° 32.102'

Difficult
routefinding!
GPS coordinates:
N 39° 39.105
W 105° 32.245

Don't go
this way

Goliath
Peak   12,216

Mount
Goliath
TH
11,540

Mt. Goliath Trail

1.5

Good
trail

2.8

Resthouse Meadows Trail

Echo Creek

Porcupine
Hill
10,208

10,991

Captain
Mountain
9,869

9,740

Burn
area

TH

12,150

Upper Goliath
TH

4.9

11,146

Captain Mountain Trail

Area closed
Jan. 1 - Jun. 14 to
all human activity
(wildlife closure)

2.4

Captain
Mountain
TH
9,070

TH

Mount Evans Road

12,448

11,670

Lincoln
Lake

Lincoln Lake Trail

0.7

Burn
area

11,460

Beaver Meadows Trail

Camp Rock
TH

Camp Rock Rd

Steep descent
to trailhead

TH   CG

Camp Rock
CG

0.9

These trails link to
doubletrack roads
that lead to the
Mt. Evans State Wildlife
Area TH

For trails to the west
of here, see "Echo Lake,
Chicago Creek, & the Mount
Evans Road" (pp. 227-231)

1.2

Burn
area

Resthouse
Meadows

2.2

Old
campground

1.3

8,790

0.9

9,010

Bear Creek

10,400

Burn
area

10,253

Burn
area

Lost Creek Trail

0.5

9,200

Summit Lake Trail

4.4 mi to
Summit Lake

1.7

Overlook

4.0

Beartrack Lakes Trail

Cub Creek Trail

Indian Creek Trail

To Summit
Lake

Little
Beartrack
Lakes

Tumbling Creek

10,500

3.8

10,245

2.1

12,182

11,170

0.2

10,750

10,860

Lost Creek

Area closed
Jan. 1 - Jun. 14 to
all human activity
(wildlife closure)

9,060

Beartrack Lakes Trail

0.8

11,000

0.4

Beartrack
Lakes

2.0

11,402

10,810

11,410

2.1

Cub Creek Trail

Cub Creek
Trail (closure
ahead due to
private property)

1.5

Roosevelt Lakes Trail

Roosevelt
Lakes

11,750

2.6

Rosedale
Peak

Cub Creek Trail

Rosalie
Peak

13,575

0.8

11,970

12,227

11,825

Good
campsites

10,640

Rocky and
loose!

For trails to the south
of here, see "Guanella
Pass & Mt. Evans South"
(pp. 238-242)

Meridian Trail
(to Meridian TH,
3.3 mi)

Tanglewood Trail
(to Deer Creek TH)

Lincoln Lake

the Cub Creek Trail just south of Resthouse Meadows (intersection of Resthouse Meadows Trail with the Beaver Meadows Trail and Cub Creek Trail). This area was the site of the 1964 Resthouse Meadows Fire, which burned 1,076 acres.

Lost Creek Trail: The trails emanating from the Lost Creek TH are used quite infrequently, but there is some great terrain to the south of the Camp Rock Rd. Begin at the Lost Creek TH and the Lost Creek Trail heads south and southwest and intersects the Cub Creek Trail after 5.0 mi.

Indian Creek Trail: Begin the Lost Creek Trail but after 1.2 mi take a left onto the Indian Creek Trail. There are several trails that branch off of the Indian Creek Trail after about 0.9 mi, 2.1 mi, and 2.6 mi; the Indian Creek Trail intersects the Cub Creek Trail after 4.7 mi.

Beartrack Lakes Trail: A gradual climb through a burn area (1998 Beartracks Fire) then along a broad, forested ridge to the intersection with the Cub Creek Trail after 4.0 mi. Near the intersection with the Cub Creek Trail there is also evidence of another fire (1964 Resthouse Meadows Fire); the forests are recovering nicely, however. The Beartrack Lakes Trail continues another 0.4 mi to Beartrack Lakes, a superb place for an overnight backpacking trip.

Roosevelt Lakes Trail: Just below Beartrack Lakes, the Roosevelt Lakes Trail climbs a steep, forested slope (routefinding difficult) to treeline, then contours southeast and south to the small yet scenic Roosevelt Lakes with the imposing walls of Rosalie Peak looming high above. A faint trail continues to a high pass, where the Tanglewood Trail (see p. 241) continues south.

Marsh marigolds and globeflower

Mount Evans and Mount Bierstadt reflect in a tarn near Guanella Pass

Tanglewood Trail: From the high pass at the top of the Roosevelt Lakes Trail (see previous page), the Tanglewood Trail descends through pine and spruce forests to the Deer Creek TH. See this trail description on page 241 (next section).

Meridian Trail: The Meridian Trail descends from the eastern end of the Cub Creek Trail towards Harris Park outside of Bailey to the Meridian TH. See this trail description on page 241 of the next section.

Guanella Pass & Mount Evans South

Secluded and wild, the southern part of the Mount Evans Wilderness is quite unique. Large stands of limber pine are found on many south-facing slopes and spruce and fir are found higher up. On the south side of Mount Evans is a large, treeless flat area that allows unparalleled views of the south side of the mountain and beyond. Abyss Lake also lies in a deep alpine valley between two 14,000-ft. peaks (Mt. Evans and Mt. Bierstadt). This region cannot be accessed easily from the Mount Evans Rd., resulting in relatively few people. The Rosalie Trail, in particular, makes a great setting for extended backpacking trips.

Access

Bailey: The town of Bailey is located in the foothills southwest of Denver. From the intersection of C-470 and US 285, take US 285 southwest for 28 mi to the town of Bailey.

Grant: The town of Grant is located in the foothills southwest of Denver. From the intersection of C-470 and US 285, take US 285 southwest for 28 mi to the town of Bailey then proceed an additional 13 mi to the town of Grant.

Meridian TH:  From the intersection of C-470 and US 285 in southwest Denver, take US 285 for about 25 mi to just northeast of Bailey (12.5 mi from Conifer). At a stoplight just to the north of Crow Hill, take a right onto CR 43A. Proceed on CR 43A, which quickly becomes CR 43 (aka Deer Creek Rd.). From the stoplight, drive for 6.7 mi on CR 43 to a Y-junction. Here, take a right onto Clark Rd./CR 47. Continue on this road for 1.4 mi then take a left onto CR 65/FS 102 (also labeled Prospectors Way) at a 4-way junction. Proceed an additional 1.0 mi on dirt to the Deer Creek TH. In winter, the road is generally not maintained all the way to the trailhead but there is parking lower down along FS 102.

Deer Creek TH: Follow directions to the Meridian TH (above) but instead of taking the right at the Y-junction after 6.7 mi on CR 43, proceed left. After an additional 2.1 mi you will reach the Deer Creek TH. The last mile or so is dirt road but is usually in pretty good shape. In winter, the road is plowed to the campground but no further.

Threemile TH: Follow directions to the town of Grant (see above). Turn right (north) and drive along CR 62 (Guanella Pass Rd.) for approximately ... you guessed it, three miles! The parking area and trailhead is found on the east side of the road.

Abyss TH: Follow directions to the Threemile TH (see above) but continue another 2.3 mi on CR 62 (Guanella Pass Rd.) to a high meadow with a parking area and the Abyss TH on the right (east) side of the road.

Krummholz near Roosevelt Lakes

Guanella Pass & Mount Evans South

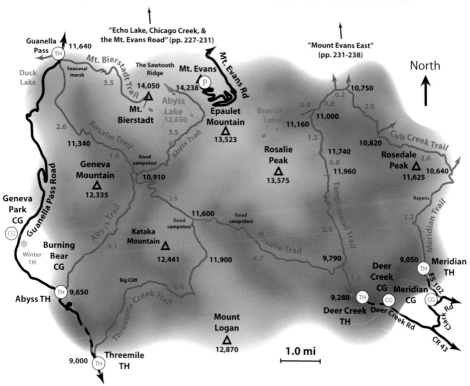

Guanella Pass: Guanella Pass is most easily accessed from the north from the town of Georgetown along I-70 but can also be accessed on the south side from the town of Grant along US 285. To access from the north, take I-70 west from the I-70/C-470 junction in west Denver for 32 mi to I-70 Exit 228 at Georgetown. Drive through town and follow signs for Guanella Pass. Continue up the Guanella Pass Rd. for about 11 mi to the parking area at the top of the pass. To access from the south, follow directions to the town of Grant (see p. 239) along US 285. Turn right (north) onto CR 62 (Guanella Pass Rd.) and proceed about 13 mi to the top of the pass. The Colorado Department of Transportation usually plows to the top of Guanella Pass in winter from the north but not from the south; in general, winter maintenance of the southern part of the Guanella Pass Rd. ends somewhere around the Duck Creek Picnic Area (see map).

The broad, flat area at a high point of the Rosalie Trail

Recommended Routes

Meridian Trail: Start at the Meridian TH. This trail ascends a very nice, rather smooth trail along a slope forested with limber pine. About halfway up the moderate climb, you will enter an idyllic aspen forest. Atop the climb are some great camping spots if you are backpacking. 3.3 mi and 1,700 ft. of elevation gain to the intersection with the Cub Creek Trail.

Tanglewood Trail: Beginning at the Deer Creek TH, Tanglewood Creek keeps you company as you ascend the Tanglewood Trail through spruce and limber pine forests. The lower section of the Tanglewood Trail is relatively easy but the difficulty and rockiness increase as you continue past the Rosalie Trail. Near treeline you will visit a small stand of bristlecone pine and it is a short ways to a high pass, which marks the end of the Tanglewood Trail. From the pass, the Roosevelt Lakes Trail continues north. It is 4.0 mi and 2,730 ft. of elevation gain to the pass.

Rosalie Trail: A 12-mi trail connecting Guanella Pass with the Tanglewood Trail near the Deer Creek TH. You will experience a variety of terrain on this trail - rocky climbs, traverses through high alpine meadows, aspen forests, stream crossings, and beaver ponds. Have a shuttlebunny drop you off on Guanella Pass and trek downwards to one of the other trailheads in the area. A high, flat, lofty area near the intersection with the Threemile Trail is a perfect spot for an

overnight adventure, with views of Mount Evans and Square Top Mountain. From west to east, this trail climbs about 1,600 ft. and descends a total of 3,400 ft. The broad area atop Guanella Pass is a fun place to ski and snowshoe in winter.

Mt. Bierstadt Trail: Several high peaks can be accessed throughout the year from Guanella Pass, including Mt. Bierstadt, Mt. Evans, Square Top Mtn, Argentine Pk, Grey Wolf Mtn, and Mt. Spalding.   By far the most popular is Mt. Bierstadt from Guanella Pass. The climb of Bierstadt is relatively short (3.5 mi) but climbs 2,850 ft. Many folks enjoy snowshoeing in the vicinity of Guanella Pass and Mt. Bierstadt in winter. The area to the east of Guanella Pass is known for its wet, marshy terrain during certain times of the year (i.e., spring).

Abyss Trail: Begin at the Abyss TH off of the Guanella Pass Rd. The Abyss Trail leads east, intersects the Rosalie Trail after 4.1 mi, but ultimately continues for an additional 3.5 mi above treeline to a spectacular lake (Abyss Lake, 12,650 ft.) situated in a deep valley between Mt. Bierstadt and Mt. Evans. It is 7.6 mi and 3,200 ft. of elevation gain to Abyss Lake. There are some nice campsites near the intersection of the Abyss Trail and the Rosalie Trail.

Threemile Creek Trail: The Threemile Creek Trail begins at the Threemile TH. After skirting alongside some private property and traversing to Threemile Creek, the trail climbs northeast up a secluded valley, making several stream crossings along the way.   The trail then climbs steeply near treeline then traverses north along willows and tundra to intersect the Rosalie Trail at an elevation of 11,600 ft. after 6.6 mi. This broad area near the intersection of the Rosalie Trail would make a spectacular place for an overnight campsite. This lower part of the trail is also a prime place for cross country skiing and snowshoeing in winter, conditions permitting.

Backpacking in the Mount Evans Wilderness

The Mount Evans Wilderness is a prime place for single- or multi-night overnight backpacking trips because there are few people, plentiful water sources, diverseness in terrain, and multiple access points. Outlined below are several recommended backpacking trips. Strong hikers and trail runners could do some of these trips in a single day if weather allows. This is wild country, so navigation and things as simple as just staying on the trail can be quite challenging - be prepared!

Beaver Meadows: A short overnight to a beautiful setting. Begin at the Camp Rock

Square Top Mountain as seen from the Rosalie Trail

TH and hike the Beaver Meadows Trail. Great campsites along the meadow only 1.3 mi up near the old campground. Continue higher to Resthouse Meadows for a longer trip. Plenty of water available. This would be an excellent trip for beginner backpackers or for those with limited time.

Rosalie Trail: There are some great campsites along the Rosalie Trail and the traverse of the Rosalie Trail would make a superb out-and-back or point-to-point trip from Guanella Pass.

Resthouse Meadows: The Resthouse Meadows is a relatively mellow trail and there are plenty of campsites off the trail for overnight trips. Lincoln Lake is a prime place to spend some time. Otherwise, continue south from near Lincoln Lake to Resthouse Meadows, a scenic area tucked in a broad valley.

Mt. Evans Semi-Circumnavigation: ◆ This would be a big trip but nice for a week-long backpacking adventure. Have someone drop you off at Guanella Pass or set up a car shuttle with friends and leave a car at Echo Lake for the return. From Guanella Pass, take the Rosalie Trail southeast all the way to the Deer Creek TH. Good campsites near the top of the Threemile Trail and also just below treeline at the head of Deer Creek. Continue north on the Tanglewood Trail (difficult climb) and over the pass to the Roosevelt Lakes and Beartrack Lake area. Camp at Roosevelt Lakes or continue to Beartrack Lake, where there are some nice campsites to the east of the lake. Hike north on the Cub Creek Trail to the Resthouse Meadows/Lincoln Lake area and stay a night here. Finally, take the Resthouse Meadows Trail to Echo Lake. Treat yourself to a celebratory meal at the Echo Lake Lodge!

Charlie's Picks for the Mount Evans Area

This chapter is a relatively short one, so I've provided only my top 5 picks:

1. Beaver Meadows Trail (p. 234)

2. Abyss Trail (p. 242)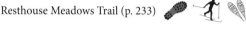

3. Resthouse Meadows Trail (p. 233)

4. Hell's Hole (p. 230)

5. Chicago Lakes Trail (p. 228)

Breckenridge Ski Resort, early summer

Chapter 7: Summit County

The areas comprising this chapter present tremendous recreational activities, ranging from the high adrenaline endeavors such as mountain biking and downhill skiing to peaceful hikes along trickling creeks and forays into untamed wilderness areas. There is a dramatic contrast between the rustic elegance of Frisco, Silverthorne, Keystone, and Breckenridge and the wilderness experiences available in the Eagle's Nest Wilderness and the Mohawk and Crystal Lakes area where you may feel no one has ever visited. Hiking trails to high alpine lakes can literally be accessed within minutes of Breckenridge. An extremely well-maintained and extensive paved bike path system invites cyclists of all abilities. High ridge traverses between thirteen thousand foot peaks challenge the advanced hiker. In winter, many of the hiking and biking trails provide settings for ski and snowshoe adventures. Colorado Ski Country truly is a place where everyone, regardless of abilities or experience in the outdoors, will find something special in all seasons of the year. Remember to take it easy on your first day in this outdoor recreation paradise if you are traveling from sea level and allow your body to acclimatize.

Summit County

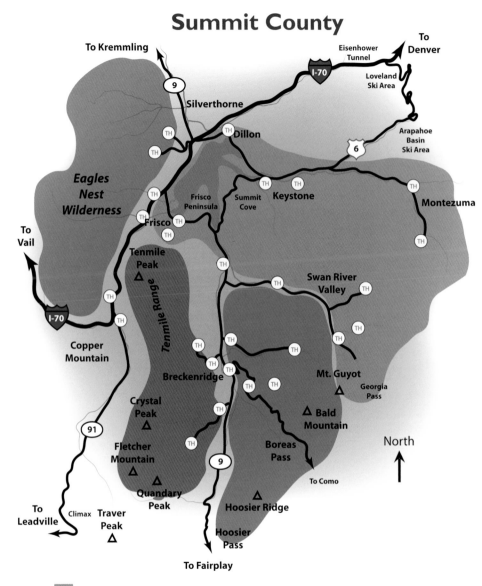

To Kremmling

To Denver

Eisenhower Tunnel

I-70

Loveland Ski Area

9

Silverthorne

Dillon

6

Arapahoe Basin Ski Area

Eagles Nest Wilderness

Frisco Peninsula

Summit Cove

Keystone

Montezuma

To Vail

Frisco

Tenmile Peak

Tenmile Range

I-70

Copper Mountain

Swan River Valley

Breckenridge

Mt. Guyot

Georgia Pass

Crystal Peak

Bald Mountain

91

Fletcher Mountain

Boreas Pass

North

To Como

Quandary Peak

9

Hoosier Ridge

To Leadville

Climax

Traver Peak

Hoosier Pass

To Fairplay

Legend:

- Frisco, Lake Dillon, Keystone, and Montezuma (pp. 247-264)
- Boreas Pass Road, Breckenridge, & the Golden Horseshoe (pp. 265-276)
- Breckenridge Ski Area and the Tenmile Range (pp. 277-290)
- Eagle's Nest Wilderness - Frisco Side (pp. 291-297)

The view of Lake Dillon from near Swan Mountain

Frisco, Lake Dillon, Keystone, and Montezuma

The combination of diverse year-round activities, great shops and restaurants, and ease of access make the towns and surrounding regions of the Lake Dillon area popular among weekenders and vacationers alike. Some of the best mountain biking in the state can be found near Keystone at Summit Cove and along the Colorado Trail; these trails also make for excellent day hikes as well as first-rate ski and snowshoe trails in winter. Adventurous mountain biking and hiking prospects abound near the quaint town of Montezuma, which is quite different than the bustling resort areas found elsewhere in the region.

Maps: Sky Terrain "Summit, Vail, & Holy Cross" and Latitude 40° "Summit County Trails." For Trails Illustrated maps, you will need both "Vail, Frisco, Dillon (#108)" and "Idaho Springs, Georgetown, Loveland Pass (104)" for full coverage of this region.

Best Time of Year: The best time of year for this area is mid to late June (depending on snowfall) through mid to late October. The season can be extended for the trails lower down (e.g., Summit Cove area) but snowfall usually shuts down trails that are at higher elevations by early November at the latest. Many of the trails in the vicinity can be traveled by snowshoe or cross country skis in the winter.

Camping: Several National Forest Campgrounds are found along the shores of Lake Dillon, including Heaton Bay, Peak One, Pine Cove, Prospector, Windy Point, and Lowry Camp Campgrounds. Some of these may be currently closed due to pine beetle hazards. You can obtain more information regarding these campgrounds by calling the Dillon Ranger District of the White River National Forest at 970-468-5400 or visiting the following website: www.fs.fed.us/r2/whiteriver. Campground reservations for this area can be made either at www.recreation.gov or www.reserveamerica.com. Many

Welcome to Montezuma!

informal campsites can be found on National Forest land (Tiger Rd. as well as CR 5 that goes to Montezuma). Showers are available in the Silverthorne Recreation Center, located at 430 Rainbow Drive in the area to the north of the I-70/HWY 9 intersection.

Access

Frisco: From the I-70/C-470 intersection west of Denver, take I-70 west for about 61 mi to Exit 203. Frisco is just south of this exit.

Silverthorne/Dillon: From the I-70/C-470 intersection west of Denver, take I-70 west for about 58 mi to Exit 205 to Silverthorne. Dillon is located a mile or so southeast of here along US 6.

Keystone: Keystone is located southeast of Dillon. Follow directions above (Silverthorne/Dillon) to I-70 Exit 205 near Dillon then proceed south along US 6 for 7.5 mi to Keystone.

Montezuma: From Keystone, take the Montezuma Rd. (CR 5) at the eastern end of the valley towards Montezuma. This road begins just as US 6 starts its climb east towards Arapahoe Basin. After a little over 5 mi you will reach Montezuma.

NOTE: All of the trailheads listed below are plowed and easily accessible in winter.

Frisco Bay Marina: Bike paths can be accessed from the Frisco Bay Marina. At the end of your ride, stop into the Island Grill for a bite to eat or a drink! From the intersection of HWY 9 and Main Street in Frisco, travel east a short ways to the marina. Plenty of parking here.

Dickey TH: From I-70 Exit 201 in Frisco, proceed south on HWY 9 for 3.0 mi (this is outside of town east of signs for the Peninsula Recreation Area). There is a dirt road on your left that leads to the Dickey Day Use Area.

Gold Hill TH: From the intersection of HWY 9 and Main Street in Frisco, travel south on HWY 9 from Frisco for 5 mi to the obvious trailhead on your right (west), just off of the highway.

Tenderfoot TH: Follow US 6 south and east from I-70 for 1.2 mi. Take a left on Dillon Drive at the stoplight, and immediately take a sharp right on CR 51 and follow this another 0.6 mi to the TH, which is past the Forest Service Work Center.

Dillon Bay TH: This trailhead is popular among users of the Summit County paved bike paths. From I-70 Exit 205 in Silverthorne, drive south on US 6 for about 3.5 mi. There is a parking area just off the road to your right (south).

Cemetery TH: Follow directions to the Dillon Bay TH (above). Just across US 6 on the north side is a dirt road that leads a short ways to an obvious parking area by a locked gate. This trailhead provides access to the east end of the Oro Grande Trail.

Cove TH: From I-70 in Silverthorne, follow US 6 south for 4.5 mi. Take a right on Swan Mountain Rd. and start measuring here. Take a left on Cove Blvd. after 0.1 mi, right on Royal Coachman Blvd. after 0.8 mi, then a left on Forest Glen Rd. at 1.6 mi. The trailhead

Peak One and a lupine-covered meadow on the Frisco Peninsula

is on the right after 0.1 mi.

Dredge Boat TH: Follow HWY 9 from Frisco 7 mi to Tiger Rd. Take a left (east) and drive 2.5 mi. Just before the pavement turns to dirt is a trailhead parking lot on your left (north).

Keystone Gulch TH: From I-70 Exit 205 in Silverthorne, follow US 6 south towards Keystone. At the first stoplight getting into the Keystone area (well past Swan Mountain Rd., 6.1 mi from I-70), take a right onto W. Keystone Rd. Take an immediate left and follow signs to Keystone Ranch. After 0.4 mi from the stoplight, take a right on Soda Ridge Rd. and follow this another 0.5 mi to the Keystone Gulch Rd. (Forest Service Rd.). Take a left onto Keystone Gulch Rd. and after a tenth of a mile you will find parking and the Keystone Gulch TH.

Peru Creek TH: This trailhead is located on a double switchback just 0.8 mi before the town of Montezuma (see p. 248).

Webster Pass Road TH: From the center of the town of Montezuma (see p. 248), continue 1.4 mi on CR 5 to a parking area (summer and winter). This is just past one of the two roads that ultimately joins with the Webster Pass Rd.

Keystone Ski Resort: There is plenty of parking at the base of the Keystone Ski Resort. From the first stoplight in town at US 6 and W. Keystone Rd., proceed an additional 1.5 mi west (7.7 mi from I-70) and there are signs that direct you to free public parking.

Summit Stage: This free bus service offered by Summit County can be super valuable in setting up one-way hiking and biking adventures in this area as well as other areas in Summit County. The Summit Stage has bus stops in Breckenridge, Boreas Pass, Frisco, Copper Mountain, Silverthorne, Dillon, Keystone, and Leadville. Bikes can be placed on the buses from May 1st to October 31st, before sunset. For information, visit www.

Mt. Guyot and Bald Mountain at sunrise

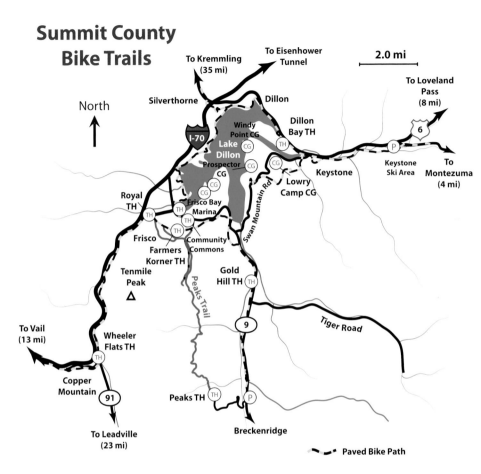

Summit County Bike Trails

North

To Kremmling (35 mi)

To Eisenhower Tunnel

2.0 mi

To Loveland Pass (8 mi)

Silverthorne

Dillon

I-70

Windy Point CG

Dillon Bay TH

6

Lake Dillon

CG

CG

Keystone Ski Area

To Montezuma (4 mi)

Prospector CG

CG

CG

Keystone

CG

Lowry Camp CG

Royal TH

TH

Swan Mountain Rd

TH

Frisco Bay Marina

TH

Frisco

TH

Community Commons

Farmers Korner TH

Peaks Trail

Tenmile Peak △

Gold Hill TH

TH

To Vail (13 mi)

Tiger Road

9

Wheeler Flats TH

TH

Copper Mountain

91

Peaks TH

TH

P

To Leadville (23 mi)

Breckenridge

Paved Bike Path

summitstage.com.

Bike Rentals: Road and mountain bikes can be rented at many places in the Summit County area. Pick up a local phone book, search for bike rentals online, or just keep an eye out for one of the many sporting good or bike stores in the area. There is probably no better place in the state to tour by bicycle than Summit County due to the spectacular network of paved and unpaved bike trails.

Lodgepole and lupines on Frisco Peninsula

Recommended Routes

Summit County Bike Trails

There are close to 200 miles of paved bike trails in Summit County and the Vail valley. Suitable for mountain bikes and road bikes alike, these trails connect the towns of Breckenridge, Frisco, Dillon, Silverthorne, Keystone, Copper Mountain, and Vail. Don't have a bike? There is no shortage of shops in the area that offer short- and long-term bike rentals. Trail maps can be found in many stores and shops as well. The bike trails can be accessed from a variety of points in Summit County, including Royal TH, Farmers Korner TH, Frisco Bay Marina, Community Commons, Gold Hill TH, and Dillon Bay TH, among other locations. So grab a bike, pack a picnic, and explore the Summit County and Vail areas! The trails can also be snowshoed and cross country skied in winter, depending upon conditions and recent snow coverage.

Frisco Peninsula

Frisco Peninsula hosts some exceptional singletrack hiking and biking trails that can be traveled in spring, summer, and fall. In winter, the Frisco Nordic Center grooms many of these trails (and more) and other trails can be accessed by skis and snowshoes. Over the last decade the peninsula has been hit very hard by the pine beetle (see p. 36). Extensive

Frisco Peninsula

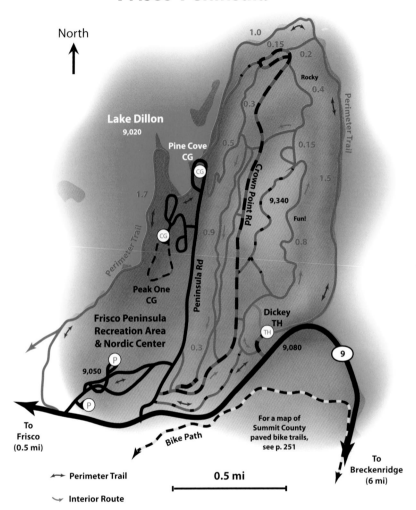

North

Lake Dillon
9,020

1.0
0.15
0.2

Rocky
0.4

Perimeter Trail

0.3

Pine Cove
CG

CG

0.5
0.15

1.5

Crown Point Rd
9,340

Fun!

1.7

CG

0.9

Peak One
CG

Perimeter Trail

0.8

Peninsula Rd

Dickey
TH

TH

Frisco Peninsula
Recreation Area
& Nordic Center

0.3

9,080

9

P

9,050

P

To
Frisco
(0.5 mi)

Bike Path

For a map of
Summit County
paved bike trails,
see p. 251

To
Breckenridge
(6 mi)

↞→ Perimeter Trail

⤳ Interior Route

0.5 mi

logging operations have thinned many of the trees here. However, the wide-open meadows that have resulted are chock full of wildflowers in the summer and provide stellar views of Lake Dillon. Combined with the forested regions that remain, there is tremendous variety on the Frisco Peninsula and there are trails for everyone.

Here are a few good hiking/mountain biking loops that will keep you on some of the best terrain the peninsula has to offer:

Perimeter Trail: The Perimeter Trail hugs the coastline of Lake Dillon quite tightly. Begin at either the Frisco Nordic Center or the Dickey TH. If beginning near the Nordic center, find some dirt roads and head northwest until you

reach the shore of Lake Dillon and the trail hugs the edge of the water. Caution is advised; the trail drops off precipitously to the water in a few spots! Overall easy but be aware of these few technical spots just feet from an icy plunge into Lake Dillon. 5 mi for the loop.

Interior Route: Some of the trails on the northern side of the peninsula are quite rocky and this route avoids those trails. Begin at the Dickey TH and find a steep, rocky trail that leads west starting a few hundred feet south of the

trailhead. Continue up this rocky trail and find the singletrack trail that leads north. Follow arrows for this route on the map on the opposite page. The trails on the western side of the peninsula are great, weaving through lodgepole pine forests and lupine-covered meadows. Return to your car via the highway or dirt roads on the south side of the peninsula. When conditions are good, this area offers some fantastic skiing and snowshoeing in winter.

Additional Wintertime Activities

The Frisco Nordic Center and Frisco Adventure Park are both found on the Frisco Peninsula and offer exciting recreational opportunities in winter.

❄ **Frisco Nordic Center:** 💲 The Frisco Nordic Center has over 45 km of cross country ski trails and over 18 km of snowshoe trails that innervate the Frisco Peninsula. Ski lessons are offered as well as snowshoe tours. The lodge area has a retail shop, snack bar, and even a fire pit to roast marshmallows over. For more information, contact (970) 668-0866 or visit www.breckenridgenordic.com.

❄ **Frisco Adventure Park:** 💲 The Frisco Adventure Park has a lift-served tubing hill and snowboarding terrain park in winter as well as dinner sleigh rides. For more information call (970) 668-2558 or visit www.townoffrisco.com/adventure-park/winter.

Lake Dillon

Tenderfoot Trail: Bring your sweetie or soon-to-be sweetie up this trail for a scenic, romantic sunset. There are great views of Lake Dillon! Start at the Tenderfoot TH and follow the Tenderfoot Trail 0.3 mi to a trail intersection. The Tenderfoot Trail goes left

(east) and climbs up aspen-, sage-, and pine-covered slopes to a bench near the end of the trail after 1.3 mi and a climb of just over 500 vertical ft.

Oro Grande Trail: An easy doubletrack trail that contours along the hills to the east of Dillon. Start at the Tenderfoot TH, continue straight after 0.3 mi (the Tenderfoot Trail goes left), then continue to a 4-way junction after 2.1 mi total. Take a right and descend the gulch, past the cemetery to the Cemetery TH. Take the dirt road down for a tenth of a mile and there will be a trail entering the meadow on your left, which leads through a tunnel underneath US 6 and to a bike path, which can be followed on the west side of US 6 all the way back to the stoplight at Dillon Rd. It is a quick ride back to the trailhead.

Summit Cove Area Trails

Nothing but fun! If you love smooth singletrack biking, the Summit Cove area is the place for you. Or go by foot and explore all the nooks and crannies of this unique landscape. This area has a plethora of fun loops. Whether you are out for just an hour or so or are looking for an epic trail run or mountain bike ride, there is something for everyone. One could easily put together a

bike ride in this area of 20+ miles or even a burlier one if incorporating the Keystone Gulch area trails or Swan River Valley area trails (Colorado Trail). Choose your own adventure, but make sure to bring a map and compass. Be sure to check out Blair Witch; it is one

Summit Cove, late fall

spooky, winding intestine of a trail and is not to be missed!

Three loop rides/hikes are outlined here and the routes are shown on the map on the following page - one easy, one moderate, and one difficult.

Blair Witch Loop: ● Begin at the Dredge Boat TH, ascend past the Colorado Trail to the 5-way junction, traverse the rolling, winding, and fun Blair Witch Trail, returning via the Colorado Trail. 4.1 mi round trip with 560 ft. of elevation gain.

Ranch Loop: ■ Begin at the Summit Cove TH. Follow singletrack trails south (see map) first ascending then descending through a broad valley to a creek. Turn left and continue descending along the creek until you end up near the Keystone Homestead. From here, ascend up to the 5-way intersection; either proceed south to the Colorado Trail or traverse Blair Witch Trail, your choice. Descend north to the creek and return the way you came. A great lollipop loop with only a few short but strenuous climbs. 9.9 mi and 1,600 ft. of climbing.

Colorado Trail/Red's Loop: ◆ The descent of Red's Trail to the homestead is spectacular but requires an eastward climb up the Colorado Trail, which is rather strenuous.

Begin at the Summit Cove TH, follow singletrack south to the 5-way intersection. The traverse of Blair Witch Trail is optional but highly recommended. Regardless, make your way to the Colorado Trail just north of the Dredge Boat TH. Start the climb up the Colorado Trail. Red's Trail is not signed, but there is a wooden marker in the middle of a meadow a small ways up a slope; it is easy to miss this left turn (the Colorado Trail continues to the right). Descend Red's Trail all the way to the intersection with the West Aqueduct Trail (fun!), then return west via singletrack the way you came (or a slight variation). With Blair Witch this lollipop loop is about 15 mi and has around 3,000 ft. of climbing/descending.

Along the Colorado Trail

Summit Cove Trails

North

To Royal Coachman Blvd

Neighborhood
9,100

Summit
Cove TH   TH
9,150

Keystone

0.5

9,310

Keystone Ranch

Tree house

0.9

1.1

1.0

To Keystone Gulch TH
(4.2 mi from Homestead)

Swan Mountain   10,796

0.2

0.3

10,971

For trails to the
east of here, see
pp. 260-264

9,490   1.0

9,260

9,320

0.3   Spring

0.4

To Frisco
(4 mi)

?   ?
10,324   10,210

Not recommended

0.8

1.8

9,630

0.7

10,207

9,360

Homestead

0.15   1.0

9,846

0.6

Faint trail

1.0

9,490

Red's Trail   1.8

9

Gold Hill TH   TH

9,260

Trail difficult to
follow - heads east
across clearing

9,650

Blair Witch

0.4   1.5

5-way
intersection

Colorado
Trail

9,200

Colorado Trail

2.0

9,964

9,680

0.9

10,100

2.6

olorado
Trail
ee p. 282)

0.9

9,922

0.7

9,460

0.5

10,006

Colorado Trail

10,408

10,460

To Breckenridge
(3 mi)

Tiger Road

9,430

Dredge
Boat TH   TH

To Swan
River Valley

→ Blair Witch Loop (Easy)
→ Ranch Loop (Moderate)

1.0 mi

Keystone

Aqueduct Trail

Aqueduct Trail: This is a great trail for beginner mountain bikers or those looking for a nice evening activity. A great place to start is the Keystone Gulch TH. It requires a short but steep 0.2-mi climb west from the trailhead up to the actual aqueduct, but after this it is an easy hike or bike ride to the homestead. Be careful around the unburied aqueduct. It is just over 4 mi to the homestead.

Keystone Gulch

Upper Aqueduct Trail: The Aqueduct Trail intersects the Keystone Gulch Rd. a short ways south of the Keystone Gulch TH. South of this intersection, the Upper Aqueduct Trail continues south for approximately 2.2 mi where it once again intersects the Keystone Gulch Rd. A moderate

hike but somewhat technical bike ride due to roots, stream crossings, and rocks. The trail is not as well-worn nor well-maintained as the Aqueduct Trail.

Map labels:
Keystone
6
Soda Ridge Rd
W. Keystone Rd
Keystone Gulch TH
TH
9,290
North
0.35 9,330
0.4
Aqueduct Trail
△ 10,360
2.5
Aqueduct Trail
Upper Aqueduct Trail
Keystone Gulch Road
Bike Path
10,870 △
10,980 △
2.2
9,960
9,340
Red's Trail (see p. 261)
10,990 △
10,100
11,080 △
For trails to the south of here, see pp. 260-264
1.0 mi

West Ridge Lollipop: From Keystone Gulch TH, spin up the well-maintained dirt road to the Outback Express lift. The road passes by beautiful beaver ponds and meadows. Just after the lift, take a right at a gate (4.5 mi); 0.3 mi past this gate watch for a right turn (well marked) onto singletrack. Follow this down a bit, cross the creek, then climb on

The author biking beneath Mt. Guyot along the Colorado Trail

West Ridge Lollipop

singletrack and double track, winding through spruce and fir trees until you eventually make it to the Colorado Trail (6.7 mi total). The trail is well marked with a red sign that has a bicycle on it. Once you reach the CT, take a break if you wish to rest the legs then continue right (west). Cruise the stellar trail, looking for a fork after being on the Colorado Trail for 1.1 mi. Take a right here and soon the trail turns into a dirt road; follow the dirt road as it zigzags down (loose at times) and ultimately intersects the Keystone Gulch Rd. that you came in on. An okay descent if you are short on time; otherwise, better to spend your well-earned altitude on a longer, more fun descent (see next description)! Follow the road back down to the TH. 14.0 mi and close to 3,000 ft. of elevation gain.

Bonus: If you get hungry during the climb up Keystone Rd., change your plans and at the Outback lift, climb west 1,000 ft. and 2.0 mi to the top of the Outback where you can purchase food and drinks.

West Ridge Superloop: Follow the West Ridge Lollipop as described above. However, instead of taking the right turn that brings you back down to the Keystone Gulch Rd., stay left on the Colorado Trail. You will be rewarded with stellar singletrack for almost 5 mi. Stay left at a sharp left in the trail

West Ridge Superloop

(not well marked) in a clearing (top of Red's Trail). Continue through a few short climbs and some more awesome descents through wildflower-studded meadows and eventually the trail intersects a dirt road underneath some powerlines (12.6 mi total). Take a right and climb a short 0.9 mi to a small saddle and trail intersection. Go over the saddle and veer right. Follow this trail all the way down to the homestead, cross the dirt road and stay left at a trail intersection. Follow the Aqueduct Trail, staying in the trees. After 4.0 mi on the Aqueduct Trail, you will close the loop and the trailhead is at the base of the Keystone Gulch Rd. Take a left and return to the Keystone Gulch TH. The loop is 19 mi and has 4,100 ft. of elevation gain/loss.

Variation: Red's Trail will cut off much of the climbing and mileage towards the end of this loop. After the 5-mi descent from the West Ridge down the CT, there is a very sharp left turn in a meadow, as described above. Red's Trail heads straight along the hillside and down into the trees and eventually intersects the Aqueduct Trail down near the homestead.

Keystone Ski Resort: There are quite a number of activities available at the Keystone Ski Resort. Park at the resort and the best option is to visit the Adventure Center for information on current biking and hiking trails. A number of activities for adults as well as kids are available, including boating, fishing, and bike rentals.

Rainbow and campsite, Swan River Valley

Swan River Valley & the Colorado Trail

NOTE: Due to the many snowmobiles here in winter, a better option in winter is to start from the Dredge Boat TH or Gold Hill TH to avoid snowmobiles. If you do decide to ski and snowshoe here, the winter trailhead is found approximately 5 mi up Tiger Rd. (see map).

North Fork Option: Park at Dredge Boat TH, bike up Tiger Rd. 3.2 mi to the North Fork of the Swan River (CR 354). Take a left just before a bridge. This is a half mile before Good Times Adventures. You can also park at the bottom of this if you want. Bike up CR 354 for 0.8 mi until the Colorado Trail

North Fork of the Swan

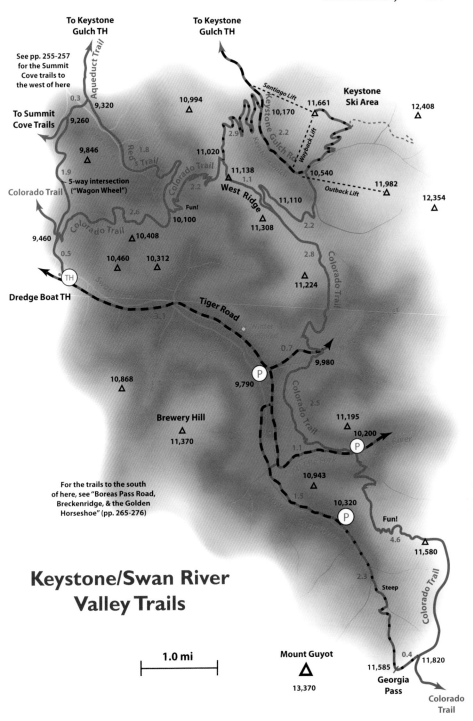

To Keystone
Gulch TH

To Keystone
Gulch TH

See pp. 255-257
for the Summit
Cove trails to
the west of here

Aqueduct Trail

Santiago Lift

Keystone Gulch Rd.

Keystone
Ski Area

0.3
9,320

10,994

11,661
10,170

12,408

Wayback Lift

To Summit
Cove Trails

9,260

2.9

Red's Trail

1.8

9,846

11,020

2.2

Colorado Trail

Keystone Gulch

11,138
1.1

10,540

Outback Lift

11,982

12,354

1.9

Colorado Trail

5-way intersection
("Wagon Wheel")

2.2

West Ridge

11,110

2.6

Fun!
10,100

11,308

2.2

9,460

Colorado Trail

10,408

0.5

Swan

TH

10,460

10,312

2.8

Colorado Trail

11,224

Dredge Boat TH

3.3

Tiger Road

Winter
10,868

0.7

P
9,790

9,980

Brewery Hill

11,370

2.5

Colorado Trail

11,195

10,200

P

1.1

For the trails to the south
of here, see "Boreas Pass Road,
Breckenridge, & the Golden
Horseshoe" (pp. 265-276)

10,943

1.5

10,320

P

Fun!

4.6

11,580

**Keystone/Swan River
Valley Trails**

2.3   Steep

Colorado Trail

1.0 mi

Mount Guyot

0.4

11,820

13,370

11,585

Georgia
Pass

Colorado
Trail

(CT) crosses the road; hang a left (west) here. Be sure you don't follow the motorized trail, which is less than a hundred yards down from the actual CT – make sure there is a CT sign. You are now on the mighty CT! This trail ascends steeply at times, flattens out at the top, then zigzags way down. Follow this and eventually you will come out on a dirt road just below a power line. Follow this dirt road left (south) back to the Dredge Boat TH. The loop is 13.1 mi and has 2,000 ft. of climbing/descending.

Middle Fork Option: Instead of taking the N. Fork (CR 354), continue up the Tiger Rd. an additional 2.4 mi (5.6 mi from the Dredge Boat TH) past a beaver meadow on your right to the Colorado Trail, which crosses the road. Hang a left and follow the Colorado Trail as it rolls along the hillside. You will most likely hear a pack of sled dogs down the hill and the trail will ultimately make its way to the N. Fork Rd. From here, follow the N. Fork option back to the trailhead as described in the previous description. You can also bail out here and go down to Tiger Rd. 17.2 mi with 2,900 ft. of elevation gain/loss.

South Fork Option: This is a big one but worth it. The only thing stopping this part of the CT from being one of the best sections for mountain biking is the rocky, rooty, technical section near the bottom. Either way you cut it, getting to the top of Georgia Pass from the west side is a

grunt. However, you will be rewarded with one of the finest singletrack descents around, at least for the first 4 mi or so. The beautiful trail winds gently through spruce and fir and flowers. Begin at the Dredge Boat TH and bike the Tiger Rd., taking a right onto the Georgia Pass Rd. (CR 355). Easy going gives way to steep, rocky terrain; any forks in the

The Snake River winding its way down from the Montezuma area

Curious mountain goats with Mt. Guyot in the distance

road usually lead back to the same spot. Stay left at around 11,000 ft. as the road descends to the east a bit. Hike-a-bike, granny gear it, do whatever you can to get up to the top of Georgia Pass! Hang a left (north) at Georgia Pass and continue to climb and you will intersect the CT. Here, follow the CT through rolling terrain for just over a mile and then the downhill begins! Enjoy. The trail spits you out on the upper part of Tiger Rd. Continue along the CT or, if you are pooped, you can call it a day here and cruise the Tiger Rd. back to the Dredge Boat TH. 25 mi and 4,800 ft. of climbing/descending.

Variation: Alternatively, the S. Fork option can be done by itself. In this case, it is best to park near a bridge that crosses the S. Fork of the Swan to the west (0.8 mi past Good Times Adventures). A short dirt road leads to an intersection with the Georgia Pass Rd., continue left (south) up to Georgia Pass and continue down the CT as described above. This loop by itself is 10.4 mi with 2,300 ft. of elevation gain/loss. *Bonus:* For the uber-adventurous: from Georgia Pass, it is a moderate hike to the summit of Mt. Guyot.

Montezuma

Peru Creek Trail: An old dirt road that leads along Peru Creek. Park at the Peru Creek TH (see p. 250). The old jeep road passes through private land in spots, crosses to the north side of Peru Creek after about a mile, traverses through several open meadows, and

Montezuma Lungbuster

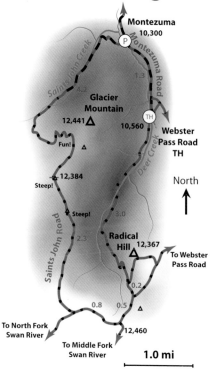

Montezuma
10,300

Glacier
Mountain
12,441

Fun!

12,384
Steep!

Steep!

Saints John Road

Radical
Hill   12,367

North

10,560

Webster
Pass Road
TH

Deer Creek

To Webster
Pass Road

0.2

0.5

12,460

0.8   0.5

To North Fork
Swan River

To Middle Fork
Swan River

1.0 mi

ultimately leads to a small lake at about 12,170 ft. Crank your neck and look way up high above you - Grays Peak towers overhead. The mountain biking begins easy lower down but gradually becomes quite difficult after about 5 mi. It is a climb of 2,230 ft. to the end of the road at the lake. In winter, the lower parts of this road are excellent for snowshoers and cross country skiers.

Montezuma Lungbuster Loop: You better have some strong legs and be willing to hike your bike a bit. This is a stellar loop reminiscent of jeep roads in the Silverton area of southwestern Colorado. Begin in the town of Montezuma or at the Webster Pass Rd. TH. Bike up Montezuma Rd. and keep going past the Webster Pass Rd. Continue up steep and rocky terrain, following the Montezuma Rd. all the way up to the top, where a road heads straight to the Middle Fork of the Swan River. Continue right to a

Montezuma
Lungbuster Loop

high area (straight takes you to the North Fork of the Swan River) and take a right on Saints John Rd. The route follows the crest of a ridge and on your left and right you can look down into basins far below! Eventually, the Saints John Rd. descends quickly back down to Montezuma. The loop is 12.3 mi in length with 3,100 ft. of elevation gain/loss. The entire loop is not recommended in winter (avalanche terrain) nor for hikers, but the Montezuma Rd. and Saints John Rd. are excellent places to hike in summer and ski and snowshoe in winter (be careful of snowmobiles).

Deer Creek: In winter, Montezuma Rd. (CR 5) is plowed to the Webster Pass Road TH (see p. 250). From here, skiing or snowshoeing up the Montezuma Rd. is a fun wintertime activity. Be sure to watch out for snowmobilers on this multi-use road.

Boreas Pass sunrise

Boreas Pass Road, Breckenridge, & the Golden Horseshoe

The town of Breckenridge is nestled in a valley bordered on the west side by the Tenmile Range and on the east side by a high ridge connecting Hoosier Pass to the south with Bald Mountain to the north. To the northeast of town, the Golden Horseshoe is a geographical area that was known for the high number of gold deposits, making it one of the richest mining areas in the state of Colorado. Gold was discovered here in 1859 and this quickly led to the founding of Breckenridge. The Golden Horseshoe envelopes the French Gulch area, ranging from the Sally Barber mine on the south side of the valley to the Minnie Mine and present-day Flume Trails on the northern side. The Boreas Pass Rd. on the east side of town was an early route for prospectors to approach the Breckenridge area in the early 1860s; the route was widened to accommodate wagon trains in the late 1860s. In 1882 the Union Pacific Railroad lay down narrow gauge track, which at the time was an impressive engineering feat. Today, the old railway bed has been converted to a road and many relics remain along the Boreas Pass Rd. Several trails are found to the east of Breckenridge that can be easily accessed from town or from the Boreas Pass Rd.

Maps: Sky Terrain "Summit, Vail, & Holy Cross" or Latitude 40° "Summit County Trails." This area lies right at the intersection of three National Geographic Trails Illustrated maps: "Vail, Frisco, Dillon" (#108), "Idaho Springs, Georgetown, Loveland Pass" (#104), and "Breckenridge & Tennessee Pass" (#109).

Best Time of Year: The recreational activities in this area, like many in the high country, are dependent upon seasonal snowfall to be in shape. In general, the trails in this area don't come into riding and hiking shape until mid to late May. The higher trails aren't suitable until late June to early July. Most of these trails can be used well into late fall until snow shuts them down. Many of the trails and the Boreas Pass Rd. turn into great ski trails in winter.

Camping: There are several campsites along the Boreas Pass Rd., especially the farther you progress (starting around Baker's Tank). Otherwise, the pickings are slim right around Breckenridge but you can always find spots high up Tiger Rd., north of town. Showers are available at the Breckenridge Rec Center (north side of town) as well as the Ice Rink (base of the Boreas Pass Rd.). See pp. 247-248 for campgrounds around the Lake Dillon area; it is just a quick drive from Breckenridge from Lake Dillon.

Access

Breckenridge: From the I-70/C-470 intersection west of Denver, take I-70 west for about 61 mi to Exit 203 in Frisco. If approaching from the east, take I-70 east through Vail and over Vail Pass to the Frisco exit (Exit 203). Travel south through Frisco on HWY 9 and Breckenridge is reached after about 10 mi.

Ken's Cabin and Boreas Pass Section House: Ken's Cabin and the Section House are two ski huts located along the Boreas Pass Rd. Ken's Cabin was built in the 1860s and the Section House in 1882; both were built to house the personnel involved with the construction and maintenance of the historic railway. Today, the huts can be reserved in winter by skiers and snowshoers; it is a lengthy (6.5 mi) but gradual ski/snowshoe to the huts from the Baker's Tank TH. Visit www.summithuts.org, www.huts.org, or call (970) 925-5775 for more information about these and other huts.

Summit Stage: This free bus service offered by Summit County can be super valuable in setting up one-way hiking and biking adventures in this area as well as other areas in Summit County. The Summit Stage has bus stops in Breckenridge, Boreas Pass, Frisco, Copper Mountain, Silverthorne, Dillon, Keystone, and Leadville. Bikes can be placed on the buses from May 1st to October 31st, before sunset. For information, visit summitstage.com.

Breckenridge Recreation Center: From the large traffic circle at the intersection of HWY 9 and Main Street as you enter Breckenridge from the north, continue right on HWY 9 to the first stoplight at Airport Rd. and North Park Ave (HWY 9). Proceed north (right) onto Airport Rd. and travel a quarter of a mile. Follow signs to the recreation center. There is plenty of parking here and this is a great access point to the paved bike paths.

Carter Park: From Main St. in Breckenridge, take Lincoln Ave. six blocks east to High St., then proceed three blocks south to Carter Park. If the parking is full, you can park along

High St. but obey all parking signs.

Ice Rink/Illinois Creek TH: From the southern end of Breckenridge, proceed south on HWY 9 a short ways to the last stoplight in town at Boreas Pass Rd. Turn left (east) and proceed a quarter of a mi to the large parking lot at the southeastern end of Stephen C. West Ice Rink.

Lupine along the Blue River Trail

Baker's Tank TH: The Baker's Tank TH is a popular trailhead located 3.7 mi up the Boreas Pass Rd. from the Ice Rink (see above). The road is plowed to this point in the winter.

B&B TH: Take HWY 9 north from Breckenridge. Just outside of town, look for a gas station at a stoplight. Take a right onto Huron Rd./CR 450 and proceed past some commercial buildings and the road turns into Reiling Rd. and ultimately turns into the French Gulch Rd. Be sure to take a left at the T-intersection after 1.1 mi. The B&B TH is located on the right side of the road 2.3 mi from the stoplight.

Reiling Dredge TH: Follow directions to the B&B TH (see above). Continue an additional 0.7 mi on the French Gulch Rd. and there is a parking area and trailhead on the left side of the road.

Lincoln TH: From the Reiling Dredge TH (see above), continue east on the French Gulch Rd. an additional 0.9 mi to a parking area on the south side of the road. Several hundred yards up the road the Sallie Barber Rd. exits to the right behind a closure gate. The Sallie Barber Rd. proceeds down a short ways to a creek crossing then climbs southwest out of French Gulch, ultimately passing the Sallie Barber Mine and exiting at the Sallie Barber TH.

Gold Run TH: From the north end of Breckenridge, travel approximately 3 mi on HWY 9 to the stoplight at Tiger Rd. Take a right and proceed 1.5 mi to Gold Run Gulch Rd. Take another right and drive 0.8 mi to a T-junction and stop sign. Turn right (still on Gold Run Gulch Rd.) and after 0.6 mi there is a parking area at the end of the road.

Baldy TH: From the intersection of HWY 9 and the Boreas Pass Rd. in southern

Breckenridge, travel the Boreas Pass Rd. east for just over 2 mi to Baldy Rd. (CR 520). Continue on Baldy Rd. as it climbs then levels off. After 1.4 mi on Baldy Rd. the road switchbacks sharply left but at this switchback there is a bus stop and a parking area (winter trailhead). In summer, continue straight (east) along FS 520. Most vehicles can make it to a road intersection after 0.7 mi on FS 520; after this point the Baldy Rd. (FS 520) becomes quite rocky and requires 4WD.

Sallie Barber TH: Follow directions to Baldy Rd. (CR 520) as described in description for Baldy TH (above). From the intersection of the Boreas Pass Rd. and Baldy Rd., drive 0.9 mi and take a left on Sallie Barber Rd. Continue for 0.25 mi to an obvious parking area and trailhead. In winter, this road is plowed to the trailhead and the Sallie Barber Rd. behind the trailhead is popular among snowshoers and cross country skiers.

Recommended Routes

Boreas Pass Road & Blue River Trails

Boreas Pass Road: Great for beginner mountain bikers or as an approach to adventures elsewhere. Begin at the Baker's Tank TH or higher up along the road and enjoy the rather mellow old railroad grade. Baker's Tank is reached after about 2.7 mi, the Section House at the top of Boreas Pass is reached after 5.7 mi. Spectacular setting for summer and winter adventures with the view of the Tenmile Range and Breckenridge Ski Area spread out before you across the valley to the west.

Baker's Tank Trail: A popular trail in all seasons and for folks of all skill levels. Begin at the Baker's Tank TH. Hikers and snowshoers can do an out-and-back on the trail but mountain bikers will want to make it a loop by biking up the gradual Boreas Pass Rd. for 2.7 mi to the obvious Baker's Tank, where the southern end of the Baker's Tank Trail meets the Boreas Pass Rd. The trail is then overall downhill from this point, making it a fun singletrack descent. The Mountain Pride Trail intersects

the Baker's Tank Trail 0.9 mi from its southern terminus; the Mountain Pride Trail climbs gradually then descends 1.6 mi to near the Baldy TH. Continuing straight at the Mountain Pride intersection, a 4-way intersection is reached at around 10,700 ft.; the southern spur heads to the Boreas Pass Rd. and the northern spur heads to a residential area. The Baker's Tank Trail is 2.8 mi from the Baker's Tank TH to Baker's Tank.

Aspen Alley: A difficult, singletrack climb punctuated with comforting traverse through a sublime aspen grove. The bottom of this trail is found just south of a large hairpin turn in the Boreas

Boreas Pass Area

For trails to the north of this area, see "Golden Horseshoe" map on p. 275

To Frisco (8 mi)

Breckenridge

Firecracker inbound from Prospect Hill area

Reiling Dredge TH
10,070

B&B TH

French Gulch Rd

Lincoln TH 10,340

Ski Hill Rd

Carter Park 9,650

See detail on p. 271

Barney Ford

9,960   B&B

1.5 Turk's Trail

Sallie Barber Rd 1.3

Firecracker outbound (continues up French Gulch)

1.3

Juniata

Sallie Barber TH
10,430

10,670

North

9,680

Burro TH

Winter TH
10,900

1.2

10,990

Ice Rink 9,690

0.5

Aspen Alley

1.0

Wakefield Ranch   10,370

Baldy TH

Baldy Rd

Burro Trail

Goose Pasture Tarn (private)

1.4

Baker's Tank TH

Baker's Tank

1.6

Mountain Pride

3.2

Spruce Creek Rd

0.2   0.9

11,060

0.9

Bald Mountain

△

13,684

Blue River Trail

1.5

10,100

1.4

Stables Trail

0.6

Indiana Trail

1.0

10,860

Private Road (bikes permitted)

Indiana Creek Rd

Baker's Tank Trail

1.2

Boreas Pass Rd

10,580

Spruce Creek TH
10,350

0.25

0.35   0.7

Mount Argentine
△
11,412

1.2

10,560

10,460

1.1

0.5   0.6

Spruce Creek Trail

Blue River 10,020

Pennsylvania Creek

1.3

1.3

10,870   0.6

9

For trails to the west and south of here, see "Breckenridge Ski Area & the Tenmile Range" pp. 277–290

11,170

Boreas Pass

To Como

To Hoosier Pass & Alma

Red Mountain
△
13,229

Red Peak
△
13,215

Hoosier Ridge

Hoosier Ridge
△
13,352

1.0

Firecracker Route

Pass Rd. (see map on opposite page) just north and east of the entrance gate to the private Wakefield Ranch. Begin at the Ice Rink. This trail can be connected to the Blue River Trail by taking a short singletrack trail that begins on the west side of the entrance gate.

Mountain Pride Trail: The Mountain Pride Trail is a rather smooth but muddy-at-times trail gradually descending from the Baker's Tank Trail to Iowa Mill Rd. Mostly singletrack. In combination with Nightmare on Baldy, a nice way to connect the Boreas Pass area to the Sallie Barber Mine area.

Nightmare on Baldy: A zigzagging, super fun trail descending from the Baldy Rd. area to the Sallie Barber Rd. Quite loose as the trail nears the Sallie Barber Rd. but fun for hiking or biking. Roughly 1.2 mi and a drop of 350 ft.

Baldy Road: Baldy Rd. is a challenging climb to the northern ridge of Bald Mountain. This makes a great hike but a difficult mountain bike ride. The road ends but a trail leads to the top of Bald Mountain. In winter, park near the bus stop at the end of Baldy Rd. (see winter TH in the Baldy TH description) and ski or snowshoe up this road.

Sallie Barber Road: Leading to the historic Sallie Barber Mine, the Sallie Barber Rd. connects Baldy Rd. with French Gulch. Fun for hiking and mountain biking in the dry months and skiing and snowshoeing in winter. It is 2.8 mi from the Sallie Barber TH to the Lincoln TH.

Barney Ford Trail: A fun descent from the Sallie Barber Rd., winding its way through forests. The easiest way to get to the top of the trail is to take the paved Boreas Pass Rd. from the Ice Rink to the Sallie Barber Rd. (follow driving directions to the Sallie Barber TH).

Carter Park Trails: Several trails are found to the south of the Barney Ford Trail just above and east of Carter Park. The Juniata Trail is a fun, moderate singletrack trail descending from the western terminus of the Sallie Barber Rd. to the top of the Moonstone Trail, which is a continuation of the Barney Ford Trail. Containing several optional terrain features (jumps, boardwalks), the B-Line Trail is mostly built for downhill mountain bikes but is ridable for experienced cross

Carter Park
& Ice Rink Detail

Carter
Park
Trail

**Carter
Park**
9,650

Moonstone   0.25
0.2

Barney Ford Trail   1.2

Sallie Barber
Road

0.25   0.3   10,200

0.25

0.1

0.5

Sunbeam

Hermit Placer

0.4   B-Line   0.4   10,100   Boreas Pass Road   0.25

Baldy Road

Juniata Trail

10,430

TH

**Sallie Barber
TH**

**Ice
Rink**   P   9,690

Jack's Cruel Joke

Illinois Gulch Road

0.6

10,420

Illinois Crk Trail   0.4

Southside Trail   0.5

Aspen Alley   1.0

North

↑

9   0.2   **Private**

**Wakefield
Ranch**

Blue River Trail

10,370   TH   **Baker's Tank
TH**

1.4 mi
to Indiana
Creek Rd

country mountain bikers. Test your ability to balance on beams and maybe pop off a small jump or two. The Hermit Placer Trail traverses above Carter Park along an old water ditch; from the southern end of this trail you can try to descend the steep and technical Jack's Cruel Joke. Sunbeam Trail is an easy trail that heads south from Carter Park towards the Boreas Pass Rd. Most of these trails are easy to moderate in difficulty and are suitable for hiking and mountain biking in summer and fall and snowshoeing in winter.

Blue River Trail

Blue River Trail: A superb trail. Begin at the Ice Rink. Follow the Boreas Pass Rd. east for 0.8 mi to the Wakefield Ranch. Take a right here but do not pass the gate. Just on the right side of the ranch gate, follow the singletrack trail, which is the Blue River Trail. This climbs gently then rolls down to the Pennsylvania Creek Rd. (1.4 mi from Boreas Pass Rd.). Cross the road and continue to the town of Blue River (2.9 mi of singletrack) along relatively easy terrain. Alternatively, take the Southside Trail (see next page) from the Ice Rink to the Wakefield Ranch area. Unfortunately, there is no access at Pennsylvania Creek Rd. (private property) nor the town of Blue River (no parking on side streets). Return the way you came, or continue through the town of Blue River and take HWY 9 back to Breckenridge.

Southside Trail: An easy, fun singletrack trail connecting the Ice Rink to the Wakefield Ranch area, where the Blue River Trail begins. Great for hikers and mountain bikers; several other trails in the area going this way and that.

Blue River/Indiana/Pennsylvania Loop: Start at the Ice Rink and follow Southside Trail and the Blue River Trail to the Pennsylvania Creek Rd. Take a left and follow the pavement and continue past where the road turns to dirt. Stay right at a fork at around 10,460 ft. (3.9 mi total), crossing to the south side of the drainage. Climb way up to the ridge. Take a right turn atop this saddle and the road turns to singletrack. The

trail climbs northwest along the ridge crest to the top of Mount Argentine (6.5 mi total). Descend singletrack on the west side of Mount Argentine to the Pennsylvania Creek Rd. Take a right and follow this road down to a neighborhood; a singletrack trail leads from one of the switchbacks to the very south end of the Blue River Trail (steep!). Return via HWY 9 or via the Blue River Trail. 12.5 mi and 2,500 ft. of climbing for the round trip from the Ice Rink and returning via Blue River Trail & Southside.

Firecracker: This "barbell"-shaped route follows more or less the Firecracker 50 race course (www.mavsports.com), a 2-lap race that takes place every 4th of July to the east of Breckenridge. Routefinding is difficult but the course is depicted in the maps on p. 269 and p. 275 with purple arrows. Start at Carter Park and head south on Sunbeam to the Boreas Pass Rd. Take the Boreas Pass Rd. all the way up past the Baker's Tank TH and continue to Baker's Tank. Take a left onto the Baker's Tank Trail and after 0.9 mi you will reach a fork in the trail. Continue right onto Mountain Pride for 1.6 mi to Baldy Rd./Baldy TH. Near the Baldy TH, continue up on the north fork of Baldy Rd., staying left at an intersection. A doubletrack road turns into the singletrack Nightmare on Baldy. Take this enjoyable trail as it switchbacks down to the Sallie Barber Rd. near the old mine. Turn right and take the Sallie Barber Rd., take another right onto the French Gulch Rd., then continue 0.8

Bald Mountain from French Gulch

mi to a closure gate; 0.5 mi past the gate take a left and climb up Little French Gulch. All but the strongest will need to hike their bike on some of this terrain. At the top near treeline, the trail cuts back across the drainage and a singletrack trail proceeds north along an old pipeline to reach a road intersection near Humbug Hill. Continue north on doubletrack then routefinding is very difficult but you want to stay on the Lincoln Park Rd. and take it generally west to the Prospect Hill Rd., then along the north side of Prospect Hill until you intersect the Prospect Gulch Rd. From here, find the singletrack Sidedoor Trail and proceed gently uphill then down X10U8 to the Reiling Dredge TH. Bike up the French Gulch Rd., west along the Sallie Barber Rd., then descend awesome the fun switchbacks of the Barney Ford, Moonstone, and Carter Park Trails. The loop is 27 mi and has 4,800 ft. of climbing!

Krummholz trees and windswept snow

Golden Horseshoe Area Trails

NOTE: There are many forest roads in this area, all of which are not shown on the map. Navigation in the Golden Horseshoe area is quite challenging - trails and roads heading this way and that. It is recommended to bring a map and compass if you have a particular route in mind, or just go exploring! I have only mentioned the more popular trails below. There are many loops that can be put together. Hikers will probably want to stick to B&B Trail, Turk's Trail, Sidedoor/X10U8/Minnie's Trails, and the Flume Trails. These can be accessed readily from the Reiling Dredge TH. Little French Flume Trail also makes a fine hike.

Flume Trails: Begin near the base of Huron Rd./CR 450 on the north end of Breckenridge. Keep an eye out for a fire hydrant on the north (left) side of the street

Flume Trails

after about 0.2 mi from HWY 9. A singletrack trail leads north near a stand of trees and intersects the Flume Trails. The Lower Flume Trail heads left (north) and the Upper Flume Trail heads right and up. The Lower Flume Trail follows an old aqueduct and contours through forests and meadows to an intersection with Mike's Trail after 1.3 mi. Mike's Trail heads up and intersects the Middle Flume Trail and Upper Flume Trail (see map). The Middle Flume Trail connects the short Mike's Trail with the Gold Run Gulch area. A moderate climb as the trail heads east. The Upper Flume Trail is a moderate route above the Lower Flume Trail. The Flume Trails are great for hiking, biking, cross country skiing, and snowshoeing.

Toxic Forest Trail: Connects the Gold Run Gulch Rd. with the east end of the Upper Flume Trail. The trail contours along forested slopes to just below the remnants of the Jumbo Mine, whose toxic tailings have poisoned the nearby forests. Good for hiking or mountain biking. If approaching from the Gold Run Gulch Rd. (southeast), it is difficult to find the trail but it is marked with a small marker just west of a switchback in the road.

Turk's Trail: A singletrack trail winding through trees and over a few bridges, great for the beginner mountain biker wanting to improve to the moderate level, but even great for the expert biker. Perfect for any hiker. This trail can be biked

with other trails, biked from town, or done as a short loop from the B&B TH (preferred for hikers). In any case, bikers will want to bike up the French Gulch Rd. and enter the B&B Trail from across the road from the Reiling Gulch TH and do Turk's Trail in the east-to-west direction. Turk's Trail is about 1.5 mi long.

B&B Trail: An easy doubletrack trail that is great for a quick hike or bike ride. Traverses along the southern side of French Gulch through pine forests. Can also be used to access Turk's Trail (see above). Excellent cross country skiing and snowshoeing in this area in the winter.

Minnie Mine Trails: Above French Gulch on the south-facing slopes are several stellar trails near the old Minnie Mine. If fun, moderate singletrack floats your boat, check out these trails, which include Sidedoor Trail, Minnie Mine Trail, and X10U8.

French Gulch Rd.: In summer, the French Gulch Rd. provides for a spectacular, relatively easy mountain bike

Golden Horseshoe Trails

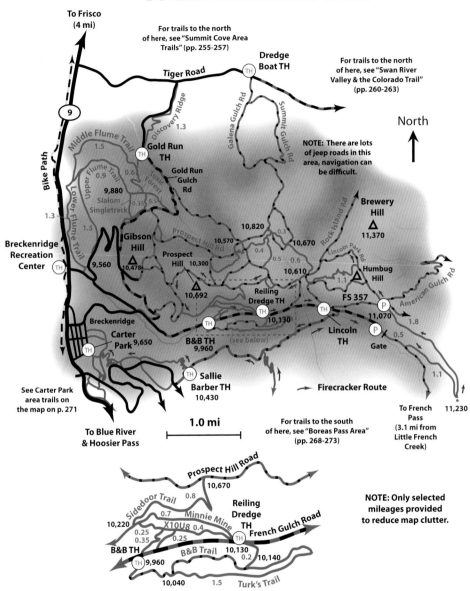

To Frisco
(4 mi)

For trails to the north
of here, see "Summit Cove Area
Trails" (pp. 255-257)

Dredge
Boat TH

Tiger Road

For trails to the north
of here, see "Swan River
Valley & the Colorado Trail"
(pp. 260-263)

North

Galena Gulch Rd

Summit Gulch Rd

Discovery Ridge

9

Middle Flume Trail
1.5

Gold Run
TH

1.3

NOTE: There are lots
of jeep roads in this
area, navigation can
be difficult.

Upper Flume Trail
0.9   0.6

Gold Run
Gulch
Rd

Fossil Forest

Brewery
Hill
11,370

Rock Island Rd

Bike Path

9,880
Slalom
Singletrack
0.35   0.5

10,820

Lincoln Park Rd

1.3

Lower Flume Trail

1.5

Gibson
Hill

Prospect Hill Rd

10,570

0.3

10,670

Breckenridge
Recreation
Center

9,560

10,478

Prospect
Hill   10,300

0.4

10,610

0.5   0.6

Humbug
Hill

American Gulch Rd

TH

10,692

Reiling
Dredge TH

1.1

FS 357

11,070   P

1.8

Breckenridge

Carter
Park   9,650

B&B TH
9,960

TH
10,130

(see below)

TH

Lincoln
TH

P

Gate

0.5

TH

Sallie
Barber TH
10,430

Firecracker Route

1.1

See Carter Park
area trails on
the map on p. 271

1.0 mi

For trails to the south
of here, see "Boreas Pass Area"
(pp. 268-273)

To French
Pass
(3.1 mi from
Little French
Creek)

11,230

To Blue River
& Hoosier Pass

Prospect Hill Road

10,670

Sidedoor Trail
0.8

Reiling
Dredge
TH

French Gulch Road

NOTE: Only selected
mileages provided
to reduce map clutter.

10,220

0.7
0.25
0.35

Minnie Mine
X10U8   0.4

0.25

B&B TH

B&B Trail   10,130

TH   9,960

0.2   10,140

10,040   1.5   Turk's Trail

ride. Awe-inspiring views surround you on all sides. Begin at the Lincoln TH in summer or winter and proceed east from here. You can actually continue an additional 0.8 mi past the Lincoln TH and park a tenth of a mile west of a closure gate in summer. The French Gulch Rd. continues all the way to French Pass as doubletrack then singletrack, although the trail gets significantly rougher and less defined the further you go. From the closure gate, it is about 3.6 mi to French Pass.

Little French Gulch Trail: Begin at the Lincoln TH. Approximately 0.5 mi up the French Gulch Rd. from the Lincoln TH, a doubletrack trail heads left (east) up Little French Gulch. The road is quite steep and rocky at times and is a difficult

Little French Gulch Trail

climb. Ultimately, near treeline at around 11,500 ft. the trail becomes singletrack and exits left and north across the drainage, following an old flume northeast. Here, the trail is easy and doesn't lose too much elevation. For a more gradual route, take FS 357 from near the Lincoln TH to the northwest end of the Little French Gulch Trail and take this southeast into the magnificent Little French Gulch drainage.

Additional Wintertime Activities

Gold Run Nordic Center: $ The Gold Run Nordic Center, which is run by the Breckenridge Recreation Department, offers extraordinary cross country skiing and snowshoeing as well as ice skating, sleigh rides, ski lessons, a retail shop, and the Clubhouse restaurant. The center grooms over 22 km of skate and classic trails and maintains 10 km of snowshoe trails. Visit www.townofbreckenridge.com or call (970) 547-7889 for more information.

Lower Mohawk Lake

Breckenridge Ski Area and the Tenmile Range

The Tenmile Range is surrounded by Breckenridge to the east, Frisco to the north, and Copper Mountain to the west. The trails of the Tenmile Range are accessed readily from the valleys below. The terrain here is quite diverse, ranging from dense forests, steep climbs to alpine lakes, and ridge traverses. Breckenridge Ski Area hosts some excellent hiking and biking trails and to the north and south of the ski area, the Peaks Trail and Burro Trail provide stellar, year-round avenues for adventure.

Maps: Sky Terrain "Summit, Vail, & Holy Cross" or Latitude 40° "Summit County Trails." For National Geographic Trails Illustrated maps, you will need "Vail, Frisco, Dillon" (#108) and "Breckenridge & Tennessee Pass" (#109).

Best Time of Year: Many of the high alpine hiking and biking trails of the Tenmile Range can only be traveled once the snow has melted, which is usually mid to late June, depending upon snowfall. The Burro Trail and Peaks Trail usually thaw out sooner than others in this region. Snowfall shuts down these trails by mid to late October. During the winter months (December through late March or April), the low-lying trails offer some of the area's best ski tours. Telemark skiing and alpine touring are popular above Francie's Cabin.

Camping: There are plenty of campgrounds in the Lake Dillon area. See pp. 247-248 for these camping options. Overnight backpacking trips can be taken to pretty much any area on National Forest; just be sure to read all signs and Forest Service information.

Showers are available at the Breckenridge Rec Center (north side of town) as well as the Ice Rink (base of the Boreas Pass Rd.).

Access

Breckenridge: From the I-70/C-470 intersection west of Denver, take I-70 west for about 61 mi to Exit 203 in Frisco. If approaching from the east, take I-70 east through Vail and over Vail Pass to the Frisco exit (Exit 203). Travel south through Frisco on HWY 9 and Breckenridge is reached after about 10 mi.

Frisco: From the I-70/C-470 intersection west of Denver, take I-70 west for about 61 mi to Exit 203. Frisco is just south of this exit. Main Street is reached about 1.1 mi south of I-70 along HWY 9.

Copper Mountain: From Frisco (above), travel I-70 west for about 5 mi to Exit 195. From Vail, take I-70 east over Vail Pass for 19 mi to Exit 195.

Francie's Cabin: Francie's Cabin can be accessed from the Spruce Creek TH or the Burro TH. The hut is open in the summer from July 1st through September 30th and in the winter from Thanksgiving through April. Contact the Summit Huts Association for more information and to make a reservation: www.summithuts.org or (970) 453-8583. Stay for

Early morning in early summer, Tenmile Range

Early morning in early summer, Tenmile Range

a night as a stopping point during a multi-day excursion or use it as a base camp for area activities. Francie's Cabin is located 1.2 mi from the Spruce Creek TH up the Crystal Lake Rd. a tenth of a mile before reaching the Wheeler Trail. Follow a road to the right (north) for less than a quarter mile.

Summit Stage: This free bus service offered by Summit County (www. summitstage.com) can be super valuable in setting up one-way hiking and biking adventures in this area as well as other areas in Summit County. The Summit Stage has bus stops in Breckenridge, Boreas Pass, Frisco, Copper Mountain, Silverthorne, Dillon, Keystone, and Leadville. Bikes can be placed on the buses from May 1st to October 31st, before sunset.

Wheeler Flats TH: Take I-70 to Exit 195 (Copper Mountain). At the stoplight south of the interstate, take a left and drive past the Conoco gas station for 0.4 mi to the Wheeler Flats TH.

Royal TH: The Royal TH is located near the west end of Main Street in Frisco, just east of I-70 Exit 201 and on the south side of Main Street. Access either from Frisco or from I-70.

Farmer's Korner TH: From Main St. in Frisco, find 2nd Ave. and go south for about 0.4 mi to the end of 2nd Ave. Park here, but the official trailhead is located a short walk away across the bike path. Signs will lead you to the beginning of the Peaks Trail.

Rainbow Lake TH: From the stoplight at the intersection of HWY 9 and Main Street in Frisco, continue south on HWY 9 just over a tenth of a mile and take a right onto 8th Ave. Continue south a quarter of a mile and take a right onto Belford St. Go one block west then left on 7th Ave; continue up 7th about a quarter of a mile until you intersect the bike path. Parking can be found along 7th St. just north of the paved bike path.

Community Commons/Miner's Creek TH: From the intersection of Main Street and

HWY 9 in Frisco, travel 0.5 mi south to a stoplight at CR 1004. Turn right (south) and quickly take a left at Nancy's Place. Veer left and park in the Community and Senior Center parking lot. There is no overnight parking here – the Miner's Creek TH is located just up the bike path (shared bike path/road) and you can park overnight here if need be. To get to the Miner's Creek TH and/or the bike path from Community Commons, follow signs for the Miner's Creek Trail from the bike path just west of Community Commons across CR 1004.

Watson/Riverwalk Parking: These two parking areas are found on the east side of Park Ave/HWY 9. The Watson Parking lot is found to the northeast of the intersection of Park Ave and Watson Ave. The Riverwalk Center parking is found just southeast of the intersection of Park Ave and Four O'Clock Rd.

Snowflake TH: From the intersection of Park Ave and Four O'Clock Rd., proceed west on Four O'Clock Rd. for 0.25 mi and take a left onto King's Crown Rd. The Snowflake TH is located just to the southwest at the beginning of King's Crown Rd.

Breckenridge Nordic Center TH: Take Ski Hill Rd. west and up from Park Ave for 0.9 mi. Just after Windwood Cir. you will see signs for the Breckenridge Nordic Center. This is about 0.4 mi past the big hairpin turn and Shock Hill sign. Park here in the large parking area.

Winter sunrise

Peaks TH: Located at the southern terminus of the Peaks Trail. From N. Park Avenue (HWY 9) in Breckenridge, follow Ski Hill Rd. west past the base of Peak 8 and park shortly after the road turns to dirt (2.3 mi from N. Park Avenue/HWY 9).

Burro TH: From S. Park Avenue (HWY 9) in Breckenridge, turn west on Village Rd. Follow this up a quarter of a mile to the Beaver Run Resort parking area on your left (south). There is also a "Breckenridge Stables, 1 mile" sign here. Officially, parking at this paved lot is reserved for Beaver Run Resort visitors. Therefore, it is best to park beyond the parking lot by driving through the lot and taking CR 751 a short ways. You may park along the county road beneath the ski lift. You can take one of the town's free shuttles to the trailhead if you park elsewhere. From the parking area, it is just over a tenth of a mile to the official National Forest Service sign, which is located south across the ski hill near the trees at the top of the T-bar lift. In winter, this parking area cannot be accessed but snowshoers and skiers can still access the Burro Trail.

Spruce Creek TH: Drive HWY 9 south of Breckenridge for 2.0 mi from the last stoplight in town. Just after Goose Pasture Tarn (more like a lake than a tarn) take your first right turn, which is Spruce Creek Rd. Follow this dirt road 1.2 mi to Spruce Creek TH, making sure to veer left after a tenth of a mile.

Mohawk Lake TH: To access the Mohawk Lake Trail, 4WD vehicles can proceed 1.8 mi up the Spruce Creek Rd. (see above in Spruce Creek TH description) past the intersection with the Wheeler Trail (1.2 mi) to the end of the road where there are several parking spots just below the start of the Mohawk Lake Trail. Some high-clearance 2WD vehicles can make it most of the way. There is some additional parking about 0.2 mi down the road from the Mohawk Lake TH. The Spruce Creek Trail emerges just below this trailhead area.

S. Wheeler TH: From the last stoplight (Boreas Pass Rd.) in Breckenridge as you are leaving town, drive south on HWY 9 for approximately 7.3 mi to CR 850. Take a right onto CR 850 then an immediate right onto CR 851 (McCullough Gulch Rd.), following signs for the Quandary Peak TH. The McCullough Gulch TH is reached after 2.2 mi on CR 851, staying right at a road intersection after 1.6 mi; the trailhead is located at a switchback in the road. Additional parking and some limited camping can be found just past this switchback. 2WD vehicles will likely not make it all the way to the trailhead and will have to be parked somewhere along this road after the Quandary Peak TH. CR 851 is not passable in winter.

McCullough Gulch TH: Follow directions to the S. Wheeler TH (above) but stay left at the road intersection 1.6 mi up CR 851. After 0.5 mi is a parking area near a closure gate. Depending on conditions, you may or may not be able to get here with 2WD.

Northern Tenmile Range

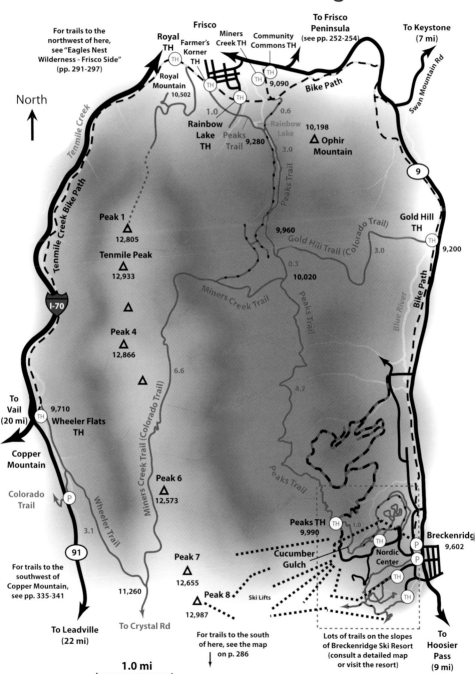

For trails to the
northwest of here,
see "Eagles Nest
Wilderness - Frisco Side"
(pp. 291-297)

North

Royal
TH

Frisco

Farmer's
Korner
TH

Miners
Creek TH

Community
Commons TH

To Frisco
Peninsula
(see pp. 252-254)

To Keystone
(7 mi)

Royal
Mountain
10,502

9,090

Bike Path

Swan Mountain Rd

Tenmile Creek

Rainbow
Lake
TH

Peaks
Trail
9,280

Rainbow
Lake

1.0

0.6

3.0

10,198
△ Ophir
Mountain

9

Tenmile Creek Bike Path

Peak 1
△
12,805

Peaks Trail

9,960

Gold Hill Trail (Colorado Trail)

Gold Hill
TH
TH
9,200

3.0

Tenmile Peak
△
12,933

0.3

10,020

Peaks Trail

Blue River

Bike Path

I-70

△

Miners Creek Trail

Peak 4
△
12,866

△

6.6

Miners Creek Trail (Colorado Trail)

4.7

To
Vail
(20 mi)

9,710
TH
Wheeler Flats
TH

Copper
Mountain

Colorado
Trail
P

Wheeler Trail

Peak 6
△
12,573

Peaks Trail

Peaks TH
9,990
TH

1.0

Breckenridge
9,602

P

Nordic
Center

TH

P

TH

91

3.1

Cucumber
Gulch

TH

For trails to the
southwest of
Copper Mountain,
see pp. 335-341

11,260

Peak 7
△
12,655

Ski Lifts

TH

△ Peak 8

12,987

To Leadville
(22 mi)

To Crystal Rd

For trails to the south
of here, see the map
on p. 286

Lots of trails on the slopes
of Breckenridge Ski Resort
(consult a detailed map
or visit the resort)

To
Hoosier
Pass
(9 mi)

1.0 mi

Mayflower TH: This trailhead is located 5.8 mi south of Copper Mountain just off the east side of HWY 91. The trailhead provides access to the Mayflower Trail.

Recommended Routes

Peaks Trail: A popular hiking and mountain biking trail in the Frisco/Breckenridge area. A moderate hike but bikers will encounter several technical and rooty spots and therefore it is best to bike in the south-to-north direction. There are several ways to do the Peaks Trail. It can be done as an out-and-back, a loop with a return via the bike paths, or as a shuttle with cars parked at either end. The southern terminus of this trail is about a thousand feet higher than the northern terminus; therefore, it is much easier to do this route from Breckenridge to Frisco. The Summit Stage can also be utilized to get back to the starting point (or to get to the trailhead); buses stop at Community Commons. The Peaks Trail connects the Peaks TH in Breckenridge with the Farmers Korner TH in Frisco but the Peaks Trail can also be accessed quite readily from Community Commons/Miner's Creek TH. Schuss along on skis or tramp through the snow on snowshoes for a fun winter outing. It is about 8.0 mi from the Peaks TH to Community Commons and about the same to the Farmer's Korner TH. **NOTE:** There are many beetle kill trees in the area; avoid this trail during high winds (see p. 36).

Along the shores of Lower Mohawk Lake

Peaks Loop: This loop begins in Breckenridge, traverses to Frisco via the Peaks Trail, then returns to Breckenridge via bike paths. The southbound Peaks Trail rolls along over Ewok Village raised bridges and gains only 200 ft. of elevation over the first 2 mi, then descends gradually and climbs again after 3.7 mi. Many small pristine streams trickle down from the left (west). After 4.5 mi, the final 2.4-mi hair-raising descent over roots and pine needles takes you screaming down to where the singletrack ends. Continue left at this point past Rainbow Lake for an additional 1.0 mi to the Farmer's Korner TH. Or, head down the dirt road for 0.6 mi and you'll intersect the main Frisco bike path. If you continue straight it will take you to the Frisco Community Commons, where you can pick up a Summit Stage bus back to Breckenridge. Alternatively, take a right at the intersection with the bike path and it is 8.6 easy miles back to City Market in Breckenridge and another 2 mi and 500 ft. of climbing back to the Peaks TH.

Cucumber Gulch Wildlife Preserve: Start at the Breckenridge Nordic Center TH. Make your way to the Nordic center building and a doubletrack trail leads northwest to the Cucumber Gulch Wildlife Preserve. Find the

Cucumber Gulch Trail and head west then north. Alternatively, park at the Peaks TH and across Ski Hill Rd. the Cucumber Gulch Trail can be accessed. Cucumber Gulch has occasional seasonal closures in the spring and no dogs are permitted here. This trail is about a mile long.

Breckenridge Ski Area Trails: There are numerous hiking and biking trails on the slopes of the Breckenridge Ski Area. Bikers will want to park in town at the Watson or Riverwalk THs and bike up Ski Hill Rd. or 4 O'Clock Rd. then descend some of the superb singletracks on the ski hill. It is recommended that hikers start at the Snowflake TH and take the trails up towards the small reservoir. A difficult but extremely fun trail is the Game Trail, which begins at the base of Peak 8. The Shock Hill area up Ski Hill Rd. also has some fun trails to hike or bike. For more information on the trails, please consult the "Hiking and Biking Trail Map" produced by the Town of Breckenridge and available in the Breckenridge Welcome Center at 203 S. Main St.

Burro Trail: Winding its way along the west side of the Breckenridge valley to the south of town, the Burro Trail is a pleasant an popular trail that can be hiked or biked in summer and cross country skied or snowshoed in winter.

Access is easy and is within minutes of Breckenridge. The Burro Trail connects the Burro TH in Breckenridge to the Spruce Creek TH south of town. Begin at either of these trailheads. It is 3.2 mi between the two trailheads and a climb of 1,000 ft. (100 ft. descent) in the north-to-south direction. Great for a trail run!

Spruce Creek Trail: An easy, beautiful hike along a creek surrounded by spruce and fir. Suitable by itself for a hike, bike, snowshoe, or ski, or as a route to get to the Mohawk Lakes (see below). It is 2.0 mi from the Spruce Creek TH to the Mohawk Lakes TH.

Mohawk Lakes Trail: The Mohawk Lakes are nestled in a deep valley with high peaks all around. A great way to get to the Mohawk Lakes is via the Spruce Creek Trail, especially if you don't have a high clearance vehicle. From the Spruce Creek TH, follow the Spruce Creek Trail as it follows the

beautiful Spruce Creek and makes its way through spruce and fir trees. The trail intersects the Wheeler Trail after 1.5 mi and emerges from the trees at the upper part of Spruce Creek Rd. after 2.0 mi. From this point, it is 0.5 mi to Mayflower Lake (a side trip), 1.0 mi to Lower Mohawk Lake, and 1.3 mi to Upper Mohawk Lake along the Mohawk Lake Trail. This trip makes a great backpacking trip since it is close to a trailhead and is very scenic. The beautiful Continental Falls pour down the cliffs and several short side trips enable one to get close to the falls. The 14,000-ft. peaks Grays and Torrey are visible in the distance to the north.

Crystal Lakes: The Crystal Lakes basin is as beautiful of a high mountain cirque as the Mohawk Lakes basin but far less crowded. It is an alpine atmosphere that will rival the best and is one of the shortest hikes from a highway to a beautiful alpine area in all of Colorado. Two tenths of a

mile past the Spruce Creek TH on the right is a jeep road that climbs steeply for 2.1 mi to Lower Crystal Lake; Upper Crystal Lake can be reached via a faint trail that heads west on the north side of Lower Crystal Lake, then up the southeast face of Peak 10. Descending the section of the Wheeler Trail south of Crystal

A rolling cascade near Mohawk Lake

Southern Tenmile Range

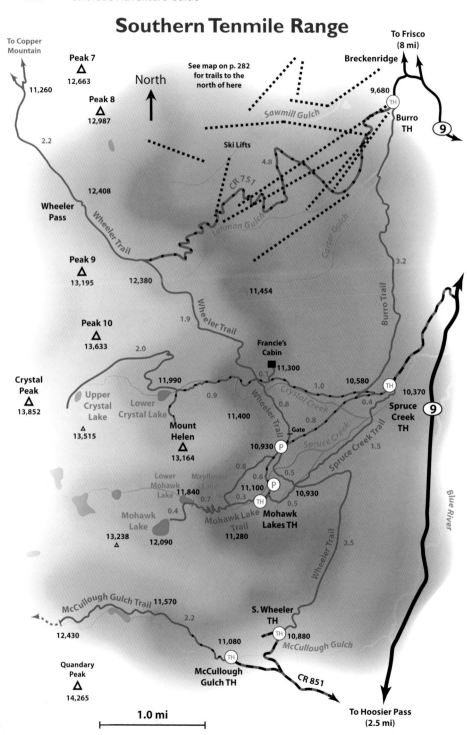

To Copper Mountain

To Frisco (8 mi)

Breckenridge

Peak 7
△
12,663

See map on p. 282 for trails to the north of here

North

Peak 8
△
12,987

9,680
TH
Burro TH

9

2.2

Sawmill Gulch

Ski Lifts

12,408

4.8

CR 751

Wheeler Pass

Wheeler Trail

Lehman Gulch

Carter Gulch

Peak 9
△
13,195

12,380

3.2

11,454

Burro Trail

Peak 10
△
13,633

1.9

Wheeler Trail

Francie's Cabin

Crystal Peak
△
13,852

2.0

△
13,515

11,990

11,300

0.1

1.0

10,580

TH
10,370

Upper Crystal Lake

Lower Crystal Lake

0.9

Crystal Creek

0.8

0.4

Spruce Creek TH

9

Mount Helen
△
13,164

11,400

Wheeler Trail

0.8

Gate

0.8

Spruce Creek

Spruce Creek Trail

Blue River

10,930
P

1.5

Lower Mohawk Lake

Mayflower Lake

0.8

0.6

0.5

11,840

0.7

11,100
P

10,930

Mohawk Lake

0.4

Mohawk Lake Trail

0.3

TH
Mohawk Lakes TH

0.5

△
13,238

12,090

11,280

2.5

Wheeler Trail

McCullough Gulch Trail   11,570

S. Wheeler TH

12,430

2.2

11,080

TH
10,880

McCullough Gulch

Quandary Peak
△
14,265

TH
McCullough Gulch TH

CR 851

To Hoosier Pass (2.5 mi)

1.0 mi

Lake Rd. and return via Spruce Creek Rd. makes a good loop trip. It is roughly 2.5 mi to Lower Crystal Lake. Mountain bikes are allowed on this road as well as on the Spruce Creek Rd. *Variation*: Alternatively, the return trip from Crystal Lake can be made via the Spruce Creek Trail by continuing south on the Wheeler Trail across the Spruce Creek Rd. and intersecting the Spruce Creek Trail.

Burro Trail to Spruce Creek Trail: This is a great easy to moderate mountain biking adventure suitable for beginner and intermediate bikers or trail runner. Starting in Breckenridge at the Burro TH, follow the Burro Trail 3.1 mi south to the intersection of the Crystal Lake Rd. Cross the rocky road and continue on the short singletrack section

to the Spruce Creek Rd. Take a right on this road and continue 1.4 mi up to near the end of the jeep road where the Spruce Creek Trail emerges from the forest. Take the Spruce Creek Trail down for 2.0 mi as you zoom, bounce, and wind through tree roots and spruce and fir trees, exiting at the Spruce Creek TH. Either return via the Burro Trail (just up the Crystal Lake Rd. 0.3 mi on the right) or ride the 3.2 mi to Breckenridge by descending the Spruce Creek Rd. to HWY 9. Return via the Burro Trail makes the trip a perfect 10.0-miler. *Variation:* Instead of returning to Breckenridge via the Burro Trail, ride the Spruce Creek Rd. down to HWY 9, turn right and ride for 1.3 mi south on HWY 9 to the town of Blue River. Take a left, cross over the Blue River, and follow the roads through town, staying left when you can. At the end of a dirt road, you can hit the Blue River Trail (see map) and ride this stellar singletrack all the way to Breckenridge.

Colorado Trail/CDT Marker

Wheeler Trail: The Wheeler National Recreation Trail is a long trail traversing from McCullough Gulch near Hoosier Pass and Quandary Peak to Copper Mountain. Sections of the trail make great day hikes or parts of mountain bike loops but the trail is also great for overnight backpacking trips,

perhaps even with a side trip to Mohawk Lakes. Follow directions on p. 281 to the McCullough Gulch TH to access the southern terminus; the northern terminus is accessed just off I-70 in Copper Mountain at the Wheeler Flats TH. From south

Looking up towards Atlantic and Fletcher Peaks from near Fremont Pass

to north, the complete trail is 10.8 mi long and has 2,600 ft. of climbing and 3,800 ft. of descending.

McCullough Gulch

McCullough Gulch Trail: Begin at the McCullough TH. Take an old mining road west for about 0.5 mi just past a small lake on the left (south) side of the road, taking a left at a fork. From here, follow singletrack trail. After about a mile, you can take a side trip to White Falls and/or continue west and up the valley through forests then meadows as the trail eventually fades away after 2.2 mi near some small lakes. Quandary Peak looms over you to the south. This is an extraordinary basin, similar to the two basins to the north (Mohawk Lakes and Crystal Lake).

Mayflower Trail: Start at the Mayflower TH south of Copper Mountain. This easy trail climbs about 2.0 mi gradually up the valley past some old mines to the base of Fletcher Mountain.

Mayflower Trail

Tenmile Range Crossings

There are several options to cross up and over the Tenmile Range from Breckenridge to Copper Mountain, and all three of these options require fit individuals and an early start. All of them can be done by both hikers and mountain bikers, although you might be crazy to push your bike up and over the route described in Option #3. If hiking, you will either need to have someone pick you up at the end, hike back, take the Summit Stage, or have a bike pre-stashed in the Copper Mountain area.

Tenmile Crossing #1:   Best for hikers but doable via mountain bikes, the route explained here links Breckenridge to Copper Mountain via the Burro Trail and the Wheeler Trail. Begin at the Burro TH, take the Burro Trail south to the Crystal Lake Rd., and climb steeply for 1.1 mi to the junction with the Wheeler Trail, which is a tenth of a mile past the turnoff to Francie's Cabin. Hang a right and do whatever you can to get to the top of the steep and rocky old doubletrack trail (difficult for bikes). At about 12,400 ft. the trail becomes relatively flat and contours north then west then northwest to an intersection at the top of the Peak 9 Rd. (CR 751). Stay on the Wheeler Trail (singletrack) as it contours, descends, then climbs again to Wheeler Pass (12,400 ft.). Carefully descend the Wheeler Trail all the way down to Wheeler Flats, staying left on the Colorado Trail at a trail intersection. When the trail crosses a bridge and joins the bike path, take a left to arrive at the Wheeler Flats TH or turn right and bike to Frisco then Breckenridge for a loop or hop on the Summit Stage for a ride back to Breckenridge. 11.3 mi from the Burro TH to the Wheeler Flats TH with approximately 3,200 ft. of climbing and descending.

Tenmile Crossing #2:   Similar to Option #1 but this route climbs the Peak 9 Rd. (CR 751) to the Wheeler Trail intersection as described in the previous route. From the parking area along CR 751 near the Burro TH, continue on CR 751 west up the ski resort slopes. Veer right and then

left by the Quicksilver chairlift and then another left at a fork and climb this road past the Peak 9 restaurant. Continue through rocky terrain and go straight at a fork above Chairlift B. Climb up to the top of the Peak 9 Road to the intersection with the Wheeler Trail (4.8

Tenmile Range from the west

mi). Continue over Wheeler Pass as in Option #1. Return via a pre-arranged shuttle, the Summit Stage, or take the bike paths back to Breckenridge. 10.1 mi for the one-way trip with 3,000 ft. of climbing and descending.

Tenmile Crossing #3: This is the most difficult of the three Tenmile Range Crossing options and is best suited for hikers and trail runners. A lot of time will be spent above treeline; thus, an early start is necessary to avoid afternoon thunderstorms. Begin at the Farmer's Korner TH or Community Commons in Frisco. Take the Peaks Trail to the intersection with the Miner's Creek Trail (also the Colorado Trail at this point). Climb west on steep slopes and switchbacks to treeline and continue on difficult terrain to the top of the ridge to a high point of around 12,500 ft. Take in the views! Continue south as the trail drops gradually then steeply to treeline. Shortly after reaching treeline on the west side of the Tenmile Range, the trail intersects the Wheeler Trail. Take a right and follow the Wheeler trail all the way down to the Wheeler Flats TH. Return either via pre-arranged shuttle or via the Summit Stage. From Community Commons to the Wheeler Flats TH it is 12.8 mi with 3,700 ft. of climbing and 3,000 ft. of descending. Also makes a great, challenging trail run.

Additional Wintertime Activities

Breckenridge Nordic Center: $ The Breckenridge Nordic Center is open generally mid November through late March or early April. Follow directions as indicated on p. 280. The Breckenridge Nordic Center has over 30 km of groomed cross country ski terrain and over 18 km of spectacular snowshoe trails. The cozy lodge hosts a retail store and woodburning fireplace. The center offers ski lessons, rentals, and guided tours. Call (970) 453-6855 or visit www.breckenridgenordic.com for more information.

Wildflowers for as far as the eye can see along the Gore Range Trail

Eagle's Nest Wilderness - Frisco Side

There are few places in Colorado where one can access a wilderness area as readily as the Frisco and Copper Mountain areas. The Eagle's Nest Wilderness contains the mighty Gore Range and there are ample hiking opportunities here. While the trailhead areas can be crowded and parking can often be difficult, few people venture more than a few miles into the Eagle's Nest Wilderness. Whether you are out for a multi-day backpacking adventure or a quick hike while passing through the area, this area has something for everyone. Beginner backpackers will find this area quite attractive due to the ease of access. Like all wilderness areas, mountain bikes are not allowed in the Eagle's Nest Wilderness.

Maps: Sky Terrain "Summit, Vail, & Holy Cross", Latitude 40° "Summit County Trails", or National Geographic Trails Illustrated "Vail, Frisco, Dillon" (#108).

Best time of the year: Late June through early October, depending upon snowfall. Like many trails in Colorado, the higher elevations melt out later and get snowy sooner. The lower parts of the North Tenmile Creek, Meadow Creek, and Gore Creek Trails are all popular ski and snowshoe destinations in the winter. Consider visiting this area in the fall when the aspen trees display their fall colors (usually during the last two weeks in September).

Camping: A multitude of National Forest Service campgrounds provide intimate overnight campsites while in the Summit County area. These campgrounds include the Heaton Bay, Peak One , Pine Cove, Prospector, Windy Point, and Lowry Camp Campgrounds. Some of these may be currently closed due to pine beetle hazards. The Blue River Campground north of Silverthorne along the Blue River is another option. You can obtain more information regarding these campgrounds by calling the Dillon Ranger District of the White River National Forest at 970-468-5400 or visiting the following website: www.fs.fed.us/r2/ whiteriver. Campground reservations for this area can be made either at www.recreation. gov or www.reserveamerica.com. Many informal campsites can be found on National Forest land in the area. Showers are available in the Silverthorne Recreation Center, located at 430 Rainbow Drive in the area to the north of the I-70/HWY 9 intersection.

Access

Frisco: From the I-70/C-470 intersection west of Denver, take I-70 west for about 61 mi to Exit 203. Frisco is just south of this exit. Main Street is reached about 1.1 mi south of I-70 along HWY 9.

Wildflowers and rocks

Copper Mountain: From Frisco (above), travel I-70 west for about 5 mi to Exit 195. From Vail, take I-70 east over Vail Pass for 19 mi to Exit 195.

NOTE: All of the following trailheads in this area are accessible in winter. Additional access points are found in the northern parts of the Gore Range Trail (not discussed here) but many of these are not necessarily accessible in winter.

North Tenmile Creek TH: This trailhead is just off of I-70 (Exit 201) on the west side of the interstate.

Meadow Creek TH: From the Frisco exit of I-70 (Exit 203), take CR 1231, which

Sunrise reflections near Red Buffalo Pass

runs parallels I-70 on the north side of the interstate, for just over half mile.

Mesa Cortina TH: From I-70 Exit 205 in Silverthorne, go north on HWY 9 for a tenth of a mile and take a left at the first stoplight (Wildernest Rd.). Proceed on Wildernest Rd. for a quarter of a mile and take a right on Adams Rd. Almost immediately, take a left on Royal Buffalo Drive (marked as Buffalo Mountain Dr.). Follow this road for 0.7 mi, take a right on Lake View Drive, proceed 0.4 mi and turn left on Aspen Drive, and after a tenth of a mile or so the TH is on your right.

Buffalo Cabin TH: From I-70 Exit 205 in Silverthorne, go north on HWY 9 for a tenth of a mile and take a left at the first stoplight (Wildernest Rd.). Continue up Wildernest Rd. for about 3.5 mi to near the end of the road where there is an obvious parking area. The TH is found on the northwest side of the parking area.

Lily Pad Lake TH: Within a tenth of a mile of the Buffalo Cabin TH, just to the south. Same parking area, follow directions to the Buffalo Cabin TH.

South Gore Range TH: This trailhead is just north of Copper Mountain in a rest/

scenic area. From Frisco, drive I-70 for about 5 mi. About a mile before Exit 195 (Copper Mountain), turn into the rest/scenic area. The trailhead can be found here and the Gore Range Trail heads south towards Exit 195 before heading up to the northwest. If approaching from the west, you should drive to Frisco (Exit 201) and turn around and return to access the rest area since this rest/scenic area cannot be accessed from eastbound I-70.

Summit Stage: This free bus service offered by Summit County can be super valuable in setting up one-way hiking and biking adventures in Summit County. The Summit Stage has bus stops in Breckenridge, Boreas Pass, Frisco, Copper Mountain, Silverthorne, Dillon, Keystone, and Leadville. Bikes can be placed on the buses from May 1st to October 31st, before sunset. For information, visit summitstage.com.

Recommended Routes

Gore Range Trail: Named after Sir St. George Gore, an Irish nobleman who led a hunting expedition in this area back in 1853, this trail begins in Copper Mountain and makes its way 45 mi to just south of Green Mountain Reservoir. Many adventures abound along this trail! There are many other access points to the Gore Range Trail north of Silverthorne

Red Buffalo Pass from Eccles Pass

Eagles Nest Wilderness - Frisco Side

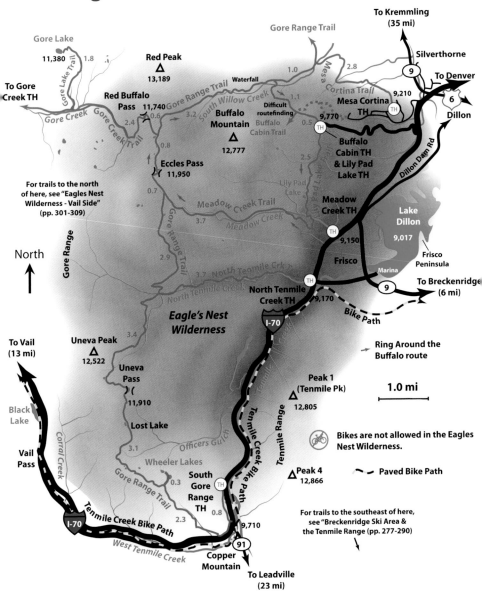

Gore Lake
11,380   1.8

Red Peak
△
13,189

Gore Range Trail

To Kremmling
(35 mi)

Silverthorne

9

To Denver

To Gore
Creek TH

Red Buffalo
Pass 11,740

Gore Range Trail

Waterfall

1.0

South Willow Creek

Mesa Cortina Trail

2.8

9,210

Mesa Cortina
TH

TH

6

Dillon

Gore Creek   Gore Creek Trail

2.4   0.6

3.2

Buffalo
Mountain
△
12,777

Difficult
routefinding

1.1

Buffalo
Cabin Trail

0.5

9,770

TH

Buffalo
Cabin TH
& Lily Pad
Lake TH

Dillon Dam Rd

0.8

Eccles Pass
11,950

2.5

Lily Pad
Lake

Meadow
Creek TH

Lake
Dillon
9,017

For trails to the north
of here, see "Eagles Nest
Wilderness - Vail Side"
(pp. 301-309)

0.7

Meadow Creek Trail

3.7

Meadow Creek

TH
9,150

Frisco

Frisco
Peninsula

North
↑

Gore Range

Gore Range Trail

2.9

3.7 North Tenmile Crk Tr

Marina

9

To Breckenridge
(6 mi)

North Tenmile
Creek TH

TH
9,170

Bike Path

North Tenmile Creek

Eagle's Nest
Wilderness

To Vail
(13 mi)

Uneva Peak
△
12,522

3.4

I-70

Ring Around the
Buffalo route

Peak 1
(Tenmile Pk)
△
12,805

1.0 mi

Uneva
Pass
(
11,910

Tenmile Creek Bike Path

Tenmile Range

🚳 Bikes are not allowed in the Eagles
Nest Wilderness.

Black
Lake

Lost Lake

Officers Gulch

Peak 4
△
12,866

Vail
Pass

Corral Creek

Wheeler Lakes

3.1

Gore Range Trail

0.3

South
Gore
Range
TH

TH

〰 〰 Paved Bike Path

I-70

Tenmile Creek Bike Path

0.8

For trails to the southeast of here,
see "Breckenridge Ski Area &
the Tenmile Range (pp. 277-290)

2.3

West Tenmile Creek

9,710

91

Copper
Mountain

To Leadville
(23 mi)

to the west of the Blue River (HWY 9). The most popular part of the Gore Range Trail is the section Meadows Creek Trail and Copper Mountain. Consult a map for points north along this trail.

North Tenmile Creek Trail: Easily accessible and fun, the trail follows North Tenmile Creek 3.4 mi (gain of 900 ft.) to the intersection with the Gore Range Trail. Do an out-and-back on this trail or use it to access the heart of the Eagle's Nest Wilderness.

Lily Pad Lake Trail: Begin from either the Lily Pad Lake TH or the Meadow Creek TH. The hike to the lakes requires less elevation gain from the Lily Pad Lake TH but is slightly longer (1.7 vs. 1.6 mi) than the hike from the Meadow Creek TH. An easy trail with occasional rocky sections passing through aspen groves, lodgepole pine, and spruce and fir.

Meadow Creek Trail: This trail is a scenic one that gets you quickly to the heart of the Eagle's Nest Wilderness. Mainly lodgepole pine lower down giving way to spruce higher up. Intersects the Gore Range Trail in a stellar high meadow after 4.3 mi; a nice way to approach Eccles Pass and Red Buffalo Pass. Begin at the Meadow Creek TH.

Buffalo Cabin/Gore Connector Trail: This trail connects the Gore Range Trail to the Buffalo Cabin and Lily Pad Lake area. Extremely difficult to find this trail from it's north side. From the intersection with the Gore Range Trail, the trail gently climbs south up to an old ditch. The trail follows the ditch but then takes a sharp right and climbs the hill. The trail up this hill is difficult to follow. Don't make the mistake of staying on the ditch as this will likely not get you where you are going. It is about 1.6 mi from the Gore Range Trail to the Buffalo Cabin TH. Much easier to follow going south to north.

Buffalo Cabin Trail: Follow the Buffalo Cabin/Gore Connector Trail 0.5 mi from the Buffalo Cabin TH. At the trail intersection, take a left (west) and climb 0.6 mi to the old Buffalo Cabin.

Ring Around the Buffalo: An excellent loop hike, trail run, or overnight backpacking trip that completely circumnavigates Buffalo Mountain. Very scenic. Start at the Meadow Creek TH, hike up the Meadow Creek Trail

to the intersection with the Gore Range Trail, proceed up to Eccles Pass, continue north past the intersection with the Gore Creek Trail, and continue to follow the Gore Range Trail all the way down to the intersection with the Buffalo Cabin/Gore Connector Trail. Follow the Buffalo Cabin/Gore Connector Trail (see navigational difficulties on previous page) all the way to the Buffalo Cabin TH. Continue from the Lily Pad TH on the Lily Pad Trail south past Lily

Tina Lewis on the Gore Range Trail with Copper Mountain Ski Resort in the distance

Pad Lake and back to Meadow Creek TH. The loop is 14.1 mi with 3,800 ft. of ascent/descent. See map on p. 295 (route marked with green arrows).

Mesa Cortina Trail: This is an easy trail for all seasons. It is easily accessible from Silverthorne. Drive to the Mesa Cortina TH. The trail winds its way initially through aspen groves then through a clearing and eventually through pine forests, much of which have been affected by pine beetle. The trail intersects the Gore Range Trail after 2.8 mi.

Wheeler Lakes: A quick trip to beautiful lakes, great for the beginner backpacker or for those just passing through or looking for a morning or afternoon hike. Start at the S. Gore Range TH and follow the Gore Range Trail 3.1 mi to the Wheeler Lakes Trail intersection. Another 0.3 mi will bring you to the lakes.

Uneva avenU: A great adventure! Park in Frisco either at the North Tenmile Creek TH or at the large parking lot a quarter mile east of I-70 along Frisco Main Street. Hike the North Tenmile Creek Trail 3.7 mi to the intersection with the Gore Range Trail. Follow the Gore Range Trail south over Uneva Pass (at 7.1 mi total) all the way to Copper. Grab some food in Copper Mountain and take the Summit Stage back to Frisco (bus stops in the village and also at the entrance to the ski area near the stoplight). This route can also be done in reverse. This route is 12.5 mi with 3,300 ft. of climbing and 2,750 ft. of descending.

Charlie's Picks for Summit County

1. Montezuma Lungbuster Loop (p. 264)

2. Summit Cove Trails (p. 255-257)

3. Ring Around the Buffalo (p. 296)

4. West Ridge Superloop (p. 259)

5. Mohawk Lakes Trail (p. 285)

6. Middle Fork of the Swan River (p. 262)

7. Uneva avenU (p. 297)

8. Tenmile Crossing #3 (p. 290)

9. Burro Trail to Spruce Creek Trail (p. 287)

10. Blue River Trail (p. 271)

Campsite in Summit County with the Gore Range in the distance

Vail Village

Chapter 8: Vail & Copper Mountain

During the summer months, the Vail Valley turns into a mountain playground. There are plenty of activities ranging from bagging peak summits, mountain biking along aspen-covered ridges, and hiking to alpine lakes. Mountain bikers will find excellent biking north of town as well as south of and near the Vail Ski Area. The Gore Range and its labyrinth of rocky creeks and high alpine lakes provide hikers and backpackers a diverse set of wilderness adventures. In winter, there are plenty of options outside of the ski resort. Cross country ski or snowshoe on one of the many trails emanating from the Vail valley. And there is always much to do at the end of a hard day of playing in the high country - check out the exquisite shops, restaurants, and bars in the town of Vail while your body recovers for tomorrow.

Vail & Copper Mountain

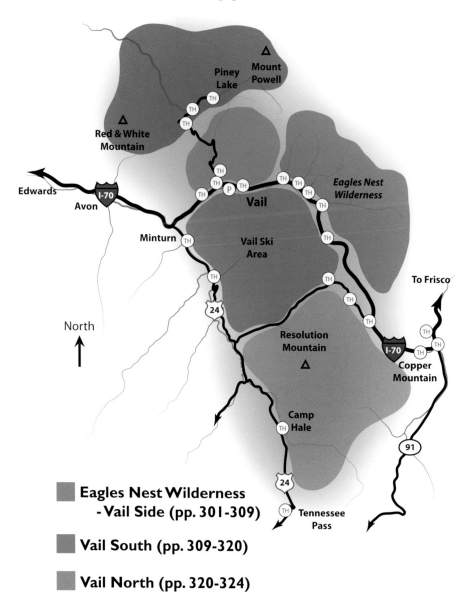

Eagles Nest Wilderness - Vail Side (pp. 301-309)

Vail South (pp. 309-320)

Vail North (pp. 320-324)

Upper Piney River (pp. 325-334)

Copper Mountain to Tennessee Pass (pp. 335-341)

Eagle's Nest Wilderness - Vail Side

There are few places in Colorado where one can access a wilderness area as readily as the Vail, Frisco, and Copper Mountain areas. The Eagle's Nest Wilderness contains the mighty Gore Range and there are ample hiking opportunities here. Surprisingly few people venture more than a couple of miles into the Eagle's Nest Wilderness. Whether you are out for a multi-day backpacking adventure or a quick hike while passing through the Vail valley, this area has something for everyone. Like all wilderness areas, mountain bikes are not allowed in the Eagle's Nest Wilderness.

A tarn deep in the Eagle's Nest Wilderness

Maps: Latitude 40° "Summit County Trails", National Geographic Trails Illustrated "Vail, Frisco, Dillon" (#108), or Sky Terrain's "Summit, Vail, & Holy Cross".

Best time of the year: Late June through early October, depending upon snowfall. Like many trails in Colorado, the higher elevations melt out later and get snowy sooner. The lower parts of the North Tenmile Creek, Meadow Creek, and Gore Creek Trails are all popular ski and snowshoe destinations in the winter. Consider visiting this area in early fall when the aspen trees display their fall colors (usually during the last two weeks in September).

Camping: Unfortunately, there isn't a lot of camping right in the Vail valley. However, informal campsites can be found along the Shrine Pass Rd. (see directions to the Shrine Pass TH in the "Vail South" section on p. 310) or the Red Sandstone Rd. (see access directions in "Vail North" on p. 322). Otherwise, the Gore Creek Campground south of Vail is a great option. First come, first serve, no reserved sites. For more information, call 970-945-2521. If you are up for the drive, there are many other National Forest Service campgrounds in the Summit County area (Lake Dillon and north of Silverthorne along the Blue River).

Access

Vail: Vail is located at Exit 176 of I-70. The East Vail and West Vail exits are Exit 180 and Exit 173, respectively.

Copper Mountain: Copper Mountain is located at Exit 195 of I-70. This is about 5 mi west of Frisco and 19 mi east of Vail.

Vail Bus: The town of Vail offers a free bus service throughout the Vail Valley. Stops range all along the valley floor, including stops up Bighorn Rd. (the last stop very close to the Gore Creek TH), near the base of Pitkin and Booth Creeks, the base area of the Vail Ski area, various stops in Vail Village, Red Sandstone Rd., and the Trappers Run TH area. Visit www.vailgov.com for more information about this great bus service. The bus service is a great way to access the trailheads of the Eagle's Nest Wilderness. In addition, if you are interested in setting up more advanced loop or point-to-point adventures in this area, the bus can aid in these endeavors.

Gore Creek

Booth Creek TH: Take I-70 to the East Vail exit (Exit 180). Go west (left) along the north side frontage road for 0.9 mi to Booth Falls Rd. Turn right and follow this up a quarter of a mile to the parking area. In winter, parking is limited to 3 hours and no parking between 11 pm and 7 am. If the parking is full, you might be able to park back down the road at the school, but check the signs.

Pitkin Creek TH: Take I-70 to Exit 180 (East Vail). Go east (right) immediately on Fall Line Rd., located on the north side of I-70. Take this road 0.3 mi to the trailhead. Open in winter.

Along the Booth Creek Trail

Bighorn Creek TH: Take I-70 to Exit 180 in East Vail. On the south side of I-70, take Bighorn Rd. east 0.8 mi. Turn left (north) on Columbine Drive and proceed 0.2 mi (crossing underneath I-70) to the trailhead. Very limited parking in winter.

Gore Creek TH: From the East Vail exit of I-70 (Exit 180), take the Bighorn Rd. on the south side of I-70 east for 2.2 mi to the trailhead. Towards the TH you will pass under I-70. In winter, parking is limited to 3 hours (no parking between 11 pm and 7 am for snow removal activities) and the trailhead is located quite a bit down the road just west of the I-70 overpass.

NOTE: Additional free *winter* parking can be found at various locations in the Vail Valley, although some of these areas are quite distant from the trailheads above. Consult www.vailgov.com for more information.

South Gore Range TH: This trailhead is just north of Copper Mountain in a rest/scenic area. From Frisco, drive I-70 for about 5 mi. About a mile before Exit 195 (Copper Mountain), turn into the rest/scenic area. The trailhead can be found here and the Gore Range Trail heads south towards Exit 195 before heading up to the northwest. If approaching from the west, you should drive to Frisco (Exit 201) and turn around and return to access the rest area since this rest/scenic area cannot be accessed from eastbound I-70.

Recommended Routes

Booth Creek Trail: Absolutely spectacular. It is rare for a single trail to have such variety in both vegetation and terrain. The trail takes you first through lush aspen and cow parsnip then you will climb through spruce and fir trees (don't forget to view Booth Falls after 2.0 mi). Finally, you will contour through wildflower-peppered meadows and finish with a rocky ascent to Booth Lake at 11,476 ft. It is a climb of 4.7 mi with 3,050 ft. of elevation gain to Booth Lake.

Pitkin Creek Trail: A steep beginning but then the trail levels out to a large meadow with Pitkin Falls crashing down. Another steep bench (with Upper Pitkin Falls - great campsites here) and the trail finishes at Pitkin Lake, located in a surreal alpine amphitheater. The one-way trip to Pitkin Lake is 4.8 mi and a climb of 2,875 ft.

Booth Creek to Pitkin Creek: It is possible to traverse from the Booth Creek drainage to the Pitkin Creek drainage by utilizing a pass that is southeast of Booth Lake and due west of Pitkin Lake. This pass requires some easy scrambling to ascend so is not for the inexperienced. You will need to walk back along

Near Gore Lake

Eagles Nest Wilderness - Vail Side

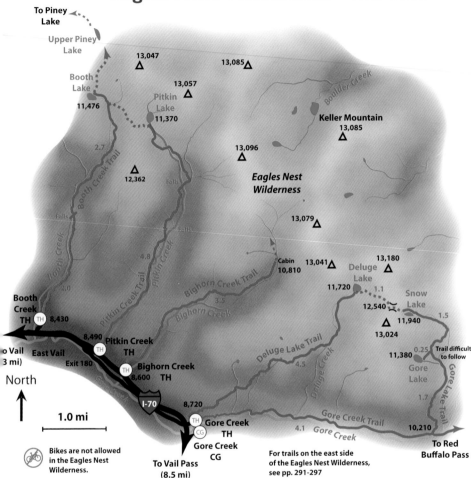

To Piney Lake

Upper Piney Lake

13,047

13,085

Booth Lake

13,057

Pitkin Lake
11,370

11,476

Keller Mountain
13,085

2.7

Booth Creek Trail

13,096

Eagles Nest Wilderness

12,362

Falls

Falls

13,079

Troubh Creek

Falls

4.8

Cabin
10,810

13,041

Deluge Lake

13,180

Snow Lake

11,720

2.0

Pitkin Creek Trail

Bighorn Creek Trail

12,540

11,940

Booth Creek TH 8,430

3.5

Bighorn Creek

13,024

1.5

Trail difficult to follow

8,490 **Pitkin Creek TH**

Deluge Lake Trail

11,380

0.25

o Vail **East Vail**
(3 mi) **Exit 180**

Bighorn Creek TH
8,600

Deluge Creek

4.5

Gore Lake

North

I-70

1.7

1.0 mi

8,720

Gore Creek TH

Gore Creek Trail

4.1 Gore Creek

10,210

Bikes are not allowed in the Eagles Nest Wilderness.

Gore Creek CG

To Vail Pass (8.5 mi)

For trails on the east side of the Eagles Nest Wilderness, see pp. 291–297

To Red Buffalo Pass

the frontage road in Vail from the Pitkin Creek TH to the Booth Creek TH or set up a car shuttle. The entire route is about 11 mi with approximately 3,820 ft. of elevation gain.

Bighorn Creek Trail: Start at the Bighorn Creek TH. The trail climbs steeply for 300 vertical ft., mellows out, then climbs through beautiful aspen forests before the final steep and rocky climb to the final bench, where an old cabin is located. It is a 3.5-mi hike and a gain of 2,200 ft. to the Bighorn cabin.

Bighorn Creek Trail

Snow Lake

Deluge Lake Trail: A steep, very consistent climb to a beautiful lake above treeline. Begin at the Gore Creek TH but take the Deluge Lake Trail. The trail levels out after 2.5 mi for a bit but then the last 0.5 mi gets steep again. 4.5 mi and 3,000 vertical ft. to the lake (at around 11,720 ft., not the 11,178 ft. as shown on most maps). Short but not so sweet.

Gore Lake Trail: Absolutely spectacular, one of my favorite destinations in the Gore Range. Gore Lake is surrounded by jagged peaks, and small streams trickle all around you. Plan to spend some time up here! Start at the Gore

Creek TH and ascend the Gore Creek Trail 4.1 mi to the intersection with the Gore Lake Trail on your left. There is also an old grave located here. Climb steeply up the Gore Lake Trail for 1.9 mi as the trail winds through creeks and meadows and ultimately brings you to around treeline, where the lake sits. 6.0 mi to the lake and a climb of 2,670 ft. The first couple of miles are moderate and are suitable for snowshoers and skiers if you have skins.

Snow Lake: This small lake sits above Gore Lake in a rocky setting. A nice side trip if camped at Gore Lake. The trail is not used often and is difficult to follow at times. A great alpine setting. An additional 600 vertical ft. and 1.5 mi past Gore Lake.

Deluge Creek to Gore Creek: This makes a long yet fulfilling day in the mountains or is a great 2- to 3-day backpack trip. Ascend to Deluge Lake from Gore Creek TH as described above. There is a high pass at around 12,550 ft. to the southeast (not directly east) of Deluge Lake. From the

Storm clearing from the Gore Range

Stormy sunrise near Shrine Pass

lake, a game trail is visible that ascends to the pass. Climb talus then steep grass slopes to gain this trail and take the trail to the saddle. Descend the east side of the pass towards Snow Lake, eventually finding a small cairned trail on the north side of the lake. Take this trail east down the creek then south and southwest, intersecting the Gore Lake Trail. Visit Gore Lake if you wish, then return to Gore Creek TH. Most parties will take 6-10 hours if done in a day, but why rush through this beautiful area?! 4,120 ft. of total elevation gain/loss and 7.3 mi.

Gore Creek Trail to Red Buffalo Pass: Hike just a mile or two or travel all the way to Red Buffalo Pass. As you emerge from the Eisenhower Tunnel and descend I-70 into Dillon, Buffalo Peak looms over Dillon and appears to have been scooped out by a large ice cream scoop; Red Peak is to the right of this and Red Buffalo Pass behind Buffalo Peak. Begin at the Gore Creek TH. The trail follows Gore Creek as it passes by

Gore Creek to Red Buffalo Pass

several short waterfalls. The trail climbs steeply initially through aspen and pine forests, giving way to fir and spruce higher up. You will encounter a mandatory stream crossing at 4.1 mi, depending upon snowmelt and recent rain. Additionally, your feet will likely get wet along the mile of trail after the stream crossing and again at mile 5.8. Jaw-dropping panoramas to the west will reveal themselves and help ease the pain of the final climb out of timberline and up to the pass (6.5 mi). The trail can be difficult to follow above treeline but large cairns mark the trail. Turn around here or continue your adventure – it's up to you! If you are continuing beyond the pass, there is usually a large cornice/snowfield perched on the east side of Red Buffalo Pass. 6.5 mi, 3,000 vertical ft., and 2.5-4 hours to Red Buffalo Pass; less on return trip.

Vail South

Nestled between I-70 on the north and the Shrine Pass Rd. on the south, the south side of Vail offers some great hiking and biking options. Excellent trails can be found on the slopes of the Vail Ski resort and there are some longer and more adventurous routes south of the ski area towards Minturn, Redcliff, and Vail Pass.

Maps: Latitude 40° "Summit County Trails", National Geographic Trails Illustrated "Vail, Frisco, Dillon" (#108), or Sky Terrain's "Summit, Vail, & Holy Cross".

Best Time of Year: Most of the trails described here are relatively high up. As such, they usually are inaccessible after mid to late October, depending on snowfall. The trails on the lower reaches of the Vail ski area may be usable a bit later into the season. The fall colors are spectacular along the trails of the Vail ski area. Wildlife closures exist along the Two Elks Trail as well as the Mill Creek Rd. from May 6 - July 1. Many of these trails, especially Bowman's Shortcut Trail, the Shrine Pass Rd., and the Lime Creek Rd., can be cross country skied in the winter, if you can tolerate snowmobile traffic.

Camping: There are a limited number of informal campsites along the Shrine Pass Rd. The Gore Creek Campground south of Vail is the only official campground in the Vail area. First come, first serve, no reserved sites. For more information, call 970-945-2521. If nothing else, campsites can be found 5-8 mi up the Red Sandstone Rd. or in Summit County.

Access

Vail: Vail is located at Exit 176 of I-70. The East Vail and West Vail exits are Exit 180 and Exit 173, respectively.

Vail Village Parking Structure: Parking is free in this parking structure May through November. From the main Vail exit (Exit 176), follow the S. Frontage Rd. east for about 0.3 mi to the parking structure, which is on your right (south side).

Lionshead Parking Structure: Parking is free here too May through November. From the main Vail exit (Exit 176), follow the S. Frontage Rd. west for about a half mile, the parking structure is on the left (south) side of the road.

10th Mountain Division Huts: Go online to www.huts.org or call the 10th Mountain Division at (970) 925-5775 for more information about the Shrine Mountain Inn (Jay's, Chuck's, and Walter's Cabins) that are near Shrine Pass.

Along the Commando Run in winter

Vail Bus: The town of Vail offers a free bus service throughout the Vail Valley. Visit www. vailgov.com for more information about this great bus service. Use the bus service to set up point-to-point hikes or bike rides. Bikes are allowed on the bus.

Game Creek TH: From the Minturn exit (Dowd's Junction) of I-70 west of Vail (Exit 171), drive south on US 24 into the town of Minturn (1.7 mi), taking a left at Chilly Willy's onto North Main St. Take a right after the Minturn Saloon onto Railroad Ave then veer right onto Taylor Street. Continue to the end of Taylor Street and park at a parking area a hundred yards or so down from the Game Creek TH (no parking right at the TH).

Two Elk East TH: From the East Vail exit of I-70, take the Bighorn Rd. on the south side of I-70 east for 2.3 mi, just past the Gore Creek TH. To get to the official Two Elk East Trailhead, you will need to hike (or bike - bring a bike lock to lock your bike to a tree) 1.9 mi up the paved recreation path. Difficult to get to in winter.

Two Elk West TH: From the Minturn exit (Dowd's Junction) of I-70 west of Vail (Exit 171), drive south on US 24 for 2.7 mi into Minturn and take a left at Cemetery Rd., crossing the bridge and train tracks. Continue to a fork in the road and take the right fork but then at a second fork take a left turn. Park at the end of the road (about 1.8 mi from US 24).

Shrine Pass TH: From the west side of Vail Pass (Exit 190 of I-70), follow signs to the Vail Pass Rest Area. Within a tenth of a mile, turn right onto the Shrine Pass Rd. (FS 709, suitable for 2WD vehicles). Begin measuring here. Drive the Shrine Pass Rd. and park at the parking area at 2.3 mi.

Bowman's TH: Drive to the Shrine Pass TH as described above, measuring from the start of the Shrine Pass Rd. Continue past the Shrine Pass parking area and down to the intersection with the Lime Creek Rd. (FS 728) after 3.8 mi. Take a right and drive up the Lime Creek Rd. (suitable for 2WD vehicles) taking a left at the fork after 4.3 mi and continuing another tenth of a mile (4.4 mi total from Vail Pass) and a sign for Bowman's Shortcut will be on your right. Be sure to park well off the road; there is a good pull-off on the south side of the road.

Vail Pass Rest Area: Just off of I-70 at the Vail Pass exit (Exit 190) on the west side. Park in the upper lot (recreation parking, available daily from 6 am to 7 pm). Restroom facilities and drinking water are available here.

NOTE: $ In winter (roughly late November through early to mid April) the White River National Forest assesses a Vail Pass Winter Recreation Area (VPWRA) fee (daily fee per person or season passes available) to utilize the trails in the Vail Pass, Shrine Pass, and Corral Creek areas. The 55,000-acre area lies roughly west of the Eagle's Nest Wilderness area and Copper Mountain, north of but including Camp Hale, east of US 24 and Red Cliff, and south of the Vail Ski Area. For more information, please visit www.fs.usda.gov and search for Vail Pass Winter Recreation Area.

Recommended Routes

Shrine Pass: It is an easy bike ride, hike, or ski from the Vail Pass Rest Area up the Shrine Pass Rd. to Shrine Pass. In summer, restroom facilities are available at Shrine Pass.

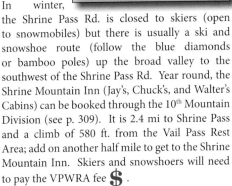

In winter, the Shrine Pass Rd. is closed to skiers (open to snowmobiles) but there is usually a ski and snowshoe route (follow the blue diamonds or bamboo poles) up the broad valley to the southwest of the Shrine Pass Rd. Year round, the Shrine Mountain Inn (Jay's, Chuck's, and Walter's Cabins) can be booked through the 10th Mountain Division (see p. 309). It is 2.4 mi to Shrine Pass and a climb of 580 ft. from the Vail Pass Rest Area; add on another half mile to get to the Shrine Mountain Inn. Skiers and snowshoers will need to pay the VPWRA fee $.

Two Elk Pass

Bowman's Shortcut Trail: Connecting the Lime Creek Rd. to the Vail Ski area, this trail can be taken as an out-and-back or incorporated into longer loop or point-to-point routes. For a short hike or bike, follow Bowman's Shortcut to The Top of the World, a high point overlooking the Vail Valley with superb views of the Gore Range. The bottom portion of this trail is easy but then it steepens as you approach the top. Skiers will need to pay the VPWRA fee **$** .

Shrine Pass Road: The Shrine Pass Rd. connects the town of Redcliff on the west with Vail Pass on the east. This road travels along Turkey Creek and is a popular destination for off-road vehicles and ATVs in the summer and snowmobiles in the winter. However, this road can be a fun bike ride as it is a fairly gradual

climb from Redcliff to Shrine Pass. This road can be driven by most higher clearance 2WD vehicles and is a great way to access the backcountry in this area. Despite the annoying-at-times buzzing of snowmobiles in the winter, cross country skiers will find fast and moderate ski terrain along this road. An easy and fun ski in the winter is to set up a (somewhat long) car shuttle, one car at Vail Pass and another in the town of Redcliff, and cruise the mostly downhill Shrine Pass Rd. from Vail Pass to Redcliff. A great winter weekend getaway is to ski down from Vail Pass to Redcliff, stay the night in Redcliff (several options for lodging), then ski back uphill to Vail Pass the next day. The climb from Redcliff to Vail Pass requires 2,475 ft. of elevation gain (loss of 580 ft.) over 11.7 mi.

Lime Creek Road: A fast road for biking or skiing, also suitable for 2WD vehicles. This is usually incorporated into other adventures. The far west end of the Lime Creek Rd. turns into a very rocky section that descends south to meet the Shrine Pass Rd. This section is not recommended for vehicles other than the burliest 4WD vehicles. Skiers must pay the VPWRA fee **$** .

Commando Run: The 10th Mountain Division ski troops trained on areas of this route, which traverses from Vail Pass to the town of Vail. The route is mostly downhill and a car shuttle is recommended. Skiers should be experienced in avalanche safety and be prepared with

beacons and shovels as this route crosses avalanche terrain (although prudent route-finding can almost alleviate avalanche danger). The Commando Run is a serious winter endeavor. Park one car at Vail Pass Rest Area and another in the town of Vail (one of the two parking structures). From Vail Pass, bike or ski the Shrine Pass Rd. all the way to the Lime Creek Rd. (FS 728) after 3.8 mi. Continue up this road for another 0.6 mi, staying left at a fork at 0.5 mi. Look for the Bowman's Shortcut sign and head up on this singletrack trail. Initially easy but then a steep climb, then the trail contours along ridge tops and descends then climbs again before a final descent to Two Elks Pass. There is a 4-way junction at Two Elks Pass but disregard the left (west) turn since this is an old trail and goes nowhere. From Two

Vail South

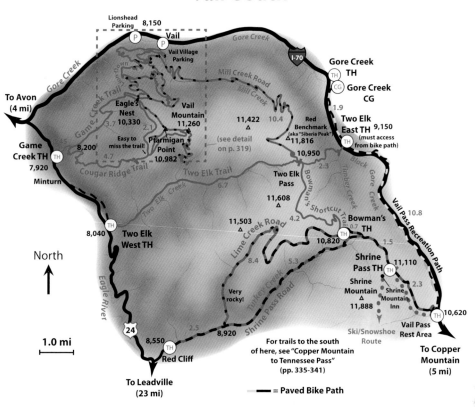

Elks Pass, mountain bikers should ascend the trail and dirt road towards Siberia Peak then descend the Mill Creek Rd. to the town of Vail. Skiers can either ascend the ridge of Siberia Peak directly or an easier and safer alternative (avoids avalanche terrain) is to enter the back bowls of Vail and ascend the cat tracks to the top of the ski area. Skiers will need to pay the VPWRA fee $. An alternative would be to traverse ski maintenance roads west and descend some of the Vail Ski Area trails. From Vail Pass, it is approximately 19.1 mi via the summer route with 3,000 ft. of climbing and 5,000 ft. of descending.

Two Elk Trail

Two Elk Trail: This trail is a designated National Scenic Trail. Spectacular, although the aesthetic value has been slightly diminished because of the Vail Ski Area expansions in recent years. There are many options for hiking or biking the Two Elk Trail. For hikers, it is recommended either to do an out-and-back from either side (east or west) or set up a shuttle (drop a car or bike off at one

Fresh snow in the Vail backcountry

side. Mountain bikers will find it difficult to ascend the east part of this trail from the Vail Valley side, but there are two great bike rides summarized here.

Vail Pass to Minturn via the West Two Elk Trail: This is a great point-to-point ride. Start at Vail Pass and ride to Two Elks Pass as in the Commando Run (see p. 312). Instead of taking the Mill Creek Rd. down to Vail, continue west on the Two Elks Trail to the Two Elks West TH near Minturn. This is a

Vail Pass to Minturn via the West Two Elk Trail

spectacular, organ-tossing descent at times and gets pretty technical and rocky towards the bottom. Nevertheless, it should not be missed. If you don't have a car shuttle set up, ride the Cemetery Rd. out to Minturn, take US 24 to Dowd's Junction, and find the bike path just west of I-70 and return to Vail Pass via bike paths (a long climb!). This route receives the "difficult" rating because of the technical nature of the lower Two Elks Trail as well as for the strenuous climbs up Vail Pass and Bowman's Shortcut. It is 15.4 mi from Vail Pass to the Two Elk East TH with 2,250 ft. of ascent and 4,900 ft. of descent.

East Two Elks Trail

East Two Elks Trail: A shorter alternative to the route just described. Follow the same route as above to Two Elks Pass. Take the right (east) turn and immediately you will descend very steeply down a steep and rocky trail. If biking, your forearms will be burning from squeezing the brakes! Towards the bottom you will ride across three bridges, then a short ascent will leave you at the Two Elks East TH along the Vail Pass recreation path. Either bike down to a car in Vail (either in the town of Vail or near the Gore Creek TH) or bike back up to Vail Pass Rest Area. 11.0 mi and 2,300 ft. of ascent/3,700 ft. of descent from Vail Pass to the East Two Elks TH. If hiking, you'll want to begin at the Two Elks East TH and do a manageable out-and-back hike.

Grand Traverse to Cougar Ridge: This route is best for mountain bikes but there is plenty of hiking in this area. Begin at the base of the Vista Bahn ski lift, located just to the south of the Vail Village Parking Structure. Choose your route to the top of the Eagle Bahn gondola (Eagle's Nest area - see pp. 317-318). It is a long climb, close to 2,000 vertical ft. but the trails  are good. Alternatively, you can purchase a lift pass and take the gondola to the Eagle's Nest area. From Eagle's Nest, find Grand Traverse, which starts near the base of Kloser's Klimb. Traverse along Game Creek Bowl. After exiting Game Creek Bowl on the south side of a broad ridge, be on the lookout for an unmarked trail on the right, shortly *before* crossing under a ski area boundary rope. This is the Cougar Ridge Trail and it takes the ridge down on your right, rolling initially, a few small climbs, then a huge descent with excellent views all the way down to the Game Creek TH in Minturn. Return via bike paths to Vail. Eagle's Nest to Game Creek TH: 600 ft. of climbing (another 2,000 ft. if you start in town), 3000 ft. of descent, 7.2 mi. About another 7 mi return to Vail Village Parking Structure via bike paths.

Fall gives way to winter in the Vail Valley

Game Creek Trail: A nice hike from the town of Minturn to Eagle's Nest in the Vail Ski Area. Grab a bite to eat up at the top for lunch! This trail takes you initially through a somewhat overgrown creek area then climbs to the top of an aspen-covered ridge. Very scenic with views of Mount of the Holy Cross to the  west. Begin at the Game Creek TH in Minturn and after 0.5 mi take a left and ascend the 3.7-mi trail to Eagle's Nest atop the Vail Ski Resort. 2,400 ft. of elevation gain. The bottom parts make for a good snowshoe outing.

Vail Pass Recreation Path: Climb to the top of Vail Pass from Vail or have someone drop you off at the top of Vail Pass and scream down to Vail on this paved and popular bike path. When snow persists in the spring or has shut down trails in the fall, this trail can be a great outing and will challenge even the mightiest biker. This trail also serves as a relatively easy way to get back to Vail Pass if doing some of the more difficult mountain bike rides in the back bowls of Vail if a shuttle cannot be set up. From central Vail (near Exit 176 of I-70) to Vail Pass it is about 16 mi and a climb of around 2,500 ft. of climbing. From Copper Mountain to Vail Pass, it is about 5.5 mi and a climb of around 1,000 ft.

Corral Creek: Great for snowshoers and skiers. The trail changes year to year (and throughout the year!) but begins on the east side of the overpass over I-70 (Exit 190). A small  climb to a high point and then choose your own adventure! Users of this area in winter are required to pay the VPWRA fee.

The Gore Range is an awe-inspiring sight from the slopes of the Vail Ski Area

Along Hank's Hideaway

Vail Ski Area Trails

In summer and fall, there are some super fun trails along the slopes of the Vail Ski Area, ranging from beginner to expert. You can also purchase a day-long gondola ticket to access trails at the top of the slopes or hike/bike to the top yourself. Recommended biking trails include Village Trail, Gitalong Rd., Lion Down, Cub's Way, Fred's Lunch, Onza Alley, and especially Hank's Hideaway. Here are a few recommended loops:

Kloser's Klimb to Grand Traverse Trail: Begin the Kloser's Klimb on the southwest side of the top of Eagle Bahn gondola (see p. 315 "Grand Traverse to Cougar Ridge"). Kloser's Klimb begins as singletrack but then takes doubletrack up and over Ptarmigan Point and east towards the top of Vail Mountain. As you climb the final bit to the top of Vail Mountain, find the

Grand Traverse trail on your right (south). Grand Traverse is only open to mountain bikers and contours along the top of Sundown Bowl then Game Creek Bowl as it returns to Eagle's Nest.

Fred's Lunch/Hank's Hideaway Loop: A great loop for mountain bikers. From the base of the Vista Bahn lift, ascend Village Trail to Mid Vail (or take the gondola to Eagle's Nest and descend to Mid Vail). Descend the primo singletrack of Fred's Lunch as it zigzags down through forests and open slopes, then proceed down Hank's Hole to Gitalong Rd., and ultimately traverse west on Lion Down to the top of Hank's Hideaway (see map). From

Along the Berry Picker Trail, Vail Ski Area

the bottom of Hank's Hideaway you can easily make your way back to the gondola or Vail Village by going north or east, respectively, after a short climb. It is a descent of 2,000 ft. over 5.4 mi from Mid Vail to the base of the Eagle Bahn Gondola.

Berry Picker Trail: Ascending the ski slopes of the Vail Ski Area, the Berry Picker Trail picks its way over roots, through aspen groves, the occasional clearing, and waist- to shoulder-high cow parsnip - a near jungle experience! Higher up, the vegetation thins and the trail zigzags through pine forests and

grassy ski slopes to just east of Eagle's Nest. It is a climb of about 2,200 ft. over 2.9 mi from the bottom of the gondola to Eagle's Nest (west spur) and 2,000 ft. over 3.3 mi via the east spur (near bottom of the Vista Bahn lift).

Additional Wintertime Activities

Vail Nordic Center: Looking for some additional winter-time activities in the Vail area? Check out the Vail Nordic Center, where you can cross country ski on 17 km of groomed trails and snowshoe on 10 km of trails. Rentals and lessons available. The trail fee is very reasonable. Visit www.vailnordiccenter.com for directions and more information.

Vail Ski Area Trails

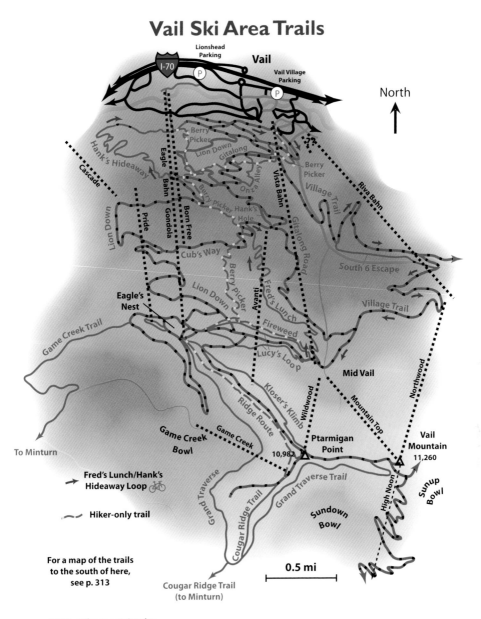

Lionshead Parking

Vail

I-70

Vail Village Parking

North

Berry Picker

Eagle Bahn Gondola

Lion Down

Gitalong

Oh? a Alley

Berry Picker

Vista Bahn

Berry Picker

Village Trail

Riva Bahn

Hank's Hideaway

Cascade

Pride

Born Free

Berry Picker Hank's Hole

Gitalong Road

South 6 Escape

Lion Down

Cub's Way

Berry Picker

Lion Down

Avanti

Fred's Lunch

Village Trail

Eagle's Nest

Fireweed

Lucy's Loop

Game Creek Trail

Kloser's Klimb

Ridge Route

Wildwood

Mid Vail

Mountain Top

Northwood

To Minturn

Game Creek Bowl

Game Creek

10,982

Ptarmigan Point

Vail Mountain 11,260

Fred's Lunch/Hank's Hideaway Loop 🚲

Grand Traverse

Cougar Ridge Trail

Grand Traverse Trail

High Noon

Sunup Bowl

Hiker-only trail

Sundown Bowl

For a map of the trails to the south of here, see p. 313

0.5 mi

Cougar Ridge Trail (to Minturn)

NOTE: Mileages omitted to reduce map clutter.

Vail North

Some of Vail Valley's best hiking and biking trails can be found on the north side of I-70. Specifically, the North Trail system provides many opportunities for shorter hikes and rides or longer link-ups. The Buffehr Creek Trail and the Son of Middle Creek Trail climb higher up the aspen-covered slopes and offer the biker spectacular descents through pine and aspen forests.

Maps: Latitude 40° "Summit County Trails", National Geographic Trails Illustrated "Vail, Frisco, Dillon" (#108), or Sky Terrain's "Summit, Vail, & Holy Cross".

Best Time of Year: This area is relatively low in elevation so is one of the first places to melt out in the spring and one of the last places to get snowed over in the winter. However, despite this area's easy access and long season, the North Trail is closed from April 15 - June 15 and the Son of Middle Creek Trail is closed from May 1 - June 15 for elk calving and soil protection during seasonal runoff. Due to the abundant aspen trees in the area, the North Trail makes a spectacular venue for fall hiking and biking exploits.

Camping: The Gore Creek Campground south of Vail is the only official campground in the Vail area. First come, first serve, no reserved sites. For more information, call 970-945-2521. Free camping in the Vail area is somewhat limited unless you are willing to drive a bit. There are many informal campsites 8.5-9.7 mi up the Red Sandstone Rd. just before the Piney Lake area. The Piney Crossing Campground seen on many maps is currently closed

Winter sunrise near the Ben Eiseman Hut with Vail ski slopes in the distance

Ben Eiseman Hut in summer

due to beetle kill logging as are campsites near Piney Lake. The Moniger Rd. (FS 701) has abundant campsites as well; this road branches off of the Red Sandstone Rd. to the west at about 7.2 mi from Vail.

Access

Vail: Vail is located at Exit 176 of I-70. The East Vail and West Vail exits are Exit 180 and Exit 173, respectively.

10th Mountain Division Huts: Go online to www.huts.org or call the 10th Mountain Division for more information about Shrine Mountain Inn and the Ben Eiseman Hut that are both in the Vail area.

Vail Bus: The town of Vail offers a free bus service throughout the Vail Valley. Stops range all along the valley floor, including stops up Bighorn Rd. (the last stop very close to the Gore Creek TH), near the base of Pitkin and Booth Creeks, the base area of the Vail Ski area, various stops in Vail Village, Red Sandstone Rd., and the Trappers Run TH area. Please visit www.vailgov.com for more information about this great bus service. The bus service is a great way to set up point-to-point hiking and biking adventures. Bikes are allowed on the bus.

Tina Lewis, North Trail

NOTE: For the five North Trail access points below, parking is limited to 3 hours and there is no parking allowed between 11 pm and 7 am. The trailheads are open in the winter.

Trapper's Run TH: From the roundabout on the north side of the West Vail exit (Exit 173) of I-70, follow the frontage road 0.3 mi to the trailhead.

Cortina Lane Trailhead: There is no parking here, but this neighborhood street provides access to the North Trail. From the Trapper's Run TH, continue up Arosa Drive 0.3 mi and take a left on Davos Trail, follow Davos Trail a short distance and take a right on Cortina Lane. Follow Cortina Lane another 0.3 mi and the pavement turns to dirt. This can be followed a short way to gain access to the North Trail.

Buffehr Creek TH: From the roundabout on the north side of the West Vail exit (Exit 173) of I-70, follow Chamonix Rd. 0.2 mi north and take a right on Chamonix Lane. Follow Chamonix Lane another 0.2 mi and take a left on Buffehr Creek Rd. Follow this for yet another 0.2 mi, continue straight at a stop sign and the trailhead is up a short distance on the left.

Red Sandstone TH: From the roundabout on the north side of the West Vail exit (Exit 173) of I-70, follow the frontage road east 0.9 mi to Red Sandstone Rd. Take a right at Red Sandstone Rd. and go north for 0.4 mi and at a hairpin turn in the road the Red Sandstone TH is on your left. You can also access Red Sandstone Rd. from the main Vail exit (Exit 176) by taking the north side frontage road 1.0 mi from the roundabout.

Spraddle Creek TH (aka Middle Creek TH): From the roundabout on the north side of the main Vail exit (Exit 176), take the Spraddle Creek Rd. a short tenth of a mile to the trailhead.

Red Sandstone Winter Gate: The winter closure gate for Red Sandstone Rd. currently differs from what is shown on most maps. Follow directions to the Red Sandstone TH. Continue another 0.9 mi on the Red Sandstone Rd., staying left (straight) when the road turns to dirt. The winter closure is located at a sharp left turn. Parking is available here throughout the year and is most popular for utilizing the North Trail and/or the Son of Middle Creek Trail.

Vail North

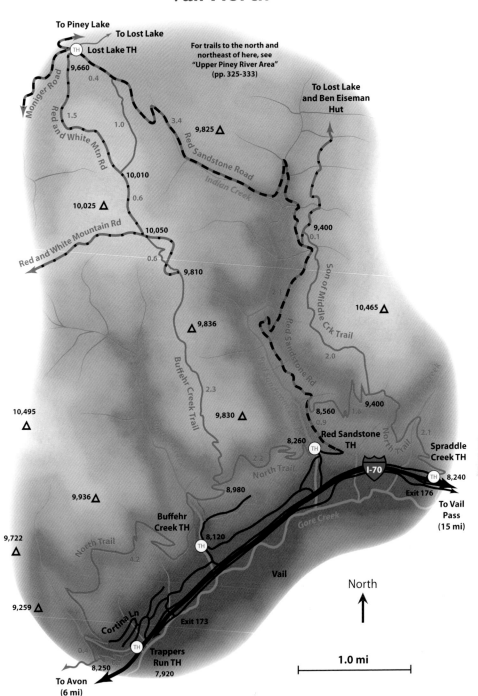

To Piney Lake

To Lost Lake

Lost Lake TH
9,660

Moniger Road

Red and White Mtn Rd

0.4

1.5   1.0   3.4

For trails to the north and
northeast of here, see
"Upper Piney River Area"
(pp. 325-333)

9,825

Red Sandstone Road

To Lost Lake
and Ben Eiseman
Hut

Indian Creek

10,010

10,025   0.6

Red and White Mountain Rd

10,050   9,400
0.1

0.6

9,810

Son of Middle Crk Trail

10,465

2.1

9,836

2.0

Red Sandstone Rd

Buffehr Creek Trail

2.3

9,830

9,400

10,495   8,560   1.6

Red Sandstone
TH   North Trail   2.1

8,260

9,936   North Trail   2.2   Spraddle
Creek TH
8,240

I-70

Exit 176

8,980

9,722   Buffehr
Creek TH
8,120   To Vail
Pass
(15 mi)

North Trail   Gore Creek

4.2   Vail

9,259   North

Cortina Ln

Exit 173

Trappers
Run TH
7,920

8,250

To Avon
(6 mi)   1.0 mi

Recommended Routes

Red Sandstone Road: A moderate dirt road that provides access to the northwestern part of the Gore Range and the Piney Lake area. In winter, the road is popular among snowmobilers but skiers and snowshoers can utilize the road as a nice winter excursion or to access ski terrain near the Ben Eiseman Hut.

North Trail: A spectacular trail winding its way mainly through aspen groves, grass, and evergreen forests along the north side of the Vail Valley from Spraddle Creek down to Trapper's Run in West Vail. There are five access points (see trailheads on p. 322) for accessing the trail. There are several steep hills but they are short. Approximate one-way distances between trailheads: Spraddle Creek TH to Red Sandstone TH: 4.6 mi; Red Sandstone TH to Buffehr Creek TH: 3.2 mi; Buffehr Creek TH to Trappers Run TH: 4.7 mi. **NOTE:** The North Trail is closed from April 15 - June 15.

Son of Middle Creek Trail: Great singletrack hiking and biking trail through aspens and pine. If on bike, ride up the Red Sandstone Rd., take a right at the Lost Lake Rd., and after 0.15 mi the Son of Middle Creek Trail is found on the right. Follow this

down for 2.0 mi to a junction with the North Trail. **NOTE:** The Son of Middle Creek Trail is closed from May 1 - June 15.

Buffehr Creek Trail: Hikers will want to do an out-and-back (up-and-down) of the Buffehr Creek Trail from the North Trail. Begin at the Buffehr Creek TH, ascend the North Trail east, then climb the Buffehr Creek Trail from there. A nice loop for mountain bikers is one that starts from Red Sandstone TH. Ride the Red Sandstone Rd. way up to 0.4 mi before the West Lost Lake TH. This comes 0.6 mi after a pair of switchbacks in the Red Sandstone Rd. At this point, look for a marked singletrack trail on your left. Take this 1.0 mi and it spits you out on the Red and White Mountain Rd. Or take the Red and White Mountain Rd. from the Red Sandstone Rd. Regardless, you are looking for a sharp switchback in the Red and White Mountain Rd. with a road leaving to the left. There should be a sign for Buffehr Creek Trail. Either take the singletrack located on the right several hundred yards down or take the road; both lead to the same place and will take you to the Buffehr Creek Trail. Nothing but spectacular singletrack through aspen groves until you intersect the North Trail. Go left (east) to the Red Sandstone TH or right (west) to the Buffehr Creek TH. From the Red and White Mountain Rd., it is a descent of just over a thousand vertical feet over 3.0 mi to the intersection with the North Trail. It is another 2.2 mi back to the Red Sandstone TH, where many folks will park. The loop is 13.1 mi with 2,100 ft. of climbing and descent.

Upper Piney River Area

Nestled in an idyllic Colorado mountain valley on the west side of the rugged Gore Range is the Upper Piney River area. This region, generally speaking, contains the headwaters for the Piney River, which ultimately winds its way northwest where it intersects the mighty Colorado River near the town of State Bridge. Ranging from jagged and remote thirteen thousand foot peaks like Mount Powell to creekside trails around Piney Lake to the overlooks of Red & White Mountain, this area boasts some of the best hiking around and bikers will have plenty of options to choose from. In winter, skiers will enjoy the trip to the Ben Eiseman Hut. The northern-central part of this area, which consists of areas north and west of Piney Crossing TH, are not well traveled but can be explored by the adventurous.

Maps: Latitude 40° "Summit County Trails", National Geographic Trails Illustrated "Vail, Frisco, Dillon" (#108), or Sky Terrain's "Summit, Vail, & Holy Cross".

Best Time of Year: The trails in this area receive significant snowfall during the winter. Depending on snowfall, most of these trails will be accessible by mid to late June with the higher trails like the Upper Piney Trail drying up a few weeks later.

Magnificent views north from Red and White Mountain towards the Lower Piney River area

(pp. 326-327: Fall in the Piney River area)

Camping: There are many informal campsites 8.5-9.7 mi up the Red Sandstone Rd. just before the Piney Lake area. The Piney Crossing Campground seen on many maps is currently closed due to beetle kill logging as are campsites near Piney Lake. The Moniger Rd. (FS #701) has abundant campsites as well. This road branches off of the Red Sandstone Rd. to the west at about 7.2 mi from Vail.

Access

Vail: Vail is located at Exit 176 of I-70. The East Vail and West Vail exits are Exit 180 and Exit 173, respectively.

Ben Eiseman Hut: Bike to this 10th Mountain Division Hut for the day or stay the night. High-clearance vehicles can make it to just below the hut. Excellent views, a well-traveled 4WD road. From the roundabout on the north side of the West Vail exit (Exit 173) of I-70, follow the frontage road east 0.9 mi to Red Sandstone Rd. Take the Red Sandstone Rd. 3.3 mi from Vail to a road intersection. Take a right here (Lost Lake Rd. - FS 786) and after 1.3 mi there is a fork - the Lost Lake Rd. continues straight (left) and FS 719 climbs up and to the right. Turn right and climb and additional 4.9 mi up to the hut. If driving this road, there is a parking area just before the hut; a short 0.1 mi hike in will bring you to the hut. The hut is open but you cannot drive to it in winter. Visit www.huts.org for information about reserving this fantastic ski hut.

East Lost Lake TH: A high clearance vehicle is required to get to this trailhead, which provides access to the east side of Lost Lake. Follow directions above for the Ben Eiseman Hut but instead of taking a right onto FS 719, continue left (straight) and drive the Lost Lake Rd. (FS 786), taking a left after 1.5 mi in a clearing. Continue another 1.4 rocky mi to the trailhead.

Lost Lake TH: From the roundabout on the north side of the West Vail exit (Exit 173) of I-70, follow the frontage road east 0.9 mi to Red Sandstone Rd. Take a right at Red Sandstone Rd. and reset your odometer here. When the road turns from pavement to dirt after 0.8 mi, stay left (straight). Continue on the Red Sandstone Rd. for a total of 7.2 mi; the road ascends, descends, then ascends again and shortly after a few switchbacks in the road the Lost Lake TH is on your right (east side of road) at the top of a flat area.

Piney Lake TH: Shortly after the Lost Lake TH, the Red and White Mountain Rd. (FS 734) splits off to the left (south), the Moniger Rd. (FS 700) also splits off to the left (southwest) and the Red Sandstone Rd. (FS 701) continues north. Continue on the Red Sandstone Rd. as it descends several switchbacks and makes its way to the Piney Crossing TH just after the road crosses the Piney River (2.5 mi from the Lost Lake TH). Continue east along the Piney River (follow signs for Piney River Ranch) for 1.4 mi to a parking area

Along the upper part of Piney River

Upper Piney River Area

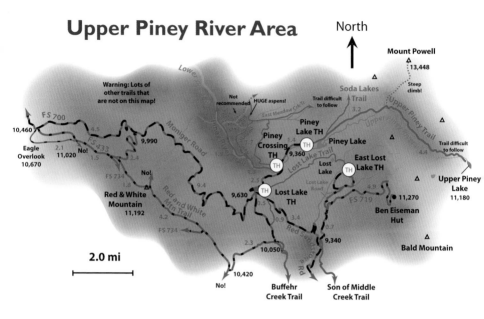

just outside the private Piney River Ranch. The Upper Piney Trail begins just to the north of this parking area across the dirt road.

Piney Crossing TH: From the roundabout on the north side of the West Vail exit (Exit 173) of I-70, follow the frontage road east 0.9 mi to Red Sandstone Rd. Take a right at Red Sandstone Rd. and reset your odometer here. When the road turns from pavement to dirt after 0.8 mi, stay left (straight). After 7.2 mi, the Moniger Rd. (FS 700) splits off to the left. Continue on the Red Sandstone Rd. (FS 701) for another 2.5 mi to the Piney Crossing TH just after the road crosses the Piney River.

Recommended Routes

Lost Lake Trail: A nice hike or bike. Start from either the Lost Lake TH along the Red Sandstone Rd. or from the East Lost Lake TH at the end of Lost Lake Rd. (FS 786). Both trails bring you to Lost Lake, nestled among pine trees with excellent views of the Gore Range peaks. The hike is 0.7 mi from the East Lost Lake TH and about 3.3 mi from the Lost Lake TH along Red Sandstone Rd.

Upper Piney Trail: This is spectacular, classic Colorado. Begin at the Piney Lake TH. Hike along the west side of Piney Lake and continue up the valley. The trail ascends gradually through aspen forests and grass with magnificent views of the river valley below. Shortly after a small descent you will find some small waterfalls. This is a great place for a picnic. If you are inclined and are adventurous, continue up the valley. There are lots of marshes and streams so your feet will definitely get wet! The trail is difficult to follow at times but persevere and you will be rewarded with a surreal alpine lake surrounded by high jagged peaks - Upper Piney Lake. This makes a great backpacking trip. About 3 mi (1 hr.) to the waterfalls; 3-4.5 hours to Upper Piney Lake (7.6 mi). Rated "difficult" for hike to Upper Piney Lake; easy hike to the waterfalls. *Variation:* The Booth Lake area can be accessed from the Upper Piney Lake area - the only thing separating the two drainages is a steep, 12,100-ft. pass. Great for an extended backpacking trip.

Mount Powell: A difficult high 13,000-ft. peak, only for those experienced with peak climbing. Just past the waterfalls along the Piney River Trail, there are several trails leaving to the left (north). The trails are marked with cairns and they all lead essentially to the same place - up! The trail climbs very steeply

and ultimately makes its way to a saddle below the summit. Follow the ridge to the top, a great climb but requires a lot of energy.

The Piney River snakes its way to Piney Lake

Piney Lake at sunset

Looking up at The Spider from the Upper Piney Trail

Red, White, and Bruised: This is a big bike ride, especially if you aren't able to set up a shuttle. Grab some friends or convince a shuttlebunny to help out with this one. A map and compass and the ability to use them is a must as there are many forks and unmarked roads going off here and there. Use the map on the opposite page for the exact route and mileages but be warned that there are lots of roads going here and there that are not shown on the map. Begin at the west end of Red and White Mountain Rd. (FS 734) at its junction with FS 700, also know as the Moniger Rd. (see map). Either take the Red and White Mountain Rd. or a better, more scenic, alternative is to take an unmarked road just south of this junction southwest to Eagle Overlook. At a junction with the Red and White Mountain Rd. go left (north) for a short ways to another junction with FS 433. Continue right (east) and you will come to another junction; stay on FS 433. At yet another junction, FS 433 will descend down (north); shortly after this, you will want to take a right on a road (unmarked) and continue on this until the doubletrack ends and obscure singletrack begins (again, stay on the ridge). Routefinding is difficult but stay on the ridge. Finally, you will arrive near the summit of Red and White Mountain. The trail descends in the trees and contours east and you arrive at another road intersection with a view of the red and white sandstone cliffs that the mountain is named for. Take a right and descend way down and continue through rolling terrain to the intersection with the Red and White Mountain Rd. (FS 734). Go left (southeast) to an intersection, continuing left (east then north) on FS 734. You will come to a sharp left turn in the road with another road going right; continue down the Buffehr Creek Trail as in the description on p. 324. A big day but worth it! 17.5 mi and 2,100 ft./4,400 ft. of elevation gain/loss for the one-way trip. Rated "difficult" because of the strenuous nature but not technically difficult.

Piney River Trail: This trail follows the lower Piney River, below Piney Crossing (below Piney Lake). Begin at the Piney Crossing TH and follow the Piney River Trail as it descends nearly 500 vertical ft. and 3.2 mi to some old ruins in a pristine meadow. The Piney River Trail continues north from these ruins.

Piney Crossing Trail: Follows an old road west and north from the Piney Crossing TH, linking up to the East Meadow Creek Trail.

Fall in the Piney River area

Sunset on Copper Mountain

Copper Mountain to Tennessee Pass

Unbeknownst to many high country travelers is a hidden pocket of wilderness located to the south and west of Vail Pass and Copper Mountain extending west to Camp Hale and south to Tennessee Pass. The Colorado Trail from Copper Mountain to Tennessee Pass is an exciting leg that is open to both hikers and mountain bikers and will bring you to remote areas with excellent views of the Gore Range to the north, the Tenmile Range to the southeast, and the Sawatch Range to the south. There are several doubletrack roads that make excellent routes for mountain biking in the summer and fall and for skiing in the winter. There are additional snowmobile-packed ski routes, making this a great place to cross country ski and snowshoe in winter.

The history of Camp Hale is quite interesting. Camp Hale was a military base initiated in 1942 that trained the 10th Mountain Division Ski troops for cold and mountainous conditions until 1945. Many of the ski troops saw action in the Italian Alps during WWII. On the night of February 18th, 1945, the troops surprised the Germans by scaling a 1,500-ft. face of Riva Ridge that was thought impossible to climb; thus, the Germans had only protected the ridge with a single battalion. The Germans were caught off guard and the troops were able to conquer Riva Ridge. This led to the subsequent securement of Mt. Belvedere, which in turn was instrumental in ousting the Germans from Italy. The 10th Mountain Division suffered one of the highest casualty rates of any division in the war (in 114 days of fighting, 992 troops were killed and 4,154 were wounded). From 1959 to 1965, the CIA secretly trained 259 Tibetan guerrillas at Camp Hale.

Maps: Sky Terrain's "Summit, Vail, & Holy Cross" or you will need both the National Geographic Trails Illustrated "Vail, Frisco, Dillon" (#108) and "Breckenridge/Tennessee Pass" (#109).

Best time of the year: This area is relatively high in elevation compared to other places nearby. The best time of year for hiking and mountain biking is late June through early October, depending upon snowfall. Once the snow starts to fall (usually November through April), there are many cross country ski opportunities here. Several backcountry ski huts lie in this area (see "10th Mountain Division Huts below), contributing to this region's popularity among backcountry skiers and snowshoers in winter.

Camping: Informal campsites can be found along the Shrine Pass Rd. as well as the Camp Hale area. The Tigiwon, Hornsilver, Blodgett, Camp Hale, and East Fork (also at Camp Hale) Campgrounds are nearby; visit www.recreation.gov for information and to reserve a site.

10th Mountain Division Huts: There are several 10th Mountain Division Huts in this area. Equipped with wood-burning stoves, propane stoves for cooking, dishes, and more, these huts provide a rustic but very comfortable experience to backcountry travelers. Normally open during the winter season, some of them are available in summer too and would provide stop-over points on multi-day excursions. Go online to www.huts.org or call the 10th Mountain Division at (970) 925-5775 for more information. Huts in the Copper Mountain/Tennessee Pass area include Janet's Cabin, the Shrine Mountain Inn (3 cabins), the Fowler-Hilliard Hut (re-built in the fall of 2010 after it burned down), and the Jackal Hut. Janet's Cabin is owned by the Summit Huts Association (www.summithuts.org).

Evening light near Fremont Pass

Access

Copper Mountain: Copper Mountain is located at Exit 195 of I-70. This is about 5 mi west of Frisco and 19 mi east of Vail.

Leadville: From Copper Mountain, drive south on HWY 91 for 23 mi over Fremont Pass to the town of Leadville. If approaching from the south, Leadville is located 35 mi north of Buena Vista on US 24.

Minturn: Minturn is located 2 mi south of I-70 Exit 171, which is about 7 mi west of Vail (see directions to Vail on p. 328) and 55 mi east of Glenwood Springs.

Red Cliff: From Minturn, drive south on US 24 for about 8 mi. Just

Janet's Cabin

before the big bridge across the river, take a left onto High Rd. and proceed about a half mile to Red Cliff. Park on side streets in town (obey parking signs) or find the Shrine Pass Rd. (aka Turkey Creek Rd.) on the northeast side of town and drive up this to a parking area near a water tank (1.0 mi from town). In winter, you will need to start in town.

Wheeler Flats TH: Take I-70 to Exit 195 (Copper Mountain). At the stoplight south of the interstate, take a left and drive past the Conoco gas station for 0.4 mi to the Wheeler Flats TH.

Union Creek TH: The Union Creek TH provides access to the Colorado Trail and the Vail Pass paved bike path. **In summer:** Take I-70 to Exit 195 (Copper Mountain). At the stoplight south of the interstate, take a right onto Copper Rd. and drive on Copper Rd. for 1.2 mi to the Union Creek Lot on the right side of the road. The Union Creek TH is located just west of here near the river. **In winter:** Park at the Alpine and Far East parking lots at the base of the mountain just southwest of the stoplight at HWY 91 and Copper Rd. then take the free shuttle to Union Creek TH.

Shrine Pass TH: From the west side of Vail Pass (Exit 190 of I-70), follow signs to the Vail Pass Rest Area. Within a tenth of a mile, turn right onto the Shrine Pass Rd.

(FS 709, suitable for 2WD vehicles). Begin measuring here. Drive the Shrine Pass Rd. and park at the parking area atop a high saddle area after 2.3 mi. There are toilets here.

Max Nuttelman skiing to the Fowler-Hilliard Hut

Vail Pass Rest Area: Just off of I-70 at the Vail Pass exit (Exit 190) on the west side. Park in the upper lot (recreation parking, available daily from 6 am to 7 pm). Restroom facilities and drinking water are available here.

Camp Hale TH/Pando TH: From Minturn, drive south on US 24 (10th Mountain Division Memorial Highway) for about 13.5 mi to CR 702, just after crossing a bridge over the railroad tracks. Take a left here (this is the Pando TH, which is used in winter to access the Fowler-Hilliard Hut), veer right after 0.1 mi, and continue on CR 702 (Resolution Mountain Rd.) for a total of 1.1 mi. Take a right onto CR 714 and drive about 2.2 mi to an obvious trailhead on your left or another parking area after another 0.7 mi. Alternatively, 0.1 mi back from the first parking area, you can take a right (south) and go 0.3 mi to another access point for the Colorado Trail at a 90° right turn, just north of the East Fork of the Eagle River. In winter, continue on US 24 for an additional 1.6 mi past CR 702 to a plaque and stone gates; park here or at another parking area 0.7 mi south on US 24. These two parking areas provide closer access to the southeast part of Camp Hale in winter.

Tennessee Pass TH: Tennessee Pass is located approximately 20 mi south of Minturn and about 10 mi northwest of Leadville on US 24. Atop the pass on the west side of the highway is an obvious parking area and trailhead used to access the Colorado Trail.

Recommended Routes

NOTE #1: 💲 In winter (roughly late November through early to mid April) the White River National Forest assesses a Vail Pass Winter Recreation Area (VPWRA) fee ($6 per day per person; season passes available for $40) to utilize the trails in the Vail Pass, Shrine Pass, and Corral Creek areas. The 55,000-acre area lies roughly west of the Eagle's Nest Wilderness area and Copper Mountain, north of but including Camp Hale, east of US 24 and Red Cliff, and south of the Vail Ski Area. For more information, please visit www.fs.usda.gov and search for Vail Pass Winter Recreation Area.

Copper Mountain to Tennessee Pass

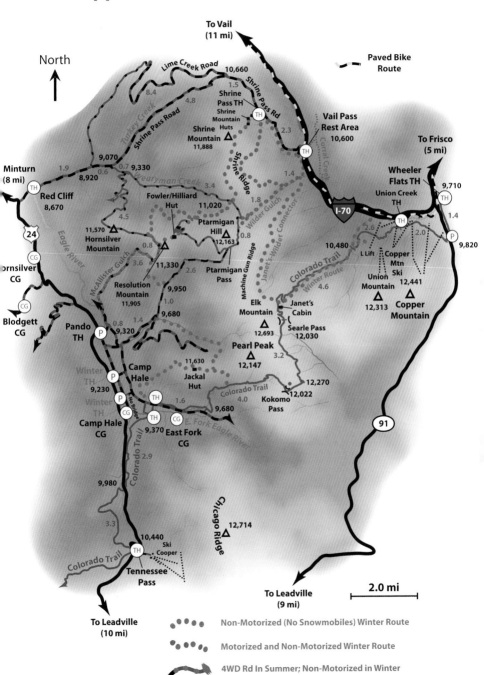

North

To Vail
(11 mi)

Paved Bike
Route

Lime Creek Road   10,660
8.4   1.5
4.8   Shrine
Pass TH
Shrine
Mountain   Huts
Shrine   11,888
Mountain
2.3

Vail Pass
Rest Area
10,600

To Frisco
(5 mi)

Minturn
(8 mi)   1.9   9,070   0.7   9,330   3.4   1.4

Wheeler
Flats TH   9,710
Union Creek
TH   1.4

Red Cliff   8,920   0.6
8,670

Fowler/Hilliard
Hut   11,020   1.8

Ptarmigan
Hill
12,163   0.8

10,480

L Lift   2.6   2.0   P
9,820

Hornsilver   11,570
Mountain   0.8   11,330   2.6

Copper
Mtn
Ski
12,441

Resolution
Mountain
11,905   9,950   1.0

Union
Mountain
12,313

Copper
Mountain

ornsilver
CG

Pando TH   0.8   1.4   9,320   9,680

Janet's
Cabin

Searle Pass
12,030

Blodgett
CG

Elk
Mountain
12,693

Camp
Hale   11,630   Pearl Peak
12,147   3.2

Winter
TH   9,230   Jackal
Hut   1.6   12,270
12,022

Winter
TH   9,370   East Fork
CG   4.0   Kokomo
Pass

Camp Hale
CG   2.9

9,680

91

9,980

3.3   12,714

10,440
Ski
Cooper

Tennessee
Pass

To Leadville
(9 mi)

2.0 mi

To Leadville
(10 mi)

•••• Non-Motorized (No Snowmobiles) Winter Route

•••• Motorized and Non-Motorized Winter Route

4WD Rd In Summer; Non-Motorized in Winter

The Tenmile Range from the Copper Mountain area

NOTE #2: There are numerous dirt roads in this area that can be hiked or biked in summer through fall and there are several designated non-motorized trails in the VPWRA. Not all of these trails are discussed in this section, but many are denoted on the map on p. 339.

Colorado Trail: The Colorado Trail out of Copper Mountain makes a great out-and-back day hike to Kokomo Pass. Or, continue on the trail to Searle Pass and beyond to Camp Hale. Access at the Wheeler Flats, Union Creek, or Camp Hale trailheads. You can also access the Colorado Trail about 1.0 mi south of Copper Mountain along HWY 91; there is a small parking area on the east side of the highway. A larger group could set up a shuttle quite easily and leave one car at Camp Hale. It is 19.3 mi from Copper Mountain to Camp Hale via the Colorado Trail with 3,500 ft./3,800 ft. of elevation gain/loss.

Shrine Pass Road: The Shrine Pass Rd. is great for mountain biking adventures in summer and fall and cross country ski touring adventures in winter. Start at Vail Pass or in the town of Red Cliff and explore this road. Heavy ATV use at times. Snowmobiles use this road in

winter but there are numerous side roads going this way and that to explore. In winter, there is a skier/snowshoe route down in the broad drainage to the west of the Shrine Pass Rd. The road is snowmobile-only until Shrine Pass.

Shrine Ridge Trail: A short hike to a scenic ridge that overlooks Mount of the Holy Cross to the west and the Gore Range to the northeast. Bikes are not permitted. An easy hike in the summer, moderate ski/snowshoe in the winter (there are a few avalanche prone slopes in winter).

Wilder Gulch Trail: A single-track hiking trail in summer closed to mechanized transportation but becomes a snowcat-groomed snowmobile route in winter. This trail provides access to the Ptarmigan Pass area and is a common access route for the Fowler-Hilliard Hut in winter. The lower sections of this trail is relatively easy and is great for beginners. Watch for snowmobiles!

Janet's Cabin: Regardless of whether you are staying here overnight or not, the ski up Guller Creek in winter is spectacular. Begin at the Union Creek TH (park at the Alpine or Far East parking lot and take the free shuttle to Union Creek TH in winter). From Union

Creek TH, ski up the far west (right) side of Roundabout ski run to the base of the L lift, then the far west side of "West Tenmile" run. At about 10,640 ft., a gate leads out of the resort. Follow blue diamonds all the way up Guller Creek to near treeline, which is where Janet's Cabin sits. Please do not go into the cabin if you are day-trippers (not paying guests). Janet's Cabin can also be accessed via Vail Pass, although this is not a popular route.

Fowler-Hilliard Hut: Similar to the trip to Janet's Cabin, the trip to the Fowler-Hilliard Hut is a fun winter outing, although tough. From the Pando TH on the north side of Camp Hale, ski or snowshoe up McAllister Gulch (jeep road in summer) to below Resolution Mountain. The trail leaves the road and traverses the north side of Resolution Mountain before dropping down to the hut. The cabin can also be accessed from Vail Pass via Wilder Gulch and winter ski and snowmobile routes.

The newly rebuilt Fowler-Hilliard Hut; the old one burned down in the summer of 2009

Charlie's Picks for the Vail & Copper Mountain Area

1. Upper Piney Trail (p. 331)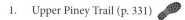

2. Gore Lake (p. 307)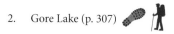

3. Booth Creek Trail (p. 304)

4. North Trail (p. 324)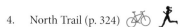

5. Commando Run (p. 312)

6. Vail Pass to Minturn via the West Two Elk Trail (p. 314)

7. Deluge Lake Trail (p. 307)

8. Grand Traverse to Cougar Ridge (p. 315)

9. Colorado Trail from Copper Mountain (p. 340)

10. Snow Lake (p. 307)

In the backcountry near Ptarmigan Pass

Summer sunset, near Rabbit Ears Peak

Chapter 9: Steamboat Springs

Tucked away in a quaint valley in the northern part of the state, the greater Steamboat Springs area has a uniqueness that sets it apart from other mountain communities of Colorado. Relatively low-lying for a ski town, Steamboat Springs is only at an elevation of about 6,700 ft. However, the slopes of the Steamboat Ski Resort climb steeply from the valley floor with Mount Werner rising to an impressive 10,568 ft. The region has a rich trapping and ranching history and is without a doubt one of the state's cross country skiing centers. Howelsen Hill Ski Area is still the training center for many Olympic ski jumpers and Nordic skiers. In fact, more skiers have been sent to international competition from Howelsen than any other ski resort in North America and more than 64 Olympians have trained here. A variety of hiking and mountain biking trails can be found all over the Steamboat Springs area with some of the area's best trails within minutes of town. If you are attracted to the serene and pristine nature of wilderness areas, the nearby Mount Zirkel Wilderness is well worth the drive. After a day full of activity and adventure, be sure to soak your weary legs in the Old Town Hot Springs in town or the Strawberry Park Hot Springs located north of town.

Steamboat Springs

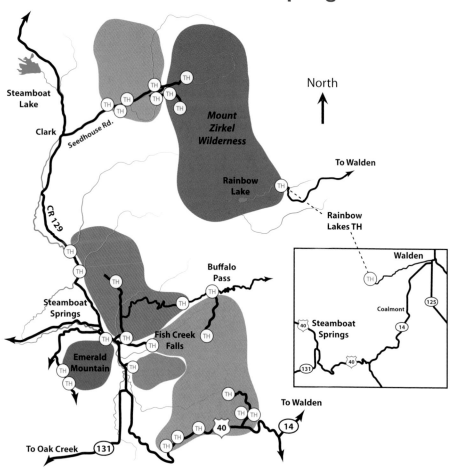

North ↑

Steamboat Lake
Clark
Seedhouse Rd.
CR 129

Mount Zirkel Wilderness

Rainbow Lake
To Walden
Rainbow Lakes TH

Buffalo Pass

Steamboat Springs
Fish Creek Falls
Emerald Mountain

To Oak Creek   131

To Walden

40   14

Walden
Coalmont   125
40   Steamboat Springs   14
131   40

Steamboat Ski Resort (Mout Werner) (pp. 345-351)

Rabbit Ears Pass to Buffalo Pass (pp. 352-364)

Howelson Hill & Emerald Mountain (pp. 365-370)

Steamboat Springs North (pp. 371-376)

North Routt County (pp. 377-384)

Mount Zirkel Wilderness (pp. 385-393)

The Steamboat Ski Resort slopes in summer

Steamboat Ski Resort (Mt. Werner)

The slopes of the Steamboat Ski Resort offer year-round recreational opportunities in an extraordinary setting. In summer, start your hiking or mountain biking adventures at the base of the resort (6,900 ft.) or purchase a ticket and take the gondola to Thunderhead (9,080 ft.) and begin there. Many folks like to hike or bike down the trails from Thunderhead. There are several hiker- and biker-only as well as multi-use trails of varying ability that climb above Thunderhead. In winter, snowshoeing presents an alternative to downhill skiing; several snowshoe trails crisscross ski slopes and adjacent areas. Like in summer, you can ride the gondola and begin your adventure at Thunderhead, where you can grab a bite to eat. Regardless of the season, the view of the Steamboat valley far below is impressive!

Maps: Sky Terrain Maps "Steamboat Springs & Mt. Zirkel" or National Geographic Trails Illustrated "Clark, Buffalo Pass" (#117) and "Steamboat Springs, Rabbit Ears Pass" (#118). The Routt County Riders "Steamboat Springs Mountain Bike Map", available in local outdoor stores, is also an excellent map, most suitable for mountain biking in this area.

Best time of the year: Outdoor recreation opportunities abound on the slopes of the Steamboat Ski Resort in summer and winter. Trails are generally open in late May or early June but some of the trails, especially atop Mt. Werner, can be closed even through late July, depending upon the previous winter's snowfall. The gondola is open daily from mid June through Labor Day weekend, in general, on weekends through the end of September, weather permitting, and again during ski season (late November through early April). The aspen trees in the area display their fall colors in late September, and this is a great time of year to explore these trails. Winter trails can be utilized from late November through early April. Please visit www.steamboat.com for up-to-date summer and winter trail conditions and more information about recreation at the Steamboat Ski Resort.

Camping: Several National Forest Campgrounds are located within 10-20 mi or so of Steamboat Springs. These include the Dry Lake, Summit Lake, and Granite Campgrounds in the vicinity of Buffalo Pass and the Buffalo Pass Rd., the Dumont Lake Campground on Rabbit Ears Pass, and the Seedhouse and Hinman Campgrounds along Seedhouse Rd. northeast of Clark (north of Steamboat Springs on CR 129. Additional informal and dispersed camping can be found on National Forest lands in the region. Contact the Routt National Forest at (970) 870-2299 for more information about campgrounds; some of these campgrounds can be reserved at www.recreation.gov.

Access

Directions to Steamboat Springs: Steamboat Springs is located approximately 150 mi from Denver. From the intersection of C-470 and I-70 in the foothills west of Denver, take I-70 west for 56 mi to Exit 205 in Silverthorne. From here, travel north for 38 mi on HWY 9 to the town of Kremmling. Proceed on US 40 west (north) over Rabbit Ears Pass for 52 mi to the town of Steamboat Springs. If approaching from the west, take I-70 east to Exit 157 (Wolcott/Steamboat Springs) then proceed north on HWY 131 for about 70 mi past the towns of Toponas, Phippsburg, and Oak Creek to the junction of HWY 131 and US 40. It is a short 4 mi from this junction north to Steamboat Springs along US 40. Alternatively, if driving from west of the Rifle area, take I-70 east to Exit 90 (Rifle/Meeker), proceed north for 90 mi on HWY 13 to Craig, then take US 40 east for 42 mi to Steamboat Springs.

Along the Steamboat Ski Resort slopes in winter

The view of the Yampa Valley from Thunderhead Peak (top of the gondola)

Knoll Parking Lot/Gondola Square: Free parking is available year-round at the Knoll Parking Lot (additional pay parking is available closer to the ski resort base area). At the first stoplight in Steamboat Springs as you approach from Rabbit Ears Pass, take a right (east) onto Mt. Werner Rd. Proceed about a mile to the Knoll Parking Lot, which is on your left. Be sure to stay straight after 0.7 mi as the road turns into Mt. Werner Circle. Gondola Square at the base of the mountain is located a short distance to the northeast.

Recommended Routes

There are quite a few trails on Mt. Werner. Some of the more popular trails as well as a few suggested mountain biking loops are provided below. Start at the Knoll Parking Lot near Gondola Square for the easiest access.

NOTE: Hiking and running are technically allowed on any of the trails on Mt. Werner; however, it is highly recommended that hikers and runners utilize the Thunderhead Hiking Trail as bikers can fly around corners at any time on many of the popular biking trails.

Thunderhead Hiking Trail: The 2,000-ft. climb to the top of the gondola and Thunderhead Peak is a daunting challenge. Thankfully, the Thunderhead Hiking Trail has been designed to make this feat surmountable due to the many switchbacks and the occasional flat section of trail.

The resort generally provides gondola rides in the downhill direction for free as a reward for your hike to the top; otherwise, you will need to pay a fee to ride the gondola up. The trail progresses through meadows and lush aspen forests. This trail is off limits to bikes.

Mount Werner Trails

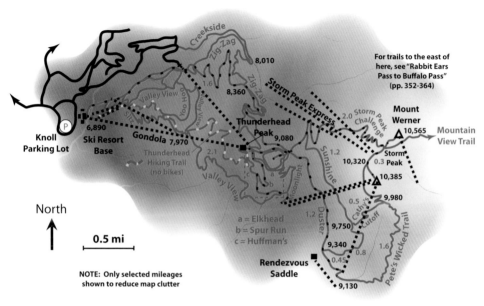

For trails to the east of here, see "Rabbit Ears Pass to Buffalo Pass" (pp. 352-364)

North

0.5 mi

NOTE: Only selected mileages shown to reduce map clutter

Map labels: Creekside, Zig-Zag, 8,010, 8,360, 1.6, Storm Peak Express, Valley View, 8,360, Thunderhead Peak 9,080, 2.0 Storm Peak Challenge, Mount Werner ▲ 10,565, Mountain View Trail, Knoll Parking Lot, P, 6,890, Ski Resort Base, Gondola 7,970, Thunderhead Hiking Trail (no bikes), 2.1, Valley View, Sunshine, 1.2, 10,320, Storm Peak, 0.3, ▲ 10,385, 9,980, a = Elkhead, b = Spur Run, c = Huffman's, Duster, 1.2, 9,750, 0.5, Cathy's Cutoff, Pete's Wicked Trail, 9,340, 0.8, 1.6, 0.45, Rendezvous Saddle, 9,130, Moonlight

Zig-Zag Trail: A fun trail that winds through aspen forests to Thunderhead. A moderate way to bike up the resort and one heck of a fun trail to descend!

Creekside Trail: A fun but technical trail descending along a scenic creek. The trail ends at Burgess Creek Rd., which must be ascended a short ways back to the resort.

Zig-Zag/Creekside Loop: Climb Zig-Zag and descend Creekside. A strenuous, relatively short loop with a zoom-through-the-forests finish.

Cathy's Cutoff Trail: Cathy's Cutoff connects Sunshine Trail to Pete's Wicked Trail and eliminates the top section of Pete's Wicked so that the difficult Storm Peak Challenge must not be ascended in order to descend Pete's Wicked.

Sunshine Trail: A moderate trail that climbs from Storm Peak Challenge to the base of Cathy's Cutoff Trail then descends to near Rendezvous Saddle at the top of the South Peak lift. A stellar traverse.

Storm Peak Challenge: A rocky, steep at times doubletrack road that switchbacks up to near the summit of Mount Werner. Loose in spots, making it a challenging uphill mountain bike ride.

Pete's Wicked Trail: In many regards, Pete's Wicked Trail seems like a true wilderness experience as it descends from the top of the Steamboat Ski Resort through the back bowls and arrives at the base of Sunshine Express lift. Those who venture on this trail will be treated with spectacular views of the Flattops and the Yampa River valley to the southwest and west. There are a few rocky sections to the south of the intersection with Cathy's Cutoff but otherwise Pete's Wicked Trail is quite rideable and fun. The best way to climb Mt. Werner is via Storm Peak Challenge to Sunshine to Cathy's Cutoff; most folks actually skip the very top section of Pete's Wicked and begin the descent at the top of Cathy's Cutoff. Unfortunately, there is a short stinger climb at the conclusion of singletrack and a doubletrack road must be taken from the base of the South Peak lift up to Rendezvous Saddle. However, the excellent descent is well worth the added effort.

Aspen and spruce, near Steamboat Ski Area

Valley View Trail: Another incredible singletrack trail great for the intermediate or advanced mountain biker. There are several technical spots and short tenuous climbs that can catch you off guard, but otherwise this trail is nothing but fun. Several spots to take a break and enjoy the view of the town below. The

first part of the official Valley View Trail is on a doubletrack road, so most people will take Elkhead to Moonlight to Valley View (see next trail description). The lower part of Valley View Trail contours northwest along forested slopes with a few short climbs then descends all the way down to the intersection with the bottom portion of Zig-Zag.

Moonlight to Valley View: Either take the gondola to Thunderhead Peak or bike to Thunderhead via a climb up Zig-Zag or another trail. From Thunderhead, head due east on Duster (doubletrack). After you contour around the north side of a small peak, you will reach a 4-way intersection at a saddle. Take a right onto Elkhead, follow this singletrack trail a short ways to Moonlight, descend Moonlight to a doubletrack road, and find Valley View a short ways up the road and heading down and to the west. Continue on Valley View as described above (Valley View Trail).

Pete's Wicked to Valley View: A lengthy, magnificent descent with a variety of terrain on mostly singletrack trails. From the top of Mt. Werner (easiest way to the top is via Storm Peak Challenge to Sunshine to Cathy's Cutoff), take Pete's Wicked to the base of the Sunshine Express lift and climb back to Rendezvous Saddle (top of South Peak lift). Descend the doubletrack Duster Trail (road) to a 4-way intersection at

a saddle area. Find the singletrack Elkhead Trail on the left (south side of 4-way junction) and take Elkhead a short ways to the top of Moonlight. Descend Moonlight and Valley View to the base of the resort as described in "Moonlight to Valley View" above.

Steamboat Springs Area Ski & Snowshoe Trails

Mt. Werner Snowshoe Trails: There are numerous snowshoe trails on Mt. Werner in winter. Unlike other ski resorts where uphill traffic is prohibited, the Steamboat Ski Resort allows uphill travel on snowshoes and skis, as long as you stick to the sides of the slopes near the trees. Like in summer, you can catch a free ride down on the gondola if you get yourself to the top of Thunderhead Peak. Otherwise, grab a ticket for the gondola and there are several trails emanating from the Thunderhead area. Visit the Steamboat Information Center at the base of the resort or call Steamboat Central Reservations at 1-877-237-2628 for more information.

The ski touring centers listed below are part of the Steamboat Springs Nordic Center of the

Rockies. There are over 100 kilometers of groomed cross country ski trails. Snowshoeing is also permitted in many areas. You can contact each touring center individually or you can visit the website for the Nordic Center of the Rockies at www.steamboatxcski.org.

Steamboat Ski Touring Center: $ The Steamboat Ski Touring Center is located just north of Mountain Village. Rentals and lessons are available, snowshoers can use over 10 km of trails, and visitors can even grab a "picnic basket" that contains homemade breads, soups, hot and cold drinks, and cookies! Visit online at www.nordicski.net or call them at (970) 879-8180.

Howelsen Hill Nordic Center: $ Although groomed, the cross country ski trails of Howelsen Hill are strenuous and difficult and have been part of the Nordic Combined World Cup cross country course. The Howelsen Hill Nordic Center does not offer lessons or rentals (bring your own or rent from elsewhere in town) but they do have a snack bar. Plenty of challenging snowshoe trails, too. For directions or more information, please call (970) 879-4300.

Lake Catamount Ski Touring Center: $ Situated south of town, this ski touring center is situated on a private development yet is open to the public. Over 30 km of mostly easy groomed ski trails. Rentals available and lessons by appointment only. They serve lunch Wed-Sun 11:00 am to 3:00 pm.

Colorado Columbines near Rabbit Ears Pass

The distinctive rock formations that give Rabbit Ears Pass its name

Rabbit Ears Pass to Buffalo Pass

The area to the north of Rabbit Ears Pass, south of Buffalo Pass, and east of Steamboat Ski Resort is a year-round playground for outdoor sports enthusiasts. Mountain bikers and hikers will appreciate the Wyoming Trail (part of the Continental Divide Trail) that connects Buffalo Pass to Rabbit Ears Pass and beyond, as well as other trails in the area. This relatively flat area contains many small lakes and ponds and is high in elevation yet below treeline, making it home to many wildflowers. Moreover, the trails are rather easy, requiring few big, strenuous climbs. Access is relatively straightforward and stress-free, especially from Rabbit Ears Pass. The Mountain View Trail connects the Wyoming Trail to the Steamboat Ski Resort, providing a popular bike route from Rabbit Ears Pass to the town of Steamboat Springs. In winter, skier- and snowshoe-specific trails are plentiful and begin at four different winter trailheads near Rabbit Ears Pass. Fortunately, these ski and snowshoe trails are closed to snowmobiles (snowmobiles are permitted on the east side of the pass), providing a peaceful wintertime setting.

Maps: Sky Terrain Maps "Steamboat Springs & Mt. Zirkel" or National Geographic Trails Illustrated "Clark, Buffalo Pass" (#117) and "Steamboat Springs, Rabbit Ears Pass" (#118). The Routt County Riders "Steamboat Springs Mountain Bike Map", available in local outdoor stores, is also an excellent map, most suitable for mountain biking in this area.

Best time of the year: As winter storms approach from the west and northwest and the clouds are pushed up to the Continental Divide from the Yampa Valley, the moisture is squeezed out like a sponge, resulting in abundant rain in the summer and snow in the winter and early spring months. Because of the large snowpack each year, you probably want to wait to recreate in this area until well into the summer (July and August). However, low snow years may warrant earlier exploration of these trails, and they are usable

Enchanted forests along the Wyoming Trail

until snow shuts them down, which typically occurs as early as late September or mid October. Worry not, because there is plenty of skiing and snowshoeing to be had in the winter!

Camping: The Dumont Lake Campground is currently the only campground open on Rabbit Ears Pass. Other dispersed camping can be found on Forest Service roads near Rabbit Ears Pass. There are many other campgrounds near Steamboat Springs; see the "Camping" section for the "Steamboat Springs/Mt. Werner" section on p. 346 for more options. For information on the Dumont Lake Campground, please contact the Routt National Forest at (970) 870-2299 or reserve a site at www.recreation.gov.

Access

Steamboat Springs: The Fish Creek Falls and Mountain View Trails can be accessed from the west side near the town of Steamboat Springs (the Mountain View Trail is accessed near the top of the Storm Peak Express lift near the top of the ski area). See directions to Steamboat Springs on p. 346.

Fish Creek TH: **$** Approach downtown Steamboat Springs from the south along US 40 (Lincoln Ave). Take a right (northeast) onto 3rd St. and take the next right onto Fish Creek Falls Rd. Continue east on Fish Creek Falls Rd. for about 3 mi to the parking area. There is a fee to park here. The entrance station is located a short ways before the parking area. Additional parking can be found near the entrance station.

Dry Lake TH/Buffalo Pass Winter TH: From downtown Steamboat Springs, take 7th St. northeast for a few blocks to a stop sign. Veer right onto Missouri Avenue and you should see signs for the Buffalo Pass Rd. Missouri Ave will take a left then turn into

Strawberry Park Rd. and the road will take a right turn. Proceed on Strawberry Park Rd. to a T-junction with Amethyst Rd. and continue left on CR 36. After about 0.9 mi from this intersection take a right onto CR 38 (Buffalo Pass Rd./FS 60). The paved road quickly becomes dirt. Continue up the Buffalo Pass Rd. and the Dry Lake TH and winter parking area can be found after about 3.3 mi.

Buffalo Pass TH: From the Dry Lake TH (see previous page), continue on the Buffalo Pass Rd. (FS 60) for an additional 7.6 mi to a high point. Summit Lake and Summit Lake Campground are off to the left (north), the Buffalo Pass Rd. continues east and down, and if you continue south then after about 0.2 mi there is a parking area and the Buffalo Pass TH. The Wyoming Trail (CDT) can be accessed to the south of the parking area.

Fish Creek Reservoir TH: Follow directions to the Buffalo Pass TH (see previous page). Continue along FS 310 south for about 4.7 mi to a gate, passing Granite Campground after about 4 mi. A high-clearance vehicle is recommended. Park at the gate and be sure to read all signs.

Dumont Lake TH: There is a fee to park at Dumont Lake TH, but it will cut off about a half mile of hiking north along the Continental Divide Trail (Wyoming Trail) compared to if you start at the Dumont TH (see below).

Dumont TH: This trailhead is an alternative to the Dumont Lake TH and will eliminate the fee for parking at Dumont Lake. From Steamboat Springs, drive approximately 20 mi south and west on US 40 and follow signs to Dumont Lake. This is about 0.6 mi east of the Department of Transportation maintenance area. Take a left (north) off of US 40, travel north and east on FS 315/CR 199 for 1.5 mi to FS 311, just past the Dumont Lake Campground. Take a left onto FS 311 and travel a short ways to the parking area off either side of the road. The Continental Divide Trail passes through this trailhead.

Base Camp TH: Follow directions to the Dumont TH (see above). Continue on the rough and rocky-at-times FS 311 (Base Camp Rd.) for 4.3 mi to a trailhead in the trees on the north side of the road. The Wyoming Trail heads north and down from here.

Recommended Routes

Rabbit Ears Peak: A fun hike to the namesake of Rabbit Ears Pass. Follow directions to the Dumont TH. Park here, or you may

Rabbit Ears Peak

The spectacular Fish Creek Falls just minutes from downtown Steamboat Springs

travel another 0.2 mi (rough road but passable for high clearance 2WD and 4WD vehicles) along FS 311 (Base Camp Rd.) to park at the beginning of FS 291. Regardless, make your way to FS 291 and hike along the rough doubletrack through forests and meadows, then the last quarter mile of the hike is quite steep to the summit. Enjoy the view! 2.7 mi and close to 1,000 vertical ft. to the top.

Fish Creek Falls Trail: Fish Creek Falls is a popular destination and for good reason. It is only a short 1/4-mi hike to the raging, beautiful falls. The Fish Creek Falls Trail can be continued well beyond the initial falls. This trail is a steep, rocky climb and reaches the Upper Fish Creek Falls after 2.0 mi. The trail ultimately continues to the intersection with the Mountain View Trail after 5.5 mi. Don't make the mistake I did and try to bike UP this trail, bad idea. Not recommended for bikes unless you are quite comfortable on rocky, technical descents. All bikes must be walked between the trailhead and a quarter mile above the first falls. An excellent hike, 2500 ft. of elevation gain to the intersection with the Mountain View Trail. Easy or difficult, depending upon how far you wish to go. There is also a short, easy trail that leads from the parking area to an overlook of the lower falls. The initial part of the trail can be snowshoed in winter.

Wyoming Trail: The Wyoming Trail was used historically in the early 1900s to bring sheep from Rawlins, WY, to Steamboat Springs, CO. Part of the much longer Continental Divide Trail, the Wyoming Trail links Rabbit Ears Pass to the Wyoming border, passing through the Mount Zirkel Wilderness. The section between Buffalo Pass and Rabbit

Fish Creek Falls

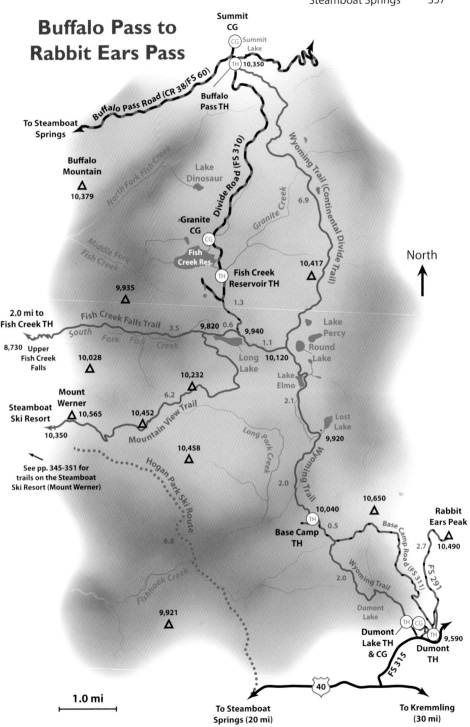

Buffalo Pass to Rabbit Ears Pass

Summit CG
CG Summit Lake
TH 10,350
Buffalo Pass TH

Buffalo Pass Road (CR 38/FS 60)

To Steamboat Springs

Buffalo Mountain
△ 10,379

Lake Dinosaur

Divide Road (FS 310)

North Fork Fish Creek

Middle Fork Fish Creek

Granite CG
CG
Fish Creek Res.

Fish Creek Reservoir TH
TH

Granite Creek

Wyoming Trail (Continental Divide Trail)

6.9

10,417 △

△ 9,935

1.3

North

2.0 mi to Fish Creek TH

Fish Creek Falls Trail   3.5

9,820   0.6

9,940

8,730 Upper Fish Creek Falls

South Fork Fish Creek

△ 10,028

Long Lake

10,120

1.1

Lake Percy

Round Lake

Lake Elmo

△ 10,232

6.2

Mount Werner
△ 10,565

Steamboat Ski Resort

△ 10,452

Mountain View Trail

10,350

See pp. 345-351 for trails on the Steamboat Ski Resort (Mount Werner)

△ 10,458

Long Park Creek

Lost Lake

9,920

2.1

Hogan Park Ski Route

Wyoming Trail

2.0

6.8

10,650 △

Rabbit Ears Peak
△ 10,490

Base Camp TH
TH
10,040   0.5

Base Camp Road (FS 311)

2.7

FS 291

Fishhook Creek

△ 9,921

Wyoming Trail

2.0

Dumont Lake

Dumont Lake TH & CG
TH CG
TH
9,590

Dumont TH

FS 315

40

1.0 mi

To Steamboat Springs (20 mi)

To Kremmling (30 mi)

Reflection along the Mountain View Trail

Ears Pass is relatively flat and rolling with few climbs more than a hundred ft. or so. Several small lakes and ponds can be found along this high, broad area. Hike or mountain bike the Wyoming Trail from either the Buffalo Pass TH or the Dumont TH atop Rabbit Ears Pass. The Wyoming Trail can also be accessed from the Base Camp TH, the Fish Creek Falls Trail and Mountain View Trail from the west, and other trailheads from the east. Backpackers would enjoy a multi-day experience along this trail.

Long Lake: There are two ways to reach Long Lake. First, the Fish Creek Falls Trail (see p. 356) can be taken for 5.7 mi to Long Lake. This is a challenging endeavor as it requires over 2,500 ft. of elevation gain over rocky terrain. Second, the lake can be reached from Fish Creek Reservoir by driving the Buffalo Pass Rd. and the Divide Rd. (FS 310) to a parking area beyond Granite Campground to a gate along FS 310 (see directions to Fish Creek Reservoir TH). From here, continue past the gate along the doubletrack service road, continuing left (south) at a fork in the road. After 1.3 mi you will intersect a singletrack trail (Fish Creek Falls Trail); take a right here and it is a short ways to Long Lake. Have a picnic at the scenic lake or hike along the Mountain View Trail (see next page).

Long Lake Loop: Begin at Buffalo Pass TH. Bike the Wyoming Trail south for 6.9 mi to the Fish Creek Falls Trail; hang a right here (Lake Percy Trail goes east) and proceed 1.0 mi to an intersection near Long Lake. After spending some time at the lake, return via

doubletrack north to Fish Creek Reservoir and gradually ascend the Divide Rd. (FS #310) then a short descent back to your starting point at Buffalo Pass TH. 13.8 mi round trip with 1,560 ft. of elevation gain/loss.

Mountain View Trail: Winding through lush spruce forests and along a ridge connecting Mount Werner (Steamboat Ski Resort) to the Continental Divide, the Mountrain View Trail is a must! Great for mountain bikers, hikers, and trail runners alike. Would make an excellent overnight backpacking trip as there are many small ponds and high points overlooking the vast Continental Divide region. If accessing this by foot, it is recommended to park past the Granite Campground near Fish Creek Reservoir and to hike to Long Lake, where you can pick up the Mountain View Trail (see map). The hike westward from Long Lake along the Mountain View Trail is actually quite strenuous as the trail climbs and descends quite a bit; it is an overall climb to the top of Mount Werner. This trail can also be accessed from the top of Mount Werner by taking the gondola up the ski resort (fee required) to Thunderhead at 9,080 ft. From there, hiking trails lead to the summit of Mount Werner (see "Steamboat Ski Resort" section on pp. 345-351), but this is a strenuous climb. For the burly, hike or run up the ski slopes from town to access this trail.

Round Lake, Lake Percy, and Lake Elmo: These three lakes can be accessed quite easily by foot from the Fish Creek Reservoir TH. Proceed to Long Lake (see directions on previous page for Long Lake) then go east on the Fish Creek Falls Trail to the Wyoming Trail (1.3 mi). Round Lake and Percy

Lake are found within a mile by proceeding east (see map); Lake Elmo is located within a mile to the south along the Wyoming Trail. This area can also be reached via the Lake Percy Trail by hiking about 2 mi west of the Lake Percy TH, but the drive to the Lake Percy TH is rather complicated and long. Finally, these three lakes can be accessed from Rabbit Ears Pass via

Indian Paintbrush near Long Lake

the Wyoming Trail from Base Camp TH or Dumont TH, but this requires at least a 4-mi hike (moderate). However, the drive to the Base Camp TH or Dumont TH is much easier than the drive to Fish Creek Reservoir, so the longer hike may be worth the shorter drive.

Fishhook and Lost Lakes: Fishhook Lake and Lost Lake can be accessed easily from the Rabbit Ears Pass area. If you have a high-clearance vehicle, drive to Base Camp TH. From here, pick up the Wyoming Trail/Continental Divide Trail and hike north. Fishhook Lake will be reached after 1.5 mi and a short trail to Lost Lake will be reached after an additional 0.5 mi. For those with 2WD vehicles, park at the Dumont TH (or Dumont Lake TH) and find the Wyoming Trail, which traverses above the northeastern side of the lake. Take this singletrack trail 3.4 mi to the doubletrack FS 311, proceed west on FS 311 for about a half mile to Base Camp TH, then continue to Fishhook and/or Lost Lakes as described here.

Buffalo Pass to Steamboat Springs: Unless you are willing to ascend the Buffalo Pass Rd., this route requires a car shuttle. Leave a car in town and drive to the Buffalo Pass TH. Take the Wyoming Trail 6.9 mi to the Fish Creek Falls Trail, then proceed west 2.6 mi to beyond the west side of Long Lake (intersection a

doubletrack road after 1.0 mi that leads north to Fish Creek Reservoir) to the intersection with the Mountain View Trail. Take the Mountain View Trail 7.6 mi to the ski area (14.5 mi total to the top of the resort with approximately 1,730 ft. of climbing and descending to this point) and choose your own adventure down the slopes. Recommended trails include Pete's Wicked Trail to Valley View (challenging) or Cathy's Cutoff/Sunshine/Zig-Zag (moderate). Approximately 24 mi total if you descend via Pete's Wicked and Valley View Trails. *Variation:* The Fish Creek Falls Trail can be descended from Long Lake, but this is a very technical, rocky descent.

Rabbit Ears Pass to Steamboat Springs: If you can set up a car shuttle, this is one of the best rides around. Start at the Dumont TH and proceed along the Wyoming Trail past Base Camp TH to the intersection with the Fish Creek Falls Trail after 7.8 mi. Take a left here (west) to Long Lake and proceed to the Mountain View Trail to the top of the ski area, which is reached after a total of 15.4 mi (2,880 ft. of elevation gain, 2,340 ft. of elevation loss). Descend a route of your choice (see section on "Steamboat Ski Resort" on pp. 345-351). Primo! About 24 mi total. *Variation:* The Fish Creek Falls Trail can be descended from Long Lake, but this is a very technical, rocky descent.

Buffalo Pass to Rabbit Ears Pass: The one-way traverse from Buffalo Pass to Rabbit Ears Pass is a worthwhile adventure that takes you through some very interesting terrain and lots of

ponds and lakes. This is a great trip for mountain bikers or for hikers and backpackers, yet logistically requires a car shuttle unless you are willing to return the way you came. If you have a group of people, leave a car on Rabbit Ears Pass at the Dumont TH, start from Buffalo Pass TH, and fetch your car atop Buffalo Pass at the end of the trip. 14.7 mi one way with 720 ft. of elevation gain and 1,480 ft. of elevation loss (north to south direction).

Rabbit Ears Pass Winter Trails

The west side of Rabbit Ears pass is closed to motorized vehicles (snowmobiles) and is a quiet place to ski in winter and early spring. These trails are open to snowshoers and skiers and they do not, for the most part, coincide with any summertime trails or roads. These routes are marked with blue diamonds on trees and blue bamboo poles in clearings. Because the routes are set at the beginning of each winter and sometimes may be difficult to follow, these ski routes may differ slightly from year to year and throughout the year. Recent snow will cover up trails. Therefore, trailbreaking and routefinding may be necessary in some cases. This area is quite expansive and it would be easy to get lost during a storm or whiteout, for example if your tracks got covered up and route markers became difficult to see. While elevation gains are not super great, most of these trails are moderate to difficult in nature for skiers primarily due to the common short climbs and descents, which can be tricky on cross country skis.

NOTE: The large pits or holes that snowshoes create essentially destroy ski tracks, rendering ski waxes and the waxless scales on the bottom of skis ineffective. It is common etiquette for snowshoers to hike off to the side and parallel to ski tracks. Recommended routes

Schussing along the Hogan Park Ski Route

Rabbit Ears Pass gets a lot of snow!

for snowshoers include the Walton Creek Loop and Bruce's Trail.

Access

West Summit Winter TH: From Steamboat Springs, take US 40 for 13 mi south towards Rabbit Ears Pass. At a noticeable high point in the road there will be parking areas plowed out on both sides of the road. There are signs located away from the highway so they are not the most noticeable. If approaching from the east, take US 40 from Kremmling for approximately 32 mi. Be on the lookout for a turnoff for the Department of Transportation maintenance area. From here, continue 5.5 mi west along US 40 to the West Summit Winter TH. (3.7 mi West Summit to Walton Creek TH)

Bruce's Winter TH: This trailhead is located on the north side of US 40, 1.8 mi east of the West Summit Winter TH. If approaching from the east, follow the instructions above (West Summit Winter TH) to the turnoff to the Department of Transportation maintenance area and continue west on US 40 for 3.7 mi to Bruce's Winter TH. There are signs here, but they are not easily visible.

Fox Curve Winter TH: This trailhead is also located on the north side of US 40. Follow the instructions above to the West Summit Winter TH but continue east on US 40 for about 2.8 mi. If approaching from the east, travel approximately 2.7 mi past the Department of Transportation maintenance area. There are signs here but they are not easily visible.

Walton Creek Winter TH: Located on the south side of US 40, this winter trailhead is located 5.5 mi east of the West Summit Winter TH (follow directions above) along US 40. If coming from Kremmling, drive to the Department of Transportation maintenance area turnoff (see West Summit Winter TH directions above) and continue another 1.8 mi to the Walton Creek Winter TH. There are signs here but they are not easily visible.

Recommended Routes

West Summit Ski Loops: There are three big ski loops atop the West Summit of Rabbit Ears Pass. Loops 1A and

West Summit Ski Loops

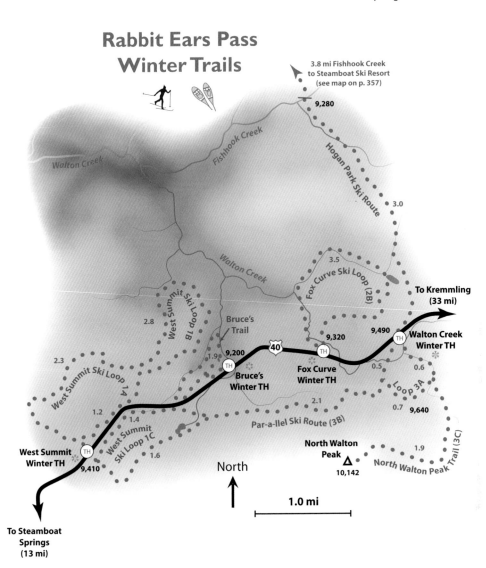

Rabbit Ears Pass Winter Trails

3.8 mi Fishhook Creek to Steamboat Ski Resort (see map on p. 357)

9,280

Fishhook Creek

Hogan Park Ski Route

Walton Creek

3.0

Walton Creek

3.5

Fox Curve Ski Loop (2B)

To Kremmling (33 mi)

West Summit Ski Loop 1B

2.8

Bruce's Trail

9,320

9,490

TH

Walton Creek Winter TH

2.3

West Summit Ski Loop 1A

1.9

9,200

TH

Bruce's Winter TH

US 40

TH

Fox Curve Winter TH

0.5

0.6

Loop 3A

1.2

1.4

West Summit Ski Loop 1C

1.6

2.1

0.7   9,640

West Summit Winter TH

TH

9,410

Par-a-llel Ski Route (3B)

North Walton Peak
△
10,142

1.9

North Walton Peak Trail (3C)

North

1.0 mi

To Steamboat Springs (13 mi)

1B begin on the north side of the parking area. Going clockwise, Loop 1A climbs through trees to the top of a broad ridge before dropping east into a drainage where the route intersects Loop 1B. Loop 1B is slightly easier than 1A and proceeds through forests with a few moderate climbs. Loop 1A by itself is about 3.5 mi and Loop 1B is 2.8 mi. Loop 1C begins on the south side of US 40 and descends to the east into an expansive creek valley. From the far east end of the loop, the Par-a-llel Ski Route (3B) heads to the east towards the Walton Creek area. Loop 1C by itself is about 3.0 mi.

Bruce's Trail: Begin at Bruce's Winter TH. There are several easy to moderate loops on the north side of US 40. Proceeding clockwise, the trail heads southwest to intersect a creek drainage, descends gradually northeast along the creek, then returns south back up to the trailhead.

Par-a-llel Ski Route (3B): This route connects Loop 1C with Loop 3A near the Walton Creek Winter TH. It is a gradual, 2.1-mi climb up the serene, wintery clearing to forests on the north side of North Walton Peak followed by a descent to the intersection with Loop 3B.

Fox Curve Ski Loop (2B): A spectacular, intimate loop varying in elevation from a low point of about 9,200 ft. to a high point of around 9,600 ft. Begin at the Fox Curve Winter TH. Going in the clockwise direction will enable you to get most of the climbing out of the way at the beginning. After descending a short ways to Walton Creek, traverse north then east and climb a broad basin to the high point. The route then drops north to a creek drainage then proceeds on the north side of the drainage west to Walton Creek. It is a rather gentle climb of just over a hundred vertical ft. back to the trailhead. 3.5 mi for the loop.

Walton Creek Loop (3A): A nice, easy loop. From the Walton Creek Winter TH, Loop 3A circles around a small mountain before descending to Walton Creek and a short climb back to the TH. 1.8 mi for the loop.

North Walton Peak: The climb of North Walton Peak is more difficult than the other winter trails in the Rabbit Ears Pass area and will require quite a bit of descending on the return trip, which is a concern for many on cross country skis. From the Walton Creek Winter TH, proceed clockwise on Loop 3A. After 0.6 mi, find a trail intersection (3C). Head south and after a ways the trail intersects a summer road, which takes you to the summit of North Walton Peak. Excellent views all around! It is 2.5 mi to the summit.

Hogan Park Ski Route: A very nice ski route. Requires a few steep climbs and descents as the trail crosses several abrupt creek drainages, but well worth the effort. As you proceed to the north side of Fishhook Creek, the views to the southwest of the Flattops are stunning. Ultimately, this trail reaches the Steamboat Ski Resort after about 6.8 mi; Fishhook Creek is reached after 3.0 mi.

The view north from Emerald Mountain

Howelsen Hill & Emerald Mountain

Howelsen Hill and its accompanying ski jumps hover over the Yampa River and downtown Steamboat Springs with impressive supremacy. Year-round activities can be found at Howelsen Hill, which is located minutes from main street. Howelsen Hill is actually part of the much larger Emerald Mountain. From atop Emerald Mountain, Howelsen Hill actually appears as just a tiny bump on the Emerald Mountain massif. In recent years, the recreational opportunities have expanded here due to the efforts of the Steamboat Rotary Club and Ben Beall, former chairman of the Emerald Mountain Partnership, who negotiated the largest land swap in Colorado history. This resulted in the 4,193-acre Special Recreation Area on Emerald Mountain. Thanks to these and other extraordinary efforts, Emerald Mountain has tremendous variety of trails, ranging from wide open, grassy meadows to lush forests of gamble oak, ferns, and spruce. Visit Emerald Mountain - it is one of the most spectacular areas in all of Colorado!

Maps: Sky Terrain Maps "Steamboat Springs & Mt. Zirkel" or National Geographic Trails Illustrated "Steamboat Springs, Rabbit Ears Pass" (#118).

Best time of the year: The elevation of Steamboat Springs is quite low for a ski town at about 6,730 ft. Emerald Mountain tops out at around 8,200 ft. Despite the relatively low elevation, cold air sinks into the Yampa Valley in the winter and allows the north and northeast sides of Emerald Mountain to hold snow for much of the winter. Consequently, skiing and snowshoeing opportunities are tremendous. Emerald Mountain thaws out in late spring and the trails here can be used quite a bit earlier than some of the other alpine trails in the region, such as the Rabbit Ears Pass and Mt. Zirkel Wilderness trails.

Camping: There isn't much camping right in the vicinity of Steamboat Springs. Several National Forest Campgrounds are located within 10-20 mi of Steamboat Springs, including the Dry Lake, Summit Lake, and Granite Campgrounds in the vicinity of Buffalo Pass and the Buffalo Pass Rd.; the Dumont Lake Campground on Rabbit Ears Pass; and the

Lush foliage on the north slopes of Emerald Mountain

Seedhouse and Hinman Campgrounds along Seedhouse Rd. northeast of Clark (north of Steamboat Springs on CR 129). Additional informal and dispersed camping can be found on National Forest lands in the region. Contact the Routt National Forest at (970) 870-2299 for more information about campgrounds (some can be reserved at www.recreation.gov).

Access

Directions to Steamboat Springs: See directions to Steamboat Springs on p. 346.

Howelsen Hill TH: From Lincoln Avenue (Main St.) in Steamboat Springs, find 5th St. and take it west across the river. Hang a right onto Howelsen Parkway and proceed a short ways to the Howelsen Hill area. Plenty of parking here.

Blackmere Drive TH: From Lincoln Avenue (Main St.) in Steamboat Springs, find 13th St. and take it west across the Yampa River. After a quarter of a mile, take a left onto Gilpin St. and follow it about a tenth of a mile. Take a left on Fairview Ave, right on Routt St., then at the high point of Routt as it turns back into Fairview the parking area and trailhead are found. Blackmere Drive heads up and south from here behind the closure gate.

A ski jump on Howelsen Hill

Cow Creek TH: From the northern-most stoplight in Steamboat Springs at the intersection of Lincoln Avenue (US 40) and Elk River Rd. take a left (west) onto Elk River Rd. for a tenth of a mile, then go left (south) on Shield Dr. for 0.4 mi, crossing on a bridge over the Yampa River. At a T-junction, take a right onto CR 33 (aka "Twentymile Road"). From here, proceed 5.4 mi to CR 45 (dirt). Take a left onto CR 45 and continue about a mile to an obvious parking area on the left (east side of road).

Beall TH: This trailhead is located 2.1 mi up CR 45 from the Cow Creek TH and provides access to the west end of the Beall Trail.

Recommended Routes

Emerald Mountain Singletrack Trails: There are too many singletrack trails to describe each in detail here, but the trails on Howelsen Hill are spectacular and diverse. You could literally lose yourself in these trails for hours, either on bike or on foot. If on foot, just go exploring! If on bike, the easiest route to the top of Emerald Mountain is Blackmere Drive/Lain of Pain;

Emerald Mountain Trails

however, many of the trails can be ascended without too much difficulty. Regardless, the climb to the top of Emerald Mountain is strenuous. Popular singletrack trails down include Lupine, Emerald, MGM, Forest Loop, and the fantastic Quarry Mountain Trail. Trails here range from easy to difficult, with the easier trails located near the bottom (Bluffs Loop, Overlook). Enjoy!

Ridge Trail

Ridge Trail: The Ridge Trail ascends the west side of Emerald Mountain from CR 45 (aka "Cow Creek Rd.") through gamble oak and grassy meadows. The singletrack trail is in great shape and is a worthy add-on

Abby's Trail on the lush northeast side of Emerald Mountain

Emerald Mountain Overview

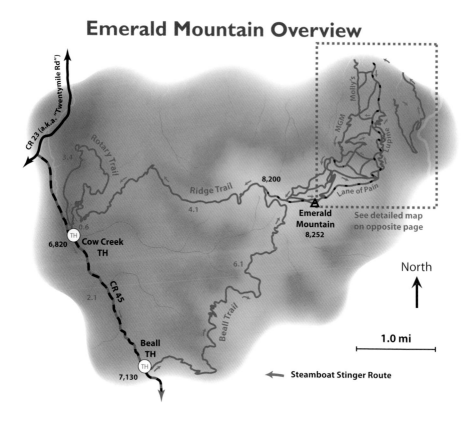

to adventures in the Emerald Mountain area. During the heat of the summer, start early on this trail as there is little shade on the west side of the mountain. 4.7 mi long.

Beall Trail: Finished in the fall of 2010, this trail has vastly improved mountain biking and hiking options in the Steamboat Springs area. Like the Ridge Trail, the Beall Trail links the top of Emerald Mountain with Cow Creek Rd. (CR 45). There is perhaps no other trail around that maximizes the use of elevation drop like the Beall Trail - 6.1 mi of sweet singletrack is jammed into this trail, which drops only slightly more than 1,000 ft. The Beall Trail takes you through a variety of vegetation ranging from ferns and firs to oak and sage near the base. Take this trail either by itself or incorporate it into a loop combined with the Ridge Trail (see Steamboat Stinger below).

Steamboat Stinger: Named after an annual bike race (www.honeystinger.com/steamboatstinger.html), this route is a spectacular, 25-mi loop that begins and ends

Emerald Mountain Detailed

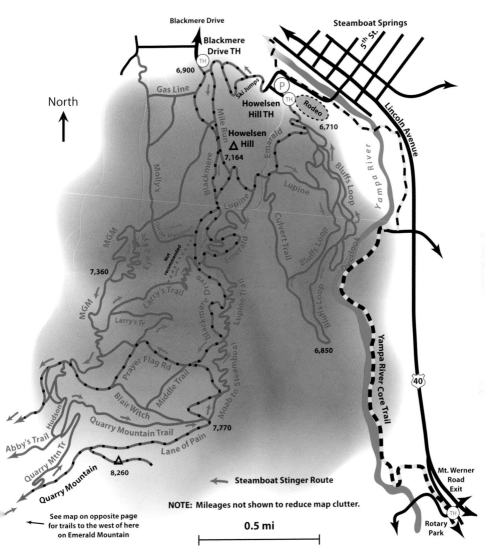

North

Blackmere Drive

Blackmere
Drive TH
6,900

Gas Line

Steamboat Springs

5th St.

Ski Jumps

Howelsen
Hill TH

P

Rodeo

6,710

Howelsen
Hill
7,164

Lincoln Avenue

Molly's

Blackmere

Mile Run

Emerald

Lupine

Lupine

Bluffs Loop

Yampa River

Onion Meadows

Eye 2 Eye

Lupine

Emerald

Culvert Trail

Bluffs Loop

Bluffs Loop

MGM

7,360

Not recommended

Larry's Trail

Larry's Tr.

Blackmere Drive

Lupine Trail

Overlook

MGM

6,850

Prayer Flag Rd

Middle Trail

Moab to Steamboat

40

Blair Witch

Yampa River Core Trail

Abby's Trail

Hudson

Quarry Mountain Trail

7,770

Lane of Pain

Quarry Mtn Tr

Quarry Mountain

8,260

Mt. Werner
Road
Exit

Steamboat Stinger Route

TH

Rotary
Park

See map on opposite page
for trails to the west of here
on Emerald Mountain

NOTE: Mileages not shown to reduce map clutter.

0.5 mi

Grassy meadow along MGM Trail, Howelsen Hill

at Howelsen Hill and utilizes the Emerald Mountain trails and the Ridge and Beall Trails on the west side of Emerald Mountain. Beginning at the base of Howelsen Hill, take Mile Run and Blackmere Drive then take a right onto Orton Meadows. From there, ascend the stellar Eye 2 Eye to MGM, then take the doubletrack Prayer Flag Rd. past some recent logging to Abby's. Abby's may be hard to find; otherwise just take Stairway to Heaven. Regardless, ascend the top of Stairway to Heaven, which spits you out on the doubletrack at the top of Emerald Mountain. Proceed west then descend the spectacular, stupendously fun Ridge Trail all the way to the Cow Creek TH. Take a left, climb CR 45 to the Beall TH, then ascend the equally fun Beall Trail all the way to the top, through sage, spruce, ferns, and fir to the top of Emerald Mountain. Return down Root Canal, Quarry Mountain Trail, Moab to Steamboat, Larry's, lower part of Lupine, and throw on a bonus of the Bluffs Loop if you are so inclined. The loop is about 25 mi and has close to 4,000 ft. of elevation gain/loss.

Rotary Trail: A new trail finished in 2011, the Rotary Trail adds some relatively easy terrain to the northwest side of Emerald Mountain near the bottom of the Ridge Trail. From end to end, the Rotary Trail is about 3.4 mi long and winds along grassy slopes and through patches

of scrub oak. The enclosed loop with the Ridge Trail is 4.0 mi long. Great for hikers and mountain bikers. For bikers, the loop is best done in the counterclockwise direction.

Additional Wintertime Activities

Howelsen Hill is truly a winter wonderland. Watch future Olympians train for ski jumping, ride the magic carpet to the top of a slope and ride a tube down, or cross country ski or snowshoe the challenging trails that traverse Howelsen Hill. See p. 351 for information on skiing and snowshoeing at Howelsen Hill.

The Mad Creek Barn

Steamboat Springs North

To region to the north of Steamboat Springs consists of rolling terrain with wide open meadows, churning rivers, and relatively low-lying hills consisting of sage, oak, and spruce. The popular Hot Springs Trail leads to the Strawberry Hot Springs, where you can soak in some extravagant natural springs. Just outside of town is the Spring Creek Trail, which is suitable for hiking, mountain biking, trail running, cross country skiing, and snowshoeing. The Mad Creek Trail ascends high above Mad Creek along a steep embankment yet reaches a lush, serene meadow just outside the Mt. Zirkel Wilderness area. Hikers and bikers will enjoy just about any of these trails. Mountain bikers can put together some longer, more adventurous rides that start and end in town. In winter, check out the Spring Creek and Hot Springs Trails for worthwhile snowshoeing excursions.

Maps: Sky Terrain Maps "Steamboat Springs & Mt. Zirkel" or National Geographic Trails Illustrated "Clark, Buffalo Pass" (#117) and "Steamboat Springs, Rabbit Ears Pass" (#118). The Routt County Riders "Steamboat Springs Mountain Bike Map", available in local outdoor stores, is also an excellent map, most suitable for mountain biking in this area.

Best time of the year: Early May through October. North-facing slopes will accumulate significantly more snow than south-facing slopes. For the Steamboat Springs area, the south-facing trails in this region (Mad Creek, Saddle Trail, Lower Bear Creek Trail, and most of the Hot Springs Trail) are some of the first trails to be usable in spring to late spring. Consequently, some of the first wildflowers to appear in summer are to the north of Steamboat Springs and in the North Routt County area.

The Spring Creek Trail crosses Spring Creek many times

Camping: The closest campgrounds in the vicinity of the northern Steamboat Springs area are the Dry Lake and Summit Campgrounds (the latter may require 4WD) along the Buffalo Pass Rd. (see directions for the Buffalo Pass Rd. on p. 354). Otherwise, there are several dispersed campsites along the Buffalo Pass Rd. after the Dry Lake Campground. The Seedhouse and Hinman Campgrounds along Seedhouse Rd. northeast of Clark are also possibilities. Contact the Medicine Bow-Routt National Forest at (970) 870-2299 for more information about campgrounds. Some of these campgrounds can be reserved at www.recreation.gov.

Access

Directions to Steamboat Springs: See directions to Steamboat Springs on p. 346.

Spring Creek TH: From Lincoln Avenue (Main St.) in downtown Steamboat Springs, take 3rd St. northeast for a block and take a right onto Fish Creek Falls Rd. Proceed 0.3 mi up a hill to Amethyst Dr. and take a left here. Drive about 0.4 mi and just past a church is Spring Creek Rd. There is plenty of parking here at the base of the road.

Mad Creek TH: From the intersection of Lincoln Ave. (Main St./US 40) and CR 129 (Elk River Rd.) on the northwest end of Steamboat Springs, proceed north on CR 129 for 5.5 mi and look for the large parking area and trailhead on the right (east) side of CR 129.

Red Dirt TH: Follow directions to the Mad Creek TH (above) but continue an additional 1.2 mi north on CR 129 to the parking area and trailhead, which is just off the highway.

Lower Bear Creek TH: From Lincoln Ave (Main St.) in downtown

Old ski lift near Strawberry Hot Springs

The upper part of Spring Creek Trail

Steamboat Springs, take 7th St. northeast for a few blocks to a stop sign. Veer right onto Missouri Avenue and you should see signs for the Buffalo Pass Rd. Missouri Ave will take a left then turn into Strawberry Park Rd. and the road will take a right turn. Proceed on Strawberry Park Rd. to a T-junction with Amethyst Rd. and continue left on CR 36. Take CR 36 from this T-junction for 4.6 mi (dirt after about 3.2 mi) and the trailhead is located on the right (east) side of the road.

Dry Lake TH: Follow directions to the T-junction at Strawberry Park Rd. and CR 36/ Amethyst Rd. From this intersection, continue north on CR 36 for 0.9 mi and take a right onto CR 38 (Buffalo Pass Rd./FS 60). The paved road quickly becomes dirt. Continue up the Buffalo Pass Rd. and the Dry Lake TH can be found after about 3.3 mi. The road is plowed to this point in the winter.

Recommended Routes

Spring Creek Trail: A popular, multi-use trail for all seasons. Begin at the Spring Creek TH. The trail follows a rather wide doubletrack road for 1.7 mi before becoming singletrack. Progressing through aspen and spruce forests, the trail crosses Spring Creek at least a dozen times on wooden bridges. Much of the trail is moderate in difficulty but there are a few short climbs. It is 5.3 mi and 1,920 ft. of climbing from the Spring Creek TH to the Dry Lake TH, which offers top-down access to the trail.

Steamboat North

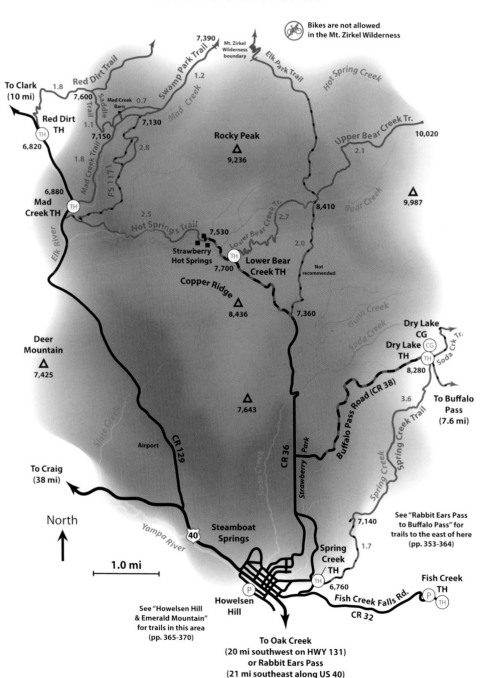

Bikes are not allowed
in the Mt. Zirkel Wilderness

7,390

Mt. Zirkel
Wilderness
boundary

Red Dirt Trail

Swamp Park Trail

Elk Park Trail

Hot Spring Creek

To Clark
(10 mi)

1.8

7,600

Saddle

0.7

Mad Creek
Barn

Upper Bear Creek Tr.

10,020

Red Dirt
TH

6,820

7,150

1.1

7,130

Mad Creek

2.1

Rocky Peak

△

9,236

Mad Creek Trail

FS 1171

1.8

2.8

6,880

Mad
Creek TH

Elk River

2.5

Hot Springs Trail

Lower Bear Creek Tr.

8,410

Bear Creek

9,987

△

7,530

2.7

Strawberry
Hot Springs

Lower Bear
Creek TH

2.0

7,700

Not
recommended

Copper Ridge

△

8,436

7,360

Gunn Creek

Soda Creek

Dry Lake
CG

Dry Lake
TH

Soda Crk. Tr.

Deer
Mountain

△

7,425

8,280

Slate Creek

△

7,643

Buffalo Pass Road (CR 38)

3.6

To Buffalo
Pass
(7.6 mi)

Airport

CR 129

Soda Creek

CR 36

Strawberry Park

Spring Creek Trail

Spring Creek

To Craig
(38 mi)

See "Rabbit Ears Pass
to Buffalo Pass" for
trails to the east of here
(pp. 353-364)

North

↑

7,140

1.7

1.0 mi

Yampa River

40

Steamboat
Springs

Spring
Creek
TH

6,760

Fish Creek
TH

P

Howelsen
Hill

P

Fish Creek Falls Rd.

CR 32

See "Howelsen Hill
& Emerald Mountain"
for trails in this area
(pp. 365-370)

To Oak Creek
(20 mi southwest on HWY 131)
or Rabbit Ears Pass
(21 mi southeast along US 40)

Soda Creek Trail: An easy, 1.7-mi out-and-back trail starting from the north side of the Buffalo Pass Rd. across from the Dry Lake TH. In winter, this is a great place to snowshoe or ski.

Hot Springs Trail: A secret (or not-so-secret) trail leading from near the Mad Creek TH to essentially the back door of Strawberry Hot Springs. Biking, hiking, or snowshoeing the Hot Springs Trail and soaking in the relaxing hot springs is a great way to spend a day in the

mountains. Begin at the Mad Creek TH but the Hot Springs Trail is accessed approximately 0.2 mi south along CR 129. A dirt road (FS 128) leads east and the Hot Springs Trail forks right after another 0.3 mi. For more information on Strawberry Hot Springs, please visit www.strawberryhotsprings.com. It is 3.1 mi from the Mad Creek TH to the hot springs.

Bear Creek Trail: Begin at the Lower Bear Creek TH off of FS 323 near Strawberry Hot Springs. The Lower Bear Creek Trail switchbacks up sage-covered slopes to a high point then descends through aspens to the intersection with the seldom used Elk Park Rd. (FS 314) after 2.7 mi. The trail continues northeast (follow FS 314 north a short ways first) as the Upper Bear Creek Trail, which climbs into a creek drainage before skirting along a ridge to a scenic high point at Summit Park (4.8 mi total), with views to the east of the high peaks of the Mt. Zirkel Wilderness.

Mad Creek Trail: You will be amazed at how this trail skirts along the side of such a steep valley carved by Mad Creek. Begin at the Mad Creek TH and climb along the west side of Mad Creek. The trail climbs steeply at first but levels out and actually descends a bit before the

intersection with the Saddle Trail. It is 1.8 mi to the Mad Creek Barn, located in a vast, lush meadow.

Swamp Park Trail: The Swamp Park Trail begins at the Mad Creek Barn and follows Mad Creek through heavy vegetation and into the heart of the Mt. Zirkel Wilderness. The trail goes all the way to the Burn Ridge TH off of Seedhouse Rd. (see p. 381). Open to mountain bikes up to the Mt. Zirkel Wilderness boundary, which is reached after 1.9 mi from the Mad Creek Barn. This trail is very easy, but requires you to ascend the steep Mad Creek Trail in order to get to it. However, the trail gets substantially more difficult as you proceed deep into the Mt. Zirkel Wilderness.

Red Dirt Trail: Climbing initially through west-facing sagebrush slopes before entering a forested creek drainage, the Red Dirt Trail is perfect for an out-and-

back hike or mountain bike ride. The trail intersects the Saddle Trail after 1.8 mi and continues through dense spruce and fir forests into the Mt. Zirkel Wilderness.

Mad Creek to Red Dirt Trail: This is a nice 5.7-mi loop for mountain bikers. Begin at the Red Dirt TH and warm up by spinning your legs down CR 129 to the Mad Creek TH. Climb the Mad Creek Trail, stay left in the meadow below the Mad Creek Barn, and find the Saddle Trail. Climb the somewhat sun-exposed oak and sage slopes of the Saddle Trail to the intersection with the Red Dirt Trail. It is a hair-raising, super fun descent to the Elk River and the Red Dirt TH, where you began. 1,650 ft. of elevation gain/loss for the loop.

Hot Mad Red Loop: If you've got a lot of energy, you might want to do this mountain bike ride, which takes you through some diverse terrain. It is recommended to park at the Red Dirt TH so that you can warm up on the roads and your car (and beer) will be waiting at the end of the last descent. Ride south

along CR 129 and left on US 40 into downtown Steamboat Springs. Take a left onto 3rd St. and follow directions on p. 372 to the Spring Creek TH. Ascend the Spring Creek Trail to the Buffalo Pass Rd. Descend the dirt road to the Strawberry Park area, then take a right on CR 36 and bike this all the way up to the Strawberry Hot Springs. Find the Hot Springs Trail at the back of the hot springs area and descend the spectacular trail (two thumbs up!) to CR 129. This is a good bail-out spot if you are too tired to continue. The loop finishes by riding the "Mad Creek to Red Dirt Trail" description above. The loop is about 23 mi with 3,700 ft. of elevation gain/loss.

Fall in the Steamboat Springs area

Just north of Steamboat Springs with Emerald Mountain in the distance

North Routt County

The Steamboat Lake area is popular among hikers, hunters, and skiers and can be enjoyed year-round. The iconic and beautiful Hahns Peak soars high above the lush valleys below. Just to the west of the Mt. Zirkel Wilderness, northern Routt County is characterized by aspen forests, wildflower- and sage-speckled meadows, and deep, subalpine forests. During July of 2002, the Hinman Fire burned to the north of the Seedhouse Rd. and into parts of the Mt. Zirkel Wilderness and in August of the same year the Burn Ridge Fire consumed forests to the south of the Seedhouse Rd. Many of the trails in this area traverse through these burn areas and it is interesting to observe the forest succession that is taking place as the forests recover.

Maps: Sky Terrain Maps "Steamboat Springs & Mt. Zirkel" or National Geographic Trails Illustrated "Hahns Pk & Steamboat Lake" (#116) and "Clark, Buffalo Pass" (#117). The Routt County Riders "Steamboat Springs Mountain Bike Map", available in local outdoor stores, is also an excellent map, most suitable for mountain biking in this area.

Best time of the year: In contrast to the high peaks of the Mt. Zirkel Wilderness area to the east, much of North Routt County is relatively low-lying and comprised of rolling terrain. In a typical year, the trails are usable by early June (snowfall dependent, of course). North Routt County hosts some of the largest, most extensive aspen forests in the state.

Visit the area in late September and you will treated to the stunning warm colors of autumn. Winter brings some spectacular skiing at Steamboat Lake and south of Seedhouse Rd. (CR 64/FS 400), which is to the east of Clark. The south side of Seedhouse Rd. is closed to mechanized transportation in winter, providing a peaceful cross country skiing and snowshoeing atmosphere.

Camping: The Hinman and Seedhouse Campgrounds are located along Seedhouse Rd. (CR 64/FS 400) and are great places to stay if you are exploring the trails to the north and south of Seedhouse Rd. Currently, dispersed camping is prohibited along Seedhouse Rd. (FS 400) but is allowed to the south along FS 443. There is also a small designated camping zone just after the winter trailhead in Hinman Park (see map) on the south side of Seedhouse Rd. along the Elk River. To the north, plenty of camping is available at the state parks, including the Sunrise Vista and Dutch Hill Campgrounds in Steamboat Lake State Park and the Pearl Lake Campground at Pearl Lake State Park. An entry fee required for both state parks. Pearl Lake State Park has yurts available, too. Finally, the Hahns Peak Lake Campground to the north of Steamboat Lake is another option. For more information about National Forest campgrounds in this area, please contact the Medicine Bow-Routt National Forest at (970-870-2299). Some of these campgrounds can be reserved at www.recreation.gov or www.reserveamerica.com. More information on the state parks can be found at: www.parks.state.co.us or by calling (970) 879-3922.

Seedhouse Guard Station: This historic Forest Service guard station is available for overnight stay from Sept. 1st through April 1st each year. It sleeps 4 people on 2 bunk beds and has propane oven and fridge, lights, a propane heater, and firewood for outdoor fires in the fall. In winter, there is no running water but a large pot is available for melting water. The cabin is located just north of the Seedhouse Campground approximately 9 mi up the Seedhouse Rd. (CR 64/FS 400) from CR 129 near Clark. In winter, you must park at the

Along the Wyoming Trail north of Seedhouse Road

Along Cutover Trail, Hinman Lake area

winter parking area (see map, about 5.8 mi from CR 129), which requires snowmobile or ski travel for about 3.2 mi. For more information and to reserve the cabin, visit www. recreation.gov or call (970) 723-2700. The cost is $100 per night.

Access

Directions to Clark & Seedhouse Road: From the north side of Steamboat Springs (see directions to Steamboat Springs on p. 346) drive CR 129 (Elk River Rd.) north for about 17 mi to the town of Clark. To access Seedhouse Rd., continue north on CR 129 for about a mile from Clark. Just after the road crosses the Elk River, Seedhouse Rd. is located on the right and is also marked as CR 64. Seedhouse Rd. becomes dirt after about 6 mi and eventually turns into FS 400.

Coulton Creek TH: Drive Seedhouse Rd. for 4.4 mi and follow signs to the Coulton Creek TH, which is located a couple hundred yards off the road on the left (north) side of the road.

South Fork TH: Drive Seedhouse Rd. for 5.5 mi to FS 440, which is on the right (south) side of the road. Take FS 440 south across the Elk River for 0.2 mi and the large parking area and trailhead are found on the south side of FS 440. In winter, FS 440 is generally plowed a bit past the South Fork TH so this area is accessible. Alternatively, in winter you can park on the north side of the river. This provides access to some ski and snowshoe trails on the south side of Seedhouse Rd.

Fall is a great time of year to explore North Routt County

Hinman TH: A small, unofficial trailhead that provides access to the Hinman Creek Trail and Hinman Lake. This parking area is located just off of Seedhouse Rd., 6.2 mi from CR 129, at the base of FS 430. Depending on conditions, you may be able to drive up FS 430 a short ways.

North Fork TH: The North Fork TH is located 8.6 mi up Seedhouse Rd. from CR 129 on the left (north) side just before crossing a bridge over the North Fork of the Elk River.

Seedhouse TH: The Seedhouse TH is located on the right (south) side of Seedhouse Rd. (CR 64) about 9.0 mi from CR 129. The parking area is located near the Seedhouse Group Campsite, which is just past the Seedhouse Campground.

Diamond Park TH: The Diamond Park TH can only be reached with a 4WD vehicle, although you can get fairly close with a 2WD vehicle. Follow directions above to the Seedhouse TH. Just past the Seedhouse TH, take a left on FS 433 (aka Lost Dog Rd.) and drive this for 3.8 mi (stay left after 3.4 mi). Take a left onto FS 44 and zigzag down to the North Fork of the Elk River (6.0 mi from Seedhouse Rd.). This is a good spot to park if you have low clearance. Otherwise, continue across the river and ascend an additional 0.9 mi to the Diamond Park TH, which is located on the north (right) side of FS 44.

Burn Ridge TH:  Drive Seedhouse Rd. for 9.5 mi to FS 443. Continue south across the Middle Fork of the Elk River for an additional 1.5 mi to the well-marked Burn Ridge TH .

Recommended Routes

Wyoming Trail: There are two trails heading north along the North Fork of the Elk River from the Seedhouse Campground area. Of the two, the Diamond Park Trail is perhaps the better one for mountain biking, but the Wyoming Trail on the east side of the creek is also superb and has a slightly more wild feel than its compatriot to the west. The Wyoming Trail north from the Seedhouse TH is rocky at times and progresses through the Hinman Fire remnants, aspens, and chest-high cow parsnip.

Diamond Park Trail: An easy trail ascending the broad valley on the west side of the North Fork of the Elk River. Begin at the North Fork TH. The trail gradually ascends an old doubletrack trail that is becoming singletrack. It is 3.8 mi to FS 44. To spice it up, ascend the Diamond Park Trail and descend the Wyoming Trail (or vice versa) and return via Seedhouse Rd.

Hinman Lake: Begin at the Hinman TH. Hike up doubletrack for about 0.9 mi, cross the creek to the west, then the short, stout singletrack climb along the Hinman Creek Trail through aspens and chest-high cow parsnip, finishing at the scenic Hinman Lake. 1.9 mi and 650 ft. of climbing to the lake.

Coulton Creek Trail: The Coulton Creek Trail is one of the finest trails in the Steamboat area. Hikers will want to do an out-and-back from the Coulton Creek TH but mountain bikers will likely want to make a loop out of this trail. Typically, bikers will ascend the Coulton Creek Trail and descend past Hinman Lake (see Coulton Creek/ Hinman Lake Loop on the next page). Alternatively, for a shorter loop you can bike up FS 429 and descend the Coulton Creek Trail. In summer, the lower part of the Coulton Creek Trail is covered with spectacular wildflowers (see photo on the next page). From top to bottom, this trail is 4.0 mi one-way and descends 1,120 ft. The Coulton Creek Trail and FS 429 are great for snowshoeing and cross country skiing in winter as well.

Cutover Trail: A relatively easy trail connecting the Hinman Lake area to the top of the Coulton Creek Trail. To get to this trail, you

A lawn of wildflowers, lower Coulton Creek Trail

must hike or bike to the Hinman Lake area on the Hinman Creek Trail (Scott's Run) or you must ascend the Coulton Creek Trail or Forest Service roads in the vicinity of Coulton Creek. Once on the Cutover Trail, it winds through forests of aspen, fir, and spruce. 1.4 mi one-way.

Coulton Creek/Hinman Loop

Coulton Creek/Hinman Lake Loop: Besides the road portion required to close this loop, this route is completely singletrack and progresses through a variety of interesting terrain and lush vegetation. The Coulton Creek Trail is a fun one to descend, but you will prefer to ascend Coulton Creek and descend the Hinman Creek Trail. Climb the Coulton Creek Trail from the Coulton Creek TH and find the Cutover Trail at the top near the edge of the burn zone. The Cutover Trail heads southeast into a stunning, lush forest. At the intersection with the Hinman Creek Trail (aka Scotts Run Trail), take a right and descend steeply on the Hinman Lake Trail through thick vegetation as the singletrack exits onto FS 430. Be sure to take the short side trip to the scenic Hinman Lake. Return via FS 430 and Seedhouse Rd. to the Coulton Creek TH. 9.5 mi and 1,500 ft. of elevation gain/loss for the loop.

Diamond Park/Scotts Run Loop: Another spectacular but challenging mountain bike loop. From the Hinman TH, take Seedhouse Rd. 2.4 mi east to the North Fork TH. Ascend the Diamond Park Trail to FS 44, climb FS 44 past the Diamond Park TH and find the singletrack Scotts Run Trail heading southwest just a short ways after crossing a creek drainage. Scotts Run Trail

Diamond Park/Scotts Run Loop

(also known as Hinman Creek Trail) is an adventurous, rocky, somewhat rutted trail. The northern (upper) part of Scotts Run traverses and gradually descends through the burn area

North Routt County

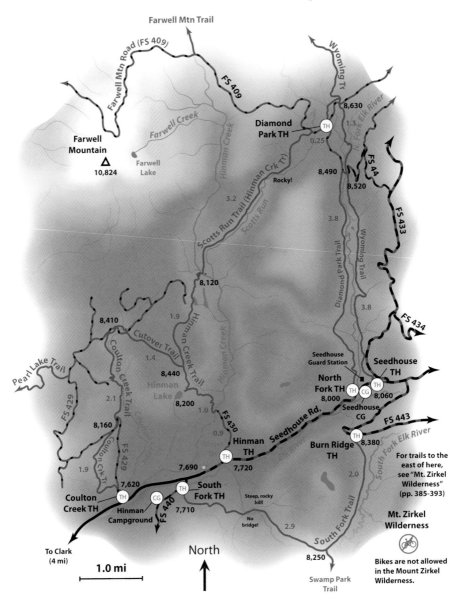

Farwell Mtn Trail

Farwell Mtn Road (FS 409)

FS 409

Wyoming Tr

8,630

Diamond
Park TH   TH   1.3

0.25

Farwell
Mountain   Farwell Creek   8,490

△   8,520   FS 44
10,824   Farwell
Lake   Rocky!

Hinman Creek   Scotts Run Trail (Hinman Crk Tr)   3.2   Scotts Run   3.8   Wyoming Trail   FS 433

8,120   3.8   FS 434

8,410   1.9   Hinman Creek Trail   Hinman Creek

Cutover Trail   Seedhouse
Guard Station   Seedhouse
TH

Pearl Lake Trail   1.4   8,440   North
Fork TH   TH   CG   TH

Coulton Creek Trail   Hinman
Lake   8,200   1.0   8,000   Seedhouse
CG   8,060

FS 429   2.1   FS 430   0.9   Seedhouse Rd.   FS 443

8,160   Hinman
TH   Burn Ridge
TH   TH
8,380   South Fork Elk River

Coulton Crk Tr   FS 429   7,690   7,720   For trails to the
east of here,
see "Mt. Zirkel
Wilderness"
(pp. 385-393)

1.9   7,620   TH   CG   TH   South
Fork TH   Steep, rocky
hill!   2.0

Coulton
Creek TH   Hinman
Campground   FS 440   7,710   No
bridge!   Mt. Zirkel
Wilderness

To Clark
(4 mi)   South Fork Trail   2.9   🚲

North   8,250   Bikes are not allowed
in the Mount Zirkel
Wilderness.

1.0 mi   Swamp Park
Trail

of the 2002 Hinman Fire to Hinman Creek, then re-enters lush forests as it climbs again towards Hinman Lake and the intersection with the Cutover Trail. Descend the Hinman Lake Trail and FS 430 back to where you began. 14.4 mi with 2,100 ft. of elevation gain/loss.

Diamond Park/Coulton Superloop: Begin at the Coulton Creek TH. Bike up Seedhouse Rd. and follow the previous route to the intersection of the Cutover Trail with the Hinman Creek Trail (Scotts Run Trail). Take a right (west) onto the Cutover Trail then descend the Coulton Creek Trail to your car. 19.5 mi and 2,650 ft. of elevation gain/loss.

South Fork Trail: The South Fork Trail connects the Burn Ridge TH (east side) with the South Fork TH (west side). There are a few very short steep and rocky sections but for the most part this trail meanders easily through aspen groves, lodgepole pine forests, and wide open meadows of grass and wildflowers. There

is a mandatory wet water crossing, so be prepared to get your feet wet. Hikers can choose to do an out-and-back from the top (Burn Ridge TH) or the bottom (South Fork TH). By bike, it is best to do as a loop in the clockwise direction by starting at the South Fork TH. The trail itself is 4.9 mi long; a loop requires a total of 10.8 mi and 940 ft. of elevation gain.

Other Recreational Opportunities

Steamboat Lake and Pearl Lake State Parks: Two outstanding state parks exist in North Routt County to the north of the town of Clark. These parks are perfect for those who like to combine camping with hiking and boating. For more information on either of these state parks, please visit www.parks.state.co.us.

Additional Wintertime Activities

Steamboat Lake State Park Touring Center: There is no better setting for cross country skiing and snowshoeing than that of the Steamboat Lake area with the impressive Hahns Peak situated at the head of the valley. Over 15 km of groomed ski trails and a 1.5-mi snowshoe trail exist within the state park and around Steamboat Lake. There are no ski rentals available here but you can find plenty of rentals in Steamboat Springs. Users must purchase a parks pass to use these trails.

Hinman Park Ski & Snowshoe Trails: In winter, trails to the north of Seedhouse Rd. are meant for motorized use (marked with orange diamonds) and those to the south of Seedhouse Rd. are meant for non-motorized use (blue diamonds). Park just south of the intersection of Seedhouse Rd. and FS 440 in Hinman Park and explore the South Fork Trail or various trails that develop just south of Seedhouse Rd. along the Elk River.

Gilpin Lake with Big Agnes Mountain (left) and Mount Zirkel (right) in the distance

Mount Zirkel Wilderness

Squeezed up near the Wyoming border to the northeast of Steamboat Springs, the Mount Zirkel Wilderness is one of the most extraordinary wilderness areas in the state of Colorado. Mount Zirkel sits at the head of three immense basins that were carved by glaciers 15,000 years ago during the Pleistocene epoch. Approximately 160,000 acres in size, the Mount Zirkel Wilderness was one of the original Colorado wilderness areas designated by the Wilderness Act of 1964 and additions were made in 1980 and 1993. In October of 1997, a peculiar wind event uprooted over 4 million spruce and fir trees and created patches of blowdown in an area 30 mi long and 5 mi wide. In all, over 20,000 acres of forest were affected. The peaks of the Mt. Zirkel Wilderness are not super high, but their jagged and lofty summits float high above some of the largest lakes and river valleys found in the state. One of the most spectacular sections of the Continental Divide Trail in the state traverses through the Mt. Zirkel Wilderness. Whether you are out for a week-long backpacking trip with a group of friends or a morning hike to one of the many spectacular crystal-clear lakes, the Mt. Zirkel Wilderness area will not disappoint. Presented in this chapter are just a handful of the more popular destinations for hikers (bikes are not permitted in the Mt. Zirkel Wilderness) and backpackers. Don't be discouraged by this bit of information, but remember to bring your mosquito repellent to the Mt. Zirkel Wilderness.

Maps: Sky Terrain "Steamboat Springs & Mt. Zirkel" or National Geographic Trails Illustrated "Hahns Peak, Steamboat Lake, N. Mt. Zirkel Wilderness" (#116) and "Clark, Buffalo Pass, S. Mt. Zirkel Wilderness" (#117).

Best time of the year: Like the Rabbit Ears Pass area to the south, the Continental Divide in this region squeezes out significant moisture throughout the year. Snowfall depths in the Mt. Zirkel Wilderness can be tremendous. Depending upon snowfall, these areas are not recommended until late June at the earliest. Fall is a great time to explore and significant snowfall does not accumulate until sometime in November.

Sunflowers, Mt. Zirkel Wilderness

Camping: On the west side of the Mt. Zirkel Wilderness, the Hinman and Seedhouse Campgrounds are located along Seedhouse Rd. (CR 64/FS 400) and are close to the Slavonia, Seedhouse, Three Island Lake, and North Lake trailheads. Currently, dispersed camping is prohibited along Seedhouse Rd. (FS 400) but is allowed to the south along FS 443. There is also a small designated camping zone just after the winter trailhead in Hinman Park (see map) on the south side of Seedhouse Rd. along the Elk River. On the east side of the Mt. Zirkel Wilderness, the Hidden Lakes and Teal Lake Campgrounds are located near the base of the east end of the Buffalo Pass Rd. to the west of Coalmont. Otherwise, dispersed camping is always available on national forest, but obey all signs. For more information about National Forest campgrounds in this area, please contact the Medicine Bow-Routt National Forest at (970) 870-2299.

Backpacking in the Mt. Zirkel Wilderness: There is no overnight camping within a quarter of a mile of Gilpin Lake, Gold Creek Lake, and Three Island Lake.

Seedhouse Guard Station: This historic Forest Service guard station is available for overnight stay from Sept. 1st through April 1st each year. This cabin is located just off

Seedhouse Rd. and would provide a nice "civilized" lodging option the night before heading out on an extended backpacking trip. Or, use as a fall retreat for exploring the west side of the Mt. Zirkel Wilderness via day hikes. See more details on p. 378 or for more information, visit www.recreation.gov or call (970) 723-2700. The cost is $100 per night.

Bikes stop at the wilderness boundary!

Sunset in the Mt. Zirkel Wilderness

Access

Directions to Clark & Seedhouse Road: From the north side of Steamboat Springs (see directions to Steamboat Springs on p. 346) drive CR 129 (Elk River Rd.) north for about 17 mi to the town of Clark. To access Seedhouse Rd., continue north on CR 129 for about a mile from Clark. Just after the road crosses the Elk River, Seedhouse Rd. is located on the right and is also marked as CR 64. Seedhouse Rd. becomes dirt after about 6 mi and eventually turns into FS 400.

Walden: Walden is located on the east side of the Continental Divide northeast of Rabbit Ears Pass. From I-70 Exit 205 in Silverthorne, take HWY 9 north for 38 mi to the town of Kremmling. Proceed on US 40 west (north) for about 27 mi to HWY 14. Continue on HWY 14 north for 33 mi to the intersection with HWY 125; take a left onto HWY 125 and Walden is reached after another mile.

Seedhouse TH: The Seedhouse TH is located on the right (south) side of Seedhouse Rd. (CR 64) about 9 mi from CR 129. The parking area is located near the Seedhouse Group Campsite, which is just past the Seedhouse Campground.

Slavonia TH: The Slavonia TH is located at the very end of Seedhouse Rd. (FS 400), 11.8 mi from CR 129.

Three Island Lake TH:  Take Seedhouse Rd. for 9.5 mi and turn right onto FS 443. Drive 3.1 mi to the roadside parking area and the trailhead for the Three Island Lake Trail.

North Lake TH: Follow directions above to the Three Island Lake TH. Continue up FS 443 for an additional 1.4 mi to the obvious trailhead and parking area. The road is passable for most 2WD vehicles, depending on conditions.

Rainbow Lakes TH: This trailhead is a bit difficult to get to. Most people end up driving to the town of Walden, which is located along HWY 14 northeast of Rabbit Ears Pass. From the intersection of HWY 14 and CR 12W to the west of Walden, take CR 12W west for 5.2 mi. At the bottom of a steep hill, take a left onto CR 18. From this intersection, travel 4.5 mi on CR 18 then take a left onto CR 5 (state wildlife area sign here). You will turn onto a dirt road, and continue on this road for about 9 mi to the Rainbow Lakes TH. The road turns into CR 22 after 1.8 mi and stay right at an intersection between mile markers 4 and 5. You know you are getting close when you ascend a winding road near some homes. The trailhead is located at the end of the road.

Big Agnes Mountain from the south

Recommended Routes

Gilpin Lake Trail: Gilpin Lake is one of my favorite destinations in the state of Colorado! A spectacular moderate hike through aspen groves, fir, and spruce as the trail climbs

Gilpin Lake Trail

higher. Gilpin Creek is never far away and there are stunning waterfalls before the final climb to the lake. The lake is located in an incredible alpine basin with high, glaciated rock walls and Big Agnes Mtn. and Mt. Zirkel looming high overhead. From the Slavonia TH, the lake is reached after 4.5 mi and 2,000 ft. of climbing. Continue beyond the lake up to the pass to the south of the lake for an amazing view (0.7 mi and 400 vertical ft.).

Mount Zirkel Wilderness - West Side

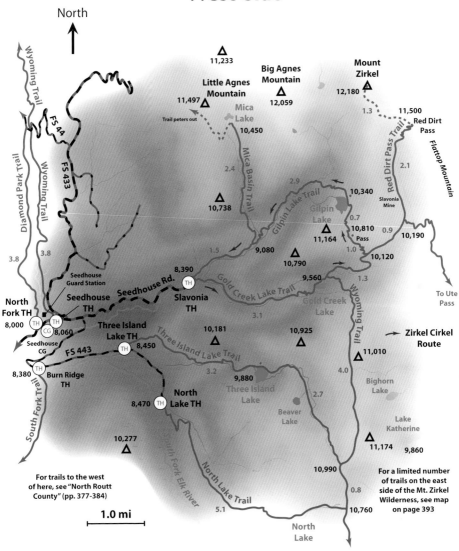

North

11,233

Little Agnes Mountain
11,497

Big Agnes Mountain
12,059

Mount Zirkel
12,180

FS 44

FS 433

Trail peters out

Mica Lake
10,450

1.3

11,500
Red Dirt Pass

Diamond Park Trail

Wyoming Trail

Mica Basin Trail

2.4

10,738

Gilpin Lake Trail

2.9

10,340

Slavonia Mine

Red Dirt Pass Trail

Flattop Mountain

2.1

Gilpin Lake
11,164

0.7

10,810
Pass

0.9

10,190

3.8

3.8

1.5

9,080

10,790

1.0

10,120

Seedhouse Guard Station

Seedhouse Rd.

8,390
TH

Gold Creek Lake Trail

9,560

1.3

Wyoming Trail

To Ute Pass

North Fork TH
8,000

Seedhouse TH

Slavonia TH

Gold Creek Lake

Zirkel Cirkel Route

TH   TH
CG   8,060

Three Island Lake TH

3.1

10,181

10,925

Seedhouse CG

FS 443

TH   8,450

11,010

8,380

Burn Ridge TH

Three Island Lake Trail

3.2

9,880

4.0

Bighorn Lake

South Fork Trail

TH

North Lake TH

Three Island Lake

2.7

Lake Katherine

8,470   TH

Beaver Lake

11,174   9,860

10,277

South Fork Elk River

North Lake Trail

10,990

0.8

For trails to the west of here, see "North Routt County" (pp. 377-384)

5.1

10,760

North Lake

For a limited number of trails on the east side of the Mt. Zirkel Wilderness, see map on page 393

1.0 mi

Norris Creek below Slide Lake

Gold Creek Lake Trail: The Gold Creek Lake Trail begins at the Slavonia TH. Take the Gilpin Lake Trail for 0.1 mi then turn right. After proceeding through some aspen groves, the trail climbs along Gold Creek, overcoming some steep terrain and switchbacks before arriving at Gold Creek Lake after 3.0 mi and 1,200 ft. of climbing. The trail continues beyond the lake. Ultimately, Red Dirt Pass can be reached after 7.3 mi and 3,300 ft. of elevation gain.

Three Island Lake Trail: The Three Island Lake Trail progresses through easy to moderate aspen-covered slopes culminating in a final climb along a cascading creek to a large meadow just below the lake. It is 3.2 mi to the lake with 1,600 ft. of elevation gain. The trail continues an additional 2.7 mi (1,130 ft. of climbing) to a spectacular viewpoint high on the Continental Divide at the intersection with the Wyoming Trail.

Wyoming Trail: Remote and somewhat difficult to follow in places adds to the appeal of the Mt. Zirkel segment of the Wyoming Trail. Spectacular views of Mt. Ethel to the south and Big Agnes Mountain and Mt. Zirkel to the north. The Wyoming Trail can eventually be accessed by starting at the Slavonia, Three Island Lake, or North Lake trailheads. A nice loop is to ascend the Three Island Lake Trail to the Wyoming Trail then descend the Gold Creek Trail, but this requires setting up a car shuttle. The difficulty varies between moderate and difficult, in general.

Zirkel Haute Route: A stunning traverse of the Continental Divide linking the North Lake TH with Slavonia TH. Best for a multi-day backpacking trip but possible for one *very* long day on foot. You will need to set up a car shuttle or will have to add on 6.9 mi of hiking on roads to complete the loop. Ascend the North Lake Trail from the North Lake TH, travel north on the Wyoming Trail to Gold Creek, then finish by hiking up and over to Gilpin Lake and descending Gilpin Creek to Slavonia TH. The route is 17.3 mi long with 4,300 ft. of elevation gain and loss.

North Lake: From the North Lake TH, this trail climbs steeply to a ridge then ascends southeast as the trail gets easier before reaching the lake after about 4.0 mi and 1,900 ft. of climbing. The trail intersects the Wyoming Trail 1.2 mi east of the lake.

North Lake TH to Buffalo Pass: If you are looking for an extraordinary multi-day backpacking trip, a long hike, or a long trail run, this section of the Continental Divide has a little of everything. Like the Zirkel Haute Route above, this section of trail will leave you breathless. You will need to set up a car shuttle, leaving a car at Buffalo Pass (see p. 354). It is approximately 20 mi with 5,100 ft. of climbing from North Lake TH to Buffalo Pass along the Wyoming Trail. Consult a detailed map for the exact route.

Mount Zirkel: Forget about the over-hyped and crowded Fourteeners (14,000-ft. peaks of Colorado) and head to Mount Zirkel. Mount Zirkel is only 12,180 ft. tall but the wild

country surrounding the peak make this an extraordinary adventure. Start at Slavonia TH and ascend the Gold Creek Lake Trail to Red Dirt Pass. From Red Dirt Pass, ascend the ridge to the summit. It is about 8.6 mi to the top with 4,000 ft. of elevation gain.

Treeline stream near the Continental Divide

Mica Basin Trail: Begin at the Slavonia TH and ascend the Gilpin Lake Trail for 1.5 mi to the intersection with the Mica Basin Trail, which heads north. The trail is quite steep for the first mile, passing through the narrow opening of Mica Basin with high rock walls on both sides. The trail eventually eases in difficulty and

Mica Basin Trail

Mica Lake is reached after 4.0 mi and 2,150 ft. of elevation gain from Slavonia TH. The lake sits in a high alpine basin framed by Big Agnes and Little Agnes Mountains. A trail continues west and up from the lake to the south ridge of Little Agnes Mountain.

Mount Zirkel Cirkel

Mount Zirkel Cirkel: This is a favorite among hikers, backpackers, and trail runners. Backpackers are the big winners here as they will be spending some quality time in one of the most spectacular alpine basins in all of Colorado. From Slavonia TH, hike up the Gold Creek Lake Trail past the lake and past the intersection with the Wyoming Trail. Continue north over the high pass to Gilpin Lake and descend the Gilpin Lake Trail back to Slavonia TH. The loop is 10.6 mi with 2,600 ft. of elevation gain/loss.

Rainbow Lake Trail: The trail to Rainbow Lakes and beyond progresses through a variety of vegetation. Begin at the Rainbow Lake TH. The trail is easy to moderate until Rainbow

Lake, which is one of the biggest natural lakes around. It is 3.4 mi to Rainbow Lake and a climb of 1,400 ft. Continue on the Rainbow Lake Trail and Upper Slide Lake is reached after an additional 3.6 mi and 1,200 ft. of climbing. The trail ultimately intersects the Wyoming Trail (Continental Divide Trail) after 8.7 mi. There are some amazing campsites at treeline near Slide and Upper

Rainbow Lake Trail

Slide Lakes with Mount Ethel keeping you company at the head of the drainage.

Roxy Ann Lake: Begin at the Rainbow Lake TH and take the Rainbow Lake Trail past Rainbow Lake and Upper Slide Lake to just before the Continental Divide. After 8.2 mi (1.3

Mount Ethel reflects in a mountain tarn

Mount Zirkel Wilderness - Rainbow Lake Area

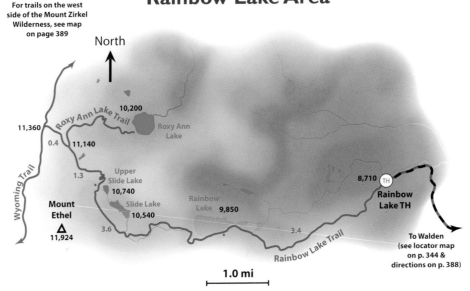

For trails on the west side of the Mount Zirkel Wilderness, see map on page 389

North

Roxy Ann Lake Trail

10,200

11,360

0.4   11,140

Roxy Ann Lake

Wyoming Trail

1.3   Upper Slide Lake
10,740

8,710   TH

Rainbow Lake TH

Mount Ethel

△

11,924

Slide Lake
10,540

Rainbow Lake   9,850

3.6

3.4

Rainbow Lake Trail

To Walden
(see locator map on p. 344 & directions on p. 388)

1.0 mi

Roxy Ann Lake

mi past Upper Slide Lake at around 11,140 ft.), descend the Roxy Ann Lake Trail for an additional 1.8 mi to the rather large Roxy Ann Lake. This is a nice setting for an overnight trip.

Grizzly-Helena Trail: Traversing the eastern edge of the Mt. Zirkel Wilderness, the Grizzly-Helena Trail is a mostly singletrack trail connecting the Grizzly TH in the south with the Helena TH in the south. Also open to motorbikes. Many adventures are possible here, so go explore on foot or by bike.

Grizzly-Helena Trail

Other Possibilities in the Mount Zirkel Wilderness

Outlined in this chapter are the most popular destinations in the Mt. Zirkel Wilderness. There are numerous other extraordinary and worthwhile destinations that are not covered in this chapter. Most of these destinations are quite secluded and difficult to get to, making them rather unpopular. However, seldom-traveled trails can make for some adventurous trips. Some of these seldom-visited areas not discussed here include the Roaring Fork, Swamp Park, and Luna Lake Trails that are located between the Mad Creek and North Fork TH areas, as well as the Lake Katherine, Ute Pass, Twin Lakes, and Blue Lake areas on the east side of the divide. Consult a map for trails elsewhere in the Mt. Zirkel Wilderness.

Charlie's Picks for Steamboat Springs

1. Beall Trail (p. 368)

2. Zirkel Haute Route (p. 391)

3. Coulton Creek Trail (p. 381)

4. Hogan Park Ski Route (p. 364)

5. Mountain View Trail (p. 359)

6. Emerald Mountain Trails (p. 367)

7. Wyoming Trail, north of Rabbit Ears Pass (p. 356)

8. Fish Creek Falls Trail (p. 356)

9. Rainbow Lake Trail (p. 392)

10. Pete's Wicked to Valley View (p. 350)

The shores of Rainbow Lake

Byers Peak in early summer

Chapter 10: Winter Park, Fraser, Indian Peaks West, and Granby

Don't be misled by the name - there is quite a bit to do in Winter Park and the surrounding areas of Grand County in all seasons, not just winter. Sure, the cross country and snowshoeing opportunities in Winter Park are numerous, but once the snow melts there are plenty of mountain biking and hiking possibilities. Touted as "Mountain Biking Capitol USA," Winter Park offers spectacular biking opportunities, and many of these trails can enjoyably be hiked. The nearby, lower-lying Fraser Valley boasts its own set of trails. For those who enjoy the solitude of wilderness, two of the lesser known wilderness areas in Colorado - the Vasquez Peak Wilderness and Byers Peak Wilderness - are southwest of Winter Park. Here, you can explore alpine lakes and some of the most extensive, easy-to-travel high ridge systems. Few people venture into the Vasquez Peak and Byers Peak Wilderness areas, so you can encounter extreme solitude. The west side of the Indian Peaks Wilderness can be accessed from northeast of Fraser near Lake Granby as well as Rollins Pass. For some spectacular moderate trails, check out the Strawberry Bench area near Grand Lake.

Winter Park, Fraser, Indian Peaks West, and Granby

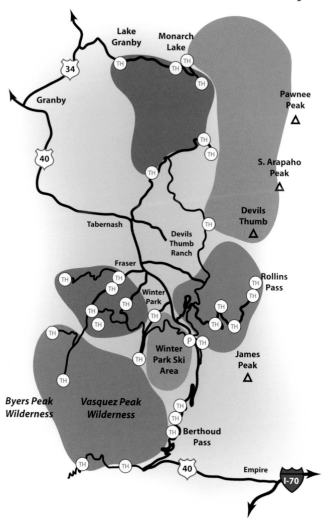

Winter Park Central (pp. 397-403)

Winter Park East (pp. 404-416)

Fraser Valley (pp. 417-425)

Byers Peak Wilderness, Vasquez Peak Wilderness, and Berthoud Pass (pp. 426-433)

Indian Peaks Wilderness - West Side (pp. 434-443)

Strawberry Creek & Monarch Lake (pp. 444-449)

Welcome to Winter Park!

Winter Park Central

The slopes of the Winter Park Resort and vicinity are home to some notable trails that zigzag through forested slopes and meadows in a serene mountain environment. Visible from the slopes of Winter Park is the lofty Continental Divide, running north to south to the east of town. James and Parry Peaks are quite impressive as are the Indian Peaks to the northeast of town. Vasquez Creek is tucked in a secluded valley to the west of the ski resort. Some great singletrack trails are found in the area between the ski resort and Vasquez Creek. In winter, the ski resort abounds with downhill skiing excitement. The Vasquez Creek area is a worthwhile area for snowshoeing and cross country skiing outings and this area can be reached quickly from town. At the end of the day, explore shops and restaurants in the town of Winter Park.

Maps: Backcountry Bound "Winter Park and Fraser, Colorado – Mountain Bike Map" and National Geographic Trails Illustrated "Winter Park, Central City, Rollins Pass" (#103).

Best time of the year: Winter maintains its icy grip on the high alpine trails of the Winter Park Resort well into early to mid June in most years. The north-facing slopes do not see a lot of sun until late spring. Late July through sometime in late September or early October is the normal summer and fall season here. Sufficient snows for skiing and snowshoeing do not generally arrive until mid to late November.

Camping: The Idlewild and Robbers Roost Campgrounds are located near Winter Park. Advanced reservations are recommended, especially for the scenic and popular Idlewild Campground. It is located within a few minutes of Winter Park, just a mile south of town along US 40. The Robbers Roost Campground is located at the base of Berthoud Pass, 7 mi south of Winter Park on US 40. Contact the Sulfur Ranger District at (970) 887-4100 for more information on these campgrounds. There is plenty of dispersed camping along the Vasquez Creek Rd. From the first stoplight in town, take Vasquez Rd. After 1.0 mi, continue straight on CR 7/FS 148 (dirt). There are lots of campsites adjacent to this road, most of them are higher up the road. There is additional camping on National Forest lands along the Rollins Pass Rd. and Elk Creek Rd. to the southeast of Fraser. Showers are available for a very reasonable fee at the Grand Park Community Recreation Center [(970) 726-8968], which is located between Winter Park and Fraser on the west side of US 40.

Access

Winter Park: From I-70 and C-470 to the west of Denver, travel I-70 for 28 mi to Exit 232 (Empire/Granby/US 40). Proceed on US 40 through the towns of Empire and Berthoud Falls then up and over Berthoud Pass. From I-70, Winter Park is reached after 28 mi.

Winter Park Resort Summer Parking: This is the place to park if you are exploring trails of the Winter Park Ski Resort or for hiking or biking the Serenity Trail and over to Vasquez Creek. From the town of Winter Park, take US 40 south for about 1.5 mi and keep an eye out for Winter Park Dr. Follow Winter Park Dr. for 1.6 mi (taking a right turn at 1.1 mi), take a right onto Nystrom Ln., and there are some parking spots and parking structure with plenty of parking for all but the busiest of days. If coming from the south, Winter Park Dr. is the first stoplight when approaching on US 40. Take a left at the stoplight and Nystrom Ln. is reached after a half mile. Overflow parking can be found in the vicinity. You will have to pay to park here in winter.

Fraser River TH: Located where US 40 crosses over the Fraser River between the ski area and the town of Winter Park. From the town of Winter Park, drive about 1.5 mi south to where the highway crosses over the Fraser River. On the west side of the highway follow signs for "Town of Winter Park Public Works." There is a parking area here with access to the Fraser River Trail.

Aspen tree trunk

![National Forests mean year round fun sign]

Twin Bridges TH: From the first stoplight as you enter Winter Park from the south (Vasquez Rd.), take a left and proceed west for about a mile on Vasquez Rd. At this point, continue straight as the road turns to dirt; also labeled as CR 7 and FS 148. Continue 0.2 mi from here and the Twin Bridges TH is located just off the left (east) side of the road. The Twin Bridges Trail is found just down the road.

Vasquez Creek Winter TH: As you drive into Winter Park from the south (Berthoud Pass), take a left on the first stoplight in town (Vasquez Rd.). Follow Vasquez Rd. west then southwest as it crosses train tracks (0.4 mi) and passes through a neighborhood. After 1.0 mi, continue straight onto Vasquez Rd. (CR 7/FS 148). From here, the winter parking area can be found after 0.9 mi.

Recommended Routes

Vasquez Road: The Vasquez Rd. can be used as an easy biking route by itself or to access other mountain biking or hiking trails in the area. Start at the Twin Bridges TH. In winter, the Vasquez Rd. is a great place to cross country ski or snowshoe (begin at the Vasquez Creek Winter TH).

Fraser River Trail: A paved bike and pedestrian path connecting the Winter Park Ski Resort with the towns of Winter Park and Fraser. Through the town of Winter Park the trail takes a break but you can follow the sidewalk on the west side of US 40. The trail resumes again on the north side

Along the paved Fraser River Trail

of town. Great for an walk, run, or bike ride. The southern terminus can be accessed off of Trademark Dr. near the base of the ski area. This is just north along Winter Park Dr. from the intersection of Winter Park Dr. and Old Town Dr. (park at the base of the resort). The Fraser River TH is also a more straightforward parking spot and the trail can be accessed from ample parking near the Grand Park Community Recreation Center, located between Winter Park and Fraser. The northern terminus is near the stoplight in Fraser.

Serenity Trail: A peaceful, wooded trail that parallels the Fraser River to the northwest of the ski resort base. Find the train tracks at the base of the resort and the trail heads into the trees on the west side of the tracks. Also a setting for the perfect winter adventure on skis or snowshoes. The Serenity Trail is 1.4 mi long.

Twin Bridges Trail: A popular trail that heads east from the Twin Bridges TH to an intimate location along Vasquez Creek. After crossing the two bridges, the trail heads south to the intersection with the Blue Sky Trail. A nice

short hike, 0.5 mi long. Continue west on the Blue Sky Trail if you are inclined.

Blue Sky Trail: An easy to moderate trail for hiking and biking in summer and cross country

Winter Park Central

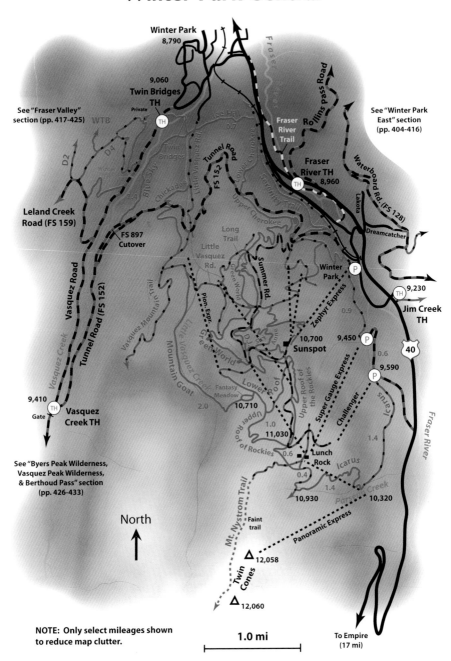

Winter Park
8,790

9,060
Twin Bridges
TH
Private

See "Fraser Valley"
section (pp. 417-425)

WTB

D2

D4

Fraser River Trail

Rollins pass Road

See "Winter Park East" section (pp. 404-416)

Fraser River TH
8,960

Waterboard Rd (FS 128)

Lakota

Dreamcatcher

Leland Creek Road (FS 159)

FS 897 Cutover

Tunnel Road

FS 152

Upper Cherokee

Long Trail

Little Vasquez Rd.

Summer Rd.

Winter Park

P

Zephyr Express

0.9

9,230

TH

Jim Creek TH

Vasquez Road

Tunnel Road (FS 152)

Vasquez Creek

Vasquez Mountain Trail

Little Vasquez Creek

Mountain Goat

Pion. Expr.

Green World

9,410

Gate

Vasquez Creek TH

See "Byers Peak Wilderness, Vasquez Peak Wilderness, & Berthoud Pass" section (pp. 426-433)

10,700
Sunspot

10,710

Fantasy Meadow

2.0

Lower Roof of Rockies

1.0

11,030

Upper Roof of Rockies

0.6

9,450

P

Super Gauge Express

Challenger

0.6

9,590

P

Icarus

1.4

Fraser River

40

Lunch Rock

0.4

10,930

Icarus

1.4

Parsenn Creek

10,320

North

Mt. Nystrom Trail

Faint trail

Panoramic Express

△ 12,058

Twin Cones

△ 12,060

NOTE: Only select mileages shown to reduce map clutter.

1.0 mi

To Empire (17 mi)

skiing and snowshoeing in winter. Start at the Twin Bridges TH, find the Twin Bridges Trail just down the Vasquez Rd., and head down to the creek. At the intersection past the bridges, take a right on the Blue Sky Trail and take this as far as you wish. Ultimately, the trail intersects the FS 897 cutover after 1.1 mi.

Blue Sky-Ice Hill-Serenity: A nice moderate mountain bike ride. Begin at the Twin Bridges TH and bike 0.9 mi up Vasquez Rd. to the FS 897 cutover to near the Tunnel Rd. Find the south end of the singletrack Blue Sky Trail, which is found at a 3-way road intersection (see map). Enjoy the 1.5 mi of moderate to easy singletrack as you zoom through the forests and exit at the Little Vasquez Rd. Cross the road and continue on Ice Hill and descend to the railroad tracks. Head south along the tracks and follow the sign for the Serenity Trail, which gradually climbs through forests to the ski resort base. Return via the Fraser River Trail and Vasquez Rd. 9.7 mi for the loop.

Little Vasquez to Vasquez Mountain: A strenuous, difficult climb for hikers or mountain bikers. Begin at the Twin Bridges TH, take the Twin Bridges Trail east and at the intersection with the Blue Sky Trail go left 0.1 mi to Little Vasquez Creek. Take a right onto FS 156 and climb all the way up to the Tunnel Hill Rd. Find a dirt road on the west side of Little Vasquez Creek. Take this road and after 0.5 mi there is a fork. Go right and climb the Vasquez Mountain Rd. After about 4.5 mi from the Twin Bridges TH the road peters out near treeline. A nice climb on foot or by bike with nice views from the top.

Winter Park Resort Bike Trails

NOTE: There are plenty of biking trails on the slopes of the Winter Park Ski Resort. The trails here are not recommended for hiking. The ski resort maintains quite a few downhill bike trails ranging in difficulty, but only a select few of these trails are described here. Routes change from year to year so please inquire about the full opportunities at the resort by visiting the website for the Trestle Bike Park at www.trestlebikepark.com. For those who are looking to earn their turns, take the Summer Rd. from the Tunnel Hill Rd. to the top of the Zephyr Express lift near Sunspot, a climb of 1,600 ft. in 3.8 mi.

Icarus: Start at the bottom of the Zephyr lift at the base of the ski area. Find a maintenance road that goes south from the base area along the edge of the forest, passing under a bridge just before exiting near the Mary Jane base. Follow the dirt road as if you are exiting the ski area. You will climb up a hill and there will be another parking lot. At the southwest end of the large lot, find a summer maintenance road to the bottom of the

Panoramic Express and Sunnyside ski lifts. From here, the trail becomes singletrack and heads up the ski slopes, zigzagging through forests and the occasional meadow to the base of the old Parsenn Bowl ski lift (no longer in use). Follow a dirt road right and northeast up to near Lunch Rock where the top of 3 lifts are found. Just before the top, Icarus continues a short ways as a singletrack trail north to intersect the Roof of the Rockies Trail. It is a climb of 2,200 ft. in 4.8 mi to Lunch Rock.

Roof of the Rockies: Upper Roof of the Rockies does a big horseshoe in the basin to the northwest of Lunch Rock. From the top of the Olympia Express lift, find Upper Roof of the Rockies (east side of service road). Take this up the ridge and pass a few maintenance roads and you'll come to a high point

and trail intersection (top of Icarus). Continue right as the trail zigzags through spruce forests to the intersection with Lower Roof of the Rockies. Lower Roof of the Rockies is singletrack between the top of the Olympia Express lift to below Fantasy Meadow near the top of the Pioneer Express lift then follows a maintenance road down to the intersection with Green World (see below). The upper part is intermediate, the lower part is slightly easier.

Mountain Goat: Find your way to Fantasy Meadow via Lower Roof of the Rockies from the top of the Olympia Express lift. About halfway around the easy Fantasy Meadow loop, the Mountain Goat Trail heads west into Little Vasquez Creek. The descent is rocky at times and ends at the Little Vasquez Rd. It is a descent of 1,030 vertical ft. in 2.0 mi from Fantasy Meadow to Little Vasquez Rd.

Green World: A fun, well-maintained trail that descends from the top of the Olympia Express lift west into the very top of Little Vasquez Creek then traverses over to the top of Cooper Creek. Many other downhill trail emerge from or intersect with Green World as it snakes its way 5.2 mi to the base of the resort.

Lower Cherokee: A fun, steep but not too technical 0.8-mi descent from the Tunnel Hill Rd. to the Serenity Trail area. Do this by itself by climbing the Tunnel Hill Rd. from the base of the ski resort or add on at the end of a longer bike ride. It is a gradual climb along the Serenity Trail back to the ski resort base.

Additional Summertime Fun

There are a lot more activities to partake in at the Winter Park Ski Resort, including disc golf, bungee jumping, mini zip line, a climbing wall, chairlift rides, Colorado's longest alpine slide, mini golf, and a human-sized maze.

Winter Park East

Visit the Winter Park area and it is difficult not to notice the high peaks hovering over the Grand Valley to the east and southeast of town. To the east of Winter Park and Berthoud Pass is the Continental Divide, stretching north to south and separating the waters that go to the Pacific Ocean (on the west side) and the Atlantic Ocean (east side). The Rollins Pass area to the east of Winter Park has a unique history. A wagon road over the pass was established in the mid 1860s by a man of the name John Quincy Adams Rollins. It wasn't until 1903 that a railroad was built over the pass by David H. Moffat. The town of Corona soon sprouted atop Rollins Pass and the town was complete with a restaurant, hotel, and housing. Near Riflesight Notch along the railroad, the railway corkscrewed around a small peak, going underneath the mountain via a tunnel then crossing over Riflesight Notch via a trestle bridge, which still remains. In 1928 the Moffat Tunnel was built underneath the Continental Divide, eliminating many of the hardships encountered by the railway workers in the winter atop Rollins Pass. Today, many recreational opportunities abound in the Winter Park area year-round. The Rollins Pass Rd., which follows the old railway bed, provides excellent access to many trails to the east of town. Rollins Pass provides a starting point for hiking adventures to the north and to the south.

Maps: Backcountry Bound "Winter Park and Fraser, Colorado – Mountain Bike Map" and National Geographic Trails Illustrated "Winter Park, Central City, Rollins Pass" (#103).

Best time of the year: The west side of the Continental Divide gets buffeted by some pretty harsh weather in winter and significant snows accumulate in the alpine and subalpine zones. While the Rollins Pass Rd. (CR 80/FS 149) and the Waterboard Rd. (FS 128) provide for some of the best cross country ski touring around, these trails do not thaw out until early June, at the earliest. The low-lying Idlewild Trails do tend to melt out sooner, although there

Forest along the Serenity Trail

Cascading waterfall, near Berthoud Pass

are several pockets that accumulate quite a bit of snow, providing muddy spots well into early summer.

Camping: The Idlewild and Robbers Roost Campgrounds near Winter Park are nice campgrounds, if you can get reservations here. Advanced reservations are recommended. The Idlewild Campground is located within a few minutes of Winter Park, just a mile south of town along US 40. The Robbers Roost Campground is located at the base of Berthoud Pass, 7 mi south of Winter Park on US 40. Contact the Sulfur Ranger District at (970) 887-4100 for more information on these campgrounds. Additional limited camping can be found along the Rollins Pass Rd. Showers are available for a very reasonable fee at the Grand Park Community Recreation Center [(970) 726-8968], which is located between Winter Park and Fraser on the west side of US 40.

Aspens along Broken Thumb Trail

Access

Winter Park: From I-70 and C-470 to the west of Denver, travel I-70 for 28 mi to Exit 232 (Empire/Granby/US 40). Proceed on US 40 through the towns of Empire and Berthoud Falls then up and over Berthoud Pass. From I-70, Winter Park is reached after 28 mi.

Rollins Pass Road: From the town of Winter Park, take US 40 south. Just after the highway crosses over the Fraser River and within a quarter mile of the "Town of Winter Park Public Works" sign, turn left (east) onto the Rollins Pass Rd. (CR 80/FS 149).

Fraser River TH: Located where US 40 crosses over the Fraser River between the ski area and the town of Winter Park. From the town of Winter Park, drive

Jim Creek TH: Take US 40 south from Winter Park for 13.1 mi to the stoplight at the southern end of Winter Park Dr. (ski resort main entrance). Take a left here and turn into Lot G of the Winter Park Resort, across US 40 from the main entrance. Park near some signs and trailhead or if full you can continue into Lot G and park there.

Rollins Pass TH: Depending upon conditions and maintenance, you may or may not be able to drive your 2WD vehicle to the top of Rollins Pass, although many folks do even when the road is bad. Follow directions on the previous page to the Rollins Pass Rd. The road starts out good but gradually gets rougher, particularly after Riflesight Notch, a cleft in the mountains that is still spanned by the old trestle railway bridge. The parking area atop Rollins Pass at 11,670 ft. is about 14 mi from US 40.

Broken Thumb TH: Follow directions on the previous page to the start of the Rollins Pass Rd. From US 40, the Broken Thumb TH is located 7.0 mi up the Rollins Pass Rd. on the left (north) side of the road.

Riflesight TH: Follow directions on the previous page to the start of the Rollins Pass Rd. Drive 8.6 mi up the Rollins Pass Rd. and there is a small parking area by a closure gate at a right-turning hairpin curve (be sure to read all signs).

Rogers Pass TH: Follow directions on the previous page to the start of the Rollins Pass Rd. The Rogers Pass TH is located 10.6 mi up the Rollins Pass Rd. by the old trestle bridge.

Pumphouse Lake with Winter Park Resort in the distance

Pumphouse TH:  An informal parking area alongside the Rollins Pass Rd. that provides access to Pumphouse and Corona Lakes. Located near the top of the Rollins Pass Rd. one mile from the top of the pass. Some 2WD vehicles may be able to get here.

Idlewild TH: The main access point for enjoying the Idlewild Trail system to the east of the town of Fraser. From the north end of Winter Park, travel less than a mile north on US 40, past the Grand Park Community Recreation Center on your left, to Rendezvous Rd. (sign for a museum here). Take a right (east) and proceed up the road as it winds its way through a neighborhood. After 1.1 mi, take a right onto Friendship Drive. After another quarter of a mile there is a fire hydrant. Park along the road just after the fire hydrant. **NOTE: There is no parking allowed along these streets from 2-10 am in the months of November through April. If you are an early morning skier you are out of luck!**

Recommended Routes

Rollins Pass Road

Rollins Pass Road: The Rollins Pass Rd. can be skied in winter and hiked and biked in the summer and fall. In summer, park at the Fraser River TH or other places along the Rollins Pass Rd. (follow signs and regulations). In winter, link to the Rollins Pass Rd. from the Waterboard Rd. (FS 128) off of Dreamcatcher North (see "Additional Wintertime Activities" on p. 416). The Rollins Pass Rd. provides scenic views to the west and of the Grand Valley. Starts out moderate but gets steeper (and the air gets thinner!). If you are really ambitious, the climb to the top of Rollins Pass is a 14-mi endeavor with close to 3,000 ft. of total climbing.

Jim Creek Trail: The Jim Creek Trail officially begins at the Waterboard Rd. (FS 128). From the Jim Creek TH, go back out to US 40, hike/bike a short ways south along the highway, and find a road (Jim Creek Rd.) that leads left (east) into the woods, crosses under a pipeline, and ultimately brings you out on FS 128. Please stay off of the boardwalk, which is a handicap-accessible trail. It is about 0.8 mi to the start of the Jim Creek Trail. The Jim Creek Trail gradually ascends on a doubletrack trail a scenic valley, alternating between meadows and forests. The trail ends after about 1.8 mi.

Jim Creek Trail

Buck Creek to Broken Thumb

Buck Creek to Broken Thumb Trail: The only thing keeping Broken Thumb Trail from being a classic singletrack bike route is the fact that it is open to motorbikes, which tend to chew up the trail and make it somewhat loose in spots. Otherwise, this is a great descent and is usually combined with Buck Creek. Start either at the Fraser River TH or the Broken Thumb TH. The latter

Winter Park East

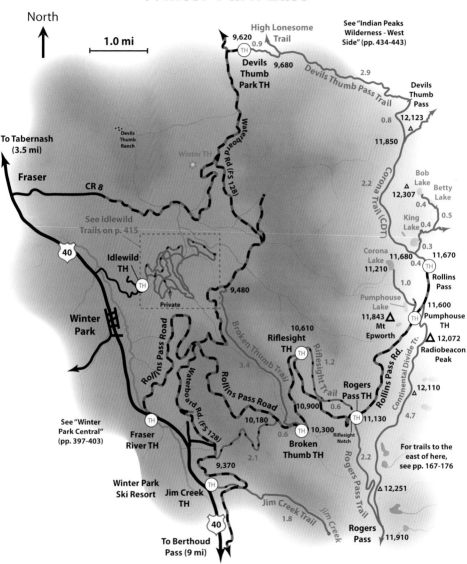

North

1.0 mi

High Lonesome Trail

9,620 0.9

Devils Thumb Park TH

9,680

See "Indian Peaks Wilderness - West Side" (pp. 434-443)

Devils Thumb Pass Trail 2.9

Devils Thumb Pass 12,123

0.8

11,850

To Tabernash (3.5 mi)

Fraser

CR 8

Devils Thumb Ranch

Winter TH

Corona Trail (CDT) 2.2

Bob Lake 12,307

Betty Lake

0.4 0.5

King Lake 0.4

0.3

40

Idlewild TH

See Idlewild Trails on p. 415

9,480

Private

Corona Lake 11,680 11,670

11,210 0.4

1.0

Rollins Pass TH

Winter Park

Waterboard Rd (FS 128)

Pumphouse Lake

Mt Epworth 11,843

11,600

Pumphouse TH

Radiobeacon Peak 12,072

Broken Thumb Trail

10,610

Riflesight TH

Riflesight Trail 1.2

3.4

12,110

Rollins Pass Road

Rollins Pass Rd.

Continental Divide Tr.

Rogers Pass TH

10,900 0.6

11,130

4.7

See "Winter Park Central" (pp. 397-403)

Fraser River TH

Waterboard Rd. (FS 128)

10,180

0.6 10,300

Broken Thumb TH

Riflesight Notch

2.1

For trails to the east of here, see pp. 167-176

12,251

Winter Park Ski Resort

9,370

Jim Creek TH

40

Rogers Pass Trail 2.2

Jim Creek Trail 1.8

Jim Creek

Rogers Pass 11,910

To Berthoud Pass (9 mi)

Sunrise atop Rollins Pass with James Peak in the distance

Lupine

is useful if you are setting up a shuttle with friends or if you don't mind the climb back to your car at the end of a ride. From the Fraser River TH, take US 40 south for a mile to the stoplight at Lakota Trail, take a left at the light and ascend a short ways to Dreamcatcher North. Take a right and follow Dreamcatcher North up until it ends at the Waterboard Rd. (FS 128). Proceed right onto the Waterboard Rd. and after a short 0.2 mi you will come to an obvious dirt road (Broken Thumb Trail) on the left with a closure gate for the James Peak Special Interest Area. Climb the doubletrack Buck Creek, staying left at a few intersections. Buck Creek will intersect the Rollins Pass Rd. after 2.1 mi. Take a right onto the Rollins Pass Rd. and climb gradually for 0.6 mi to the Broken Thumb TH and sign. Descend Broken Thumb (mostly singletrack) for 3.4 mi as it drops 1,100 ft. to the Waterboard Rd. Take a left and traverse and ascend back to the Rollins Pass Rd. then take a right and descend to US 40 and the Fraser River TH. The route described here is 13.5 mi with 2,300 ft. of elevation gain/loss.

Riflesight Trail: Relatively short, but an easy grade and some of the most impressive views around. The old railway grade gradually traverses a ridge crest with Mt. Epworth reigning supreme over the basin formed by the Middle Fork of Ranch Creek. Begin at the Riflesight TH and hike or bike up the

doubletrack trail, which passes over some old railroad ties and two rickety old bridges (be careful!). The trail reaches a fork; going straight dead-ends below the trestle bridge, the right fork brings you up to the Rollins Pass Rd. after a short but stiff climb. This out-and-back to below the trestle and a return to the Riflesight TH via the Rollins Pass Rd. makes a nice 3.5-mi hike or bike.

Moffat Trail: From the Riflesight Trail just below the cutover road up to the Rollins Pass Rd., the Moffat Trail is an old doubletrack that heads down and northwest into the head of the Middle Fork of Ranch Creek. The trail passes by some old wreckage and eventually peters out, but this makes for an interesting hike or bike ride.

Rogers Pass Trail: From the Rogers Pass TH near the trestle bridge at Riflesight Notch, the Rogers Pass Trail follows an old fading doubletrack trail for 2.2 mi to Rogers Pass. Rogers Pass sits at the border of the James Peak Wilderness. At Rogers Pass, the Continental Divide Trail (CDT) goes north (left) to Rollins

Pass or south (right) to the top of James Peak. Bikes are not allowed on the CDT here as the trail forms the border of the James Peak Wilderness. It is also popular to head east and down from Rogers Pass to the Heart Lake and Rogers Pass Lake area, which is a descent of 500-700 ft. over 0.5-0.8 mi.

Corona Lake Trail: Corona Lake and Pumphouse Lake sit at the head of Ranch Creek in the shadow of the solitary Mt. Epworth. Park at the Pumphouse TH and it is a quick hike down from the Rollins Pass Rd. It is 0.4 mi to Pumphouse Lake and an additional 0.6 mi to Corona Lake.

Corona Trail: The Corona Trail is part of the Continental Divide Trail to the north of Rollins Pass. From the pass, the going is quite easy for the first half mile to the intersection

Snowy trees

with the King Lake Trail. Don't be discouraged by the big headwall to the north of this intersection - it is easier than it looks. Once atop the high point (0.6 mi from Rollins Pass) there are 2.8 mi of easy (but high in elevation), rolling terrain and stunning views of high peaks all around. You will have a grin on your face from ear to ear.

King Lake Trail: From the top of Rollins Pass, head north on the Corona Trail for 0.4 mi to a trail intersection in a spectacular setting above King Lake. Follow the trail down and to the east to King Lake, which is reached after 0.3 mi and a loss of 200 ft. Continue on this trail if you wish, but remember it is a steep climb back to Rollins Pass!

Betty & Bob Lakes: Fortunately, Rollins Pass provides extremely easy access to some truly amazing terrain in the southern part of the Indian Peaks Wilderness. The trip to Betty & Bob Lakes is great for a day hike or an overnight adventure. From atop Rollins Pass, take the Corona Trail north for 0.4 mi to the King Lake Trail, descend the King Lake

Trail for 0.7 mi to the crossing of the S. Fork of Middle Boulder Creek. Just after the creek crossing, look for the trail to Betty & Bob Lakes. It is a climb of 330 ft. in a half mile to Betty Lake; Bob Lake is reached after an additional 0.4 mi.

Idlewild Trails

In 1961, the Idlewild Ski Area opened on the east side of Hideaway Park, which today is downtown Winter Park. At the height of operation, two lifts gave access to 400 ft. of elevation drop. A minor lift accident occurred in 1986, and it was decided at that point to close the resort. However, the Idlewild Guest Ranch was kept open as a cross country ski touring center until 1996. At times during its operation, Idlewild partnered with Devil's Thumb Ranch (see p. 425) to provide groomed ski trails connecting Fraser to Winter Park, which certainly must have been an incredible wintertime experience.

Three hikes/rides are outlined here and the routes are shown on the map on the opposite page - one easy, one moderate, and one difficult. They are denoted by green, blue, and black arrows. Unfortunately, in the fall of 2010 much of the Crosstrails Trail (see opposite) was dug up to bury natural gas pipelines. What was left behind was a 40-ft. wide swath of clearcut. Consequently, you may choose to stay off of Crosstrails.

Ditch Trail: This out-and-back is a great easy hiking or biking trail as it follows a water ditch. From the Idlewild TH, take the singletrack Meadow Trail then the Homestead Trail north to the intersection with the Ditch Trail, which proceeds to the right (southeast).

Idlewild Trails

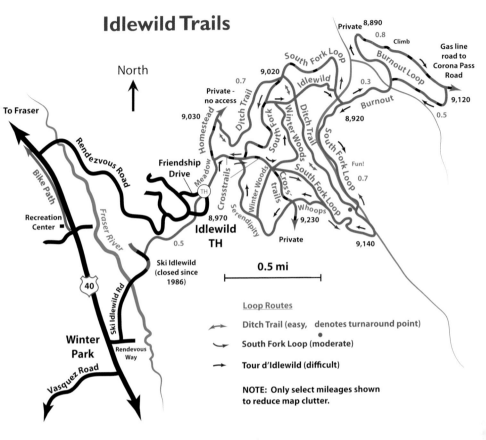

North

To Fraser

Rendezvous Road

Bike Path

Fraser River

Recreation Center ■

40

Winter Park

Vasquez Road

Ski Idlewild Rd

Rendevous Way

Friendship Drive

Meadow

TH

0.5

Ski Idlewild (closed since 1986)

8,970
Idlewild TH

Homestead

Ditch Trail

9,030

Private - no access

0.7

9,020

South Fork Loop

Idlewild

South Fork

Winter Woods

Ditch Trail

Crosstrails

Winter Woods

Serendipity

Crosstrails

South Fork Loop

Whoops

9,230

Private

Private 8,890

0.8   Climb

Burnout Loop

0.3

Burnout

8,920

Fun!

0.7

9,140

Gas line road to Corona Pass Road

9,120

0.5

0.5 mi

Loop Routes

→ **Ditch Trail** (easy, • denotes turnaround point)

↝ **South Fork Loop** (moderate)

→ **Tour d'Idlewild** (difficult)

NOTE: Only select mileages shown to reduce map clutter.

● Easy trails include:
- Meadow Trail
- Ditch Trail
- Burnout Trail

■ Moderate trails include:
- South Fork Loop
- Winter Woods Trail
- Crosstrails
- Idlewild
- Serendipity

◆ Difficult trails include:
- Burnout Loop (strenuous)
- Whoops

The Ditch Trail continues east then northeast, crosses the South Fork Loop, then continues southeast again to the intersection with the southeastern part of the South Fork Loop. Return the way you came. From the Idlewild TH, it is 1.9 mi to the intersection of the Ditch Trail with the South Fork Loop via the Meadow and Homestead Trails.

South Fork Loop: Begin at the Idlewild TH. Take Meadow Trail then Crosstrails east a short ways to the 5-way intersection (Crosstrails, Winter Woods, and South Fork Loop). Proceed on the singletrack South Fork Loop to the east and southeast. South Fork Loop climbs a bit and rolls a little then descends,

passes the Whoops Trail, then intersects the southern end of the Ditch Trail. From here, get ready for a treat! Descend South Fork Loop north through a spectacular forest along a creek. At the intersection with Burnout Trail, continue left (north) on South Fork Loop and stay on South Fork Loop all the way back to the intersection with Crosstrails. Return via Meadow Trail to the trailhead. 3.6 mi round trip.

Tour d'Idlewild: This is a "grand tour" loop composed of all the best trails at Idlewild. It has a few short, strenuous climbs but overall it is not an overly difficult loop. As with all routes here, begin at the Idlewild TH. Refer to the map on the previous page. Take Meadow Trail to Crosstrails, east (right) on Crosstrails to 5-way intersection, left (north) on Winter Woods, right on Idlewild Trail, cross the Ditch Trail and descend to South Fork Loop. Take a right on South Fork, continue left (east) on Burnout Trail, complete the Burnout Loop in the clockwise direction, and return via Burnout Trail to South Fork Loop. Ascend South Fork Loop south along the creek (awesome!), past the Ditch Trail and climb to the intersection with Whoops. Take Whoops west (a few short, difficult climbs), then descend Serendipity Trail all the way down to Crossroads and return via Meadow Trail. 5.9 mi round trip.

Additional Wintertime Activities

Waterboard Road (FS 128): For some mostly easy hiking or biking, the Waterboard Rd. (FS 128) is rather flat. In winter, this road is popular among snowmobiles but also provides an excellent ski touring setting - you can access miles and miles of gentle terrain along the Waterboard Rd. and elsewhere. The road can be accessed by driving 5.3 mi from Fraser on CR 8 (find CR 8 on the north side of Fraser) or at the end of Dreamcatcher North by driving a short ways on Lakota Trail, which is located 2.5 mi south of Winter Park on US 40.

Along St. Louis Creek with James Peak and Parry Peak in the distance

Fraser Valley

Down valley from Winter Park is the small town of Fraser, which was originally founded as a stop along the Moffat Railroad, but more recently has grown economically due to its proximity to the resort areas of Winter Park. Touted as the "Icebox of the Nation", cold air sinks into the valley in winter, making it one of the coldest places in the lower 48 states. Today, there are excellent mountain biking and hiking trails to the west and southwest of Fraser during the warm months. Eventually adjoining with the Winter Park Ski Area, these trails offer a wide variety of singletrack and doubletrack through spruce and pine forests, some of which have been heavily logged in the last few years due to beetle infestations. In winter, the trailheads are accessible for the most part and many of the Forest Service roads make excellent ski and snowshoe trails. If you are up for it, some epic mountain bike and cross country ski adventures could be put together on the singletrack, doubletrack, and Forest Service roads in this area. Explore in all seasons!

Maps: Backcountry Bound "Winter Park and Fraser, Colorado – Mountain Bike Map" and National Geographic Trails Illustrated "Winter Park, Central City, Rollins Pass" (#103).

Best time of the year: The Fraser Valley melts out earlier than some of the neighboring forests and alpine zones. In general, the trails along Elk Creek and St. Louis Creek can be used by late May or early June. However, some areas remain muddy in spots (for example, north-facing areas along the Flume Trail) into summer. Summer brings green grass, flowers, and excellent hiking and biking conditions. The brilliant colors and cooler temperatures invite fall adventures until the first snow arrives in late October to mid November. When winter comes, the landscape is transformed. Don the skis or snowshoes and explore!

Camping: The St. Louis Campground and the Byers Peak Campground are the only two campgrounds in the Fraser area. Contact the Sulfur Ranger District at (970) 887-4100 for information. Reservations are not accepted for either of these two campgrounds. Many primitive campsites can be found up Elk Creek along FS 158, after the Elk Meadow TH. Unfortunately, there is no camping adjacent to FS 160 along St. Louis Creek since this is within the Fraser Experimental Forest. Plenty of additional camping can be found along Vasquez Creek Rd. (FS 148) south of the Twin Bridges TH or along additional Forest Service roads in the area. Showers are available for a very reasonable fee at the Grand Park Community Recreation Center (970-726-8968), which is located between Winter Park and Fraser on US 40.

Access

Directions to Fraser: From the intersection of I-70 and C-470 west of Denver, take I-70 for 28 mi to Exit 232 (Empire/Granby), then travel north on US 40 through Empire and up and over Berthoud Pass. After 45 mi from I-70, you will reach Winter Park; Fraser is an additional 4 mi north on US 40.

NOTE: All trailheads below are accessible in the winter unless otherwise denoted.

Northwest Passage TH: From the only stoplight in the town of Fraser (at the Safeway), take Elk Creek Rd. (CR 72) south. Within a half mile, the road goes under the railroad tracks; continue right onto Fraser Valley Parkway for 0.8 mi, then take a left at the intersection with CR 73. From here, continue 1.7 mi to a Fraser Experimental Forest information sign on the right hand side of the road and another parking area on the left side of the

Aspen trees, Elk Creek

Along the Fraser River near the town of Fraser

road. Park at either location. The Creekside Trail begins on the left (south) side of the road and the Northwest Passage Trail begins on the right (north) side of the road.

St. Louis Campground: Just below the St. Louis Campground is a trailhead area that can be used to access the Creekside Trail and Creekside Loop. Follow directions to the Northwest Passage TH (above) but continue on CR 73 for an additional 0.6 mi and take a left, following signs to the St. Louis Campground. Non-guests of the campground must park just north of the campground. There is plenty of parking here. The Creekside Trail can be accessed from both the west and east sides of this trailhead.

Leland Creek TH: This trailhead is nowhere near Leland Creek but is at the western terminus of the Leland Creek Rd. (FS 159). The Leland Creek TH provides access to the Flume Trail and Creekside Trail as well as the eastern end of the Spruce Creek Trail. Follow directions to the Northwest Passage TH (above) but continue on CR 73, which turns into FS 160, for an additional 2.5 mi. The Leland Creek TH is located on the left near the intersection of FS 160 and FS 159. There is plenty of parking here.

Elk Meadow TH: At the only stoplight in the town of Fraser, take a left onto Elk Creek Rd. (CR 72). Start measuring from here. Veer left underneath the railroad bridge, continue up the hill (stay left at fork), and proceed 2.3 mi total to an obvious trailhead in a large meadow. This is a short ways past some ranch buildings. The road is plowed to this trailhead in the winter. The Elk Meadow TH provides access to the Chainsaw Trail and Zoom Trail and is near the northern terminus of the Elk Meadow Trail.

East Elk Creek TH: The East Elk Creek TH provides access along the Leland Creek Rd. (FS 159), a suitable parking spot if you are hiking or biking the East Elk Trail. As you drive into Winter Park from the south (Berthoud Pass), take a left on the first stoplight in town (Vasquez Rd.). Follow Vasquez Rd. west then southwest as it crosses train tracks (0.4 mi) and passes through a neighborhood. After 1.0 mi, continue straight onto Vasquez Rd. (CR 7/FS 148), which is dirt. After 1.6 mi take a right onto FS 159 (Leland Creek Rd.) and drive an additional 1.6 mi to a flat, open area near the base of some jeep roads. Park here.

Church Park TH: The Church Park TH is most useful for those wishing to utilize the Backscratch Trail and Tipperary Trail in the northwest part of the Fraser Valley. Follow directions as if you are going to the Northwest Passage TH. However, after the left turn onto CR 73, travel 1.3 mi, take a right onto CR 50-S, and proceed about 7.6 mi (CR 50-S turns into CR 50 after 1.6 mi and later turns into FS 139). The trailhead is located at the second of a pair of hairpin turns. FS 139 is plowed in winter to this point, and skiing and snowshoeing along FS 139 west from here is popular in winter.

Recommended Routes

NOTE: There are numerous short trails in the Fraser area and only the descriptions for some of the more popular ones are given here. In general, you can assume that if a trail is not described below, it is a doubletrack dirt road (e.g. D2, D3, D4, and others).

Forests along the Creekside Trail

Fraser Valley

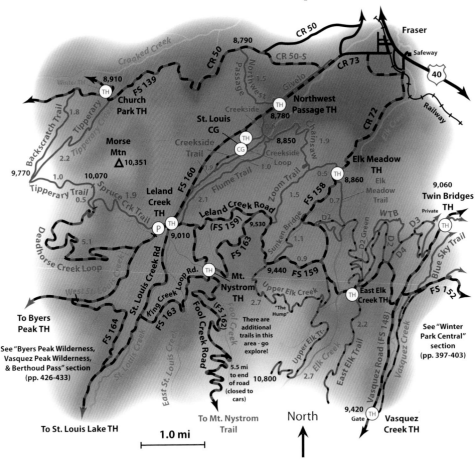

Northwest Passage: A short trail connecting CR 73 to CR 50 that traverses through a recently-logged area. Suitable for cross country skiing and snowshoeing in the winter. 1.5 mi one way.

Creekside Trail & Loop: Easy singletrack trails that parallel St. Louis Creek. Start at either the Northwest Passage TH, St. Louis Campground, or Leland Creek TH. Creekside Loop stays close to St. Louis Creek and connects the Chainsaw Trail to the Creekside Trail about halfway between the St. Louis Campground and the Leland Creek TH. Creekside Loop is 1.0 mi long and Creekside Trail is 1.9 mi long.

Creekside-Flume Loop: From the St. Louis Campground, take the Creekside Trail to Leland Creek TH, then take the stellar Flume Trail northeast and return via Creekside Trail. The Flume Trail winds through open meadows and heavily wooded forests over rooty-at-times terrain. 4.6 mi round trip. An out-and-back on the Flume Trail from Leland Creek TH also makes a nice short adventure by itself.

Chainsaw Trail: A fun singletrack trail connecting the Elk Meadow TH with the Creekside Trail. Hike or bike by itself or incorporate into longer excursions in the Fraser area. It is 1.9 mi from the Zoom Trail to the Flume Trail. Short, but a stiff climb. Recently re-routed.

Zoom Trail: The Zoom Trail singletrack ascends very gradually from the Chainsaw Trail to the Leland Creek Rd. (FS 159) along a broad ridge through forests of spruce and aspen; areas of recent logging. Great for skiing and snowshoeing in winter. 1.5 mi long.

Flume-Zoom Loop: Begin at the St. Louis Campground or the Northwest Passage TH (your choice). Navigate to the Flume Trail, which is on the south side of St. Louis Creek. Take the Flume Trail west as the trail makes its way to the Leland Creek Rd. (FS 159). Proceed east on the Leland Creek Rd. for 1.8 mi to the Zoom Trail. There is an informal parking area here and a Fraser

Post-rain aspen tree trunks in the Fraser area

Wildflowers along Creekside Trail

Experimental Forest sign at the top of the Zoom Trail. Descend the Zoom Trail and return to the trailhead via the Chainsaw Trail. 9.0 mi round trip from the Northwest Passage TH.

Upper Elk to Sunken Bridge: Begin at the Elk Meadow TH. Bike up FS 158 past the Elk Meadow Trail and D2 to the intersection with FS 159. Take a left on FS 159 but quickly find the doubletrack for Upper Elk Creek on the right. Climb this to the marked Upper Elk Trail and take a right. The doubletrack Upper Elk Creek Trail continues straight for an additional 2.7 mi to around 10,800 ft. Upper Elk Trail climbs several switchbacks with excellent views (stay right at a few road intersections) to a high point called "The Hump". The descent from here is on a mix of singletrack and doubletrack

Upper Elk to Sunken Bridge

and is spectacular. Stay right at a trail intersection. This will spit you out at FS 159. Across the road, find Sunken Bridge and drop down this doubletrack to a boardwalk across a meadow and intersect FS 158, just uphill from where you started. The loop is 7.7 mi round trip with 2,100 ft. of elevation gain/loss.

East Elk

East Elk: A moderately steep climb on an old jeep road. Great for a hike or bike ride. From the East Elk TH, travel straight south on a doubletrack road. There are a couple of different roads here and there with the left forks generally being easier. The road stops after about 2.2 mi.

Elk Meadow Trail: An easy and fun trail winding through meadows and forests to connect D2 with just south of the Elk Meadow TH. Great as an easy trail by itself (hiking, snowshoeing, or skiing) or as part of a larger mountain biking or hiking excursion. 0.7 mi long.

Elk Meadow Trail

WTB-D3 Loop

WTB-D3 Loop: WTB is one of the best sections of singletrack in the area. Loose and rooty in a few spots but otherwise excellent. This moderate loop begins at Twin Bridges TH. Ride up Vasquez Rd. (FS 148), take a right on

Leland Creek Rd. (FS 159), and ascend and contour to D2 Green, which is a well-used road leading north from FS 159. Stay right and head north, then stay right again and continue on D2 Green (east fork) to D2. Take D2 a short ways to the north, and in a clearing at the bottom of a rocky hill you will see a doubletrack trail heading right and to the northeast. A short ways further, a sign confirms you are on WTB. Follow WTB as it winds its way through a very moderate climb, then descends to a creek, then climbs a rocky trail out of the creek drainage to meet D4. Go left on D4, turn left again on D3, and descend D3 to Vasquez Rd., staying right at another fork. Return left to the Twin Bridges TH. 6.8 mi round trip.

Fool Creek Road: The 5.5-mi Fool Creek Rd. is one of the smoothest, most switchbackiest doubletrack roads around. You could probably ride a road bike up the bottom portions of this road, which is closed to cars but is carefully maintained by the Fraser Experimental Forest personnel. This makes a great 2,000-ft. climb to the border of the Vasquez Peak Wilderness. Bring your hiking boots or shoes and lock your bike at the bike rack provided and hike up towards Mt. Nystrom.

Spruce Creek Trail: Beginning at the Leland Creek TH the Spruce Creek Trail climbs steeply for 1,400 ft. to a high point after 2.4 mi. At this point, the trail levels out for a bit and descends gradually for another mile to a 3-way intersection at the top of the Tipperary and Backscratch Trails.

Deadhorse Creek Loop: Climb Spruce Creek Trail in winter and glide down Deadhorse Creek Rd. Open to hikers in the dry seasons but closed to bikes. Makes a wonderful ski/snowshoe route in winter. Do this in the counterclockwise direction on skis to avoid the steep descent down the Spruce Creek Trail. The loop is about 7.1 mi long with 2,250 ft. of elevation gain/loss.

Along the Tipperary Trail

Tipperary-Backscratch Loop: The Tipperary and Backscratch Trails are great, stout climbs that are not super technically difficult. Going up Tipperary and down Backscratch (or vice versa) makes a great adventure for hikers, trail runners, or mountain bikers. Start at the Church Park TH off of FS 139. Continue up FS 139 for 1.0 mi to the Backscratch Trail (well marked). Climb to the top of Backscratch and descend Tipperary Trail to FS 139. Take a left and return west to your car. 5.0 mi round trip with 1,900 ft. of elevation gain/descent.

Tipperary-Spruce Creek-Flume Loop: This is a big loop more suited for mountain bikers due to the large distanced covered. Climb Tipperary (or Backscratch) from Church Park TH. Descend Spruce Creek to the Leland Creek TH, continue east a short ways on FS 159 to the Flume Trail, then descend the spectacular Flume

Trail and Creekside Trail to the Northwest Passage TH. Return via Northwest Passage and CR 50/FS 139. 13.2 mi and 3,100 ft. of climbing/descending. A grand loop.

FS 158/159: Groomed in winter for snowmobile tours between Elk Meadow TH and Leland Creek TH, which makes it perfect for XC skiing (even skate skiing when conditions are good) or snowshoeing. Starts out easy but becomes a moderate climb.

Additional Wintertime Recreation

Grand County boasts two of the finest Nordic centers in the state: Devil's Thumb Ranch and Snow Mountain Ranch.

Devil's Thumb Ranch: $ Devils Thumb Ranch has a special place in my heart since this is the place my wife and I got married! So much to do in the winter, the rustic elegance is unmatched. Although the ranch has been hit hard with pine beetle infestations over the last decade, they have done a wonderful job in managing the forests and skiing through the wide-open meadows and intimate forests remains a treat. The lodge, guest cabins, and restaurants are classy and welcoming. Plan to spend some time here.

Snow Mountain Ranch: $ Snow Mountain Ranch is a YMCA-run facility that has spectacular ski trails traversing wide-open valleys, forests, and slopes. For a strenuous cardiovascular challenge, climb Blue Ridge, a 5-mi groomed trail to a high point overlooking the entire Grand Valley. The Nordic center has rentals, offers lessons, and has a cafeteria. A great place for winter outings with the family.

Sunrise in the Vasquez Peak Wilderness

Byers Peak Wilderness, Vasquez Peak Wilderness, and Berthoud Pass

To the south and southwest of Winter Park and Fraser exists a huge pocket of wild terrain. This area is characterized by forested valleys with ridge systems looming high overhead. Many options exist for the hiker in the Vasquez Peak Wilderness and in the Byers Peak Wilderness. The rolling, grassy ridges can be traversed with relative ease as there are only small drops in elevation. Several idyllic lakes can be easily accessed. In winter, the Butler Gulch area, which lies just south of the Vasquez Peak Wilderness, is quite popular among snowshoers and cross country and backcountry skiers. Bikes are not allowed in these wilderness areas but bikes can be taken right up to the border, providing nice "bike-n-hike" forays into these unspoiled areas. In fact, the Sulphur Ranger District provides bike racks at several wilderness boundary locations in the Winter Park area.

Maps: National Geographic Trails Illustrated "Winter Park, Central City, Rollins Pass" (#103).

Best time of the year: Most of the high alpine and north-facing areas of these areas do not melt out until late June at the earliest. The Vasquez Creek Rd. is a popular cross country skiing and snowshoeing destination in winter and is easily accessible.

Camping: Depending upon which side of this vast region you are trying to access, there are several camping options. A significant number of dispersed campsites exist along the Vasquez Creek Rd. below the Vasquez Creek TH. On the Fraser side, the Byers Creek Campground and St. Louis Creek Campground are nice options. Call the Sulphur Ranger District at (970) 887-4100 for more information about camping in the vicinity of Fraser and Winter Park. On the south side of this region, there are several dispersed campsites along the Jones Pass Rd. in the Henderson area.

Showers are available for a very reasonable fee at the Grand Park Community Recreation Center [(970) 726-8968], which is located between Winter Park and Fraser on the west side of US 40.

Access

NOTE: The Byers Peak Wilderness can also be accessed from several locations from the west side near Kremmling, but these points can be quite difficult to get to. Most will choose to access from the Winter Park and Fraser side (east side).

Byers Peak TH: From the only stoplight in the town of Fraser (see directions to Fraser on p. 418), take Elk Creek Rd. (CR 72) south. Within a half mile, the road goes under the railroad tracks. Continue right onto Fraser Valley Parkway, then take a left at the intersection with CR 73. Start your odometer here. Continue on CR 73/FS 160 (St. Louis Creek Rd.) all the way to the intersection with FS 164 after 6.9 mi (you will pass the Fraser Experimental Forest station after 4.3 mi, the King Creek Loop Rd. after 5.9 mi, and the Byers Creek Campground after 6.6 mi). Turn right onto FS 164 and drive 2.9 mi to a

Sunrise in the Byers Peak Wilderness

somewhat limited parking area near the top of a steep one-way loop (you will intersect FS 111 after 2.0 mi - a gate will prevent you from going right).

St. Louis Lake TH: Follow directions to the intersection of FS 160 and FS 164 in the description for the "Byers Peak TH" on the previous page. Continue left (south) on FS 160 (St. Louis Creek Rd.) for an additional 2.1 mi. You will arrive at a gate. Park on either side of the road, reading all signs.

Mt. Nystrom TH: Follow directions on p. 419 to the Leland Creek TH. From the Leland Creek TH, continue east on FS 159 (Leland Creek Rd.) for 0.5 mi and take a right onto FS 162, following signs for the Mt. Nystrom TH. Continue an additional mile to a 4-way road intersection with the King Creek Loop Rd. There is a closure gate on the south side of the intersection, which is the Mt. Nystrom TH. Make sure to read all signs.

Vasquez Creek TH: From the southern-most stoplight in the town of Winter Park (see directions to Winter Park on p. 406), take Vasquez Rd. (CR 7) southwest for 1.0 mi. At this point, the road turns to dirt and continues straight (south) as FS 148. Proceed 3.4 mi on the Vasquez Rd. and the Tunnel Rd. will intersect FS 148 from the east. Park at the obvious trailhead at this intersection. A gate will prevent you from proceeding up FS 148.

Berthoud Pass TH: A large parking area is found atop Berthoud Pass, which is located approximately 13 mi south of the town of Winter Park (see directions to Winter Park on p. 406) and 15 mi north of I-70 along US 40.

Henderson TH: This trailhead provides access to the Henderson Spur of the Continental Divide Trail, as well as Butler Gulch. Drive I-70 west from Idaho Springs for about 8 mi to Exit 232 of I-70. Take US 40 north/west for about 9 mi to the small town of Berthoud Falls. Just after Berthoud Falls, turn onto the Henderson Mine Rd. at a large hairpin turn. Follow the Henderson Mine Rd. (CR 202) and after 1.8 mi take a right onto the Jones Pass Rd. (FS 144), following signs towards Jones Pass. After an additional 0.6 mi, there is a large parking area in a clearing next to a trail marker sign for the Continental Divide Trail. In winter, most cars will be able to make it to this spot in most weather conditions; additional winter parking can be found lower down.

A curious silhouette, Vasquez Peak Wilderness

First Creek, Second Creek, and Current Creek THs: As you ascend Berthoud Pass on US 40 from Winter Park (see directions to Winter Park on p. 406), you will reach three popular winter (and to some extent summer) recreation areas, each on a sharp turn. Limited parking is available at each of these trailheads, which are reached after 9.8 mi (First Creek), 10.3 mi (Second Creek), and 11.5 mi (Current Creek) from the town of Winter Park.

Jones Pass:  Follow directions to the Henderson TH (previous page). Continue along FS 144 (Jones Pass Rd.) for an additional 3.6 mi. This road is a bit loose and steep near treeline and occasionally beyond that, but most vehicles should be able to get to the top of the pass, depending upon conditions.

Recommended Routes

Wildflowers above Berthoud Pass

Byers Peak Trail: Begin at the Byers Peak TH and ascend the wide doubletrack trail behind the closure gate (FS 111). After 1.7 mi, the road will end (there is a bike rack if you want to save some time and bike here) and a trail continues southeast then southwest along the ridge to the summit of Byers Peak. An incredible climb to a surreal spot. 4.4 mi and 3,300 ft. of elevation gain to the summit.

Bottle Peak Trail: Bottle Peak is not as serious of an undertaking as the climb of Byers Peak, but will provide you with spectacular views south towards Byers Peak. Start at the Byers Peak TH, ascend FS 111 for 1.7 mi to a singletrack trail heading to the right and up. From here, switchback through the trees to treeline, then 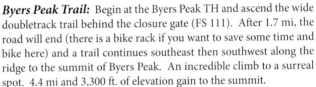 the trail peters out and you will need to hike off-trail along the ridge to the north until you reach Bottle Peak. 3.2 mi and 2,100 ft. of elevation gain to the top of Bottle Peak.

St. Louis Divide Trail: A seldom-used trail, the St. Louis Divide Trail links the Lake Evelyn area west of Byers Peak to the summit of Mt. Nystrom. The trail is difficult to follow in many spots, requiring good navigational skills. From the Fraser area, the best place to access the St. Louis Divide Trail is the St. Louis Lake TH (see previous page). A backpacking trip along this trail would be incredibly scenic.

Along the St. Louis Lake Trail

St. Louis Lake: St. Louis Lake is perhaps one of the wildest, most scenic, and undisturbed lakes that does not lie within an official wilderness area. Thankfully, the Fraser Experimental Forest has strict regulations regarding camping and off-trail travel so this area has been somewhat protected. The hike to

St. Louis Lake is superb. If you can, try to spend a night up here. Start at the St. Louis Lake TH and hike 3.4 mi up a very good doubletrack road to the old trailhead at 10,490 ft. From here, cross the bridge and ascend the trail, steep at times, to the intersection with the St. Louis Pass Trail after 4.6 mi. Continue right (north) for another 1.3 mi and the steepness eases within the last half mile to the lake. 5.9 mi and 2,150 ft. of elevation gain to the lake.

Mt. Nystrom Trail: Linking the Winter Park Resort to the Fraser Experimental Forest, the Mt. Nystrom Trail is a somewhat faint route that forms a big alpine horseshoe above Vasquez Creek. Part of this trail overlaps with the Continental Divide Trail (see p. 432). Unfortunately, this route does not see a lot of use so the trail is difficult to follow in many spots. But fortunately, because of the low use you will be treated with a wild, solitary experience. Access the western branch from the Mt. Nystrom TH, which will require a 5.5-mi hike or bike to the wilderness boundary, or from the top of Berthoud Pass (most popular). Other places to access the Mt. Nystrom Trail include the Henderson TH, Jones Pass, or even the top of the Winter Park Ski Resort (least popular). The section between Mt. Nystrom and the top of the Fool Creek Rd. is highly recommended, with views of Byers Peak to the west, Vasquez Peak to the south, and

Byers Peak Wilderness, Vasquez Peak Wilderness, and Berthoud Pass

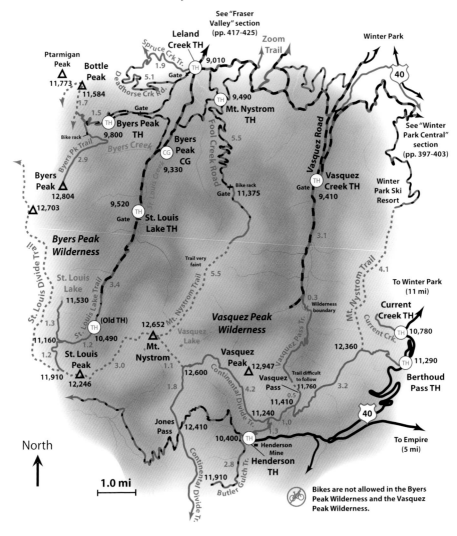

North

1.0 mi

Bikes are not allowed in the Byers Peak Wilderness and the Vasquez Peak Wilderness.

the Indian Peaks and Continental Divide splayed out to the east. Also recommended is Berthoud Pass to the Henderson TH (see next page in "Continental Divide Trail" section).

Vasquez Road

Vasquez Road: A perfect, easily accessible place to ski or snowshoe in winter. The winter trailhead is located about 1.9 mi from US 40 in Winter Park along Vasquez Rd., about 0.7 mi past the Twin Bridges TH (see p. 399).

Upper Vasquez Road: Start at the Vasquez Creek TH. Proceed past the closure gate on foot or by bike. This makes an easy hike or mountain bike ride in a superb subalpine setting with nice views all around. Bikes are allowed until the wilderness boundary, which is reached after 3.4 mi.

Vasquez Pass Trail: Follow directions above for the Upper Vasquez Rd. After 3.1 mi, a singletrack trail heads left off of the road, crosses a creek, and enters the Vasquez Peak Wilderness. From here, the Vasquez Pass Trail climbs an old doubletrack trail and singletrack to Vasquez Pass after 7.0 mi and 2,750 ft. of total climbing. The trail is hard to follow for the last half mile or so, but just make your way to the obvious pass, which is located in a pretty interesting setting. The pass can also be accessed by climbing north for 0.5 mi from the Mt. Nystrom Trail/Continental Divide Trail.

Continental Divide Trail: The Continental Divide Trail (CDT) passes through Berthoud Pass from the James Peak Wilderness. It continues west towards Vasquez Peak and Jones Pass before heading south towards the Eisenhower Tunnel area. The CDT coincides with the Mt. Nystrom Trail from near Berthoud Pass to north of Jones Pass. Several opportunities exist for hiking the CDT in this area. The

most popular being an out-and-back from Berthoud Pass to the divide (1.1 mi one way with a climb of 1,100 ft., spectacular!) and a foray to the CDT from the Henderson Spur from the Henderson TH. If you can arrange a shuttle with friends, leave a car atop Jones Pass and start from the Henderson TH, encircling the West Fork of Clear Creek, a hike of 7.3

St. Louis Lake is situated in a fantastic location below a high alpine ridge

mi. Another fine option is to have someone drop you off at Berthoud Pass and pick you up at the Henderson TH. This option has 1,800 ft./2,700 ft. of elevation gain/drop over 7.2 mi and will bring you through some extremely scenic terrain and leave you wanting more.

Vasquez Peak and Vasquez Lake

First Creek, Second Creek, and Current Creek: These are all relatively short trails that are most popular in winter but are great in summer as well. Second Creek is the most popular for winter recreation (skiing and snowshoeing). Be cautious, as all of these drainages have avalanche slopes above and near treeline. Easily accessible in winter, making these popular destinations in winter. At the time this book was written, final planning was underway for the construction of the Broome Hut, which will be located up

Second Creek and will provide an overnight hut experience. Check out www.grandhuts.org/broomehut.html for more information and to book the hut, which should be completed in November of 2012.

Butler Gulch Trail: A popular hiking destination in summer and fall that turns to an easily accessible snowshoeing and skiing area in winter. Start at the Henderson TH. The road to this trailhead is plowed in winter, in general. Continue up the Jones Pass Rd. (FS 144) for 0.1 mi to a fork in the road. Take the left fork and proceed past the closure gate. Climb the road as far as you wish. An old mine is reached after 2.8 mi. If you travel to the upper parts in winter, you may encounter avalanche terrain.

A sky pond just above Berthoud Pass

The Indian Peaks as viewed from the west side

Indian Peaks Wilderness - West Side

The Winter Park section of this guidebook would be incomplete without mention of the Indian Peaks Wilderness, whose western side can be accessed to the east of the Grand Valley. The east side of the Indian Peaks Wilderness (see Chapter 4: Northern Front Range on pp. 154-166) is considerably more popular than the west side due to its proximity to the cities of the Front Range. As a result, those who visit the Indian Peaks Wilderness from the vicinity of Winter Park and Fraser will be treated to a more secluded wilderness experience than those who explore from the east side. In fact, some of the trails on the east side are somewhat overgrown and difficult to find in spots. Remember, bikes are not permitted in the Indian Peaks Wilderness.

Maps: Sky Terrain Maps "Southern Rocky Mountain National Park & Indian Peaks Wilderness", Latitude 40° Maps "Front Range Trails", or National Geographic Trails Illustrated "Indian Peaks & Gold Hill" (#102).

Best time of the year: The Indian Peaks Wilderness is located in a high alpine environment and much of the wilderness lies above or near treeline. Consequently, the heavy snows do not generally melt out completely until sometime in June or early July, depending upon seasonal snowpack. July, August, and even early September are the preferred months to hike the trails here. In mid to late July the wildflowers peak, which is one of the best times of year to be in the Indian Peaks Wilderness. Winter is harsh here and winter access is difficult since many of the trailheads are not accessible in winter. CR 6 on the south side of Lake Granby is plowed in winter to just below the Monarch Lake TH, providing access for snowshoeing and cross country skiing (see p. 449 in the "Lake Granby and Strawberry Bench" section for more information).

Camping: The shores of Lake Granby and host several National Forest campgrounds, including the Stillwater, Arapaho Bay, Sunset Point, and Green Ridge Campgrounds. These campgrounds provide easy access to the northern part of the west side of the Indian Peaks Wilderness via the Monarch Lake TH. If accessing the Junco Lake TH via Meadow Creek, there are several dispersed campsites along the Meadow Creek Rd. (FS 129) and also near Meadow Creek Reservoir. Otherwise, there are several campgrounds to the northwest of Granby on the west side of US 34, including the Denver Creek, Bull Mountain, Sawmill Gulch, and Willow Creek Campgrounds. Some of these campgrounds may currently be closed due to hazard tree removal. Call 1-877-444-6777 or visit www.recreation.gov to reserve these campgrounds or for more information.

Backcountry Camping: Backcountry permits are required for all overnight trips to the Indian Peaks Wilderness from June 1st through September 15th each year. The fee is $5 per group regardless of duration and there are restrictions on locations where backpackers may camp. Other restrictions apply to large (8+) groups. Call the Sulphur Ranger District at

(970) 887-4100. Alternatively, day-of permits can be obtained conveniently at the Monarch and Junco Lake Wilderness Stations near Lake Granby (open every day in summer from 8 a.m. to 5 p.m.). For the most recent information regarding permits and other topics of interest to visitors to the Indian Peaks Wilderness, please contact www.fs.fed.us.gov and search for "Indian Peaks Wilderness".

Access

User Fees: $ Recently, the Arapaho National Forest has implemented a daily user fee system, which is in place at some of the trailheads in this area, including the Monarch Lake TH and the Junco Lake TH. If you visit national forests and national parks often, you may consider purchasing an Interagency Annual Pass (see information on user fees on p. 17).

An idyllic stream exiting Caribou Lake

Directions to Fraser: From the intersection of I-70 and C-470 west of Denver, take I-70 for 28 mi to Exit 232 (Empire/Granby), then travel north on US 40 through Empire and up and over Berthoud Pass. After 45 mi from I-70, you will reach Winter Park; Fraser is an additional 4 mi north on US 40.

Directions to Granby: From Fraser (see directions above), continue on US 40 north for 14 mi to the town of Granby.

Rollins Pass TH: From the town of Winter Park (see directions to Winter Park on p. 406), take US 40 south. Just after the highway crosses over the Fraser River and just after the "Town of Winter Park Public Works" sign, turn left (east) onto the Rollins Pass Rd. (CR 80/FS 149). Depending upon conditions and maintenance, you may or may not be able to drive your 2WD vehicle to the top of Rollins Pass, although many people do even when the road is bad. Follow directions on p. 406 to the Rollins Pass Rd. The road starts out good but gradually gets rougher, particularly after Riflesight Notch, a cleft in the mountains that is still spanned by the old trestle bridge. The parking area atop Rollins Pass at 11,670 ft. is about 14 mi from US 40.

Devil's Thumb Park TH: From the town of Fraser, find CR 8 near the north end of town. Head east on CR 8 (turns to dirt after about 1.6 mi). Stay left after 4.4 mi and the road takes a turn to the north. After 7.7 mi, take a right (follow signs) to the Devils Thumb Park TH. It is a short distance to the parking area and trailhead.

Junco Lake TH: $ From Fraser, follow US 40 for not quite 3 mi to CR 83 (just south of Tabernash). Take a right on CR 83 but within a half mile take a left onto CR 84/FS 129, following signs for Meadow Creek Reservoir. Drive the dirt road for 10.6

Sunset at Columbine Lake

Lone Eagle Spire above Mirror Lake

mi, past Meadow Creek Reservoir, to the turnoff for Junco Lake TH (well marked). The trailhead is located just off FS 129 in a large parking area next to the Junco Lake Wilderness Station.

Monarch Lake TH: $  From the town of Granby, continue on US 40 outside of town to the intersection with US 34. Drive north on US 34 for 5.4 mi to CR 6 on the southwest corner of Lake Granby. Take CR 6 (dirt) east for 8.8 mi to the intersection with CR 637 near Arapaho Bay. Turn right, following signs for the Monarch Lake TH. In winter, you will have to park about 0.9 mi northwest from here.

Recommended Routes

King Lake: It is an easy hike to King Lake from the top of Rollins Pass. The trip is well worth it to this high, alpine lake situated in a surreal alpine amphitheater. Drive to Rollins Pass, then hike north from the parking area into the Indian Peaks Wilderness along the Corona Trail (part of the Continental Divide Trail). After 0.4 mi, take a right (east) onto the King Lake Trail. King Lake is reached after about 0.3 mi and is approximately 250 vertical ft. *below* the parking area atop Rollins Pass.

King Lake

Bob & Betty Lakes

Bob & Betty Lakes: The Bob and Betty Lakes are, like King Lake, also very close to Rollins Pass if you are willing to make the drive. Follow directions to King Lake (see above). Continue down the King Lake Trail for an additional 0.4 mi to the intersection with the Bob & Betty Lake Trail on the east side of the creek. Follow the Bob & Betty Lake Trail about a half mile to Betty Lake. Bob Lake is reached by continuing along the trail, which is faint in spots, for 0.4 mi past the southeastern end of Betty Lake.

Corona Trail: The Corona Trail connects the Devils Thumb Park TH with Rollins Pass and most of the trail coincides with the Continental Divide Trail and/or the High Lonesome Trail

Corona Trail

Along the Corona Trail near Rollins Pass with James Peak in the distance to the south

(see below). The Corona Trail is one of the most incredible, high alpine trails around. Start at Rollins Pass for an out-and-back north to the Devils Thumb Pass area. It is 3.4 mi and 850 ft./790 ft. of climbing/descending to Devils Thumb Pass. (See also p. 165.)

High Lonesome Trail: The High Lonesome Trail begins near Monarch Lake to the north and traverses south through forests and somewhat rocky terrain to the Devil's Thumb

Park TH. This trail is open to bikes except for the northern-most section just south of Monarch Lake (wilderness). It is 6.4 mi with 1,000 ft./700 ft. of elevation gain/loss between the Junco Lake TH and the Devils Thumb Park TH.

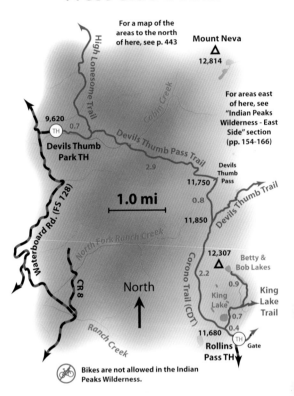

Indian Peaks - West Side South

For a map of the areas to the north of here, see p. 443

Mount Neva △ 12,814

For areas east of here, see "Indian Peaks Wilderness - East Side" section (pp. 154-166)

High Lonesome Trail

Corbin Creek

9,620 TH 0.7

Devils Thumb Park TH

Devils Thumb Pass Trail

2.9

11,750

Devils Thumb Pass

1.0 mi

Waterboard Rd. (FS 128)

0.8

11,850

Devils Thumb Trail

North Fork Ranch Creek

12,307 △

Betty & Bob Lakes

Corono Trail (CDT)

2.2

CR 8

North

0.9

King Lake

King Lake Trail

0.7

Ranch Creek

11,680

0.4

TH

11,680

Rollins Pass TH

Gate

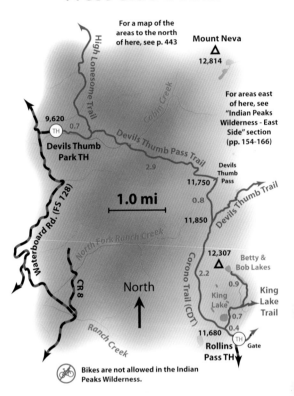

Bikes are not allowed in the Indian Peaks Wilderness.

Caribou Pass Trail to Caribou Lake: Begin at the Junco TH and head southeast on the Caribou Pass Trail, staying left after 1.7 mi. The trail climbs steeply over very loose and technical terrain, dropping down to Dorothy Lake on the east side of the Continental Divide after 3.9 mi. From here, descend north from Arapaho Pass on the Arapaho Pass Trail to Caribou Lake. It is 5.5 mi and 2,200 ft./1,100 ft. of elevation gain/loss to Caribou Lake.

Columbine Lake: The perfect trail to an absolutely splendid lake that is perfect for a morning or afternoon hike or even an overnight backpacking trip. Begin at Junco TH. The trail is quite easy except for the last mile, which conquers steep, rocky, and rooty terrain just below the lake. Overall moderate but there are a few short difficult sections. 3.0 mi and 1,000 ft. of elevation gain to the lake.

Monarch Lake Loop: A great easy 4.0-mi loop for hiking in summer and fall or skiing/snowshoeing in winter. See a detailed description for this loop on p. 449.

Devils Thumb Pass: The hike from Devils Thumb TH to Devils Thumb Pass takes you through some unique terrain to a high point. Here, you can peer east towards the plains and west with a stellar view overlooking the Grand Valley. The first mile or so is rather flat but the steepness quickly increases as the trail

climbs rocky terrain then passes through a bit of chest-high willow before arriving at the pass. Continue south along the Continental Divide Trail if you wish. 3.6 mi and 2,200 ft. of elevation gain to the pass.

Arapaho Pass Trail: The Arapaho Pass Trail is a rather long trail linking the west and east sides of the Indian Peaks Wilderness. From the west side, the Arapaho Pass Trail is accessed readily via the Monarch Lake TH. Hike southwest then southeast along the west and south sides of Monarch Lake. Southeast of the lake, follow signs for the Arapaho Pass Trail at two trail intersections. The second intersection is found on the east side of Arapaho Creek after a bridge crossing. The Arapaho Pass Trail is a lengthy trail but

starts out very gradual, slowly getting steeper near the top as the trail climbs to treeline and Caribou Lake. Plan on spending some time at Caribou Lake, which is reached after 10 mi and 3,600 ft. of climbing from Monarch Lake TH. Rated difficult for the long hike.

Cascade Creek Trail: Begin at the Monarch Lake TH and head east along the north side of Monarch Lake. The Cascade Creek Trail ambles along Cascade Creek, climbing through forests and traversing

Stream near Crater Lake

Moose on the west side of the Indian Peaks

Cascade Creek Trail

through subalpine meadows. It passes several waterfalls, ultimately ending at the intersection with the Crater Lake Trail and the Pawnee Pass Trail after 6.7 mi and 2,300 ft. of climbing. The base of this can be snowshoed or skied in winter.

Mirror & Crater Lakes: Visited by relatively few people, Mirror and Crater Lakes are nestled at the bottom of a deep and dark chasm with high, jagged peaks all around. Lone Eagle Spire is an impressive sight from these lakes. Take the Cascade Creek Trail to its eastern terminus at the base of the Pawnee Pass Trail (see previous description), then head

Mirror & Crater Lakes

south on the Crater Lake Trail for an additional 1.2 mi to Crater Lake. Mirror Lake is found along the way just below the larger Crater Lake.

Pawnee Pass Trail

Pawnee Pass Trail: Take the Cascade Creek Trail to its eastern terminus (see "Cascade Creek Trail" above). At the 3-way intersection, climb east on the Pawnee Pass Trail through difficult but rewarding terrain to Pawnee Lake. Here, stunning views abound. From the 3-way intersection, climb 3.5 mi over technical and steep terrain to the top of Pawnee Pass (10.2 mi and 4,900 ft. of climbing from Monarch Lake TH). The last mile or so to the top of the pass is quite steep and rocky.

Morning fog near Caribou Lake

Buchanan Pass Trail: Another east-west connector trail in the Indian Peaks Wilderness.   To hike the west side of the Buchanan Pass Trail, ascend the Cascade Creek Trail from Monarch Lake TH.   After 3.3 mi just before a bridge crossing over Buchanan Creek, take a left and hike 5.7 strenuous miles to the top of Buchanan Pass, which is reached after 9.0 mi from the Monarch Lake TH and a climb of 3,900 ft.

Gourd Lake Trail: Halfway up the Buchanan Pass Trail, the seldom used Gourd Lake Trail heads north and switchbacks steeply to Gourd Lake, a climb of 1,400 ft. over 2.0 mi from the Buchanan Pass Trail.

Columbines along Cascade Creek

Indian Peaks Wilderness - West Side North

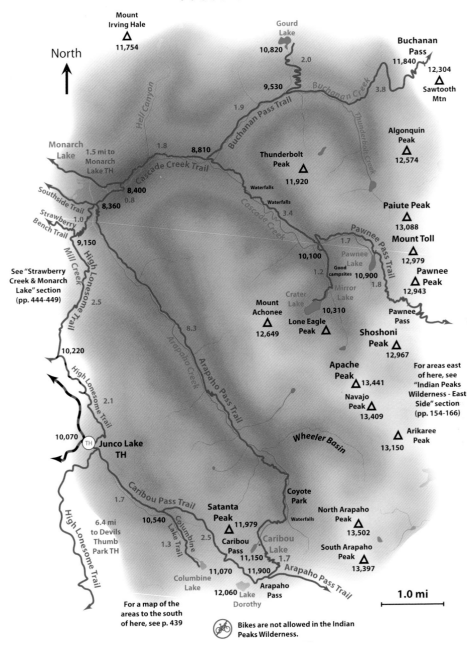

North

Mount Irving Hale
△ 11,754

Gourd Lake
10,820

Buchanan Pass
11,840

2.0

△ 12,304
Sawtooth Mtn

Buchanan Creek

9,530

3.8

1.9

Hell Canyon

Buchanan Pass Trail

Thunderbolt Creek

Algonquin Peak
△ 12,574

Monarch Lake

1.5 mi to Monarch Lake TH

1.8

8,810

Thunderbolt Peak
△ 11,920

Cascade Creek Trail

8,400

0.8

Waterfalls

Paiute Peak
△ 13,088

8,360

Southside Trail

Waterfalls

Cascade Creek

3.4

Pawnee Pass Trail

Mount Toll
△ 12,979

Strawberry Bench Trail

1.0

9,150

1.7

Pawnee Lake

Pawnee Peak
△ 12,943

Mill Creek

See "Strawberry Creek & Monarch Lake" section (pp. 444-449)

High Lonesome Trail

10,100

1.2

Good campsites

10,900

1.8

Mount Achonee
△ 12,649

Crater Lake

Mirror Lake

2.5

8.3

Lone Eagle Peak △

10,310

Pawnee Pass

Shoshoni Peak △
12,967

10,220

Arapaho Creek

Arapaho Pass Trail

Apache Peak
△ 13,441

For areas east of here, see "Indian Peaks Wilderness - East Side" section (pp. 154-166)

High Lonesome Trail

2.1

Navajo Peak △
13,409

10,070

TH Junco Lake TH

Wheeler Basin

Arikaree Peak
△ 13,150

Caribou Pass Trail

1.7

Coyote Park

North Arapaho Peak
△ 13,502

High Lonesome Trail

6.4 mi to Devils Thumb Park TH

10,540

Columbine Lake Trail

2.5

Satanta Peak
△ 11,979

Waterfalls

Caribou Lake

1.3

Caribou Pass

1.7

South Arapaho Peak
△ 13,397

11,070

11,150

11,900

Arapaho Pass Trail

Columbine Lake

12,060 Lake Dorothy

Arapaho Pass

1.0 mi

For a map of the areas to the south of here, see p. 439

Bikes are not allowed in the Indian Peaks Wilderness.

Strawberry Bench just below Strawberry Lake

Strawberry Bench & Monarch Lake

Just to the west of the Indian Peaks Wilderness is Monarch Lake and the Strawberry Bench area, a relatively wild chunk of land with some stellar hiking and mountain biking trails to the south and southeast of Lake Granby. Trails range in difficulty - you may find yourself meandering through a grassy meadow one moment but descending rocky switchbacks the next. Hikers have many trails to choose from in this area yet the options of mountain bikers are slightly fewer due to trails that connect to the Indian Peaks Wilderness.

Maps: National Geographic Trails Illustrated "Indian Peaks & Gold Hill (#102).

Best time of the year: The trails in the Strawberry Bench area are relatively low-lying. Consequently, they are the first to melt out and do not accumulate significant snows until late fall. In general, you can count on hiking or biking these trails in early June through late October. In winter, the road to Monarch Lake is plowed to just before the Monarch Lake TH, allowing the trails in the vicinity of the lake to be snowshoed and cross country skied.

Camping: Numerous National Forest campgrounds can be found near the Stillwater Campground, Arapaho Bay Campground, Sunset Point, Green Ridge (Lake Granby), Denver Creek Campground (Granby), Bull Mountain Campground (NW of Granby), Sawmill Gulch (NW of Granby), Willow Creek Campground (NW of Granby), Timber Creek Campground (Rocky Mountain National Park), Meadow Creek Reservoir area (up FS 129, north of Tabernash). Some of these campgrounds may currently be closed due to hazard tree removal. Call 1-877-444-6777 or visit www.recreation.gov to reserve these campgrounds or for more information.

Access

User Fees: **$** Recently, the Arapaho National Forest has implemented a daily user fee system, which is in place at some of the trailheads in this area, including the Monarch Lake TH. If you visit national forests and national parks often, you may consider purchasing an Interagency Annual Pass (see information on user fees on p. 17).

Directions to Fraser: From the intersection of I-70 and C-470 west of Denver, take I-70 for 28 mi to Exit 232 (Empire/Granby), then travel north on US 40 through Empire and up and over Berthoud Pass. After 45 mi from I-70, you will reach Winter Park. Granby is an additional 18 mi north on US 40.

High Lonesome Hut: The High Lonesome Hut is located south of Lake Granby and is a fun place for an overnight trip via skis or snowshoes in winter or by mountain bike or foot in summer and fall. The hut is quite comfortable, including hot water, a shower, indoor toilet, and photovoltaic panels for electricity. The hut sleeps 12 people. For more information on the hut or for reservations, please contact www.lonesome-hut.com or call (970) 726-4099. The hut is most commonly accessed from the south along the Meadow Creek Rd. via the High Lonesome Hut TH (2.3 mi along the Strawberry Trail) but can also be accessed from the Doe Creek TH.

Doe Creek TH: **$** From Granby, take US 40 to just west of town to the intersection with

Aspen trees along the Doe Creek Trail

Along the Strawberry Creek Trail

US 34. Drive north on US 34 for 5.4 mi to CR 6 on the southwest corner of Lake Granby. Take CR 6 (dirt) east for 3.5 mi to an obvious parking area and trailhead.

Strawberry Lake TH: 💲 Not an official trailhead, but you can park along CR 6 where the Strawberry Lake Trail exits the woods. Follow CR 6 from US 34 for about 7.3 mi and be on the lookout for an unmarked trail that enters the woods on the south side of the road. Park along the road.

Monarch Lake TH: 💲 ❄ Follow directions above to the Doe Creek TH but continue on CR 6 east for an additional 5.3 mi (8.8 mi from US 34) to the intersection with CR 637 near Arapaho Bay. Turn right, following signs for the Monarch Lake TH. In winter, you will have to park about 0.9 mi northwest of here.

Roaring Fork TH: 💲 At the intersection of CR 6 and CR 637 (see directions above for "Monarch Lake TH"), continue about 0.8 mi northwest on CR 637 to the Arapaho Bay Campground. The trailhead is located on the right (north) side of the road between the Moraine and Roaring Fork Loops of the campground.

High Lonesome Hut TH: 💲 From Fraser (directions to Fraser can be found on p. 436), follow US 40 for not quite 3 mi to CR 83 (just south of Tabernash). Take a right on CR 83 but within a half mile take a left onto CR 84/FS 129, following signs for Meadow Creek Reservoir. Drive CR 84/FS 129 for 3.9 mi to a sharp right-turning hairpin curve, about a mile past double hairpin curves. There is gate and an old road behind the sign.

Junco Lake TH: **$** Follow directions to the High Lonesome Hut TH but continue along the Meadow Creek Rd. (FS 129) for an additional 6.7 mi (11.1 mi from US 40) to a road leading to the Junco Lake TH, which is located just off FS 129 in a large parking area next to the Junco Lake Wilderness Station.

Recommended Routes

Doe Creek Trail: A moderate trail that heads south from the Doe Creek TH towards the Strawberry Creek area. The trail starts out relatively easy, traversing through aspen and pine forests and meadows but then climbing forested hillsides before descending to Little Strawberry Creek after 3.3 mi.

Strawberry Lake Trail: This trail begins at the Strawberry Lake TH and climbs via switchbacks south to intersect the Strawberry Bench and Strawberry Creek Trails after 1.4 mi. Strawberry Lake is a short distance (0.3 mi) beyond this intersection in a large meadow.

Strawberry Bench Trail: The 3.6-mi long Strawberry Bench Trail connects the Strawberry Lake area with the High Lonesome Trail to the south of Monarch Lake. Excellent, rolling terrain through enchanted forests.

Strawberry Trail: The Strawberry Trail connects the High Lonesome Hut TH with the Strawberry Creek Trail. Use this trail to access the High Lonesome Hut, which is reached after 2.3 mi.

Caribou Trail: The 4.2-mi long Caribou Trail connects the Meadow Creek Reservoir area with Strawberry Creek. The top section of this trail is difficult to find, but from the north side of Meadow Creek Reservoir, take a left (north) on the only dirt road that heads north then take an immediate right and park along the dirt road. You should see a small sign for the Caribou Trail.

High Lonesome Trail: The High Lonesome Trail coincides with the Continental Divide Trail and connects the Monarch Lake area in the north with the Devils

Strawberry Bench & Monarch Lake

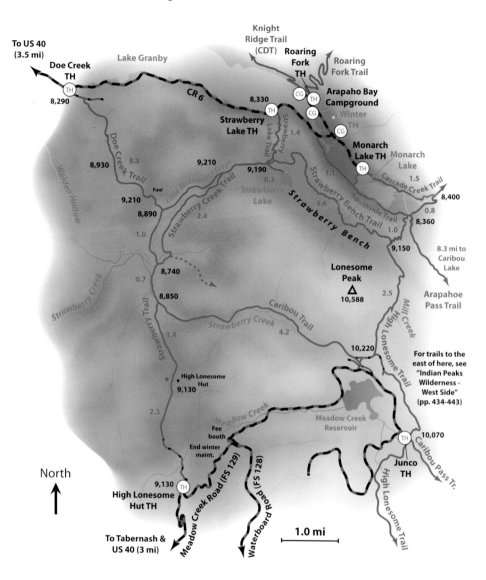

To US 40
(3.5 mi)

Doe Creek TH
8,290

Lake Granby

CR 6

Knight
Ridge Trail
(CDT)

Roaring Fork TH

Roaring
Fork Trail

8,330

Strawberry Lake TH

CG

Arapaho Bay Campground

CG

Winter TH

1.4

CG

Monarch Lake TH

Monarch Lake

Doe Creek Trail

3.3

8,930

9,210

Fun!

9,210

8,890

9,190

0.3

Strawberry Lake

1.1

Cascade Creek Trail

1.5

8,400

1.0

Strawberry Bench Trail

3.6

Strawberry Bench

Southside Trail

0.8

8,360

Walden Hollow

Little Strawberry Creek

Strawberry Creek Trail

2.4

9,150

8.3 mi to Caribou Lake

Strawberry Lake Trail

1.0

Lonesome Peak
△
10,588

2.5

Arapahoe Pass Trail

0.7

8,740

8,850

Caribou Trail

Strawberry Creek

4.2

Mill Creek

High Lonesome Trail

Strawberry Trail

1.4

10,220

For trails to the
east of here, see
"Indian Peaks
Wilderness -
West Side"
(pp. 434-443)

High Lonesome Hut
9,130

2.3

Meadow Creek

Meadow Creek Reservoir

TH

10,070

North
↑

Fee booth

End winter maint.

High Lonesome Hut TH
9,130

Meadow Creek Road (FS 129)

Waterboard Road (FS 128)

Junco TH

Caribou Pass Tr.

High Lonesome Trail

1.0 mi

To Tabernash &
US 40 (3 mi)

Thumb Park TH (see p. 436) in the south via the Junco TH. Closed to bikes just south of Monarch Lake but open again to bikes south of Meadow Creek Reservoir. A rocky trail for mountain biking but moderate by foot. It is 7.3 mi with 2500 ft./770 ft. of elevation gain/loss from the Monarch Lake TH to the Junco Lake TH.

Monarch Lake Loop: A nice easy loop for all seasons. Start at the Monarch Lake TH. Proceed either clockwise or counterclockwise. Hike the Monarch Lake Loop Trail around the lake. In the clockwise direction, the Cascade Creek Trail is reached after 1.5

mi, the Arapaho Pass Trail is reached after 2.3 mi, and the High Lonesome Trail is reached shortly thereafter. The loop is about 4.0 mi long with 500 ft. of climbing/descending. In winter, you will need to park back at the winter trailhead (see p. 446), which will add on about 0.9 mi each way.

Knight Ridge Trail: The Knight Ridge Trail begins at the Roaring Fork TH and heads west along Knight Ridge towards the west side of Rocky Mountain National Park. This trail coincides with the Continental Divide Trail. Excellent views of Lake Granby and Monarch Lake.

Roaring Fork Trail: Seldom used and difficult to follow in spots, this trail begins at the Roaring Fork TH. The trail climbs steeply via switchbacks then gradually climbs along Roaring Fork Creek before descending east into Hell Canyon. Stone Lake and Upper Lake sit in a nice meadow with spectacular

views. It is about 6.2 mi to Stone Lake and 6.6 mi to Upper Lake with approximately 4,200 ft. of elevation gain (1,800 ft. of elevation drop).

Charlie's Picks for Winter Park, Fraser, Indian Peaks West, and Granby

1. Corona Trail (p. 437)

2. Mirror & Crater Lakes (p. 441)

3. Tour d'Idlewild (p. 416)

4. Spruce Creek Trail (p. 424)

5. Byers Peak Trail (p. 429)

6. Creekside-Flume Loop (p. 422)

7. St. Louis Lake (p. 430)

8. Doe Creek/Strawberry Bench Trails (p. 447)

9. Columbine Lake (p. 439)

10. Arapaho Pass Trail to Caribou Lake (p. 440)

Index

Items in **bold** denote a map; items in *italics* denote a photo

Items in **bold** denote a map; items in *italics* denote a photo

Items in **bold** denote a map; items in *italics* denote a photo

Items in **bold** denote a map; items in *italics* denote a photo

Items in **bold** denote a map; items in *italics* denote a photo

Items in **bold** denote a map; items in *italics* denote a photo

Items in **bold** denote a map; items in *italics* denote a photo

Items in **bold** denote a map; items in *italics* denote a photo

Items in **bold** denote a map; items in *italics* denote a photo

Items in **bold** denote a map; items in *italics* denote a photo

Items in **bold** denote a map; items in *italics* denote a photo

Items in **bold** denote a map; items in *italics* denote a photo

"Red exhaustion rips at your throat
And salt sweat spills off your forehead and mats your eyelids and brows
And drips on the burning ground
And your legs start to turn to rubber and collapse like a balloon.
'Pretty soon I've got to rest.
How much farther?
What's the good of this God damn work anyway?'
The long distance runner is paid by the snap of a white thread across his chest.
You are paid by the picture at your feet."

- Terry and Renny Russell from "On the Loose"

COLORADO ADVENTURE GUIDE eMapBook

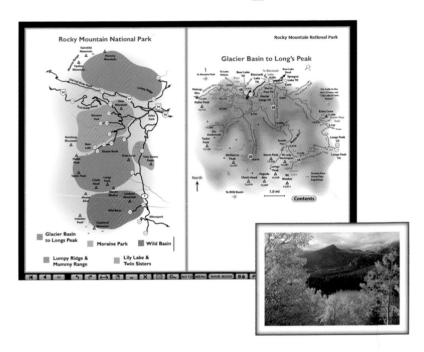

Check out the eMapBook, the perfect electronic companion to the Colorado Adventure Guide. An interactive ebook containing all maps and many photographs found in this guidebook. Demo and download the eMapBook at:

www.jaggedmountainpublishing.com/emapbook.html

About the Author

I am extremely fortunate to have lived in Colorado my entire life and am indebted to my parents for deciding to make Colorado their home. What a great state! Born and raised in Colorado Springs, I was exploring the trails in the Pikes Peak region at an early age. My family enjoyed camping and hiking outings and it was during these formative years that I acquired a love and appreciation for nature. Like many Colorado youngsters who develop an interest for the outdoors, I became interested in hiking 14,000-foot peaks ("Fourteeners") in my teens and eventually completed all of Colorado's 54 Fourteeners. During my college years spent at the University of Colorado, my weekends were filled with trail running, hiking, and climbing exploits with friends. Backcountry skiing and mountain biking were natural progressions and soon I was exploring Colorado in all seasons and by different, exciting modes. Recently, I have made "adventure" a priority and have tried to explore off the beaten path destinations not only in Colorado but also in Alaska, Peru, and Canada. In addition, over the past decade I have competed in a variety of competitive endurance events, such as ultrarunning, mountain biking, cross country skiing, and adventure racing. These competitive events have been fun and have enabled me to explore my physical and mental limits in the mountains. However, some of the most meaningful times in the wilderness have come at the end of a long day backpacking with friends, dipping my toes in an alpine lake, and listening to a pack of coyotes howl as the sun sets over the mountains.

This is my first book and I plan to publish the Central and Southern Editions of the Colorado Adventure Guide in coming years. While I'm not exploring trails, I teach chemical engineering, computing, and biology courses as an Instructor at the University of Colorado at Boulder. I live with and try to keep up with my "Energizer Bunny" wife in Boulder. I look forward to a lifetime of adventures in Colorado. See you on the trail!